# INEQUALITY

# INEQUALITY

## A Reassessment of the Effect of Family and Schooling in America

**CHRISTOPHER JENCKS**

Marshall Smith, Henry Acland,
Mary Jo Bane, David Cohen,
Herbert Gintis, Barbara Heyns,
Stephan Michelson

Basic Books, Inc., Publishers   New York • London

# PREFACE

This book summarizes the results of three years of research at the Center for Educational Policy Research. The eight coauthors were all Research Associates at the Center, and our work there was a collaborative effort. We plagiarized both ideas and data from one another. Most of us also spent a good deal of time criticizing one another's work. While each of us took primary responsibility for certain lines of inquiry, and this responsibility is recorded in appropriate footnotes, we see our research as an integrated effort which should bear all our names.

At the same time, this book offers an interpretation, not only of our research but of other people's. This interpretation is not a collective effort in the same sense as the research itself. The present text was written by Christopher Jencks. It embodies his prejudices and obsessions, and these are not shared by all the coauthors. Thus, he must bear primary responsibility for the book's judgments and interpretations, even though he is obviously and deeply indebted to his collaborators.

This collaboration has a complicated history. In the summer of 1966, James Coleman and his colleagues published the first analysis of the Equality of Educational Opportunity Survey. That fall, Daniel P. Moynihan and Thomas Pettigrew initiated a seminar at Harvard to reanalyze this data. Marshall Smith, then an instructor at the Graduate School of Education, became the research director of the seminar. At the same time, Jencks had begun work in Washington at the Institute for Policy Studies on a book about "The Limits of Schooling." Early in 1967, Jencks became a regular participant in the Harvard Seminar. Later in the year he joined the faculty of the Harvard Graduate School of Education. During this period, Smith and Jencks collaborated on several reanalyses of the data collected by Coleman and his colleagues for the EEOS. They also became convinced that the policy implications of the EEOS and other analogous bodies of data required more extensive exploration. In 1968, they joined with David Cohen, who had recently served as Staff Director of the Civil Rights Commission's study, *Racial Isolation in the Public Schools,* to establish the Center for Educational Policy Research. Theodore Sizer, Dean of the Harvard Graduate School of Education, agreed to provide a home for the Center, as well as initial financial support.

Stephan Michelson, an economist who had begun work in this same area while at the Brookings Institution, joined the Center as a Research Associate when it opened in 1968. Herbert Gintis, who had investigated the nonacademic outcomes of schooling while a graduate student in economics at Harvard, joined the Center in 1969. Barbara Heyns began a doctoral dissertation on high school tracking at the Center in 1969 and became a Research Associate in 1970. Henry Acland came to the Center in 1970 to complete a doctoral dissertation on the Plowden surveys of English primary schools. Mary Jo Bane joined the Center in 1971 and played a central role in editing this book.

Jencks administered the Center during its first year. Since then, Cohen has been the administrator. From the beginning, Smith served as an informal "research director," coordinating diverse data analyses, dealing with the vagaries of the Harvard Computing Center, and acting as a statistical consultant to all. (It is for this reason that he is listed as second author. The other coauthors are simply listed alphabetically.)

Money for our work came primarily from the Carnegie Corporation of New York, which supported the initial Harvard Seminar on the Coleman Report, Jencks' initial work on "The Limits of Schooling" (of which this book constitutes the final product), and roughly half the Center's budget, after its opening in 1968. The other half of the Center's budget came from research grants and contracts with organizations such as the Office of the Secretary of Health, Education and Welfare, the U.S. Office of Economic Opportunity, the Urban Institute, and the Massachusetts State Department of Education. During its first year, the Center also received some indirect support from the U.S. Office of Education (through Harvard's now defunct Center for Research and Development on Educational Differences) and the Ford Foundation (through the Harvard-M.I.T. Joint Center for Urban Studies). During 1968, Jencks' work on the limits of schooling was supported by the John Simon Guggenheim Memorial Foundation. The actual writing of this book was supported exclusively by the Guggenheim Foundation and the Carnegie Corporation. We are grateful to all these supporters. Needless to say, none of them is in any way responsible for the views we express here.

In addition to those listed as authors, many others have contributed to assembling the evidence presented here. We owe a particular debt to Marsha Brown and Carol Ann Moore, who did most of Jencks' computer programming. Additional computer work was done by Pamela Bulloch, Steve Chilton, Christine Cowan, John Gray, Polly Harold, Martha Kay, Michael Olneck, Paul Smith, and Randall Weiss. So many people helped type the manuscript at one stage or another that we cannot hope to acknowledge them all, but we are particularly indebted to Katherine Bowen-Woodward and Janet Lennon.

Finally, we are indebted to James Coleman and James McPartland of Johns Hopkins University and to the U.S. Office of Education for making available the data collected in the Equality of Educational Opportunity Survey; to John Flanagan, Marion Shaycoft, Lyle Schoenfeldt, and their colleagues for making available part of the data collected by Project Talent; to William Mason and the National Opinion Research Center for making available the data collected on veterans in 1964; to the late Sir Cyril Burt for making available data on his sample of identical twins reared apart; and to Otis Dudley Duncan for making available a variety of his unpublished computer runs and computations. Without this kind of data sharing, analyses of the kind reported here would be virtually impossible.

# CONTENTS

**ONE**   From Equal Opportunity to Equal Results   3

**TWO**   Inequality in the Schools   16

Access to Schools and Colleges   17

Preschools 18.     Elementary Schools 18.     Secondary
Schools 19.     Higher Education 19.     Overall
Inequality 20.     Conclusions 22.

Expenditure Differences between Schools and Individuals   23

Differences between States 24.     Differences between
Districts 25.     Differences between Schools in the Same
District 26.     Lifetime Inequalities in Expenditures on
Individuals 26.     Rich Children versus Poor Children 26.
Whites versus Blacks 27.     Conclusions 29.

Access to Privileged Schoolmates   29

Access to Fast Classes and College Curriculums   33

Conclusions about Inequality in the Schools   37

**THREE**   Inequality in Cognitive Skills   52

I: The Nature and Extent of Cognitive Inequality   53

What Standardized Tests Measure   53

The Stability of Individual Differences over Time   58

Measurement Scales 58.     Stability and Age 59.     Interpreting
Stability and Change 60.

Historical Changes in Americans' Test Scores   62

II: The Heredity/Environment Controversy   64

Genetic Influences on Test Scores   64

The Meaning of "Heritability" 65.     Estimating the Heritability
of IQ Scores 69.     Policy Implications 72.

The Effects of Family Background   76

The Effects of Economic Background   77

The Effects of Race   81

III: Schooling and Cognitive Inequality   84

The Effects of School Attendance   85
Preschool   85.        Elementary School   87.        Secondary
School   88.        Conclusions   89.

Differences between Schools   89
High Schools   89.        Elementary Schools   90.        Cumulative
Effects of Elementary and Secondary Schools   91.
Conclusions   93.

The Effects of School Resources   93
Expenditures   93.        Policies and Resources   95.

The Effects of Segregation   97
Effects on Blacks   97.        Effects on Poor Whites   103.        Effects
on Advantaged Students   103.        Conclusions   106.

The Effects of Tracking   106

Conclusions about Cognitive Inequality   109

**FOUR**   **A Note on Noncognitive Traits**   131

**FIVE**   **Inequality in Educational Attainment**   135

The Effects of Economic Background   138

The Effects of Race   141

Overall Effects of Family Background   143

Academic Aptitude and Academic Credentials   143

The Effects of School Quality on Educational Attainment   146
High Schools   146.        Elementary Schools   147.        Cumulative
Effects of Schools   148.

The Effects of High School Resources   149

The Effects of Segregation   151
Economic Segregation   151.        Racial Segregation   153.
Conclusions about Desegregation   155.

The Effects of Curriculum Placement   156

Conclusions about Educational Attainment   158

**SIX**   **Inequality in Occupational Status**   176

Measuring Occupational Status   176

The Inheritance of Status   179

The Effects of Educational Credentials   180

The Effects of Cognitive Skills    185

The Effects of School Quality    188

The Effects of Race    190

Conclusions about Occupational Inequality    191
Policies for Increasing Mobility    192.    Policies for Increasing
Equality    195.

**SEVEN**    Income Inequality    209

The Extent of Income Inequality    209

The Effects of Socio-Economic Background    213

The Effects of Race    216

The Effects of Family Background    219

The Effects of Cognitive Skills    220

The Effects of Credentials    221

The Effects of Occupation    225

Conclusions about Income Distribution    226

**EIGHT**    Inequality in Job Satisfaction    247

**NINE**    What Is To Be Done?    253

**APPENDIX A**    Estimating the Heritability of IQ Scores    266

Studies of Parents and Children    268
Dominance    270.    Assortative Mating    271.    Parent-Child
Correlations    274.    Genetic Resemblance between Adoptive
Parents and Children    277.    Estimating Heritability    279.

Studies of Children Reared Together    283
Correlations between Twins Reared Together    284.    Correlations
between Siblings Reared Together    289.    Correlations between
Unrelated Children Reared Together    290.    Summary of Observed
Correlations    292.    Path Model for Children Reared Together    295.
Estimating the Total Variance    297.    Correlations between
Genotypes of Children Reared Together    301.    Correlations between
Test Scores of Children Reared Together    304.

Studies of Related Children Reared Apart    309
Identical Twins Reared Apart    309.    Siblings Reared
Apart    315.

Conclusions    315

**APPENDIX B    Path Models of Intergenerational Mobility**    320

Variables    320

Data Sources    321

Measurement Error    330

Analytic Models    336

Conclusions    349

**APPENDIX C    A Layman's Guide to Statistical Terms**    351

Standard Deviation    351.    Coefficient of Variation    352.    Uses of the Standard Deviation    353.    Correlation Coefficients    354. Explained Variance    357.    Choice of Statistics    358.

**References**    359

**Index**    383

# INEQUALITY

# CHAPTER ONE

# From Equal Opportunity to Equal Results

Most Americans say they believe in equality. But when pressed to explain what they mean by this, their definitions are usually full of contradictions. Many will say, like the Founding Fathers, that "all men are created equal." Many will also say that all men are equal "before God," and that they are, or at least ought to be, equal in the eyes of the law. But most Americans also believe that some people are more competent than others, and that this will always be so, no matter how much we reform society. Many also believe that competence should be rewarded by success, while incompetence should be punished by failure. They have no commitment to ensuring that everyone's job is equally desirable, that everyone exercises the same amount of political power, or that everyone receives the same income.

But while most Americans accept inequality in virtually every sphere of day-to-day life, they still believe in what they often call "equal opportunity." By this they mean that the rules determining who succeeds and who fails should be fair. People are, of course, likely to disagree about precisely what is "fair" and what is "unfair." Still, the general principle of fair competition is almost universally endorsed.

During the 1960s, many reformers devoted enormous effort to equalizing opportunity. More specifically, they tried to eliminate inequalities based on skin color, and to a lesser extent on economic background. They also wanted to eliminate absolute deprivation: "poverty," "ignorance," "powerlessness," and so forth. But only a handful of radicals talked about eliminating inequality per se. Almost none of the national legislation passed during the 1960s tried to reduce disparities in adult status, power, or income in any direct way. There was no significant effort, for example, to make taxation more progressive, and very little effort to reduce wage disparities between highly paid and poorly paid workers. Instead, attention focused on helping workers in poorly paid jobs to move into better paid jobs. Nor was there much effort to reduce the social or psychological distance between high- and low-status occupations. Instead, the idea was to help people in low-status occupations

3

leave these occupations for more prestigious ones. Even in the political arena, "maximum feasible participation" implied mainly that more "leaders" should be black and poor, not that power should be equally distributed between leaders and followers.

Because the reforms of the 1960s did not tackle the problem of adult inequality directly, they accomplished only a few of their goals. Equalizing opportunity is almost impossible without greatly reducing the absolute level of inequality, and the same is true of eliminating deprivation.

Consider the case of equal opportunity. One can equalize the opportunities available to blacks and whites without equalizing anything else, and considerable progress was made in this direction during the late 1960s. But equalizing the opportunities available to different children of the same race is far more difficult. If a society is competitive and rewards adults unequally, some parents are bound to succeed while others fail. Successful parents will then try to pass along their advantages to their children. Unsuccessful parents will inevitably pass along some of their disadvantages. Unless a society completely eliminates ties between parents and children, inequality among parents guarantees some degree of inequality in the opportunities available to children. The only real question is how serious these inequalities must be.

Or consider the problem of deprivation. When the war on poverty began in late 1963, it was conceived as an effort to raise the living standards of the poor. The rhetoric of the time described the persistence of poverty in the midst of affluence as a "paradox," largely attributable to "neglect." Official publications all assumed that poverty was an absolute rather than a relative condition. Having assumed this, they all showed steady progress toward the elimination of poverty, since fewer and fewer people had incomes below the official "poverty line."

Yet despite all the official announcements of progress, the feeling that lots of Americans were poor persisted. The reason was that most Americans define poverty in relative rather than absolute terms. Public opinion surveys show, for example, that when people are asked how much money an American family needs to "get by," they typically name a figure about half what the average American family actually receives.[1] This has been true for the last three decades, despite the fact that real incomes (i.e. incomes adjusted for inflation) have doubled in the interval.

Political definitions of poverty have reflected these popular attitudes. During the Depression, the average American family was living on about $30 a week. A third of all families were living on less than half this amount, i.e. less than $15 a week. This made it natural for Franklin Roosevelt to speak of "one third of a nation" as ill-housed, ill-clothed, and ill-fed. One third of the nation was below what most people then regarded as the poverty line.

By 1964, when Lyndon Johnson declared war on poverty, incomes had risen more than fivefold. Even allowing for inflation, living standards had doubled. Only about 10 percent of all families had real incomes as low as the bottom third had had during the Depression. But popular conceptions of what it took to "get by" had also risen since the Depression. Mean family income was about $160 a week, and popular opinion now held that it took $80 a week for a family of four to make ends meet. About a quarter of all families were still poor by this definition. As a matter of political convenience, the Administration set the official poverty line at $60 a week for a family of four rather than $80, ensuring that even conservatives would admit that those below the line were poor. But by 1970 inflation had raised mean family income to about $200 a week, and the National Welfare Rights Organization was rallying liberal support for a guaranteed income of $100 a week for a family of four.

These political changes in the definition of poverty were not just a matter of "rising expectations" or of people's needing to "keep up with the Joneses." The goods and services that made it possible to live on $15 a week during the Depression were no longer available to a family with the same "real" income (i.e. $40 a week) in 1964. Eating habits had changed, and many cheap foods had disappeared from the stores. Most people had enough money to buy an automobile, so public transportation had atrophied, and families without automobiles were much worse off than during the Depression. The labor market had also changed, and a person without a telephone could not get or keep many jobs. A home without a telephone was more cut off socially than when few people had telephones and more people "dropped by." Housing arrangements had changed, too. During the Depression, many people could not afford indoor plumbing and "got by" with a privy. By the 1960s, privies were illegal in most places. Those who could not afford an indoor toilet ended up in buildings which had broken toilets. For this they paid more than their parents had paid for privies.

Examples of this kind suggest that the "cost of living" is not the cost of buying some fixed set of goods and services. It is the cost of participating in a social system. The cost of participation depends in large part on how much other people habitually spend to participate. Those who fall far below the norm, whatever it may be, are excluded. It follows that raising the incomes of the poor will not eliminate poverty if the incomes of other Americans rise even faster. If people with incomes less than half the national average cannot afford what "everyone" regards as "necessities," the only way to eliminate poverty is to make sure everyone has an income at least half the average.

This line of reasoning applies to wealth as well as poverty. The rich are not rich because they eat filet mignon or own yachts. Millions of people can now afford these luxuries, but they are still not "rich" in the colloquial sense. The rich are rich because they can afford to buy other people's time. They can hire other people to make their beds, tend their gardens, and drive their cars. These are not privileges that become more widely available as people become more affluent. If all workers' wages rise at the same rate, the highly paid professional will have to spend a constant percentage of his income to get a maid, a gardener, or a taxi. The number of people who are "rich," in the sense of controlling more than their share of other people's time and effort, will therefore remain the same, even though consumption of yachts and filet mignon is rising.

If the distribution of income becomes more equal, as it did in the 1930s and 1940s, the number of people who are "rich" in this sense of the term will decline, even though absolute incomes are rising. If, for example, the wages of domestic servants rise faster than the incomes of their prospective employers, fewer families will feel they can afford full-time servants. This will lower the living standards of the elite to some extent, regardless of what happens to consumption of yachts and filet mignon.

This same logic applies not only to income but to the cognitive skills taught in school. Young people's performance on standardized tests rose dramatically between World War I and World War II, for example. But the level of competence required for many adult roles rose too. When America was a polyglot nation of immigrants, all sorts of jobs were open to those who could not read English. Such people could, for example, join the army, drive a truck, or get a job in the construction industry. Today, when almost everyone can read English, the range of choices open to nonreaders has narrowed. The military no longer takes an appreciable number of illiterates, a driver's license requires a written examination, and apprenticeships in the construction trades are restricted to those who can pass tests. Those who cannot read English are at a disadvantage, simply because they are atypical. America is not organized with their problems in mind. The same thing applies to politics. If the average citizen's vocabulary expands, the vocabulary used by politicians and newspapers will expand too. Those with very limited vocabularies relative to their neighbors will still have trouble following events, even though their vocabulary is larger than, say, their parents' vocabulary was.

Arguments of this kind suggest that it makes more sense to think of poverty and ignorance as relative than as absolute conditions. They also suggest that eliminating poverty and ignorance, at least as these are usually defined in America, depends on eliminating, or at least greatly reducing, inequality. This is no simple matter. Since a competitive system means that some people "succeed" while others "fail," it also means that people will end up unequal. If we want to reduce inequality, we therefore have two options. The first possibility is to make the system less competitive by reducing the benefits that derive from success and the costs paid for failure. The second possibility is to make sure that everyone enters the competition with equal advantages and disadvantages.

The basic strategy of the war on poverty during the 1960s was to try to give everyone entering the job market or any other competitive arena comparable skills. This meant placing great emphasis on education. Many people imagined that if schools could equalize people's cognitive skills this would equalize their bargaining power as adults. In such a system nobody would end up very poor—or, presumably, very rich.

This strategy rested on a series of assumptions which went roughly as follows:

1. Eliminating poverty is largely a matter of helping children born into poverty to rise out of it. Once families escape from poverty, they do not fall back into it. Middle-class children rarely end up poor.

2. The primary reason poor children do not escape from poverty is that they do not acquire basic cognitive skills. They cannot read, write, calculate, or articulate. Lacking these skills, they cannot get or keep a well-paid job.

3. The best mechanism for breaking this vicious circle is educational reform. Since children born into poor homes do not acquire the skills they need from their parents, they must be taught these skills in school. This can be done by making sure that they attend the same schools as middle-class children, by giving them extra compensatory programs in school, by giving their parents a voice in running their schools, or by some combination of all three approaches.

So far as we can discover, each of these assumptions is erroneous.

1. Poverty is not primarily hereditary. While children born into poverty have a higher-than-average chance of ending up poor, there is still an enormous amount of economic mobility from one generation to the next. Indeed, there is nearly as much economic inequality among brothers raised

in the same homes as in the general population. This means that inequality is recreated anew in each generation, even among people who start life in essentially identical circumstances.

2. The primary reason some people end up richer than others is not that they have more adequate cognitive skills. While children who read well, get the right answers to arithmetic problems, and articulate their thoughts clearly are somewhat more likely than others to get ahead, there are many other equally important factors involved. Thus there is almost as much economic inequality among those who score high on standardized tests as in the general population. Equalizing everyone's reading scores would not appreciably reduce the number of economic "failures."

3. There is no evidence that school reform can substantially reduce the extent of cognitive inequality, as measured by tests of verbal fluency, reading comprehension, or mathematical skill. Neither school resources nor segregation has an appreciable effect on either test scores or educational attainment.

Our work suggests, then, that many popular explanations of economic inequality are largely wrong. We cannot blame economic inequality primarily on genetic differences in men's capacity for abstract reasoning, since there is nearly as much economic inequality among men with equal test scores as among men in general. We cannot blame economic inequality primarily on the fact that parents pass along their disadvantages to their children, since there is nearly as much inequality among men whose parents had the same economic status as among men in general. We cannot blame economic inequality on differences between schools, since differences between schools seem to have very little effect on any measurable attribute of those who attend them.

Economic success seems to depend on varieties of luck and on-the-job competence that are only moderately related to family background, schooling, or scores on standardized tests. The definition of competence varies greatly from one job to another, but it seems in most cases to depend more on personality than on technical skills. This makes it hard to imagine a strategy for equalizing competence. A strategy for equalizing luck is even harder to conceive.

The fact that we cannot equalize luck or competence does *not* mean that economic inequality is inevitable. Still less does it imply that we cannot eliminate what has traditionally been defined as poverty. It only implies that we must tackle these problems in a different way. Instead of trying to reduce people's capacity to gain a competitive advantage on one another, we would have to change the rules of the game so as to reduce the rewards of competitive success and the costs of failure. Instead of trying to make everyone equally lucky or equally good at his job, we would have to devise "insurance" systems which neutralize the effects of luck, and income-sharing systems which break the link between vocational success and living standards.

This could be done in a variety of ways. Employers could be constrained to reduce wage disparities between their best- and worst-paid workers.[2] The state could make taxes more progressive, and could provide income supplements to those who cannot earn an adequate living from wages alone. The state could also provide free public services for those who cannot afford to buy adequate services in the private sector. Pursued with vigor, such a strategy would make "poverty" (i.e. having a living standard less than half the national average) virtually impossible. It would also make economic "success," in the sense of having, say, a living standard more than twice the national average, far less common than it now is. The net effect would be to make those with the most competence and luck subsidize those with the least competence and luck to a far greater extent than they do today.

This strategy was rejected during the 1960s for the simple reason that it commanded relatively little popular support. The required legislation could not have passed Congress. Nor could it pass today. But that does not mean it was the wrong strategy. It simply means that until we change the political and moral premises on which most Americans now operate, poverty and inequality of opportunity will persist at pretty much their present level.

At this point the reader may wonder whether trying to change these premises is worthwhile. Why, after all, should we be so concerned about economic equality? Is it not enough to ensure equal opportunity? And does not the evidence we have described suggest that opportunities are already quite equal in America? If economic opportunities are relatively equal, and if the lucky and the competent then do better for themselves than the unlucky and incompetent, why should we feel guilty about this? Such questions cannot be answered in any definitive way, but a brief explanation of our position may help avoid misunderstanding.

We begin with the premise that every individual's happiness is of equal value. From this it is a short step to Bentham's dictum that society should be organized so as to provide the greatest good for the greatest number. In addition, we assume that the law of diminishing returns applies to most of the good things in life. In economic terms this means that people with low incomes value extra income more than people with high incomes.[3] It follows that if we want to maximize the satisfaction of the population, the best way to divide any given amount of money is to make everyone's income the same. Income disparities (except those based on variations in "need") will always reduce overall satisfaction, because individuals with low incomes will lose more than individuals with high incomes gain.

The principal argument against equalizing incomes is that some people contribute more to the general welfare than others, and that they are therefore entitled to greater rewards. The most common version of this argument is that unless those who contribute more than their share are rewarded (and those who contribute less than their share punished) productivity will fall and everyone will be worse off. A more sophisticated version is that people will only share their incomes on an equal basis if all decisions that affect these incomes are made collectively. If people are left free to make decisions on an individual basis, their neighbors cannot be expected to pay the entire cost of their mistakes.

We accept the validity of both these arguments. We believe that men need incentives to contribute to the common good, and we prefer monetary incentives to social or moral incentives, which tend to be inflexible and very coercive. We believe, in other words, that virtue should be rewarded, and we assume that there will be considerable variation in virtue from one individual to another. This does not, however, mean that incomes must remain as unequal as they are now. Even if we assume, for example, that the most productive fifth of all workers accounts for half the Gross National Product, it does not follow that they need receive half the income. A third or a quarter might well suffice to keep both them and others productive.

Most people accept this logic to some extent. They believe that the rich should pay more taxes than the poor, although they often disagree about how much more. Conversely, they believe that the poor should not starve, even if they contribute nothing to the general welfare. They believe, in other words, that people should not be rewarded solely for their contribution to the general welfare, but that other considerations, such as need, should also be taken into account. Our egalitarianism is simply another way of saying that we think need should play a larger role than it now does in determining what people get back from society. We do not think it can or should be the sole consideration.

When we turn from the distribution of income to the distribution of other things, our commitment to equality is even more equivocal. We assume, for example, that occupational prestige resembles income in that those who have low-prestige occupations usually value additional prestige more than those who have high-prestige occupations. Insofar as prestige is an end in itself, then, the optimal distribution is again egalitarian. But occupational prestige derives from a variety of factors, most of which are more difficult to redistribute than income. We cannot imagine a social system in which all occupations have equal prestige, except in a society where all workers are equally competent. Since we do not see any likelihood of equalizing competence, we regard the equalization of occupational prestige as a desirable but probably elusive goal.

When we turn from occupational prestige to educational attainment and cognitive skills, the arguments for and against equality are reversed. If schooling and knowledge are thought of strictly as ends in themselves, it is impossible to make a case for distributing them equally. We can see no reason to suppose, for example, that people with relatively little schooling value additional schooling more than people who have already had a lot of schooling. Experience suggests that the reverse is the case. Insofar as schooling is an end in itself, then, Benthamite principles imply that those who want a lot should get a lot, and those who want very little should get very little. The same is true of knowledge and cognitive skills. People who know a lot generally value additional knowledge and skills more than those who know very little. This means that insofar as knowledge or skill is valued for its own sake, an unequal distribution is likely to give more satisfaction to more people than an equal distribution.

The case for equalizing the distribution of schooling and cognitive skill derives not from the idea that we should maximize consumer satisfaction, but from the assumption that equalizing schooling and cognitive skill is necessary to equalize status and income. This puts egalitarians in the awkward position of trying to impose equality on people, even though the natural demand for both cognitive skill and schooling is very unequal. Since we have found rather modest relationships between cognitive skill and schooling on the one hand and status and income on the other, we are much less concerned than most egalitarians with making sure that people end up alike in these areas.

Our commitment to equality is, then, neither all-embracing nor absolute. We do not believe that everyone can or should be made equal to everyone else in every respect. We assume that some differences in cognitive skill and vocational competence are inevitable, and that efforts to eliminate such differences can never be 100 percent successful. But we also believe that the distribution of income can be made far more equal than it is, even if the distribution of cognitive skill and vocational competence remains as unequal as it is now. We also think society should get on with the task of equalizing income rather than waiting for the day when everyone's earning power is equal.

The evidence presented in this book is only relevant to part of this argument. We will try to show in some detail that traditional strategies for equalizing individual earning power will not work. But we will not try to demonstrate that a more direct approach to the problem would work. Since the argument is filled with diversions, qualifications, and exceptions, the reader may find a preliminary map helpful.

Chapter 2 examines the extent of inequality in the schools, i e. inequalities in schools' resources, in their social composition, and in students' access to desirable curriculums. It does not, however, assess the consequences of such inequalities. Chapter 3 analyzes the genetic and environmental factors, including schools, that influence scores on standardized tests. It does not examine the relationship between test scores and adult success. Chapter 4 deals very briefly with the "noncognitive" outcomes of schooling. Chapter 5 looks at the factors influencing the distribution of educational credentials. But like Chapter 3 it sidesteps the question of how educational credentials are used after they have been acquired. Chapters 6 and 7 investigate the determinants of occupational status and income, including family background, cognitive skills, educational credentials, and school quality. Chapter 8 briefly reviews what we know about job satisfaction, and Chapter 9 draws a variety of conclusions.

A number of topics are conspicuously missing from this list. There is, for example, virtually no discussion of why employers value certain traits, or whether these traits ought to be rewarded. Nor do we explore the relationship between economic inequality and inequality in other realms, like health, happiness, or political influence. This is not because we think these problems inconsequential, but because they are enormously complex and this book is already too long.

We have also taken a narrow view of the potential effects of schooling. We have looked at cognitive skills, as measured on standardized tests, and at students' decisions to stay in school or drop out. We have not looked in any detail at habits, values, or attitudes, i.e. what we will call the "noncognitive" effects of schooling. The reader should not infer that we think test scores more important than values or character. We take a very dim view of test scores, both as measures of schools' effectiveness and as measures of individual talent. But while cognitive tests have many obvious defects, most measures of attitudes, values, and character structure are even worse. In the absence of evidence, theorists must rely on intuition and personal experience. These have proven a poor guide to understanding the one thing we *can* measure, namely cognitive skills, so we have been reluctant to rely on them in explaining noncognitive differences. That is why our chapter on cognitive skills is 20 times as long as our chapter on noncognitive skills.

We have ignored not only attitudes and values but the internal life of schools. We have been preoccupied with the *effects* of schooling, especially those effects that might be expected to persist into adulthood. This has led us to adopt a "factory" metaphor, in which schools are seen primarily as places that alter the characteristics of their alumni. Our research has convinced us that this is the wrong way to think about schools. The long-term effects of schooling seem much less significant to us than they did when we began our work, and the internal life of the schools seems correspondingly more important. But we will not explore the implications of this alternative view in much detail. Instead, we will be content to document our skepticism about the importance of school "outputs."

We have also ignored extreme cases. In looking at economic inequality, for example, we have virtually nothing to say about the very rich (those with, say, capital assets in excess of $10,000,000). Such people do not show up in most surveys, and their incomes have a negligible effect on statistical analyses of income distribution. This does not mean they are unimportant. It simply means that their contribution to inequality in America is more political than economic.

Our treatment of cognitive inequality has similar limitations. We have not dealt in any detail with the effects of extreme deprivation, be it genetic or environmental. We are not, in other words, concerned with Mongoloidism or with children locked in closets. We are concerned with the more·widespread but less dramatic inequalities between "normal" children.

The same is true of schools. We have not tried to explore the effects of the handful of schools that differ drastically from the American norm. We have focused on differences among the public schools attended by large numbers of children. This means we cannot say much about the theoretical limits of what can be done in a place called a school. We can, however, estimate the extent to which existing disparities between schools contribute to adult inequality. We can also say a good deal about the probable effects of making what are now defined as "bad" public schools more like what are now defined as "good" public schools. Our concern with this issue does not reflect a belief that these allegedly good schools are good enough. It merely reflects our belief that when we assess the potential impact of school reform on inequality, we must be realistic about what reform might really achieve.

In order to document this argument, we use a lot of numbers. Given the limitations of social science, these numbers should be treated as very approximate. If we say that a year of school raises a man's subsequent income 4 percent, for example, this does not mean that the true figure is exactly 4 rather than 2 or 6. It simply means that 4 is our best estimate.[4]

We have tried to keep the text intelligible to those without statistical training, but arcane terms will occasionally creep in. The reader who finds these terms puzzling should read Appendix C, which provides a layman's explanation of this terminology. For the reader with statistical training, we have provided footnotes and two technical appendices, which document the arguments in the text. Readers familiar with path analysis will find the gist of our argument in Figure B–7, Appendix B.

The reader should also be warned that we are primarily concerned with inequality between individuals, not inequality between groups. This accounts for much of the discrepancy between our conclusions and those of others who have examined the same data. There is always far more inequality between individuals than between groups. It follows that when we compare the degree of inequality between groups to the degree of inequality between individuals, inequality between groups often seems relatively unimportant. It seems quite shocking, for example, that white workers earn 50 percent more than black workers. But we are even more disturbed by the fact that the best-paid fifth of all white workers earns 600 percent more than the worst-paid fifth. From this viewpoint, racial inequality looks almost insignificant.

Our decision to emphasize individual rather than group differences was made on political grounds. We would, of course, like to see a society in which everyone's opportunities for advancement were equal. But we are far more interested in a society where the extremes of wealth and poverty are entirely eliminated than in a society where they are merely uncorrelated with skin color, economic origins, sex, and other such traits. This means that we must focus on the causes and cures of individual inequality, even though we also discuss group differences at great length.

# NOTES

1. This material has been collected and analyzed by Lee Rainwater at Harvard University, as part of a forthcoming study of the social meaning of low income.

2. Thurow and Lucas, in "The American Distribution of Income," discuss the possibility of such constraints in some detail. The principal virtue of this approach is that it reduces the incomes of the rich *before* they are defined as "income" rather than afterwards. This means that the recipient is less conscious of what he is giving up and less likely to feel he is being cheated of his due.

3. If everyone had equal earning power we could assume that people "chose" their incomes voluntarily and that those with low incomes were those who were maximizing something else (e.g. leisure, autonomy, etc.). But as we note in Chapter 7, note 64, people's concern with income as against other objectives has no apparent effect on their actual income, at least while they are young. Thus we infer that income differences derive largely from differences in earning power and luck.

4. The statistically minded reader will probably be distressed at our willingness to combine data from disparate sources and at our frequent manipulations of distributions on the assumption that they are normal. We are aware of the hazards involved and have tried to check the validity of our assumptions wherever possible. Nonetheless, the methods we have used may involve considerable error. In self-defense, we can only say that the magnitude of these errors is almost certainly less than if we had simply consulted our prejudices, which seems to be the usual alternative.

# CHAPTER TWO

# Inequality in the Schools

Chapter 1 suggested that there were two distinct ways of looking at schools. Some people think a school's purpose is to make something happen to its students. They therefore try to judge the quality of a school by its long-term effect on its students. Other people think of schools primarily as communities where students and teachers live part of their lives. They judge the quality of a school by whether the students and teachers are interested or bored, sane or neurotic, happy or unhappy—while they are in school.

If you judge schools according to their long-term effects, if you believe that these effects are substantial, and if you are an egalitarian, you are likely to feel that everyone should get the same kind of schooling, whether they want it or not. Egalitarians of this persuasion often argue that students who want to drop out of high school should be encouraged or even coerced into returning, because otherwise they will have little chance of earning a good living. They also argue that students who do not want to attend college should be persuaded to do so, for similar reasons. They fight for systems of school finance that provide equal resources in every school, because they believe this is the only way to make the alumni of different schools equal. They demand an end to segregation because they think that this is a crucial step in eliminating the advantage of "haves" over "have-nots," and they oppose both elementary school tracking and distinctive high school curriculums on the grounds that these arrangements doom certain students to subordinate roles in adult life.

The evidence discussed in this book has convinced us, and may even convince some readers, that such arguments are misguided. Chapters 3 through 8 argue that differences between schools have rather trivial long-term effects, and that eliminating differences between schools would do almost nothing to make adults more equal. Even eliminating differences in the amount of schooling people get would do relatively little to make adults more equal. If this is true, schools ought to be

**16**

judged largely by their short-term effects. This does not, in our view, weaken the case for distributing school resources and opportunities equally. But it means that this case is no different from the case for making the distribution of public parks, trash collection, or other public services equal.

Giving everyone an equal claim on educational resources does not mean that everyone must receive equal benefits at any particular moment. If one 17 year old stays in school while another drops out, for example, they will receive unequal benefits in that particular year. Giving everyone an equal claim does, however, imply that we ought to try to create a system in which everyone gets more or less comparable benefits over a lifetime. If an individual does not want to take these benefits in the form of schooling, alternative benefits ought to be available. We begin, then, with the assumption that everyone's lifetime claim should be equal, leaving the burden of proof on those who want to justify deviations from this standard. (A case could be made for distributing educational benefits so as to compensate people for other handicaps, such as poor parents, physical handicaps, mental deficiencies, and so forth. We doubt, however, that education is usually an effective or efficient form of compensation in such cases.)

In discussing the distribution of educational opportunities, we will look first at quantitative differences, then at qualitative ones. We will begin, in other words, by examining disparities in the amount of pre-schooling, regular schooling, and higher education consumed by different individuals. We will then examine variations in the annual cost of such schooling and make tentative estimates of the resources going to the most- and least-favored portions of the population over their lifetimes. Having looked at inequality in educational expenditures, we will turn to other qualitative differences, first considering variations in children's chances of attending school with the kinds of classmates they prefer, and then considering variations in what schools try to teach different children.

## Access to Schools and Colleges

Access to education is far more equal for children between 6 and 16 than for older or younger children. Most states accepted an obligation to provide every child with free elementary schooling during the nineteenth century. Most states had also accepted a similar obligation with respect to secondary schooling by the beginning of the twentieth century. Preschooling (kindergarten and nursery school) is still not universally accepted as every child's "right," and neither is higher education.

## PRESCHOOLS

More children are in preschools today than at any time in the past. Between 1960 and 1970, the proportion of children who spent a year in kindergarten rose from 60 to 80 percent.[1] The proportion attending nursery school rose from 10 to 22 percent during this same period.[2] Increasing the proportion of children enrolled meant a decrease in inequality, at least if inequality is defined in standard statistical terms.[3]

In 1960, virtually all nursery schooling was private, and attendance was largely confined to the white middle class. By 1970, about 30 percent of all nursery schooling was public. Most public nursery schools were part of the Head Start program and were restricted to children with low-income parents. As a result, there were proportionately more blacks than whites in nursery school by 1970.[4]

Most kindergartens have been public for many years. But unlike Head Start, kindergartens have not made any special effort to recruit the poor or exclude the rich. As a result, about 82 percent of white children now attend kindergartens as compared to 70 percent of black children.[5]

Unfortunately, we cannot tell how many of the children who do not attend preschool would do so if one were available. Thus, we cannot say how much of the inequality we observe is due to variations in taste and how much is due to the vagaries in the public provision of such services. Neither can we tell to what extent the difference between black and white enrollment rates reflects differences in taste, and to what extent it reflects differences in access. Both are apparently involved to some degree.[6]

## ELEMENTARY SCHOOLS

Since the Civil War, the majority of Americans have completed elementary school (i.e. eighth grade).[7] Yet until fairly recently there have been many exceptions, particularly among children whose parents lived on farms and among ethnic minorities. As these two groups were assimilated into the majority culture, however, they adopted majority norms about schooling—norms that were increasingly backed by legal compulsion. Today 99.2 percent of all children between the ages of 6 and 13 are in school.[8] Thus, we can hardly talk about inequality in access to elementary schooling. At this level almost all inequalities are qualitative.

A little over 40 percent of all adolescents were entering high school in 1914, and about 25 percent were finishing. The average age for entering the labor force was about 15. By the mid-1960s, 94 percent of all students spent at least a year in high school and 82 percent graduated. The average age for entering the labor force was about 19.[9]

Whether students stay in school depends to some extent on their upbringing and expectations. In the middle 1960s, for example, 34 percent of all blacks left high school without graduating, compared with only 16 percent of all whites.[10] Similarly, whites from working-class families are more likely to leave high school than whites from middle-class families.[11] This does not necessarily prove that poor or black students have less opportunity to use high schools than other students. But it does prove that public funds are being used to subsidize a service which is used by the white middle classes more than by other groups.

HIGHER EDUCATION

American colleges have always been selective institutions. Except for a slight lag between World War I and World War II, about half the students who finished high school have entered college. Furthermore, about half those who entered college have graduated.[12] The proportion going on to some kind of graduate work has also been relatively constant. Thus, in the 1920s about 40 percent of the population finished high school, just under 20 percent entered college, just under 10 percent finished college, and just under 5 percent did some kind of graduate work. Today, 80 percent graduate from high school, almost 40 percent enter some kind of college, almost 20 percent graduate, and almost 10 percent do some kind of graduate work.

It is hard to say to what extent the selectivity of higher education represents a denial of equal opportunity, and to what extent it results from variation in people's appetite for education. We can say, however, that America has never tried to make college attendance strictly a matter of taste or talent. State legislatures are quite complacent about the fact that it is easier for students who get money from home to attend college than for students who get nothing from home. If students without money from home can get through college at all, by working, borrowing, and making all kinds of personal sacrifices, opportunities are equal enough to salve most political consciences. Thus it is not entirely accidental that 87 percent of all high school graduates whose families earned $15,000 or more entered college in 1967, as compared to only 20 percent of those whose parents earned less than $3,000.[13] Chapter 5 indicates that money per se accounts for only part of this difference, but it is certainly a factor of some consequence.

Money aside, America has provided higher education only for students with certain talents and interests. Definitions of what can be taught in a college and who should attend such institutions have broadened steadily for 200 years, but they are still not all-embracing. Most educators and laymen still assume that large numbers of students are not "college material," and that these students should go directly from high school into the labor force.

The net effect of all this is that public subsidies for higher education are even more concentrated on middle-class children than are public subsidies for high schools.[14] Students who are not temperamentally equipped for academic work, or who have no money from home and no appetite for self-sacrifice, get no direct benefit from these subsidies.

OVERALL INEQUALITY

The proportion of people finishing elementary and secondary school has increased much faster than the proportion entering college or graduate school. The educational "floor" has thus risen much faster than the "ceiling," making the distance between the floor and ceiling smaller. The number of years people spend in school is therefore increasingly equal.

Table 2–1 summarizes the pattern of change over the last 40 years. It presents two statistics, the "standard deviation" and the "coefficient of variation," which will be unfamiliar to many readers. Those who want an explanation should see Appendix C. One simple rule for those who merely want to interpret the table is that when the means are similar, a large standard deviation indicates more inequality than a small standard deviation. In order to make the comparison more precise, we divide the standard deviation by the mean to obtain the "coefficient of variation." This will be our measure of inequality throughout this book. Table 2–1 shows, for example, that the coefficient of variation declined from 0.42 to 0.23, or 45 percent, over a forty-year period. We will therefore say that inequality in years of schooling declined by 45 percent.

To make the statement more concrete, let us divide the population of the United States into fifths, according to the amount of schooling each individual has had. Among people born at the turn of the century, the most educated fifth received an average of 14 years of schooling,

TABLE 2-1

*Years of Regular Schooling Completed by Different Population Groups*

| Group | | Mean | Standard Deviation | Coefficient of Variation | (Median) |
|---|---|---|---|---|---|
| All Individuals | | | | | |
| Born: | 1895–1904 | 8.90 | 3.76 | 0.42 | ( 8.8) |
| | 1905–1914 | 9.94 | 3.63 | 0.37 | (10.5) |
| | 1915–1924 | 10.86 | 3.30 | 0.30 | (12.2) |
| | 1925–1934 | 11.47 | 3.21 | 0.28 | (12.3) |
| | 1935–1939 | 11.90 | 2.92 | 0.25 | (12.5) |
| | 1940–1944 | 12.20 | 2.80 | 0.23 | (12.6) |
| Males | | | | | |
| Born: | 1895–1904 | 8.77 | 3.89 | 0.44 | ( 8.7) |
| | 1940–1944 | 12.39 | 3.00 | 0.24 | (12.6) |
| Females | | | | | |
| Born: | 1895–1904 | 8.96 | 3.65 | 0.41 | ( 8.9) |
| | 1940–1944 | 11.99 | 2.57 | 0.21 | (12.5) |
| Whites | | | | | |
| Born: | 1895–1904 | 9.18 | 3.65 | 0.40 | ( 8.9) |
| | 1940–1944 | 12.31 | 2.77 | 0.22 | (12.6) |
| Blacks | | | | | |
| Born: | 1895–1904 | 5.91 | 3.76 | 0.64 | ( 5.1) |
| | 1940–1944 | 11.10 | 2.77 | 0.25 | (12.2) |

Source: Rows 1–14 were derived by Norma Raines for CEPR from U.S. Bureau of the Census "Educational Attainment in 1969," Table 1. In calculating means and standard deviations, individuals reported as having 0 to 4 years of school were allocated as follows: 25 percent to 0 years, 25 percent to 1.5 years, 50 percent to 3.5 years. Individuals reporting 5 or more years of college were allocated as follows: 50 percent to 17 years, 25 percent to 18 years, 25 percent to 19 years. Preschooling is excluded. Beverly Duncan obtained fractionally lower means using slightly different assumptions (see her "Trends in the Output and Distribution of Schooling").

while the least educated fifth received 3.7 years. Thus, the most educated fifth had spent almost four times as many years in school as the least educated fifth. The most educated fifth of those born during World War II spent only twice as much time in school as the least educated fifth.[15]

Another way to look at the trend data is to compare the difference between random individuals born at the turn of the century and 40 years later. If we picked pairs of individuals born between 1895 and 1904 at random, we would find that the difference between one and the next averaged 4.2 years. If we picked random individuals born between 1940 and 1944, the average difference would be 3.2 years.[16]

Table 2–1 also shows that blacks used to get far less schooling than whites but that the gap has been declining in both relative and absolute terms. It shows that women used to get more education than men (because they were more likely to finish high school) but that they now get less education than men (because almost everyone now finishes high school and women are less likely to attend college and graduate school). We also know from other sources that the children of white-collar workers used to get about 1.7 years more schooling than the children of blue-collar workers, and that they now get about 1.5 years more schooling.[17] The narrowing of this gap is explained by the increase in the minimum amount of education received by almost everyone. The importance of class background relative to other sources of variation in educational attainment does not appear to have changed at all.[18]

CONCLUSIONS

We draw three conclusions from all this. First, different individuals and groups get quite unequal shares of the nation's educational resources. Nonetheless, the amount of time people spend in school is more equal than most of their other experiences. Blacks get 10 percent less schooling than whites, for example, even though their parents make a third less money. Blue-collar children spend 13 percent less time in school than white-collar children whereas their parents' incomes are 26 percent lower.[19]

Our second conclusion is that access to low-cost educational services is more equal than access to high-cost services. Elementary and secondary schooling cost relatively little per student, so almost everyone gets them. Preschooling and higher education cost two or three times as much per pupil as regular schooling, so only a fraction of the population has access to them. When education is available only to a minority, this minority is usually academically talented or otherwise advantaged. Head Start is the main exception.

Inequalities of this kind are hard to reconcile with any theory of equal opportunity. Were it not for the recent shifts in the character of the Supreme Court, they might even be subject to legal challenge. If, as a series of lower courts held during 1971–1972, it is unconstitutional for a state to finance elementary and secondary education in such a way that some children receive substantially greater benefits than others, this same reasoning ought in theory to be applicable to higher education. The present system of state subsidies provides disproportionate benefits to those who happen to live within commuting distance of a public college and to those whose parents are willing and able to pay part of the cost. This violates the spirit of the equal protection clause in much the same way as a system of school finance that provides disproportionate benefits to those living in rich school districts. This seems doubly true in light of our finding, to be discussed in Chapters 6 and 7, that the amount of schooling people get influences their chances of entering a high-status occupation far more than the annual cost of their schooling.

Nonetheless, our third conclusion is that making all education free would not suffice to equalize people's actual use of either schools or colleges. Indeed, we cannot imagine *any* noncoercive way to equalize consumption of educational services. We therefore conclude that what America needs is a system of finance which provides alternative services to those who get relatively few benefits from the educational system. If people do not want to attend school or college, an egalitarian society ought to accept this as a legitimate decision and give these people subsidized job training, subsidized housing, or perhaps simply a lower tax rate.

Such a proposal will shock those who think that attending school is good for people. From their viewpoint, America has a positive interest in keeping people in school rather than giving them other alternatives. We are very skeptical about such claims. When a student feels he is not benefiting from school, we suspect he is usually right. If he decides to quit, he should not be expected to pay for the continued education of the students who remain. Instead, he should receive some other service that he values as much as they value staying in school.

## Expenditure Differences between Schools and Individuals

There are at least three distinct traditions for evaluating school quality. The first and most popular approach is to equate quality with cost. A second tradition equates quality with social exclusiveness. A third tradition equates quality with what a school teaches, or tries to teach. The next three sections of this chapter will describe inequality between and within schools from these three perspectives, looking at differences between expenditures in one school and another, differences in the racial, economic, and academic composition of different schools, and differences in what schools try to teach students enrolled in different tracks and curriculums.

Before describing expenditure differences between schools, a brief comment on the rationale for looking at expenditures may be helpful.[20] As we will see in Chapters 3 and 5, no specific school resource has a consistent effect on students' test scores or on students' eventual educational attainment. Thus if we valued school resources solely in terms of their long-term effects on students, we might well conclude that schools with few resources were as good as schools with ample resources. We do not believe this, however. Children spend between a sixth and a quarter of their lives in school. Teachers and administrators spend even more of their lives in schools. The quality of life in a school is therefore important, even if it has no effect whatever on students' chances of adult success. It is bad for children to be hungry, whether or not hunger produces brain damage, and it is bad for children to be miserable or bored in school, regardless of whether misery and boredom in school lead to misery and boredom in adult life.

We have no way of proving that the quality of teachers' and students' lives is affected by the resources available to their school. We do know, however, that both teachers and students *feel* there is a connection. Virtually everyone prefers small classes, new buildings in which the paint is not peeling off the walls, plenty of books in the school library, and teachers who are paid enough so they do not have to take a second job. We cannot say which of these expenditures does the most to improve the quality of people's lives and which does the least. All we can do is assume that each school district (and each school) does the best it can to make school life more satisfactory with whatever resources it has. This "best" may not be very good. It usually involves sacrificing some people's interests (usually children's) to other people's (usually adults'). Still, the more resources a school has, the less often it is likely to have to sacrifice anyone's interests. If there is enough to go round, even the have-nots may get something. We will therefore assume that well-financed schools are better for their students in the short run than poorly financed schools.[21] We will assume this despite the evidence, discussed at length in later chapters, that well-financed schools do not make much difference to students' long-run cognitive development or adult success.

There are three distinct sources of variation in school expenditures: differences between states, differences between districts in the same state, and differences between schools in the same district.

### DIFFERENCES BETWEEN STATES

In 1969–1970, the average American school spent $783 per pupil. Schools in New York State spent an average of $1,237, while schools in Alabama spent an average of $438. These were extreme cases, however. Thirty of the 50 states spent between $600 and $880 per pupil.[22]

Inequality between states is declining, but this is not because federal aid is increasing. The federal government paid only 9 percent of the total cost of public schooling in 1969, and these funds were not distributed in such a way as to reduce inequality much.[23]

Expenditure differences between states depend largely on differences in states' tax bases.[24] Wealth and income differences between states have been shrinking, so expenditure differences have done the same.[25]

### DIFFERENCES BETWEEN DISTRICTS

Expenditure differences between districts in the same state are probably less than the differences between states.[26] This is not because school districts in the same state have equal incomes from local sources. The tax bases of districts in the same state are as unequal as the tax bases of different states. However, state governments almost always do more to reduce expenditure differences between districts than the federal government does to reduce differences between states.[27]

The average state government pays about 40 percent of the cost of public education within its borders, whereas the federal government pays only 9 percent. This means that if the state gives the same amount per pupil to every district, without considering need, it will automatically reduce inequality between districts by a moderate amount. If, for example, one district spent $800 per pupil, while another spent $1,200, the richer would be spending 50 percent more than the poorer. If the state then gave $200 per pupil to both districts, expenditures would be $1,000 and $1,400, and the richer would be spending only 40 percent more than the poorer. A number of states go beyond this, giving more aid to poor districts than to rich ones. Formulas which purport to do this have become increasingly popular in recent years. Their implementation has, however, often been hedged with so many restrictions that the ultimate effect is not nearly as redistributive as the basic formula might lead people to expect. As a result, the degree of inequality between districts in the same state still depends largely on the percentage of local funds coming from the state and only secondarily on the specific formula governing distribution of the state's funds.[28]

We have no trend data on inequalities between districts in the same state. We suspect that disparities between rich and poor districts' tax bases have declined, since many very poor rural districts have been consolidated with somewhat more affluent ones. State aid is also more redistributive than in the past, simply because there is more of it. The percentage of school funds coming from the state rose from 17 percent in 1920 to 40 percent in 1950, although it has not risen since then.[29] This means that the "natural" level of redistribution rose until 1950 and then stabilized. Aid formulas may have become slightly more redistributive since 1950, although this is far from certain. Unless state or federal aid increases dramatically, or the Supreme Court upholds recent lower court decisions requiring state legislatures to revamp their aid formulas, there is not likely to be much movement toward equality in the forseeable future.

### DIFFERENCES BETWEEN SCHOOLS IN THE SAME DISTRICT

Unlike federal and state governments, local school boards do not have to "offset" the effects of neighborhood differences in wealth in order to ensure equal expenditures. All they have to do is give every school the same amount. Under these circumstances it is even harder to justify inequality between schools in the same district than inequality between districts. Nonetheless, such differences persist, though they are not as large as differences between districts and between states.[30] We know no trend data on these disparities.

### LIFETIME INEQUALITIES IN EXPENDITURES ON INDIVIDUALS

Inequalities in annual expenditures may be either exacerbated or offset by inequalities in the length of time students stay in school. The student who drops out at the age of 16 is likely to get less than his share of public funds, even if he attends high-cost schools prior to 16. The student who attends a publicly subsidized college and graduate school is likely to receive more than his share of public funds, even if he attends relatively low-cost institutions at each level.

We have no good data on the degree of lifetime inequality in public expenditures on individual students. We have, however, made some crude estimates. We began by ignoring expenditure differences between one school and another. On this basis, we estimated that the most extensively educated fifth of the population received about 75 percent more than their share of the nation's educational resources, while the least extensively educated fifth received about half their share.[31] Such disparities are declining because disparities in the number of years of schooling people receive are declining.[32] Some people, however, get *both* protracted schooling *and* schooling that costs a lot annually. The eventual resource disparity between the most- and least-favored students is thus at least 4 to 1, and perhaps more.

### RICH CHILDREN VERSUS POOR CHILDREN

Most people are not primarily concerned with random injustices that fall on rich and poor alike. They are concerned with expenditure differences between schools and individuals because they see this kind of inequality as part of a more general system in which the poor and the black get less than the rich and the white. Even if the effects of school expenditure on adult inequality are trivial, it is still important for poor and black children to get their share of the nation's resources while they are children.

We know that poor states spend less on education than rich ones, and that poor districts within a state spend less than rich districts in the same state. We also know, however, that many rich parents live in poor states and districts, and that many poor parents live in rich ones. As a result, expenditures on rich and poor children do not differ as much as we might expect. If two families' incomes differ by $1,000, their districts' average expenditure per pupil will only differ by an average of about $7.50 per year.[33]

Within any given district, schools serving predominantly middle-class areas typically spend a little more than schools serving poorer areas, but the differences are small and inconsistent.[34] Overall, the evidence suggests that the richest fifth of all families have their children in schools that spend about 20 percent more than the schools serving the poorest fifth.[35] For families whose incomes differ less dramatically, expenditure differences are correspondingly less. A few rich families use high-cost private schools, but this is exceptional.[36]

In a country where the top fifth of all families receives 800 to 1,000 percent more income than the bottom fifth, the fact that children from these same families attend schools whose expenditures differ by only 20 percent seems like a triumph of egalitarianism. Before a national celebration is begun, though, we must also take note of the fact that children from rich families stay in school longer than children from poor families. When we take this into account, we estimate that America spends about twice as much on the children of the rich as on the children of the poor.[37]

WHITES VERSUS BLACKS

Black children are more likely to live in poorly financed school districts than white children. This is because more black children than white children live in the South. Within either region, blacks and whites have about the same chance of being in an affluent district.[38] This may surprise readers who think of northern blacks as living in impoverished cities and of northern whites as living in affluent suburbs. Fortunately, most northern cities are not all that impoverished. Big city schools generally spend about as much per pupil as the state in which they are located. (Of course they may need more than the state average, but that is another issue.) While some whites live in affluent suburbs, many live in small towns and working-class suburbs where the schools spend less than in big cities.

We do not have good national data on differences in expenditure on blacks and whites in the same district. Local studies suggest that some districts discriminate against black children while others discriminate in their favor. Boston, where the school board is notoriously antiblack, seems to spend slightly more money on black than white pupils.[39] Chicago spent substantially less on blacks in 1961, but had apparently reduced the gap to zero by 1966 as a result of intense political pressure and help from Title I.[40] New York City moved from favoring whites in the 1950s to favoring blacks and Puerto Ricans in the late 1960s.[41] In Detroit, there was discrimination against blacks in the early 1960s and this persisted throughout the decade, despite the fact that Detroit had one of the most liberal school boards in the country. The differences were quite small, however. In 1969, for example, Detroit's predominantly black schools spent about 12 percent less than white schools.[42] Washington, D.C. is the only city for which we have recent data showing large differences (i.e. about 25 percent) between expenditures in white and black schools.[43] We assume that there was a similar pattern in many other southern cities prior to the start of wholesale busing. As southern schools desegregate, however, expenditures on black and white children inevitably even out somewhat.

All in all, blacks suffer from living in the South, and they often also suffer from being in schools that get slightly less money than the average for their district. Our best guess is that America spends about 15–20 percent more per year on the average white child than on the average black school child.[44] These disparities are probably declining, however, because blacks are moving out of the South, because blacks in the South are moving into the same schools as whites, and because some northern cities are allocating more funds to black schools in order to head off pressures for busing.

The picture is complicated by the fact that whites stay in school longer than blacks. As a result, blacks born at the turn of the century probably had less than half as much spent on their education as whites. Blacks born during World War II probably had something like two-thirds as much spent on their education as the average white. Blacks now in school will probably have three-quarters to four-fifths as much spent on them as whites do.[45]

CONCLUSIONS

America spends far more money educating some children than others. These variations are largely explained by where a student happens to live and how much schooling he gets.

Unequal expenditures do not, as we shall see, account for the fact that some children learn to read more competently than others, nor for the fact that some adults are more economically successful than others. The case for equalizing expenditures must therefore rest on a simpler logic, which asserts that public money ought to be equitably distributed even if the distribution of such money has no long-term effect. There is no evidence that building a school playground, for example, will affect the students' chances of learning to read, getting into college, or making $50,000 a year when they are 50. Building a playground may, however, have a considerable effect on the students' chances of having a good time during recess when they are 8. The same thing is probably also true of small classes, competent teachers, and a dozen other things that distinguish adequately from inadequately financed schools.

Adequate school funding cannot, then, be justified on the grounds that it makes life better in the hereafter. But it can be justified on the grounds that it makes life better right now. This suggests that students' and teachers' claims on the public purse are no more legitimate than the claims of highway users who want to get home a few minutes faster, manufacturers of supersonic aircraft who want to help their stockholders pay for Caribbean vacations, or medical researchers who hope to extend a man's life expectancy by another year or two. But neither are the schools' claims any less legitimate than the claims of other groups.

## Access to Privileged Schoolmates

Many people define a good school not as one with fancy facilities or highly paid teachers, but as one with the right kind of students. A definition of this kind makes it hard to provide good schooling for everyone. Once a "good" school starts taking in "undesirable" students (the definition of desirable being sometimes academic, sometimes social, and sometimes economic), its standing automatically declines. From this perspective, then, the quality of a school depends on its exclusiveness. Sometimes this exclusiveness is written into law, as in the case of racial segregation. Sometimes it is merely a by-product of the law, as in the case of zoning that excludes low-income families from high-income neighborhoods and hence from high-income neighborhood schools. Sometimes exclusiveness is a by-product of the "free market." This is the case in neighborhoods whose housing prices reflect the reputation of the neighborhood school. Such a neighborhood attracts only families that are willing to pay extra for what they assume is "quality" education.

Subsequent chapters suggest that people who define a good school in terms of its student body are probably wiser than those who define it in terms of its budget. We have found some evidence that an elementary school's social composition has a modest effect on students' cognitive development, as well as some evidence that a school's racial composition has a modest effect on black students' later occupational status. The effects are generally small, and the evidence is far from conclusive, but it is more convincing than the evidence purporting to show that expenditures matter.

Whatever its long-term effect, the character of the student body determines what friends a student is likely to make, what kinds of values he will be exposed to, and often whether he will be happy or unhappy. As a result, many parents make great sacrifices to get their children into a school with what they regard as the right schoolmates. Just as we accept the proposition that equalizing expenditures is part of equalizing educational opportunity, even though equalization has no long-term effects, so, too, we accept the proposition that equalizing access to desirable schoolmates is part of equal opportunity, even though its long-term effects are problematic.

Unfortunately, it is not always easy to tell what kind of schoolmates parents or children regard as desirable. Polls show, for example, that all other things being equal most black parents would rather send their children to a racially mixed school than to an all-black school. But all other things are rarely equal, and experience with open enrollment does not suggest that most black parents in the North want their children bused long distances to desegregated schools unless these schools also have other advantages.

Nonetheless, a great deal of public discussion assumes that all parents and children prefer schools in which the students are advantaged (i.e. white, middle class, academically talented, or all three). If this assumption were correct, equalizing opportunity would mean making the social composition of every school the same. Such a school system would be completely desegregated—racially, economically, academically, and in any other way that seemed relevant. Every child would have precisely the same proportion of advantaged and disadvantaged school-mates.

If everyone wanted the same kind of schoolmates, we could measure inequality of opportunity by measuring the amount of variation in the composition of different schools. The less variation we found, the closer we would say the schools had come to equalizing opportunity (opportunity in this case being defined as contact with advantaged schoolmates). The only difficulty with this approach is that some disadvantaged parents and students may not be enthusiastic about schools in which most of the parents and students are better off than they. Some black students prefer predominantly black schools, some working-class students prefer predominantly working-class schools, and some low-aptitude students prefer schools where there is little academic competition. To the extent that students prefer schoolmates like themselves, they prefer segregated rather than desegregated schools.

It can, of course, be argued that schools should be completely desegregated regardless of what people want. Those who take this position usually assume, however, that segregated schools lead to poor reading scores, exclusion from higher education, and diminished chances of earning an adequate living. They also assume that parents and students who prefer segregated schools are unaware of this cost and would change their views if they realized how much harm their parochialism was doing their children. As we shall see, the measurable effects of segregation on students' later lives are small and uncertain. Blacks and working-class whites who prefer schools they feel are their own cannot, then, be faulted on the grounds that they are denying their children equal opportunity. Their children will not usually have completely equal opportunity no matter what schools they attend, but desegregation will only make a marginal difference.

Some people accept all this but argue that schools should be desegregated for political reasons, regardless of how desegregation affects individual opportunity. Many believe, on the basis of extremely scanty evidence, that exposing children to people unlike themselves helps develop tolerance and understanding. Others see school desegregation as part of a political process in which diverse people (adults as well as children) are forced to accept the fact that they have to live with one another. They assume this will be a good thing for society in the long run, even if it increases tension in the short run. We know no way to judge the validity of this latter argument, but we have considerable sympathy with it.

The remainder of this section will discuss the extent of racial, economic, and academic segregation in America's public schools. We will not try to calculate the extent to which segregation is voluntary or involuntary, although we think it fair to assume that voluntary segregation is the exception rather than the rule.

Until recently, most American children attended schools that were either all white or all black. In the South, racial segregation was required by law until 1954, and it persisted on a de facto basis until the late 1960s. In 1965, for example, when the federal government made its Equality of Educational Opportunity Survey (EEOS), about 90 percent of the black children in the South were still attending black schools (i.e. schools that were more than 80 percent black).[46] By 1968, only 80 percent of southern blacks were in black schools, and by the fall of 1970 the figure had fallen to about 40 percent.[47] It is not clear how much further the Supreme Court will require southern school districts to go toward complete desegregation, but the proportion of southern blacks in all-black schools is likely to end up well below 40 percent.

In the North, many states have never had laws requiring segregation. Such laws as once existed were repealed well before 1954. Nonetheless, most northern schools remain racially segregated. In 1970, the Department of Health, Education and Welfare found that 57 percent of black northern children were attending segregated schools. If anything, this was an increase over 1965.[48] In general the situation is worse in elementary than in secondary schools.[49]

Economic segregation is far less pervasive than racial segregation. While it would be an exaggeration to say that every school is a microcosm of the larger society, this is certainly closer to the truth than the opposite exaggeration, which portrays every school as uniformly middle class or lower class. These terms describe the dominant group in a school, not a uniform pattern. The range of economic backgrounds in the typical elementary school is only 15 to 20 percent less than for the nation as a whole.[50] A few schools are more homogeneous than this, but hardly any public school enrolls uniformly affluent or uniformly poor students. This means that a poor child has a much greater chance of being in a school with a lot of middle-class children than a black child has of being in a school with a lot of white children.[51]

Schools are also segregated in terms of academic competence. This means that children with low test scores have a better than average chance of ending up in schools where most of the other children also score below average. This is largely because of economic and racial segregation, but there are also differences in the academic competence of students entering different schools at the same economic level. The most plausible explanation for this is that some parents in any given economic stratum have a stronger interest than others in their children's cognitive development. These parents appear to concentrate in neighborhoods where the schools have a good reputation. They also tend to have children who score above the norm for their economic group. The result is a moderate degree of academic segregation, over and above what we would expect on the basis of racial and economic segregation alone. The degree of academic segregation is about the same as the degree of economic segregation, which means it is considerably less prevalent than racial segregation.[52]

## Access to Fast Classes and College Curriculums

We suggested at the outset that there are three popular definitions of a good school: schools that spend a lot of money, schools that enroll the right students, and schools that teach the right subjects in the right way. In America, however, there is not much difference between the formal curriculums of most public schools. Studying the right subjects is largely a matter of being in the right track or curriculum within a given school.

At the elementary level, almost all children are expected to acquire the same basic skills, but some children are expected to acquire these skills faster than others. This often leads to "ability grouping" or "tracking." Tracking means putting fast learners in separate classes from slow learners. Ability grouping may involve tracking, but even when schools assign children to classes randomly, teachers often group the children by ability within the classroom.[53]

At the secondary level there are also variations in course content, which supposedly reflect variations in students' interests, as well as variations in their ability to do academic work. In many cases students are formally assigned to a "college preparatory" curriculum, a "technical" curriculum, a "business" curriculum, or a "general" curriculum. There are sometimes further distinctions between fast and slow tracks within these curriculums.

A 1967 National Education Association survey found that tracking was quite common at the elementary level. Twenty-seven percent of all districts reported that they grouped all elementary school pupils by ability, 43 percent reported that they only grouped some children, 25 percent reported random grouping, and 5 percent did not report. In districts that did not track students, some teachers presumably grouped students by ability within their classroom. At the secondary level, 85 percent of all districts reported ability grouping.[54] The practice seems to be favored by the overwhelming majority of teachers.[55]

A student's track or curriculum is the single most important determinant of what the school will try to teach him. If anything the school does to a student makes any difference, this should be it. Tracks and curriculums are by definition segregated in terms of academic ability. This almost inevitably means they are also segregated, albeit to a lesser extent, in terms of social class and race. Indeed, the character of a student's classmates depends at least as much on his track or curriculum as on the school he attends.[56] Thus if school segregation is a denial of equal opportunity, curriculum assignment is susceptible to the same objections.

Neither track nor curriculum assignment seems to have an appreciable effect on students' cognitive development.[57] High school curriculum assignment does, however, have some impact on a student's chances of attending college.[58] This means it has some indirect effect on later occupational status and earnings. In turn, elementary school track assignment may influence high school curriculum assignment. Furthermore, even if track or curriculum assignment has no long-term effects, it has important short-term effects on the lives of the children involved. For these reasons it seems important to find out how schools actually assign children to tracks and curriculums.

In northern urban high schools, EEOS found that 84 percent of all high school seniors said they were in the curriculum they wanted to be in. Ninety percent of those in the college curriculum said they wanted to go to college. Sixty-two percent of those in other tracks said they did not want to go to college.[59] Unfortunately, we cannot determine when these preferences and aspirations were first formed. We do not know whether most students were originally put in the curriculum they wanted to be in, or whether they simply adapted their tastes to reality once the school authorities had defined reality for them. Roughly 15 percent of all students in noncollege curriculums said they were still unhappy about it.

After personal preference, the next most important determinant of curriculum placement seems to be academic ability. The correlation between test scores and curriculum assignment is around 0.50.[60] (Readers who are unfamiliar with correlation coefficients may wish to read the explanation of measures of association in Appendix C. The size of a correlation coefficient can range from -1.0 to +1.0. The closer a correlation coefficient is to 0, the weaker the association between the two variables. Coefficients close to -1.0 indicate a strong negative relationship; one variable goes up when the other goes down. Coefficients close to +1.0 indicate a strong positive relationship.)

To our surprise, social class did not seem to play an important role in high school curriculum placement, except insofar as it influenced test scores. Among northern urban students with the same test scores, those with white-collar parents were only 3 percent more likely to be in the college curriculum than those with blue-collar parents.[61]

Even more surprising, EEOS showed that northern urban blacks were 2 percent more likely to be in the college track than whites with comparable test scores in the same school. When we compared blacks and whites of comparable economic background as well as comparable test scores, we found that the blacks were 7 percent more likely than the whites to be in the college track. This was partly due to the fact that the blacks had higher aspirations than whites of comparable background and ability in the same school. In addition, in the three all-black northern 4-year high schools covered by EEOS, blacks had higher aspirations and were more likely to be in the college track than similar blacks in integrated high schools. The differences were not large enough to warrant sweeping conclusions, but they certainly do not suggest that desegregation boosts a student's chances of being in a college curriculum.[62]

When we turn from high schools to elementary schools, the facts are harder to determine. The 1967 NEA survey referred to earlier provides data on how administrators say children are tracked. Most districts report using a combination of test scores and teacher recommendations, but some also say they take into account grades, social maturity, and parental desires. Larger districts place more emphasis on test scores than smaller ones. Folklore and anecdotal evidence suggest that race and class also have considerable influence, over and above test scores, but that is what the folklore led us to expect at the secondary level too, and our expectations proved wrong.

In the absence of national data on how American elementary schools actually assign children to tracks, our findings about England may be of interest. English primary schools assign children to streams largely on the basis of teachers' assessments. Teachers take account of test scores in judging students' ability, but other unidentified characteristics also play a role. Social class is among these characteristics, but its role is very small—comparable to its role in American high school curriculum assignment.[63]

The fact that schools do not discriminate directly against black or working-class students does not, of course, mean that these students are proportionately represented in the fast tracks or in college curriculums. They are invariably underrepresented, both because they are less likely to have high test scores, and because they are less likely to want to go to college.

Excluding students from the college curriculum on the basis of their test scores is widely accepted as necessary and legitimate. In our view, however, it is neither. It is true that students with low scores are less likely to do competent work in high school and less likely to enter college than students with high scores. If the college curriculum were like college itself—an expensive luxury which society perhaps cannot afford to give everyone—restricting access to it would perhaps be unavoidable. Test scores would then be one of the many factors that high schools might take into account in rationing scarce places. In point of fact, however, it costs no more to have a student in the college curriculum than in the general curriculum, and it costs less than having him in a technical curriculum. The only argument for excluding a student who wants to enter the college curriculum is therefore that he cannot possibly do the work. However, some students with quite low test scores can do the work in a college curriculum, and also in a college.[64] The use of test scores to exclude students from the college curriculum cannot, then, be justified in terms of either necessity or equity. It is mainly a matter of bureaucratic convenience and "maintaining standards."

Elementary school tracking on the basis of test scores is subject to some of the same objections as high school curriculum assignment. Test scores have a fairly strong relationship to how much and how easily children learn, but the relationship is far from perfect. In addition, some children's competence varies from one subject to another. This means that any assignment policy that applies to all different skills is bound to be wrong in some cases. Equalizing opportunities to learn requires a system that is flexible enough to respond to children's specialized abilities, to changes in their performance over time, and to discrepancies between test scores and other kinds of performance. Ability grouping by classroom almost never achieves this.

The most obvious alternative to placing students on the basis of test scores, grades, and other similar criteria is to let students place themselves. This is not feasible at the elementary level, which is one good reason not to track elementary school children at all. At the secondary level, substantial numbers of schools, especially in the West, have abandoned the whole idea of separate curriculums. They simply offer a variety of courses and allow each student to work out a program that suits his interests and plans. But even if a high school offers distinct curriculums, there is no reason why it cannot let the students decide for themselves which one they want to pursue. Some students would undoubtedly make the wrong decision, but then high schools also make a lot of mistakes when they start making decisions for students.

The evidence we have reviewed suggests that the existing system of curriculum choice is already more heavily influenced by what students say they want than by anything else. To the extent that this is so, the system provides what we think of as "equal opportunity." This does not, however, mean that the system is in any sense ideal. It can be argued that eighth and ninth graders should be discouraged from making *any* irrevocable decisions about their future. If so, perhaps everyone ought to be assigned to a college curriculum, so as to keep open the possibility of later attending college.

The evidence also underlines the limited value of equalizing "opportunity" without equalizing anything else. Students are not all equally talented, equally ambitious, or equally hard working. A system which provides everyone with equal opportunity will ensure that the more talented, ambitious, and diligent succeed, while others fail. Some will choose curriculums that lead nowhere, because such curriculums involve less work in the short run. Some will eschew college, because they dislike the idea of spending 4 more years reading books. Some will avoid high-status jobs, because they are afraid of responsibility or even of success. The fact that this happens does not prove that the students' educational opportunities were unequal; it proves that equal opportunity is not enough to ensure equal results.

## Conclusions about Inequality in the Schools

The evidence reviewed in this chapter suggests that educational opportunities are far from equal. This inequality takes several forms. First, resources are unequally distributed. Second, some people have more chance than others to attend school with the kind of schoolmates they prefer. Third, some people are denied access to the curriculums of their choice. None of these inequalities appears to us either necessary or just. What, then, might be done to remedy these problems?

Let us begin with the problem of equalizing different students' claims on the nation's educational resources. First, we need to make annual expenditures per pupil more equal. In order to equalize expenditures in different states, we would need to expand federal aid and drastically revise existing formulas for distributing such aid, so as to concentrate it on poor states. If we want perfect equality between districts in the same state, we must end the schools' dependence on local taxes and raise all school revenue from statewide taxes or federal aid. If we want to preserve some local discretion, we can rely on state aid formulas which make each district's income depend on the local tax rate, but not on the local tax base. "Compensatory" formulas of this latter kind have already been adopted in some states, although usually with severe restrictions. In effect, they compute each district's revenue by assuming that the district has as much taxable property per pupil as the wealthiest district in the state, and that it is taxing all this property at the rate that it actually applies to local property. The difference between the district's theoretical entitlement and its actual income from local taxation is made up by state aid. A formula of this kind results in some inequality, since districts have different tax rates, but the degree of inequality is far less than at present. Finally, if we want to eliminate disparities between schools in the same district, we must persuade school boards to provide extra resources to those schools that now spend relatively little. If, for example, schools in poor areas have high teacher turnover and hence have low average salaries, these schools must be given extra staff or other resources.

All these changes are easy to imagine, though not to implement. They grow naturally out of values that are already widely accepted in American society. But even if we were to succeed in equalizing annual expenditures per pupil, we would still be left with inequities that derive from the fact that some students get more education than others. Unlike differences in annual expenditure, differences in lifetime expenditure strike most people as entirely reasonable. Even those who have a generally egalitarian outlook usually assume that the ideal educational system would provide everyone with as much education as he wanted, and that we would finance this from a progressive income tax. They see no injustice in taxing high school dropouts to finance higher education, so long as the dropout is free to attend college if he wants to.

This attitude seems to us to derive from a mistaken analogy between education and other public services. In general, public services are free either because it is difficult to determine who benefits from them or because the beneficiaries are more needy than the average taxpayer. Public parks fall into the first category, while public hospitals fall into the second. Advanced education falls into neither category. It is easy to identify the primary beneficiaries of subsidies for higher education, namely the students. It is also easy to predict that on the average these beneficiaries will be better able to pay for their education than is the average taxpayer.

It can be argued, of course, that higher education provides benefits for those who do not attend college as well as those who do. Even the poor, for example, need lawyers. The mere fact of a public benefit is not, however, sufficient justification for a public subsidy. Hot dog vendors, for example, also render a public service, but they do not need a public subsidy. A public subsidy only makes sense if some necessary service will dry up in its absence. If, for example, lawyers earned so little that nobody was willing to pay for his own legal training, legal education might require subsidy. In fact, however, there are plenty of law school applicants, and there would be plenty even if would-be lawyers had to borrow against future income to finance the full cost of their training.

Public discussion of these issues is complicated by widespread acceptance of a false dichotomy. Many assume that there are only two alternatives: a system in which access to education depends on parents' ability and willingness to pay, and a system in which costs are shared by everyone. There is, however, a third alternative. We can create a system in which access to education depends on the *student's* willingness to pay—not at the time he gets his education, but later, when he is presumably enjoying its benefits. Ideally, funds for advanced education probably ought to come from a surcharge on the income tax of those who have had education beyond, say, the age of 16. Failing that, it would still be fairer to finance advanced education through long-term loans to those who attend college and graduate school than through taxes on those who do not attend.

The primary objection to such a system of educational finance is not that it would be inequitable, but that it would probably reduce the over-all demand for education. We do not know how many students would drop out of school or college if they knew they would eventually have to pay for it, but some doubtless would. Despite widespread hostility to students as a class, most Americans feel that schooling is a good thing. They are reluctant to impose what looks like a tax on virtue (i.e. staying in school) in order to reduce the cost of vice (i.e. dropping out). If we accepted this basic moral equation, we too would favor a system in which higher education was financed from general taxation. Since we reject the equation of schooling with virtue, we prefer a system in which higher education is financed by taxing those who have benefited from it directly.

Equalizing access to privileged schoolmates is even more contro-
versial than equalizing claims on resources. Busing arouses more
passion than state aid formulas. In principle, we believe that an ideal
pupil assignment system should give every student an opportunity to
attend any public school he (or his parents) find appealing. Indeed,
we would go so far as to *define* a "public" school as one that is open to
any student who wants to attend. All other schools, regardless of
formal control or financing, are to some degree "private."

If we want to give everyone equal access to every school, certain
reforms seem necessary. First, school districts ought to admit any student
in the district to any school he wants to attend, regardless of whether
he lives near the school or far from it. Second, they ought to pay the
cost of transporting any pupil to any school in his district. Thus a
student from a poor neighborhood who wants to attend a school in a
rich neighborhood ought to have precisely the same opportunity to do
so as a student who lives in the rich neighborhood. This might, of course,
mean that some schools in rich neighborhoods became overcrowded. If
this happened, demand might slack off. If it did not, the district could
expand the school, using portable classrooms or whatever other ex-
pedients seemed feasible. If expansion were really impossible—which
it rarely is—applicants could be admitted by lot. If popular schools got
too large, they could simply be divided in half. Applicants could then
be assigned randomly to one of the two new adjoining schools.

Those who believe in neighborhood schools object to this approach
on the grounds that "outsiders will take over our schools." These are
likely to be the same people who resist outsiders (i.e. blacks) moving
into "their" neighborhood. Committed integrationists also object to
such a system, on the grounds that it is simply a warmed-over version
of what the North calls "open enrollment" and the South calls "freedom of choice." Such a system does not ensure that every black child
will attend school with whites or vice versa. Blacks will only attend
school with whites if they apply to schools where whites are enrolled.
Whites can escape attending school with blacks if they can find schools
that have no black applicants. In a community where blacks are expected to stay in their place, and are subject to all sorts of sanctions if
they apply to an all-white school, a system of this kind will achieve
almost nothing. In a community where the school administration be-
lieves in desegregated schooling and encourages black parents to attend
desegregated schools, such a system could produce dramatic changes in
attendance patterns. The "liberal" alternative, which is widely viewed
as the road to racial equality, seems to be compulsory busing of blacks

to white neighborhoods, and vice versa. This implies that black parents cannot send their children to all-black schools, even if they want to, because all-black schools are *by definition* inferior. This position strikes us as both racist and politically unworkable over the long haul.

When we turn from school assignment to curriculum assignment, we again lean to "freedom of choice" solutions. This means we think schools should avoid classifying students whenever possible. At the elementary level, students should be assigned to classes randomly, and teachers should try to respond to students' individual interests rather than expecting all students to learn the same thing. At the secondary level, students should not be segregated into "college preparatory" and "noncollege" curriculums that determine what they must study, but should be free to design their own curriculums from whatever courses the school offers. Students who hope to attend college must be told what academic courses they need to take, and encouraged to take them. But if they also want to take vocational courses, that too should be possible. Students who want some kind of job training should be given it, assuming the school can devise training programs of practical value. But if these students also want to take academic courses, they should also be encouraged to do so on the same basis as anyone else.

These reforms are not likely to make students appreciably more equal after they finish school. They would, however, give every student an equal claim on educational resources, desirable classmates, and interesting subject matter while he was in school. By recognizing that every child's needs are equally legitimate, they would not only make educational arrangements more egalitarian, but might spark similar reforms in institutions that serve adults.

# NOTES

1. The Equality of Educational Opportunity Survey (EEOS) showed that among children who entered first grade in 1960 (and were therefore in sixth grade in 1965), 59 percent reported having attended kindergarten (see p. 77 in Mayeske et al., "Item Response Analyses"). The 1960 school enrollment survey (see Tables 2 and 4 in U.S. Bureau of the Census, "School Enrollment: 1960") showed that 49 percent of all 5 year olds were in kindergarten and that another 15 percent were in the first grade. No data were collected on 4 year olds, but since 15 percent of 5 year olds were in first

grade, it seems reasonable to assume that at least 10 percent of 4 year olds were in kindergarten. This would coincide with the EEOS estimate that 59 percent attended kindergarten at one age or another.

The 1970 school enrollment survey (see the U.S. Bureau of the Census, "School Enrollment: 1970") showed that 13 percent of all 4 year olds, 65 percent of all 5 year olds, and 5 percent of all 6 year olds were in kindergarten. Allowing for some repeaters, it seems reasonable to infer that about 80 percent of all 6 year olds had attended kindergarten at one time or another.

2. EEOS found that 12 percent of the children who entered first grade in 1960 (i.e. sixth graders in 1965) and 12 percent of those who entered first grade in 1963 (i.e. third graders in 1965) reported that they had attended nursery school. But first grade teachers reported that only 9 percent of the pupils who entered in 1965 had attended nursery school. (Another 10 percent had attended the summer Head Start program, but the year-round Head Start program did not begin until 1965.) It is unlikely that the percentage in preschool actually fell during the early 1960s. We assume that the apparent change is attributable to the fact that data on the younger children came from teachers rather than from pupils. Ten percent seems a reasonable compromise estimate for this period.

The 1970 school enrollment survey found that 12 percent of 3 year olds, 16 percent of 4 year olds, and 3 percent of 5 year olds were in nursery school. Virtually all those who are in school at 3 are in school again at 4, but about half of all 4 year olds are in kindergarten rather than nursery school. Of the 12 percent who enter nursery school at 3, we therefore assume that around half are in nursery school again at 4. This means that about $16 - (12/2) = 10$ percent of all 4 year olds are entering nursery school for the first time. Most of the 5 year olds in nursery school are probably repeaters. We, therefore, estimate that about 22 percent $(12 + 10)$ of those born in 1966 spent a year or more in nursery school.

3. Throughout the book, inequality is described in terms of standard deviations and coefficients of variation (the standard deviation divided by the mean). An explanation of these concepts will be found in Appendix C. An increase in the coefficient of variation signifies an increase in inequality; a small (close to 0.00) coefficient of variation indicates a low level of inequality.

The mean proportion attending kindergarten in 1960 was 0.60. The standard deviation was, therefore, $\sqrt{(0.6)(1 - 0.6)} = 0.49$, and the coefficient of variation was $0.49/0.60 = 0.82$. The mean in 1970 was 0.80, the standard deviation was 0.40, and the coefficient of variation was thus 0.50. Between 1960 and 1970 the coefficient of variation for nursery schooling dropped from $\sqrt{(0.1)(1 - 0.1)}/0.1 = 3$ to $\sqrt{(0.22)(1 - 0.22)}/0.22 = 1.88$. A Gini coefficient yields a similar result, since the percentage of people receiving 100 percent (or any smaller percent) of the preschooling rose steadily. For a discussion of different measures of inequality, see Alker and Russet, "On Measuring Equality."

4. See the U.S. Bureau of the Census, "School Enrollment: October, 1970."

5. Enrollment data are from the U.S. Bureau of the Census, "School-Enrollment, and Education of Young Adults and their Fathers: October, 1960," and "School Enrollment: October, 1970." Kindergarten utilization was estimated by comparing total kindergarten enrollment to the number of 5 year olds and subtracting 3 percent for repeaters, as in note 1.

6. EEOS found that blacks had somewhat less access to kindergartens than whites, largely because they were more likely to live in the rural South where kindergartens are exceptional (see Coleman et al., *Equality of Educational Opportunity*). In the urban North, where blacks are as likely as whites to be in districts with free kindergartens, they are still somewhat less likely than whites to attend (see Jencks, "The Coleman Report and the Conventional Wisdom").

7. See p. 136 in Folger and Nam, *Education of the American Population*.

8. See the U.S. Bureau of the Census, "School Enrollment: 1970."

9. On past attainment, see Table 173 in the U.S. Bureau of the Census, "Characteristics of the Population, Part 1, United States Summary," 1964. Estimates for 1914 are based on all those aged 60–64 in 1960. Estimates for the mid-1960s are from the U.S. Bureau of the Census, "Educational Attainment: March 1971." The figures in the text are for those aged 22–24 in 1971. The percentages "entering high school" are those finishing ninth grade. In addition, an unknown percentage entered but did not finish ninth grade. In a few cases, ninth grade was part of a junior high school. Data on age of entering the labor force were estimated from enrollment data by age group (see the U.S. Bureau of the Census, "School Enrollment: October 1970" for current data).

10. See Table 1 in the U.S. Bureau of the Census, "Educational Attainment: March 1971." The estimates are for whites and blacks aged 22–24 in March 1971.

11. See Table 1 in the U.S. Bureau of the Census, "Educational Change in a Generation," 1964.

12. There are three basic sources of data on continuation ratios: (1) comparisons of enrollment reports at different levels in successive years, (2) follow-up studies of individuals initially enrolled at some level, and (3) retrospective studies of adults who report how far they went. Studies based on enrollment statistics are plagued by incomplete coverage and inconsistent definitions. Studies based on follow-ups of individuals tend to lose large numbers of students. Since retrospective Census reports of educational attainment appear to be quite accurate (see Siegel and Hodge, "A Causal Approach"), they are probably the most reliable way of estimating selectivity.

One limitation of retrospective data is that the Census only publishes information of the highest grade an individual *completed*, not on the highest grade *entered*. Appreciable numbers of individuals enter high school or college but complete less than 1 year. Large numbers also do some graduate work, especially in education, without completing a full year of it.

For a fuller presentation of the Census data on educational attainment, see Folger and Nam, *Education of the American Population*. For attempts to reconcile attainment and enrollment data see Jencks and Reisman, *The Academic Revolution,* as well as Folger and Nam.

13. See Table 8 in the U.S. Bureau of the Census. "Factors Related to High School Graduation and College Attendance: 1967."

14. For a detailed analysis of this issue see Hansen and Weisbrod, *Benefits, Costs, and Finance of Public Higher Education,* and the controversy surrounding their work in Volumes 4 to 6 of the *Journal of Human Resources.*

15. Throughout the book, we will compare the top and bottom fifths of various distributions. In most cases, these estimates are derived from the mean and standard deviation of the distribution by assuming that the distribution is normal. By averaging Z-scores, we can show that the top fifth of a normal distribution averages 1.4 standard deviations above the mean, while the bottom fifth averages 1.4 standard deviations below the mean. Since the standard deviation of education for individuals born between 1895 and 1904 was 3.76 years, and the mean was 8.9, the best-educated fifth averaged $8.9 + (1.4)(3.76) = 14.2$ years. The other figures can be derived in the same way.

In point of fact, education is not quite normally distributed. The deviations from normality are not large enough to make much difference, however, so we have usually ignored them. For those born between 1940 and 1944, for example, an estimate based on normality implies that the bottom fifth got 68 percent as much schooling as the national average, whereas direct estimation from census tables indicates that the bottom fifth actually got 66 percent as much as the national average. The approximation implies that the top fifth received 132 percent of the national average, whereas direct estimation yielded 133 percent. For those born between 1895 and 1904, the approximation implies values of 41 and 150 percent, whereas the observed values are 42 and 158 percent. For parallel calculations see Beverly Duncan, "Trends in Output and Distribution of Schooling."

Ideally, we would like to be able to estimate "years enrolled" rather than "highest grade completed." Unfortunately, such data does not seem to exist. The disparity between years enrolled and years completed does not appear to be large, however. U.S. Bureau of the Census, "School Enrollment in 1970," Table 7, shows that the standard deviation of years completed among students who are enrolled in school or college and who are the same age is about 1 year. The standard deviation of years completed for students dropping out at any given age is probably quite similar to this. The standard deviation of years completed for all students, regardless of the age at which they quit, is now about 2.8 years. Thus, if all students had attended school continuously, the number of years they had attended would explain about 87 percent $(1 - (1^2/2.8^2))$ of the variance in the highest grade they completed. This implies that years in attendance correlates about 0.93 ($\sqrt{0.87}$) with years completed. Since some people have not been in school continuously prior to dropping out, the true correlation between years of regular enrollment and highest grade completed presumably exceeds this estimate. The standard deviation of years completed for students of any given age was about the same in 1960 as in 1969, but it appears to have been closer to 1.25 years in 1950 (see Folger and Nam, *Education of the American Population*). The standard deviation of schooling for all individuals completing school in 1950 was also higher, i.e. about 3.2 years. Thus, the correlation between years attended and years completed should be about $\sqrt{1 - 1.25^2/3.2^2} = 0.92$. Folger and Nam report evidence that students were held back more often prior to World War II than after World War II. But the variance in attainment was also higher before World War II, so the correlation of attainment with attendance was probably still about 0.9.

Tabulating years enrolled as against years completed would probably reduce the standard deviations shown in Table 2–1 slightly. It would probably also slightly reduce the differences between blacks and whites.

16. This comparison will also be used frequently in the text. The estimate assumes that the difference between random individuals is equal to the standard deviation multiplied by $2/\sqrt{\pi} = 1.13$. This estimate assumes a normal distribution, but deviations from normality do not greatly alter it.

17. See the U.S. Bureau of the Census, "Educational Change in a Generation," 1964. The estimate in the text is based on a comparison between males aged 25–34 and 55–64 in 1962. Men whose fathers worked on farms or who did not report their father's occupation are excluded.

18. See Blau and Duncan, *The American Occupational Structure*, Table 5–3, and the discussions of cohort data in that volume and in Appendix B of this volume. The correlation between father's occupation and son's education showed no trend for men born between 1897 and 1936.

19. Schooling estimated for men aged 25–34 in 1962 (see note 17). Income estimated for all families in 1960, excluding those living on a farm (see Table 230 in the U.S. Bureau of the Census, "Characteristics of the Population, Part 1, United States Summary," 1964).

20. For a quite different approach see Michelson, "The Association of Teacher Resourceness with Children's Characteristics."

21. Ideally, we would like to compare schools' resources by looking at expenditures per pupil and then adjusting this to take account of price differences between one community and another. As a practical matter, however, we will have to settle for simple dollar differences. We are not sure whether expenditure differences overstate or understate differences in purchasing power. This probably depends on what a school wants to purchase. For a discussion of the price of similar teachers in different kinds of schools, see Levin, "A Cost-Effectiveness Analysis of Teacher Selection." Construction prices would vary in quite different ways from teacher prices.

22. The figures are for "current expenditures per pupil in average daily attendance." Since average daily attendance is about 92 percent of enrollment, the current cost per pupil enrolled was about 8 percent lower than the figures in the text. Amortizing capital costs probably adds about 8 percent to "current" costs, however, so the figures in the text are also about right for total cost per pupil. The figures are from p. 122 of the *Statistical Abstract of the United States* (1970).

23. See Grubb and Michelson in "States and Schools."

24. On the determinants of states' educational expenditures, see, e.g. Shapiro, "Some Socio-Economic Determinants."

25. See Freeman, *Financing the Public Schools.* For a full analysis of this issue see Grubb and Michelson, "States and Schools."

26. Grubb and Michelson in "States and Schools" compute Gini coefficients for districts in 16 states. The average Gini coefficient is 0.08, but there is great variation in the coefficient from one state to another. The Gini coefficient for differences between states is 0.13. Katzman in *The Political Economy of Urban Schools* used coefficients of variation and concluded that there was as much inequality within states as between, i.e. both coefficients of variation were about 0.25. Katzman had a more restricted data base, but Grubb and Michelson calculated coefficients mainly for states with relatively large districts..

27. See the summary in Grubb and Michelson's "States and Schools" for 16 states. Also see Coons, Clune, and Sugarman, *Private Wealth and Public Education.*

28. See Grubb and Michelson in "States and Schools."

29. See Table 39 in the U.S. Department of Health, Education and Welfare, *Digest of Educational Statistics,* 1965.

30. See Katzman, in *The Political Economy of Urban Schools,* for data on Boston elementary schools; Burkhead et al., in *Input and Output in Large City High Schools,* for data on Chicago and Atlanta high schools; and the unpublished work of Paul Smith of the Harvard Center for Law and Education for data on Detroit elementary schools. These sources yield coefficients of inequality of 0.15 ± 0.02 for schools in the same district. An analysis of intradistrict variation in salary expenditures per pupil using the EEOS sample yields comparable results, but this sample is not very appropriate for this purpose. Owen, in "The Distribution of Educational Resources in Large American Cities," provides parallel analyses of large cities covered by the EEOS.

31. This calculation is based on the distribution of educational attainment in the U.S. Bureau of the Census "Educational Attainment: 1969." Each year of schooling was weighted according to a crude estimate of its cost relative to other years. The weights were as follows: each year of elementary schooling was weighted 1.00; each year of high school was weighted 1.50; each year of college was weighted 3.00; each year of graduate schooling was weighted 6.00. The basic distributions were derived in the same way as in Table 1. The resulting coefficient of inequality was 0.46 for all individuals aged 25–29 in 1969. The distribution being skewed, the bottom fifth received 54 percent of the average, while the top fifth received 175 percent. The ratio is thus 3.2:1.

32. Using the same weighting system as in the note 31, the coefficient of inequality for all individuals aged 65–75 in 1969 was 0.64, compared to 0.46 for those aged 25–29.

33. A 1960 survey, reported in Chapter 19 of Morgan et al., *Income and Welfare in the United States,* estimated that the poorest fifth of all families lived in districts that spent 20 percent less than the districts where the richest fifth lived. Of course, many of the richest families lived in the

same districts as the poorest families. This survey obtained excellent adult in- come information. The methods used to estimate the expenditures of school districts in which the adults lived were rather inexact, however. Since not all the families in question had children in public school, the data were not precisely comparable to what would be obtained from a survey of parents with children in school.

The EEOS surveyed students in public schools. It did not get information on their parents' incomes, but it did get information on a variety of other parental characteristics. The characteristic of parents that was most highly correlated with district expenditures was the "mean educational attain- ment" of parents in a school. Coleman et al., in the Supplemental Appendix of *Equality of Educational Opportunity,* reported correlations of 0.15 be- tween the mean educational attainment of parents in a school and the district's mean expenditures for sixth and ninth grade whites. The correla- tion was lower for twelfth grade students. Using the EEOS data, Jencks found that at least in the urban North, about half the variance in mean pa- rental educational attainment was between elementary schools in the same district. The correlation between the mean attainment of parents in a dis- trict and the mean expenditures would thus be about $0.15/ \sqrt{0.50} = 0.21$. Since Morgan and his coauthors found a slightly stronger correlation be- tween expenditures and parental income than between expenditures and parental education, we might reasonably assume a correlation between district expenditures and parental income as high as 0.25. This is the same as the correlation obtained by Miner in *Social and Economic Factors.* Coleman and his coauthors report that the standard deviation of district expenditures (weighted by enrollment) was $177. The standard deviation of family income in 1965 was about $6,000. This implies a $7.50 per pupil increase in expenditures for every $1,000 increase in family income. This is consistent with the estimates provided by Morgan and his coauthors for the bottom two-thirds of the income distribution, although it is higher than their overall average.

34. Katzman, in *The Political Economy of Urban Schools,* using 1965 data, found that the Boston elementary schools spent more on poor students. Burkhead et al., in *Input and Output in Large City High Schools,* found that Chicago and Atlanta high schools spent about the same on middle-class and working-class students. The plaintiff's briefs in *Hobson v. Hansen* and *Bradley v. Milliken* showed that Washington, D.C. and Detroit spent more on the middle classes. Owen, using data on selected schools in large cities covered by the EEOS, reported in "The Distribution of Edu- cational Resources in Large American Cities" that more was spent on the middle classes than on the working classes.

35. The U.S. Bureau of the Census, "Income in 1969," shows that the poorest fifth of all families had incomes averaging 32 percent of the national average in 1969, while the richest fifth averaged about 196 percent. The mean was $10,577, so the difference between the top and bottom fifths was $17,400. This implies an expenditure difference of about $130, assuming constant elasticities during the 1960s. Since the mean expenditure per pupil was $783, the top fifth would have received about $848 and the bottom

fifth received about $718. The difference is 18 percent. Morgan et al., in *Income and Welfare in the United States,* report reassuringly similar results.

36. Only 1 percent of all children are in nonreligious private schools (see the U.S. Department of Health, Education and Welfare, *Digest of Educational Statistics,* 1970). Religious private schools spend no more than public schools.

37. Note 31 estimates that the least educated fifth received 54 percent as much resources as the national average, while the most educated fifth received 175 percent, ignoring annual expenditure differences between schools. If the correlation of attainment with parental income is roughly 0.44 (see note 4, Chapter 5), the children of the poorest fifth receive about 80 percent as much resources as the national average and the children of the richest fifth receive about 133 percent, again ignoring annual expenditure differences between schools. Note 35 implies that the poorest fifth receive 90 percent of the national average each year they are in school and that the richest fifth receive 110 percent. Overall, then, the rich get (1.33) (1.10) = 146 percent of the national average, while the poor get (0.80) (0.90) = 72 percent.

38. See the Supplemental Appendix in Coleman et al., *Equality of Educational Opportunity.*

39. See Katzman, *The Political Economy of Urban Schools.*

40. See Baron, "Race and Status." Compare Burkhead et al., *Input and Output in Large City High Schools,* who found no discrimination at the high school level and Coons, "Chicago," who had earlier found discrimination. Also compare Bruck, "Results of a Study," who found whites getting 5–10 percent more than blacks from local funds. Exclusion of Title I funds shows that local funds are still allocated disproportionately to whites; inclusion of Title I yields rough equality.

41. See the Public Education Association "Status of Public School Education" for baseline data showing discrimination against blacks. For recent data showing discrimination in favor of blacks and Puerto Ricans, see Gittell, *New York City School Fact Book.*

42. For details, see plaintiff's brief in *Bradley v. Milliken.* These data were compiled by Paul Smith of the Harvard Center for Law and Education. For earlier evidence on Detroit, see Sexton, *Education and Income.*

43. See "Second Joint Memorandum of Plaintiffs and Defendants," (April 12, 1971), in *Hobson v. Hansen.*

44. Coleman et al., in the Supplemental Appendix of *Equality of Educational Opportunity,* show that in 1965 the average white was in a district that spent 8–10 percent more than the districts where the blacks lived. Within districts, we estimate the average disparity at 5–10 percent, including Title I of ESEA. These figures are obviously rough, but the order of magnitude is probably about right. Owen's "The Distribution of Educational Resources in Large American Cities" suggests somewhat larger disparities within districts, but his samples within districts may not be representative.

45. These estimates were derived by a two step procedure. First, we calculated the expenditure disparity on the assumption that the only source of expenditure differences between blacks and whites was the length of time

they stayed in school. Using the weighting procedure described in note 31, we estimated the mean expenditure on blacks aged 25–29 in 1969 at 82 percent of the mean for whites. For those aged 65–74, the black mean was 59 percent of the white mean. We then assumed that annual expenditures on blacks aged 25–29 in 1969 had been 80 percent of those on whites, and that annual expenditures on blacks aged 65–74 had been 70 percent of those on whites. This yielded an overall black-white ratio of 66 percent for the younger group and 41 percent for the older. For those now in school we simply extrapolated the implied trend. All these estimates are obviously very rough.

46. See Coleman et al., *Equality of Educational Opportunity*. The presentation of the EEOS statistics is a bit confusing because Coleman and his coauthors pooled the South and Southwest in their analyses.

47. See the U.S. Department of Health, Education and Welfare, *News Release*, 1971.

48. See Coleman et al., *Equality of Educational Opportunity*, and the U.S. Department of Health, Education and Welfare News Release. Figures 2.14.1 and 2.14.5 in Coleman et al. imply that 40 percent of all blacks were in segregated schools in 1965. These Figures seem, however, to have been drawn without reference to data. Tables 2.13.1 and 2.14.1 in Coleman et al. show 72 percent of Northern black first graders and 55 percent of Northern black twelfth graders in majority-black schools. This implies that if we combined elementary and secondary students, about 60 percent of the blacks would be in majority-black schools. If 60 percent were in majority-black schools, we can infer that about 45–50 percent were in 80–100 percent black schools. This can be compared to 57.4 percent in 1968 and 57.6 percent in 1970. Because the data are from different sources, we do not have much confidence that the 1965–1968 trend was real, especially since there was no such trend in the 1968–1970 comparisons, where the data sources *are* comparable.

49. See Coleman et al., *Equality of Educational Opportunity*.

50. Mayeske et al., on p. 96 of *A Study of Our Nation's Schools,* estimate the percentage of socio-economic variance that lies within schools at different grade levels in EEOS. For the ninth and twelfth grades, the percentages are 67 and 72. This implies that the standard deviation of the socio-economic index in the average high school will be 82–85 percent of the national standard deviation. The percentage of variance within schools should be slightly smaller for elementary schools. Mayeske et al. report that 72 percent of the sixth grade socio-economic variance was within schools. There may be more within-school error variance in the sixth than in the ninth and twelfth grade data. Mayeske et al. report 60 and 61 percent of the variance within schools at the third and first grade levels, but this probably understates the within-school variance due to the teachers' tendency to report the same socio-economic level for all students about whom they were not sure. (First and third grade teachers filled in the relevant items for the students.) We estimate the "true" within-school variance at 65 percent for elementary schools. The within-school standard deviation thus averages 81 percent of the national average.

51. In order to compare different kinds of segregation, we need a segregation index ($I$). The best index appears to be the ratio of the within-school standard deviation ($S_W$) to the standard deviation for the total population ($S_t$). In order to make this a segregation index rather than an integration index, we subtract it from 1. Thus, $I = 1 - S_W/S_t$. If we define all students as white or nonwhite, we find that 50 percent of the variance in race was within northern urban elementary schools in 1965. At the secondary level, the comparable figure was 58 percent. The standard deviation within elementary schools was thus $\sqrt{0.50} = 71$ percent of the total standard deviation, and the segregation index $= 1 - 0.71 = 0.29$. For high schools $I = 1 - \sqrt{0.58} = 0.24$. For economic status, $I = 0.19$ at the elementary level and 0.15 at the secondary level.

52. Mayeske et al., in *A Study of Our Nation's Schools,* estimate the between-school variance in test scores at 35 percent in all grades, using a composite achievement measure. Using any single test, the between-school variance is less than 35 percent. This is probably because the separate tests contain more random error. Socio-economic and racial variables explain 70 to 80 percent of the between-school variance in first grade scores. The rest must be explained by other kinds of selectivity. See Jencks, "The Quality of the Data Collected," for additional discussion and data.

53. Rist, in "Student Social Class," provides a good description of grouping within classrooms and some suggestive evidence on its effects.

54. See the National Education Association, *Ability Grouping.* The reliability of reports on grouping is uncertain (see Jencks, "The Quality of the Data Collected," for evidence that EEOS data on grouping is nearly worthless). Since large districts are more likely to use ability grouping than small districts, the proportion of *pupils* who are grouped is larger than the proportion of *districts* that group.

55. See the National Education Association, "Teacher Opinion Poll."

56. This is another way of saying that there is more test score variance and almost as much socio-economic variance between tracks and curriculums in the same school as between schools. Jencks found that in the Talent high school sample (see note 60), about 11 percent of the achievement variance and 22 percent of the socio-economic variance was between high schools. About 20 percent of the achievement variance and 14 percent of the socio-economic variance was between curriculums in the same high school. For similar results in English primary schools, see Acland, "Social Determinants of Educational Achievement." Heyns, in "Curriculum Assignment and Tracking Policies," found that in the EEOS sample of northern urban 4-year high schools 18.1 percent of the achievement variance and 13.1 percent of the variance in father's occupational status was between schools, while 28.7 percent of the achievement variance and 9.3 percent of the status variance was between the college and noncollege curriculums in the same school.

57. See "The Effects of Tracking," in Chapter 3 of this volume.

58. See "The Effects of Curriculum Placement," in Chapter 5 of this volume.

59. See Heyns, "Curriculum Assignment and Tracking Policies."

60. Heyns, in "Curriculum Assignment and Tracking Policies," found a correlation of 0.48 between verbal score and ninth grade track assignment in the 48 northern urban 4-year high schools covered by EEOS. The correlation was 0.44 in the 91 white, nonvocational high schools throughout the nation covered by the Project Talent ninth–twelfth grade follow-up. These correlations would presumably be higher if they were based on the tests used by the schools themselves to evaluate aptitude.

61. See Heyns, "Curriculum Assignment and Tracking Policies."

62. The studies of high school curriculum assignment reported above are more fully described in Heyns, "Curriculum Assignment and Tracking Policies." For additional data on segregation and black aspirations in EEOS, see Armor, "The Racial Composition of Schools and College Aspirations of Negro Students."

63. This research is fully reported in Acland, "Social Determinants of Educational Achievement." The findings are based on the Plowden survey of English primary schools. The first stage of this longitudinal survey is reported in Peaker, "The Regression Analysis of the National Survey."

64. See Chapter 5, "The Effects of Curriculum Placement," in this volume.

# CHAPTER THREE

# Inequality
# in Cognitive Skills

Those who see schools as instruments of social reform usually share a series of assumptions that go roughly as follows:

1. Social and economic differences between blacks and whites and between rich and poor derive in good part from differences in their cognitive skills.
2. Cognitive skills can be measured with at least moderate precision by standardized tests of "intelligence," "verbal ability," "reading comprehension," "mathematical skills," and so forth.
3. Differences in people's performance on cognitive tests can be partly explained by differences in the amount and quality of schooling they get.
4. Equalizing educational opportunity would therefore be an important step toward equalizing blacks and whites, rich and poor, and people in general.

Our research has convinced us that this line of reasoning is wrong. Chapters 6 and 7 will show that economic success has a rather modest relationship to test scores, and that even this relationship derives largely from the fact that standardized tests measure skills that are useful in getting through school, not skills that pay off once school is over. This suggests several things. First, economic success, as measured by occupational status and income, depends on a variety of factors besides competence. Second, competence depends on many things besides basic cognitive skill. Third, standardized tests do not measure basic cognitive skills with complete accuracy. We do not have any evidence that would allow us to assess which of these phenomena does the most to explain our findings. Our intuitive conviction, however, is that standardized tests *do* measure certain basic cognitive skills, such as the ability to manipulate words and numbers, the ability to understand written or oral instructions, and the ability to make logical inferences from written material. Since test scores do not relate closely to job performance, we infer that these skills are less important than most people assume. While we will use the terms "basic cognitive skills," or simply "cognitive skills," to designate whatever it is that standardized tests measure, we will not assume that these tests measure either vocational competence or what most people call "intelligence."

Our research has convinced us not only that cognitive inequality does not explain economic inequality to any significant extent, but that educational inequality does not explain cognitive inequality to any significant extent. The amount of schooling an individual gets has some effect on his test performance, but the quality of his schooling makes extraordinarily little difference. We have therefore abandoned our initial belief that equalizing educational opportunity would substantially reduce cognitive inequality among adults. This does not mean that we think cognitive inequality derives entirely from genetic inequality, or that test scores are immune to environmental influence. It simply means that variations in what children learn in school depend largely on variations in what they bring to school, not on variations in what schools offer them.

This chapter tries to explain in some detail what test scores measure, why some people do better on tests than others, and what society can do to alter these disparities. Part I contains three sections, dealing with what tests measure, how stable the results are over an individual's lifetime, and how much they have changed historically. Part II contains four sections, which discuss the effects of genes, family background, social class, and race on test scores. Part III contains five sections, which assess the effects of school attendance and the effects of variations in school quality on students' scores. We will discuss the social and economic consequences of cognitive inequality in Chapters 5, 6, and 7.

# I: THE NATURE AND EXTENT OF COGNITIVE INEQUALITY

## What Standardized Tests Measure

When we talk about "cognitive skills" we mean the ability to manipulate words and numbers, assimilate information, make logical inferences, and so forth. We are interested in these skills for two reasons. First, most schools claim to develop such skills. Second, many people feel that schools have "failed" because they do not teach these skills equally to everyone. These facts do not, however, tell us which *specific* cognitive skills are important.

One way to answer this question would be to develop external criteria for determining the value of different skills. If, for example, empirical studies showed that workers who knew English grammar were more likely to get promoted than workers who did not, we might feel justified in rating schools according to how much grammar their alumni knew. At present, however, this approach is unworkable. There is no coherent, empirically validated theory of what determines economic success.[1] Nor is there much evidence about what determines an individual's ability to reach noneconomic goals, or what determines his choice of such goals. Thus nobody can say with any confidence whether schools that teach geography are helping their alumni more than schools that teach mathematics, or whether reading comprehension is more important than general information.

In the absence of empirical evidence, some educators simply assert the intrinsic value of knowing geography, reading Dickens, or mastering Newtonian physics. Perhaps the best index of what American society as a whole thinks young people ought to learn is the formal curriculum of the public schools. This curriculum has evolved over many years in response to all sorts of conflicting pressures, and while nobody is completely satisfied with the result, it includes most subjects on which there is broad consensus and few on which there is not. That, indeed, is its major flaw.

Standardized tests have the same relationship to school curricula that curricula have to the larger body of knowledge and skills from which they are distilled. Most standardized tests cover only things that all schools try to teach. They ignore things that are taught in only a few schools. The five tests used in the Equality of Educational Opportunity Survey (EEOS), for example, were developed by the Educational Testing Service, the most influential manufacturer of tests in America. The tests tried to measure "Verbal Ability," "Nonverbal Ability," "Reading Comprehension," "Mathematics Achievement," and "General Information." There were no tests of competence in a language other than English, no tests of advanced mathematical skills, and no tests of familiarity with specific novels, plays, or poems. Thus no school could complain that its students were discriminated against because the tests covered material they had not studied but others had.

Tests like those used in EEOS measure several things. First, they measure the amount of miscellaneous information the student has picked up in school, at home, on television, and elsewhere. The tests are made up by psychologists and teachers, so they cover kinds of information psychologists and teachers think important. Second, the tests measure ability to read, understand, and make logical inferences from

written material. The "right" answer to many of the reading comprehension questions is contained within the question itself, but this is not
as obvious to some students as to others. Third, the tests measure the
student's ability to guess what the examiner wants. Some of the items
are ambiguous. This does not appear to be deliberate. Nonetheless, the
effect is that a student will do well if he is good at figuring out what the
tester had in mind. The student who does not think like a teacher/
tester will do poorly, as will the student who panics when confronted
with ambiguity and refuses to guess. Fourth, the tests measure the
student's ability to answer questions quickly. The student who works
slowly does poorly, even if he does good work. Finally, the EEOS
battery probably measures a rather special kind of motivation. There
was no "realistic" reason for a student to try to do well on these tests.
High scores were not rewarded, nor were low scores punished. Indeed,
students were not even told whether they had gotten the right answers
or whether they had done well relative to others. The only reason not
to give random answers was habit. Schools whose students had the idea
that right answers are always better than wrong answers, even when
self-interest is not involved, presumably did better than those whose
students were less perfectionist.

We do not know the relative importance of these factors in determining people's scores, but we do know that the factors influencing
performance on any one EEOS test were very similar to those influencing performance on the other four. A student's average score on four
of the five tests predicted his score on the fifth test quite accurately.
Each test also measured something unique, but the unique factors were
far less important than the common skills that influenced all five
tests.[2] The student who did well on one test and poorly on another
was quite exceptional.[3]

The fact that these five tests all measure pretty much the same thing
does not, of course, mean that *all* tests measure the same thing. There
are other tests that correlate poorly with these five tests, and with one
another.[4] But tests that do not correlate with one another seldom correlate with anything that schools think important. Scholastic ability
seems to be a more or less one dimensional concept.[5]

Assuming that EEOS and other widely used tests measure a single
dimension of cognitive skill, we need a name for it. Test manufacturers
use several different terms. Each is useful but also potentially misleading. Many distinguish, for example, between "achievement" and
"aptitude." In principle, achievement tests tell whether students have
mastered some body of material that the tester deems important. Ap-

titude tests theoretically tell whether students are *capable* of mastering a body of material the tester deems important. In practice, however, all tests measure *both* aptitude *and* achievement. The EEOS verbal test, for instance, is much like the verbal portion of the Scholastic Aptitude Test, which is widely used to predict college grades. If two students have had the same opportunity to acquire verbal skills, and if one has picked them up while the other has not, the test does indeed measure "aptitude." But if one child has been raised speaking Spanish and another English, the test measures the Spanish-speaking child's mastery of a foreign language. If the Spanish-speaking child does worse than the English-speaking, this shows lower achievement in this area, but it need not imply less aptitude.

Achievement tests also measure aptitude in many contexts. English teachers, for example, often try to make their students read their assignments by extracting short quotations from the reading and requiring students to identify the quotations on the final examination. The teacher assumes that those who have done the reading will recognize the quotations, and he views the examination as a measure of achievement. If some students do the reading and some do not, their relative performance will indeed measure achievement in this sense. However, if everyone has done the reading equally carefully, those who do well will simply be those with good memories. When everyone is equally well prepared, achievement tests become aptitude tests. When people are unequally prepared, aptitude tests become achievement tests. In light of this, we will not make any rigid distinction between aptitude and achievement. We will simply try to use the term that seems appropriate in a given context.

We have deliberately avoided equating scholastic aptitude or achievement with "intelligence." The term "intelligence" is so loaded with moral and political overtones that it is almost impossible to conduct a rational discussion once it has been introduced. Psychologists sometimes try to sidestep this difficulty by saying that "intelligence is whatever intelligence tests measure." We think this artifice disastrous. Neither psychologists nor anyone else can use a term like intelligence without assuming that it means many different things at once—all very important. Those who claim that "intelligence is what intelligence tests measure" ought logically to assume, for example, that "intelligence is of no more consequence in human life than scores on intelligence tests." Nobody uses language this way. Both psychologists and laymen attach great practical and moral importance to intelligence. Having said that "intelligence is what IQ tests measure," they conclude that what IQ tests measure *must* be important because intelligence is important. This road leads through the looking glass, and we prefer not to travel it.

Instead, we think it wiser to use a term like intelligence in its colloquial sense, to embrace every form of mental competence from the ability to learn French syntax to the ability to anticipate the future price of hog bristles. We will treat success on IQ tests, aptitude tests, and achievement tests as varieties of intelligent behavior. We will not assume that they are the *only* varieties of intelligent behavior, nor that they are necessarily the most important.[6]

While intelligence tests measure only one variety of intelligence, they do measure something. After some vacillation, we have decided to describe the things these tests measure as "IQ," simply because that is the way everyone else refers to it. There is no clear line between the skills measured by standard IQ tests and the skills measured by tests of verbal and nonverbal ability. Convention dictates, however, that the term "IQ test" be restricted to individually administered tests. We will describe group tests as "aptitude" and "achievement" tests.

Whether high scores on these tests correlate with other forms of competence remains a question for speculation and inquiry, but two bits of evidence are relevant. First, consider the relationship between test scores and school grades. The skills required to do well on standardized tests and the skills required to earn high grades in school seem quite similar. That, indeed, is an explicit criterion in selecting items for many standardized tests. Nonetheless, the correlation between test scores and grades is far from perfect.[7] There are several reasons for this. First, grades are influenced by a wide variety of factors besides performance. Different schools have different grading standards, and so do different teachers in the same school. Many teachers deliberately try to reward effort rather than ability. Even when grades depend entirely on performance, an able student may do poorly because he has not done the assigned work, while a dull student may do well because he has been unusually diligent.

The relationship between test scores and economic success is even more attenuated than the relationship between test scores and grades. To begin with, economic success depends on a wide variety of factors besides on-the-job performance. In addition, on-the-job performance depends on noncognitive as well as cognitive skills, and on attitudes and motivation. The net effect, as we will see in Chapters 6 and 7, is to reduce the association between test scores and economic success to a rather modest level. Since the remainder of this chapter is likely to convince the reader that it is quite difficult to alter an individual's performance on most standardized tests, the modest relationship between performance on these tests and performance in most other realms must be kept clearly in mind.

## The Stability of Individual Differences over Time

The national obsession with children's IQ and achievement scores rests on the assumption that those who score high when they are young will continue to score high throughout their lives, and that those who do poorly when they are young will remain at a permanent disadvantage. This assumption appears to be correct for older children, but not for very young children.

MEASUREMENT SCALES

In order to describe the relationship between test scores at different ages, we need a scale for measuring test performance. Historically, IQ scores were first calculated by comparing a child's mental age to his chronological age. If, for example, a 10 year old performed at the same level as the average 12 year old, he was said to have a mental age of 12. His "intelligence quotient" was then defined as his mental age divided by his chronological age, times 100. In the example just given, the child's IQ would be $(12/10) \times (100) = 120$. Similarly, if a 5 year old performed at the same level as the average 6 year old, his IQ would be $(6/5) \times (100) = 120$. In representative samples of American children between the ages of about 5 and 16, about one child in six usually has a mental age that exceeds his chronological by 15 percent or more, i.e. an IQ score of more than 115. Likewise, about one child in six usually has a mental age less than 85 percent of his chronological age, i.e. an IQ of less than 85. This means that two-thirds of all children usually have IQ scores between 85 and 115.

This general pattern is quite consistent, but there is some variation between tests and between children of different ages. This causes all sorts of technical problems if we want to compare a child's performance on different tests or at different ages. In order to overcome this difficulty, psychologists now calculate IQ scores in a different way. They begin by defining the IQ of the average child as 100. They then transform other children's scores so that two-thirds of all children always have scores between 85 and 115, a sixth always have scores above 115, and a sixth always have scores below 85. The transformation is also designed to ensure that 2.5 percent always score above 130, and that 2.5 percent always score below 70. This scoring system is used regardless of the actual distribution of mental ages divided by chronological ages. When the scores have been transformed in this way, they are said to have a "standard deviation" of 15 points. The reader who wants a more detailed explanation of this concept should consult Appendix C. We will use this transformation to describe not only scores on IQ tests but scores on all the other aptitude and achievement tests discussed in this book.

STABILITY AND AGE

The rate at which a child develops prior to the age of 3 tells us almost nothing about the level at which he will perform as an adult.[8] Children who learn to talk at an early age are no more likely to end up articulate than children who learn later, for example.[9] The reason for this seems to be that the skills which define precocity before the age of 2 or 3 differ drastically from the skills measured by cognitive tests later in life. This assumption is supported by the finding that infants' test scores are not related to their parents' scores.[10]

Around the age of 3, a child's precocity or retardation begins to predict his eventual level of cognitive skill. The correlations are at first quite low, but they rise steadily during the preschool years. Children's test scores at this age also begin to show some relationship to their parents' scores.[11] By the time a child is 4 or 5, his scores on a good IQ test will correlate about 0.5 with his adult IQ score.[12]

This means that 4 year olds with IQs of 120 typically have adult scores around 110. Similarly, 4 year olds with scores of 70 have an average adult score of 85. The correlation coefficient of 0.5 implies, in other words, that a relatively advantaged 4 year old will typically retain only half this advantage into adulthood, and that a low-scoring child will typically overcome half his disadvantage.[13] (This does not mean that there will be fewer adults than children with very high or very low IQs. While those who start out high or low will usually regress toward the mean, their places will be taken by others who started closer to the mean. The reader who is unfamiliar with the use of correlation coefficients to describe this recurrent phenomenom may again find it helpful to consult Appendix C.)

Once students start school, the rate at which they acquire knowledge and skills becomes an increasingly valid indication of their probable adult performance. The correlation between aptitude and IQ test scores at the age of 8 to 10 and at 18 seems to be between 0.7 and 0.8.[14] The correlation between school achievement scores at 8 to 10 and at age 18 appears to be slightly lower, but not much.[15] By the beginning of high school, achievement scores correlate 0.80 or better with scores at the end of high school. For many tests the correlation is nearly perfect.[16]

Studies of adult test scores, though few in number, all show a high degree of stability, with correlations averaging between 0.80 and 0.90 over 15–30 year periods.[17] This means that if we test adults at widely separated times, the difference between the first and second score will average 7 to 10 points. The difference between "true" scores (i.e. scores on a longer and more reliable test which involved no random error) would average 6 to 8 points.[18]

The fact that test scores at different ages are highly correlated does not mean that the absolute difference between one child and another remains constant over time. The vocabulary difference between the most adept and the least adept 12 year old, for example, is greater than that between the most and least adept 6 year old, simply because the cleverest 12 year olds have much larger vocabularies than the cleverest 6 year olds. If we compare a child who scores 85 to a child who scores 100, and if their scores are the same throughout their school careers, the child with a score of 85 will be roughly 1 year behind the child with a score of 100 when they enter school, 2 years behind when they finish elementary school, and 3 years behind when they finished high school.[19]

### INTERPRETING STABILITY AND CHANGE

The fact that test scores become relatively stable once children enter school helps explain the widespread interest in them. It does not, however, tell us much about the factors that determine test scores or about the extent to which test scores can be altered by deliberate intervention.

Some psychologists have argued that the instability of test scores in the preschool years indicates that an individual's eventual level of performance is decisively influenced by the environment to which he is exposed in early childhood.[20] This suggests that good preschools might have a decisive impact on adult test scores. This line of reasoning may be correct, but it has not yet been supported with direct evidence, and there are several alternative explanations for the indirect evidence we have been discussing. One possibility is that the tests in question measure different skills at 4 and 8, but similar skills thereafter. Alternatively, children's cognitive environments may change from one year to the next up to 7 or 8, but not after that. Or genetic factors may influence scores more as children get older.

Suppose, for example, that children are raised in very unequal home environments. Their cognitive skills when they enter school will then reflect these differences. As a result, some children with high cognitive "potential" (i.e. biological advantages) will do relatively poorly on tests administered before they enter school, because they will not have had a chance to acquire the skills the tests measure. Conversely, some children with rather limited cognitive potential (i.e. biological disadvantages) will do relatively well on the tests, because they will have had more than their share of environmental advantages.

Now imagine a school system that equalizes everyone's opportunities and incentives to learn. In such a system test scores would no longer depend on home environment. They would depend largely on "native ability." If the world worked this way, test scores at age 4, before the child entered school, might not be very highly correlated with test scores at 8 or 10. Many children who scored low on preschool tests would improve substantially when they entered school, and many who scored high would regress toward the norm for children of their age. If schools really equalized children's opportunities and incentives to acquire cognitive skills, differences in performance after entering school would be entirely due to differences in their biological potential. If the biological factors influencing test performance at different ages were the same, children's performance relative to their classmates would not change after they had been in school a few years.

The instability of test scores in early childhood and the stability of scores once children enter school may, then, mean that preschool and early school environments are more important than later environments. Or, it may only mean that children's early school environments are very similar to their later ones, but often dissimilar to their family environments. In principle, we could resolve this uncertainty by organizing a society in which students did not enter school until adolescence. If early environments were crucial, the correlation between early and late test scores would be just as high in this imaginary society as in Western societies. If schools really equalize cognitive opportunity, however, we would expect to find high correlations between scores at 5 and 10 in our hypothetical society, lower correlations between scores at 10 and at 15, and higher correlations thereafter.

The increasing stability of test scores as people get older tells us nothing about the relative importance of heredity and environment. An adult trait can be genetically determined and yet show no relationship to childhood traits. There is virtually no correlation, for example, between the amount of hair a boy has in childhood and the amount he will have at the age of 40. Nonetheless, there is plenty of evidence that baldness at 40 is influenced by genes. Conversely, a trait can be quite stable from childhood to maturity without being at all influenced by genes. The accent with which an individual speaks, for example, is usually the same at 6 and 60. This does not prove that accents are genetically determined. It simply proves that once some kinds of behavior are acquired, they are hard to change.

When trying to interpret the stability of test scores, we have found it helpful to compare test scores with weight. An infant's weight predicts his adult weight very poorly. A young child's weight predicts his adult weight considerably better. The correlations climb steadily as the individual approaches adulthood.[21] Such correlations do not prove that weight is immune to environmental influence—we all know better. Neither do they prove that an individual's weight never changes. Again, we have visible contrary evidence. So how are we to interpret the correlations? First, it is clear that weight is partly—but only partly —determined by genetic factors. Second, malnutrition in childhood seems to have some permanent effect on weight. Third, most people accept their "natural" weight more or less fatalistically. Those who are overweight make only sporadic efforts to cut it down by dieting. Thus, while weight at one age *need* not predict weight later on, it usually *does* predict it quite well.

We suspect that these same considerations also apply to test scores. Test scores, as we shall see in subsequent sections, depend partly on an individual's environment and partly on genetically determined differences in individuals' responses to that environment. Most people accept their natural level of cognitive skill as fatalistically as they accept their natural weight. They may wish they could increase the one or decrease the other, but their efforts are usually rather half-hearted. This does not prove that test scores cannot be altered. It only proves that they seldom are.

## Historical Changes in Americans' Test Scores

Good evidence regarding national trends in test performance is hard to find. The best source—and it is none too good—seems to be military records. The U.S. Army initiated the first major national testing program in 1917. Over the years the military has used three major tests to classify recruits: Army Alpha during World War I, the Army General Classification Test (*AGCT*) during World War II, and the Armed Forces Qualification Test (*AFQT*) since World War II. These military tests were initially intended to measure "intelligence," but they obviously measure "achievement" as well. They cover such things as vocabulary, ability to conceptualize spatial relationships, and familiarity with certain tools. All these military tests correlate quite highly with one another, with other standardized aptitude and achievement tests, and with IQ tests.[22]

The average level of performance on these tests rose dramatically during the first half of the twentieth century. The average man drafted in World War II, for example, outscored 83 percent of all World War I recruits.[23] Unfortunately, we have no comparable military data for the period since World War II. We know no good evidence on trends in IQ scores, but we suspect they improved too.[24] The scanty available evidence also points to a steady increase in standards of academic achievement in schools and colleges up to 1960. Since 1960, the picture is less encouraging.[25]

Since it seems clear that the gene pool has been pretty stable,[26] we must attribute any increase in achievement to environmental changes. Increasing test sophistication, radio and television, and urbanization may all play some part in this.[27] The fact that the average man left school at 15 in 1915, at 17 in 1935, and at 19 in 1965 also seems likely to explain part of the change.

Does this imply any change in the degree of cognitive inequality? The absolute amount of variation in test scores does not appear to have changed appreciably.[28] But since the average level of performance has been rising, inequality relative to the mean can perhaps be said to have declined. Furthermore, the curtailment of immigration has led to a steady increase in the proportion of the population that can take a written test in English.[29] We can hardly argue that second and third generation immigrants are more "intelligent" than their parents just because they can speak (and usually read) English. But we can certainly argue that they are better able to cope with many of the practical problems of American life. This example illustrates both the danger of equating test scores with intelligence and the danger of arguing that test scores prove nothing at all.

## II: THE HEREDITY/ENVIRONMENT CONTROVERSY

Having described the nature and extent of cognitive inequality, we now turn to its causes. Given the limited importance of test scores in adult life, the debate about what causes scores to vary has aroused extraordinary passion. This has been particularly true of theories that emphasize the role of genes. In part this is because most people have the idea that genetic differences are inerradicable, whereas environmental differences are not. Recent scientific developments suggest, however, that the opposite may prove closer to the truth. Genetic engineering may prove considerably more practical than social engineering.

This part of this chapter tries to assess the relative importance of genes, family background, social class, and race in determining test scores. We will not deal with schools until Part III. We have tried to deal with the evidence dispassionately, despite the fact that it does not support our political prejudices. Nonetheless, our conclusions will doubtless make many people angry. Readers who have this reaction may find it helpful to remind themselves at regular intervals that we are discussing the determinants of performance on quite simple-minded tests, not the determinants of "intelligence," economic success, political influence, or moral rectitude.

### Genetic Influences on Test Scores

Liberal opinion has traditionally rejected the idea that genes determine test scores or that test scores measure genetic potential. Conservative opinion has frequently embraced the idea, at least when it was applied to somebody else's children. Academic opinion has vacillated from one side to the other, according to the political mood of the times.

Since the collapse of the liberal Democratic coalition in the late 1960s, several leading academic psychologists have written articles arguing that genes play a significant role in determining IQ scores.[30] This argument, while often overstated, is undeniably correct. Many laymen have, however, jumped to the conclusion that efforts to alter children's test scores by changing their environments are bound to fail. This conclusion does not follow from the evidence about the importance of genes. This section will try to explain why.

We will begin by describing how genetic inheritance works, and what the widely misunderstood concept of "heritability" means. We will show that high "heritability" proves almost nothing about the extent to which changing the environment can change test scores. We will then review the evidence presented by hereditarians for believing that test scores are highly heritable. Whereas Arthur Jensen and others have argued that 80 percent of the variance in IQ scores is explained by genetic factors, our analyses suggest that the correct figure is probably more like 45 percent. Finally, we will consider the policy implications of our findings.

THE MEANING OF "HERITABILITY"

The relationship between genes and human development is not well understood, but certain points are generally accepted by all geneticists. Every human being has a unique combination of genes, numbering at least in the tens of thousands. An unknown but relatively small fraction of these genes varies from one individual to another. Individuals who differ genetically often respond differently to the same environment. Placed in front of the same TV set, for example, one child may remember more of what he sees than another. Confronted with subtraction, one child may "catch on" faster than another.

Genes also influence the environments to which people are exposed. The genes that affect skin color, for example, thereby influence an individual's opportunities and incentives to learn many skills. Similarly, the genes that affect height influence how much basketball coaching an individual is likely to get. The same is true of the genes that determine sex, which thereby influence peoples' opportunities and incentives to do almost everything.

We inherit half our genes from our mothers and half from our fathers. Which half of each parent's genes we inherit and which half gets "lost" is essentially random. Far from ensuring that we will be exactly like our parents, then, genes ensure that we will differ from them in unpredictable ways. This means that we also differ genetically from our brothers and sisters.

In order to analyze these relationships, geneticists have developed a large esoteric vocabulary. Two of their terms have been widely used in popular discussions of the heredity-environment question and require brief explanation. These terms are "genotype" and "heritability."

Let us begin with the concept of a "genotype." Imagine 1,000 individuals with identical genes. Suppose these 1,000 individuals had been raised in random American homes, had attended random schools, and so forth. Suppose that they then took IQ tests and that their mean score was 110. We could then say that these individuals' "IQ genotypes" had a mean value of 110. Since the mean IQ score of all individuals exposed to random environments is by definition 100, and since the mean score of our sample is 110 when exposed to these same random environments, we can attribute the 10 point difference to the fact that our sample had genes that were unusually favorable to the development of skills measured on IQ tests. This might be because their genes actually influenced the character of their environments, making the environments nonrandom. Or it might be because their genes led them to learn more from a given environment.

If all environments provided exactly the same opportunities and incentives for acquiring cognitive skills, and if tests were perfectly reliable, people with the same genes would always have the same test scores. A genotype with a value of 110, for example, would produce 1,000 individuals who all scored 110. A genotype with a value of 85 would produce 1,000 individuals who all scored 85. Genes would thus be the only source of cognitive inequality.

If, on the other hand, people's environments were sufficiently different for reasons that had nothing to do with their genes, some people whose genotype had a value of 110 might end up with a score of only 70, while others might end up with a score of 150. If environmental factors were the *only* source of variation in IQ scores, there would be as much variation among people with the same genes as in the general population. This could, however, only happen if genes had no effect whatever on test scores.

In real life, both differences in genes and differences in environmental factors that are not affected by genes contribute to cognitive inequality. The "heritability" of test scores is the percentage of the total variation that can be "explained" by genes under real life conditions. As we shall see, our best estimate is that genes explain about 45 percent of the variance in Americans' test scores, that environment explains about 35 percent, and that the tendency of environmentally advantaged families to have genetically advantaged children explains the remaining 20 percent.[31] We will return to this last point later.

The concept of heritability has several crucial limitations that are usually ignored. To begin with, the assertion that genes "explain" differences between individuals' test scores does not necessarily imply that genes affect an individual's learning capacity. Genes can also cause test score differences by affecting the environment in which an individual develops. If, for example, a nation refuses to send children with red hair to school, the genes that cause red hair can be said to lower reading scores. This does not tell us that children with red hair cannot learn to read. Attributing redheads' illiteracy to their genes would probably strike most readers as absurd under these circumstances. Yet that is precisely what traditional methods of estimating heritability do. If an individual's genotype affects his environment, for whatever rational or irrational reason, and if this in turn affects his cognitive development, conventional methods of estimating heritability automatically attribute the entire effect to genes and none to environment.

The ambiguous character of genetic influences on test scores can be illustrated by considering differences between men and women. Men generally score higher than women on quantitative tests, while the reverse is usually true on verbal tests. Using a traditional analytic model, we would say that since these differences are associated with sex, and since sex is genetically determined, the differences are "caused" by genes. This conclusion would not, however, rule out the possibility that the differences were also caused by the environment. In order to do that we would have to see if test score differences persisted when we raised boys and girls in identical environments. This is obviously impractical, since a child's sex influences the way he or she is treated.

The foregoing examples both deal with what might be called "irrational" or "non-meritocratic" relationships between an individual's genotype and his environment. By this we mean that the genes that influence an individual's opportunities or incentives to learn have no obvious relationship to his actual capacity to learn. College admissions policies based on sex, skin color, athletic ability, and the like illustrate this phenomenon. In addition, however, genes may influence an individual's opportunities or incentives to learn in ways that *are* related to his capacity to learn. These influences are widely regarded as rational, and are supported by meritocratic values. College admissions policies based on grades and test scores illustrate this phenomenon.

Genetic influences of this sort are likely to exert their influence very early, and they are likely to become more important as children get older. There seems, for example, to be an association between the amount a mother talks to her child and the child's subsequent verbal skills. If talking to the child is interesting and pleasant, most mothers will talk more than if the child is inarticulate. If the child's verbal responses to its mother are affected by its genes, as seems likely, then the mother's dealings with the child will also end up being determined partly by the child's genes. This cycle is likely to be repeated at school. The child who starts off with a small genetic advantage may learn quickly, receive encouragement, and learn more. The child who starts off with a small genetic disadvantage may learn more slowly, be discouraged by the teacher, and stop trying to learn at all. Small genetic differences may therefore end up producing big environmental differences and hence big differences in test scores.

We have no quantitative estimates of the extent to which genetic differences in learning capacity determine an individual's opportunities for further development of these same capacities, but common sense suggests a strong relationship.

The cumulative effects of both meritocratic and non-meritocratic discrimination are probably even larger. Although we have no evidence, we would not be at all surprised if they turned out to explain at least half the test score variation that is normally attributed to genes.

The second major limitation of heritability estimates is that they apply only to populations. They tell us something about the probable cause of differences between random individuals from the population for which they are calculated, but they tell us nothing about differences between nonrandom individuals. Thus, if we compare all Americans with IQ scores of 110 to all those with scores of 100, and if our estimates are correct, we can say that on the average 4.5 points of this difference is due to heredity and its consequences, 3.5 points to environmental factors that are independent of genes, and 2 points to the correlation between a genotype and environment. But if we compare students whose fathers dropped out of college to those whose fathers dropped out of high school, and if we find that their IQ scores are 110 and 100 respectively, the difference may be all genetic, all environmental, or any combination of the two. The heritability of IQ for the general population thus tells us almost nothing about the likely cause of the difference between subpopulations.

A related problem is that heritability estimates are averages. This means they do not necessarily apply to any specific pair of individuals, even if the individuals are randomly selected. Thus if we pick two random individuals from the general population and one happens to score 110 while the other scores 100, the difference may be due to genes, to environment, or to any conceivable combination of the two. The individual who scores 110 may even have a genotype that would normally yield a score below 100, while the individual who scores 100 may have a genotype that would normally yield a score above 110, and these expectations may have been reversed by atypical environments.

Heritability estimates are, then, of extremely limited value. They tell us almost nothing about differences between specific individuals, almost nothing about differences between social groups, and rather little about populations. Bearing this in mind, we turn to the problem of actually estimating the heritability of IQ scores.

### ESTIMATING THE HERITABILITY OF IQ SCORES

Estimating heritability is extremely complicated, and we have consigned most of the details of our procedure to Appendix A. Certain general points about our estimates and their limitations require attention, however. Heritability estimates are normally derived by comparing people with different genes who have been exposed to somewhat similar environments, or by comparing people with somewhat similar genes who have been exposed to different environments. Our estimates are based on four sorts of comparisons: comparisons between parents and children, comparisons between identical and fraternal twins, comparisons between siblings and unrelated children reared together, and comparisons between identical twins reared apart.

Studies of parents and children compare the degree of resemblance between natural children and their parents, between adopted children and their natural parents, and between adopted children and their adoptive parents. These comparisons do not provide clear evidence as to the heritability of test scores. They do, however, allow us to answer a crucial question about the relationship between genes and environment. Parents with favorable genes tend to have above-average cognitive skills. This means they tend to provide their children with unusually rich home environments, regardless of whether the children are genetically advantaged or not. In addition, however, parents with favorable genes usually have genetically advantaged children. These children thus end up with a double advantage. They have more than their share of the genes that make for a high IQ score, and they also have more than their share of the environmental advantages that lead to high IQ scores. This leads to a correlation between genotype and environment, making IQ scores even less equal than they otherwise would be. This is not a matter of children's genes *influencing* their environment, although that too produces a correlation between the two. Here, we are talking only about the correlation between genotype and those features of the child's environment (e.g. the parents' IQ scores) that are *not* influenced by the child's genes. Our calculations from the data on parent-child relationships suggest that this "double advantage" phenomenon (technically known as "covariance") accounts for almost 20 percent of the variation in IQ scores.[32]

In order to allocate the remaining 80 percent of the variance between genotype and environment, we need to compare children to one another. The most common comparison is between identical and fraternal twins. Identical twins come from the same egg and have precisely the same genes. Any differences between such twins' test scores must be environmental. Fraternal twins come from separate eggs and sperms. On the average, they have only about half their genes in common. As a result, their test scores differ more than the test scores of identical twins. Environmentalists argue that this may be because fraternal twins' environments differ more than identical twins' environments, but the effect of this appears to be rather minor.[33]

We have reviewed four American, four English, and two Swedish studies that compare identical with fraternal twins. These studies suggest that there are important differences between countries. The American studies yield consistently lower heritabilities than the English studies.[34] The most plausible explanation for this is that children's environments are more similar in England than in the United States. This would mean that environment explained more variance in the United States than in England, and that genes explained relatively less. After allowing for covariance, comparisons between American twins imply that genetic differences and their consequences "explain" 50 to 60 percent of the variance in IQ scores, while environmental factors unrelated to genotype "explain" about 20 to 30 percent.

Comparisons between siblings reared together and unrelated children reared together yield a very different picture. This data suggests that after allowing for the covariance, genotypes explain less than 25 percent of the variance in IQ scores, while environment explains more than 55 percent. The data on unrelated children reared together is not very consistent, so we cannot put too much weight on the comparison. But once again heritability seems to be higher in England than in America.[35]

Still another method for estimating heritability is to compare the test scores of identical twins who have been separated early in life and reared in different families. For reasons already noted, such comparisons do not provide us with an estimate of the *total* effect of environment. To the extent that environments are determined by genes, identical twins will have the same environment no matter where they are reared. In addition, twins cannot be separated at the moment of conception and are often separated some time after birth. Furthermore, the families in which they are placed after separation may resemble one another more than random families would. As a result, the observed correlation between separated twins results both from genetic resemblance and from a limited degree of environmental resemblance.

Four sets of separated identical twins have been located and tested over the past half century: one set (19 pairs) in the United States, two sets (91 pairs) in England, and one set (12 pairs) in Denmark. Making a reasonable allowance for the fact that the prenatal and immediate postnatal environments of twins are more alike than those of random individuals, for the likely resemblance of the families in which separated twins are reared, and for the fact that adoption probably lowers the correlation between genotype and environment, the American twin's scores imply heritabilities around 0.50. The estimates for England are again higher.[36]

Taken together, this evidence suggests two general conclusions. First, different methods of estimating the heritability of test scores yield drastically different results. Second, studies of different populations yield somewhat different results. There seem to be significant differences between England and America, and there may also be significant differences between one American community and another. The relative importance of genes will be greater in small homogeneous communities than in large heterogeneous ones. This may help explain why pooling data from different American communities yields internally inconsistent results.

Nonetheless, *all* the evidence suggests that genes influence test scores either directly or indirectly. Most of the evidence suggests that genes account for close to half the variation in test scores. Virtually no American study supports the claim that genes account for 80 percent of the variance in test scores. Our guess, based on all the disparate sources of evidence discussed in this section, is that the heritability of Stanford-Binet scores in the United States is around 45 percent. This estimate could easily be off by 10 percent either way, and it might be off by as much as 20 percent either way.

We do not know how the relationship between genes and test scores really works. Part of the explanation is that America, like all other societies, allocates opportunities and incentives to learn in a highly unequal way. Those with the "right" genes are systematically favored over those with the "wrong" genes. This is true even when children start off with drastically different family backgrounds. Suppose, for example, that two genetically gifted identical twins are separated, and that one is adopted by illiterate parents while the other is adopted by a pair of Ph.D.s. The twin who is adopted by illiterates is clearly at a disadvantage, but he may nonetheless find ways of acquiring many of the skills needed for success on tests. He may evoke more talk from his illiterate parents than less vocal children would have evoked. He may spend more time looking at television or reading. When he goes to school, he may fall in with schoolmates who share his talents. In the end, then, such a child may end up with an environment quite similar to that of his twin, even though the latter did not have to work as hard to create it. Of course, we do not know to what extent this happens. Evidence on the extent to which a child's genes determine his environment has yet to be collected. Still, it is hard to imagine that this does not account for some of the association between genotype and test scores.

At the same time, we do not believe that genes affect test scores *only* by affecting opportunities or incentives to learn. Some children really seem to be born with aptitudes that others lack. Exposed to identical environments, one will learn more than another. We have no way of knowing how important these differences would be if environments were truly equal, but we do not believe they would disappear completely.

### POLICY IMPLICATIONS

What are the policy implications of all this? Since genetic inequality explains only a fraction of all cognitive inequality, and since cognitive inequality in turn explains only a small fraction of the social and economic inequality among adults, it is wrong to argue that genetic inequality dictates a hierarchical society. However, it is equally wrong to argue that genetic inequality does not exist, or that those who admit its existence must be racists.

The extent of cognitive inequality in any society depends on three factors: the amount of variation in people's genes, the amount of variation in the environments to which they are exposed, and the correlation between genotype and environment. Any one of these three factors can change, either as a result of deliberate political intervention or as a result of unplanned changes in the character of a society. If such changes took place in America, the heritability estimates cited earlier in this section would no longer be accurate.

Political efforts to reduce the amount of variation in people's environments have a long and honorable history. This has been a traditional objective of egalitarian reform. Among educators, it has been widely equated with "equality of opportunity." If all environmental inequality were eliminated except that which arises in response to genetic differences, cognitive inequality would probably be reduced by 25 to 40 percent. This means the difference between random children's IQ scores would average 10 to 13 points instead of 17 points.[37] If efforts to reduce environmental inequality were abandoned, and if the effects of environmental inequality doubled as a result, the difference between random children would rise from 17 to between 24 and 27 points.[38] If we could also eliminate environmental differences that are now *caused* by genetic differences, we could presumably reduce cognitive inequality even more, although we have no idea how much. Conversely, if American society loses interest in equalizing cognitive skill, and if, as a result, we further restrict either opportunities or incentives for those who start out at a genetic disadvantage, the level of cognitive inequality might rise dramatically.

One inevitable result of eliminating environmental inequality would be to increase the correlation between IQ genotype and IQ scores. Indeed, this is often a conscious objective of educational policy. Most schools try to help students with high "native ability" realize their "potential." In effect, this also means eliminating the unfair advantage of students who have unpromising genes but come from stimulating homes. The idea seems to be that inequality based on genetic advantages is morally acceptable, but that inequality based on other accidents of birth is not. Most educators and laymen evidently feel that an individual's genes are his, and that they entitle him to whatever advantages he can get from them. His parents, in contrast, are not "his" in the same sense, and ought not to entitle him to special favors. For a thoroughgoing egalitarian, however, inequality that derives from biology ought to be as repulsive as inequality that derives from early socialization.

We do not know of any society that has made a conscious effort to equalize people's genetic endowments. Indeed, most people assume that this would require some kind of genetic engineering and shy away from the whole concept. The degree of genetic inequality in a population also depends, however, on social factors, i.e. who marries whom and how many children they have. The degree of genetic inequality therefore varies from time to time and place to place even without direct intervention.

During the years between World War I and World War II, for example, Americans with unusually high and unusually low test scores had more than their share of children. Americans with average test scores had less than their share.[39] This implies that the proportion of individuals with very favorable or very unfavorable genotypes increased slightly and that the proportion of individuals close to the mean declined slightly. This trend may well be continuing, though we cannot be sure. Like the birth rate itself, such changes are almost impossible to predict in advance.

The degree of genetic inequality in a population also depends on who marries whom—a process that geneticists have given the romantic label "assortative mating." If those who score above average mate with those who score below average, genetic inequality will decline. Sharing the genetic wealth in this way will result in many children whose genes are pretty much like the national average and relatively few children whose genes are far above average or far below average. Sharing genetic wealth is, however, even rarer than sharing capital assets. People whose test scores are above average usually marry other people who are above average, and people with below average scores usually do likewise.

Women with IQs of 120, for example, have husbands whose IQs average around 111.[40] This does not mean that women are usually cleverer than their husbands. Men with IQ scores of 120 also have wives whose scores average about 111. Those who find this confusing should recall that if people married entirely randomly, both men and women with IQs of 120 would have spouses whose IQs averaged 100. Because people do not marry randomly, there are more children with extremely favorable and extremely unfavorable IQ genotypes than would otherwise be the case.

Changes in fertility and marriage patterns are hard to predict, much less plan. We must therefore assume that the level of genetic inequality in American society will remain more or less constant. Nonetheless, it is worth noting that if we could eliminate all genetic inequality, we could probably reduce the overall level of cognitive inequality by a third to a half.[41]

Another possible strategy for reducing cognitive inequality is to accept both genetic and environmental inequality as inevitable but to alter the relationship between them. This means trying to allocate the most favorable environments to those individuals who start life with the fewest genetic advantages. By implication, of course, it also means allocating the least favorable environments to those who start with genetic advantages. If, for example, some students have more trouble than others learning to read, this strategy implies that the teacher should ignore the fast readers and give the slow learners extra help. If this does not work, a remedial reading teacher should be called in to provide intensive help of a kind not available in the regular classroom. Taken to its logical conclusion, this strategy would imply that anyone who was reading above the norm for his age should be sent home, and the entire resources of the schools devoted to the laggards. If the whole society were organized along these lines, environmental inequality would serve to offset genetic inequality. The overall level of cognitive inequality would then be considerably less than if everyone were simply treated alike.

In its less extreme forms, this strategy is often described as an effort to provide "equal opportunity." Yet it is obviously quite different from the traditional vision of equal opportunity, which seeks to treat everyone alike. For analytic purposes, it is therefore useful to distinguish between "equal opportunity" (i.e. treating everyone alike) and "compensatory opportunity" (i.e. helping the neediest). Unfortunately, conceptual clarity is precisely what the advocates of compensatory opportunity (including ourselves) feel they cannot afford. "Compensatory opportunity" is a slogan devoid of political appeal, while "equal opportunity" is still capable of rallying widespread support. Advocates of compensatory opportunity have therefore felt obliged to pretend that "equal opportunity" really implies compensatory opportunity. We see no reason for abandoning this sleight of hand, but it is also useful to recognize that treating everyone alike is not the same as helping the neediest.

The existing distribution of opportunity is only compensatory in a few minor respects. Schools are virtually the only institutions that give even sporadic lip service to such ideals. We have estimated that eliminating the correlation between family background and genotype (e.g. by requiring all parents to place their children for adoption and ensuring that adoption was random) would reduce cognitive inequality about 10 percent.[42] If we could also eliminate the direct *effects* of genotype on environment, cognitive inequality would decline even further. If we could make the overall correlation between genetic and environmental advantages negative, we would have even more equal results.

All in all, we conclude that if society were willing to manipulate children's environments in sufficiently drastic ways, it could greatly reduce cognitive inequality, despite the persistence of genetic differences. If those who started life with genetic disadvantages were given a big enough environmental advantage, and if those who started with genetic advantages were given big enough environmental handicaps, we could produce relatively equal performance in many realms where inequality now prevails. Even hereditarians concede this point. They simply argue that the social cost of distributing opportunities in this way would be intolerable. On this score they are probably right. A society committed to achieving full cognitive equality would, for example, probably have to exclude genetically advantaged children from school. It might also have to impose other handicaps on them, like denying them access to books and television. Virtually no one thinks cognitive equality worth such a price. Certainly we do not. But if our goal were simply to reduce cognitive inequality to, say, half its present level, instead of eliminating it entirely, the price might be much lower.

Mathematical estimates of heritability tell us almost nothing about these questions. Indeed, our main conclusion after some years of work on this problem is that mathematical estimates of heritability tell us almost nothing about anything important. Trial and error seem to be the only way to answer most practical questions about the causes and cures of cognitive inequality.

## The Effects of Family Background

We have already noted that environmental variations that are independent of individual genotype seem to explain something like 35 percent of the variation in people's test scores.[43] Psychologists habitually divide this environmental variation into variation between one family and another and variation within the same family. Environmental variation between families may be due to differences between children's home environments, differences between their schools, differences between their communities, or anything else that makes children raised in one family different from children raised in some other family. We will lump all these sources of inequality between families together and label them "family background." Environmental inequality within families may arise either because of differences in the way the same parents treat different children, differences in these children's experiences and opportunities outside the home, or anything else that makes siblings different from one another.

The overall effect of environmental differences between families, i.e. "family background," can be estimated in several different ways. The most direct approach is to compare identical twins reared together and apart, siblings reared together and apart, or unrelated children reared together and apart. All these comparisons suffer from limitations cited in the previous section, namely that children are adopted some time after conception and are seldom assigned to random families. In addition, the relevant studies have been small, have covered dissimilar populations, have often been skimpily reported, and have produced inconsistent results. We have therefore supplemented our direct estimates with indirect estimates based on comparisons of identical and fraternal twins. Different methods suggest that family background accounts for as little as 10 or as much as 40 percent of the overall variation in IQ scores in the United States today. We will take 20 percent as the most likely estimate. Environmental differences within families are also important. Our best guess is that they normally account for something like 15 percent of the total variance. In addition, as noted in the previous section, the correlation between genotype and family background explains about 20 percent, leaving 45 percent for genes per se.[44]

The effects of family background can be described in another way, which may help throw some light on the claim that test scores are largely determined by genes. Suppose we rank families in terms of their ability to develop their children's cognitive skills. Suppose we then compare children whose families rank in the top fifth to genetically identical children whose families rank in the bottom fifth. If our estimates are correct, the average IQ difference between these two groups of children will be about 19 points.[45] This is considerably less than the 42 points that separate the top and bottom fifths of the IQ distribution, but it is hardly trivial.

Like heritability, however, the concept of "family background" has serious limitations. To begin with, we have rather fuzzy ideas about what aspects of family background influence test scores. Indeed, the term "family background" can itself be somewhat misleading, since differences between families derive not just from differences in home environment but from differences between neighborhoods, regions, schools, and all other experiences that are the same for children in the same family. Thus we cannot say with any confidence exactly how much effect parental behavior really has on children's IQ scores.

The sections which follow examine certain specific environmental factors that are commonly presumed to influence test scores. We look first at the effects of the parents' socio-economic status, then at the effects of race, and, finally, at the effects of schools. Of these factors, socioeconomic status and race appear moderately important, while schools do not appear very important.

## The Effects of Economic Background

Social scientists often use the terms "family background," "social class," and "economic status" almost interchangeably. We think this is a mistake, and will distinguish the concepts. By "family background" we mean all the environmental factors that make brothers and sisters more alike than random individuals. Some of these factors are economic, while some are not. The way a family brings up its children is obviously influenced by its economic position. The extent of such influence is, however, a problem for investigation, not a matter of definition. If words are to mean anything at all, we have to call a prosperous doctor's family "upper-middle class," even if the parents have reduced all their children to autism. Conversely, we have to call an impoverished laundry worker's family "working class" or "lower class," even if all the children have IQs of 180 and have earned graduate degrees from exclusive universities. It follows that there can be great variation in "family background" among children who come from precisely the same social or economic class.

Considering the vast sums that have been spent testing millions of American students, reliable data on the relationship between test scores and economic status is remarkably hard to find. National testing programs have related students' scores to the students' reports of their parents' incomes, but such reports are unlikely to be reliable. Testing programs have also related test scores to students' reports on their parents' occupations, but many students misclassify their parents' jobs. Really accurate data is available only for local samples. Taking all the evidence together, however, we estimate that a family's economic status probably correlates about 0.35 with the children's test scores.[46]

This means that if we compare children whose fathers rank in the top fifth of the occupational hierarchy to children whose fathers rank in the bottom fifth, their test scores will differ by an average of 13 to 15 points.[47] If we rank children according to their father's education, the disparity between the top and bottom fifth will again be 13 to 15 points. If we rank them according to their family income, the disparity will be less than 13 points.

Class differences seem to be greatest for verbal ability and general information. Such tests tend to be highly correlated with one another as well as with IQ scores. Tests of reading comprehension, mathematical skills, nonverbal ability, and many other talents show less relationship both to IQ and to economic background.[48] Perhaps this is because these skills are largely taught in school, so that differences between homes affect them less.

The relationship between test scores and economic background also seems to be stronger in the United States than in other countries.[49] This reinforces our conviction that the range of environmental variation is greater in the United States than in most other industrial countries.

The traditional liberal explanation for these differences has been that children from economically disadvantaged families have fewer opportunities to acquire the skills measured on standardized tests. This interpretation is reinforced by examining specific questions included on most standardized tests. Answering these questions often requires at least vicarious familiarity with middle-class life and culture. But when psychologists have looked at different students' performance on a question-by-question basis, they have rarely found that poor children do better on "culture free" questions.[50] Similarly, when they have tried to develop "culture free" or "culture fair" tests, they have found the same differences between rich and poor children as on "culturally biased" tests.[51]

Conservatives have responded to these findings by arguing that there must be genetic differences between rich and poor children. They point out that children with favorable genes are likely to have high test scores, that children with high test scores are likely to get more than their share of schooling, and that people with a great deal of schooling are likely to be economically successful. It follows that economically successful adults are likely to be individuals who have more than their share of the genes that lead to high test scores.[52] If economically successful parents have more than their share of "favorable" genes, their children will also have more than their share of such genes.

As far as it goes, this argument is quite persuasive. Everyone who has studied the matter agrees that test scores have *some* genetic determinants, that there is *some* social mobility in America, and that test scores have *some* effect on a child's chances for mobility. It follows, then, that there must be *some* genetic differences between rich and poor. The real question is not whether such differences exist, but whether they are large or trivial. More specifically, the question is how much of the test score gap between rich and poor children is likely to be due to genes and how much is likely to be due to environment.

There are two ways to answer such a question. The first method is to compare the relationship between test scores and economic status among adopted and natural children. If the relationship is as strong for children adopted into a household as for children raised in the household, the cause of the relationship is probably environmental. If an adopted child's test score is more related to the status of his natural parents than to the status of his adoptive parents, the cause is probably genetic.

Studies of adopted children are usually rather messy, since middle-class children are seldom placed for adoption if they are legitimate, and information on illegitimate children's fathers is seldom very complete.

Even more serious, working-class parents who are allowed to adopt children are not necessarily typical of the working-class population. Parents who would provide extremely unfavorable environments are likely to be screened out. Recognizing these limitations, the studies still suggest that a child's test scores depend at least as much on the status of his natural parents as on the status of his adoptive parents. We can summarize the results of such studies in three propositions:

1. The correlation between a mother's status and her child's IQ score is reduced by about half if she places the child for adoption into another family at an early age.[53]

2. The correlation between an adoptive parent's status and an adopted child's IQ score averages 25 percent of the correlation between a natural parent's status and natural child's score.[54]

3. In two studies where comparable data on both foster and natural parents is available, the child's scores correlated more highly with the natural parents' status than with the foster parents' status.[55] In one study the situation was reversed.[56]

Conclusions (1) and (2) are somewhat contradictory, since if the "preadoption" effect of status is 50 percent of the total effect and the "postadoption" effect is 25 percent, we are left with 25 percent unaccounted for. Taken together, these studies are distressingly inconsistent. Yet if we had no other evidence we would conclude that at least half the difference between high- and low-status children's IQs was accounted for by genes, prenatal environment, or differences in the treatment of children during the first few months after birth.

We do, however, have some additional evidence, although it is indirect. Appendix A estimates the relationship between genes and test scores, while Appendix B estimates the relationship between IQ scores and economic success. This allows us to infer the probable relationship between a father's economic status and his children's genotypes. It suggests that about 30 percent of the observed relationship between a father's occupation and a child's test scores is explained by genes, and that about 70 percent is environmental.[57] Genes appear to play a somewhat larger role in the IQ disparity between children with well-educated parents and children with poorly educated parents.[58]

All in all, the combination of direct and indirect evidence suggests that genes account for something like half the observed relationship between parental educational attainment and test scores, and something like a third of the observed relationship between father's occupation and test scores.

What can we conclude about the overall relationship between economic status and test scores? First, we can say that economic inequality is not one of the major causes of cognitive inequality in America. Random individuals' IQ scores differ by an average of 17 points. Our estimates suggest that the direct and indirect effects of economic inequality have typically caused less than 2 points of this difference.[59]

Second, while economic inequality explains only a small fraction of the overall variation in children's cognitive skills, the gap between the most and the least economically advantaged children is still sizable. Children with fathers in the top fifth of the occupational hierarchy have IQ scores 13 to 15 points higher than children whose fathers rank in the bottom fifth.

Finally, we can say that if an economic elite wanted to pass along its privileges to its children, establishing a system in which privilege depended on test scores would not be a wise strategy. Suppose, for example, that we define the "upper-middle class" as those families that rank in the top fifth in terms of income and occupational status. If access to this elite were strictly random, one upper-middle class child in five would end up in the upper-middle class. If America were suddenly to create a system in which new recruits to the upper-middle class were selected entirely on the basis of test scores, one upper-middle class child in three would be able to maintain his or her parents' privileges.[60] This suggests that a good deal of liberal and radical rhetoric about testing ought to be reexamined. The idea that tests serve mainly to maintain the privileges of the economic elite is exaggerated.

## The Effects of Race

At least in America, the average white child scores about 15 points higher on standardized tests than the average black child. This disparity is apparent among first graders, and it persists throughout school and college. In terms of mental ages or grade levels, blacks fall further and further behind whites. The average black 6 year old is 1 year behind the average white 6 year old. By the time he is 12, the average black child is scoring at the same level as the average white 10 year old. The average black 18 year old has scores comparable to a white 14 or 15 year old.

These differences are quite consistent on both IQ and achievement tests. Some studies report racial differences of less than 15 points, while others report more, but virtually none report anything like equal performance.[61] There is no evidence in EEOS or in other research to support the theory that black children are more disadvantaged on verbal tests than on other standardized tests.[62]

There has been a recurrent debate about whether these differences in average test performance should be attributed to genes, environment, or both. The evidence is consistent with all three theories. In the only American study of identical twins reared apart, for example, 4 of the 19 twins had IQ scores that differed by 15 points or more.[63] If white children have 4 chances out of 19 of being adopted into families that produce such an IQ gap, it is easy to imagine that the difference between the average black family and the average white family could produce a similar gap.

White scores on Army Alpha also rose by 9 to 12 points between 1918 and 1943.[64] Studies in Appalachia showed a comparable increase in a single decade, apparently as a result of the introduction of schools, roads, and the like.[65] It takes no great leap of faith to suppose that the cultural differences between blacks and whites are as great as the cultural differences between white America in 1918 and white America in 1943, or between Appalachia in the late 1920s and in the late 1930s. Similarly, the classic study of unwed mothers and their children showed that the children outscored their mothers by more than 17 points—a disparity which must have been largely environmental.[66]

Unfortunately, we do not know which specific features of the environment caused these differences in test scores, so we cannot say whether such differences account for the gap between blacks and whites. We do know that economic differences explain less than a third of the test score difference between blacks and whites.[67] Cultural differences may explain far more.[68]

Even if we could identify a set of background factors that completely explained differences between black and white children's test scores, we would still have to decide whether the relevant background differences arose and persisted for genetic reasons, environmental reasons, or both. It is not very helpful, for example, to show that differences between black and white children's vocabularies are "explained" by differences between black and white parents' vocabularies. This simply pushes the problem back one generation. Explaining a difference environmentally is not sufficient to rule out genetic factors, any more than explaining the difference genetically rules out environmental factors.

These difficulties derive from the fact that an individual's genes can and do influence his environment. In a certain sense, both sides agree that genes account for the difference between black and white test scores; they simply disagree about the extent to which environment is also involved. One side argues that the genes that cause dark skin thereby influence opportunities and incentives to learn. The other side argues that the genes that cause dark skin (or other genes whose frequency varies between races) influence how much an individual learns from his environment. There is no way to resolve such disagreement in the forseeable future. We cannot expose blacks and whites to the same environments, since skin color itself influences an individual's environment. Nor can we compare the test scores of blacks and whites with identical IQ genotypes, because we do not know which specific genes influence IQ. As a result, everyone will doubtless continue to believe what his prejudices make him want to believe. The reader should not be surprised to learn that we favor environmental explanations.

While we expect this controversy to persist, we also feel that its importance has been greatly exaggerated. Suppose, for example, that blacks and whites could be raised in identical environments and that their test scores still differed by, say, 5 IQ points. This would imply a small genetic difference between the two groups, at least in that particular environment. Given the wide range of other physical differences between ethnic groups, such a difference in IQ genotypes is certainly conceivable. But what follows? For social and political purposes, differences of this magnitude are trivial compared to the differences within ethnic groups. As we will see in Chapter 7, an IQ advantage of 5 points typically translates into an income advantage of a few hundred dollars a year. Its effect on occupational status is equally trivial.

Why, then, have millions of man hours been devoted to demonstrating the genetic superiority of one race over another? As Noam Chomsky has noted, the question is of negligible scientific interest.[69] Establishing a linkage between the genes that influence learning capacity and those that influence skin color is unlikely to advance our understanding of how these genes work, or how people learn. Such a "discovery" would be no more consequential than discovering an association between, say, the genes that determine test scores and the genes that determine height.[70]

The importance of genetic differences between races is political rather than scientific. As of 1972, white people still ran the world. Those who have power always prefer to believe that they "deserve" it, rather than thinking they have won it by venality, cunning, or historical accidents. Some whites apparently feel that if the average white is slightly more adept at certain kinds of abstract reasoning than the average black, this legitimizes the whole structure of white supremacy—not just in America, but around the world. Conversely, many people seem to feel that if blacks and whites are born with the same capacity for abstract reasoning, this proves that white supremacy is illegitimate—and therefore perhaps temporary.

The whole debate is in some ways like the earlier debate about whether blacks had the same natural athletic potential as whites. Symbolically, this was once an enormously important issue. The fact that blacks now dominate many professional sports has therefore been a useful step toward destroying a foolish myth. But the symbolism can be dangerous, too. If blacks were to conclude that winning equality was a matter of athletic ability, most would end up disappointed. The same may also be true about the current controversy regarding test scores. It seems to be symbolically important to establish the proposition that blacks can do as well on standardized tests as whites. But if either blacks or whites conclude that racial equality is primarily a matter of equalizing reading scores, they are fooling themselves. As we shall see in Chapters 7 and 8, blacks and whites with equal test scores still have very unequal occupational statuses and incomes. Instead of accepting the myth that test scores are synonymous with "intelligence" and that "intelligence" is the key to economic success, we would do better to recognize that economic success depends largely on other factors. We could then try to tackle economic inequality between blacks and whites directly.

## III: SCHOOLING AND COGNITIVE INEQUALITY

The next five sections examine schools' effects on cognitive inequality. Before doing this, we must again remind the reader that we have defined cognitive inequality in fairly narrow terms, as the ability to use language easily and accurately, the ability to understand and make logical inferences from printed material, the ability to use numbers with facility, and the ability to absorb and retain miscellaneous information. These are the skills measured by standard tests of verbal ability, reading comprehension, arithmetic, and general information. Every school tries to teach these skills. There are other skills, such as the ability to speak French or the ability to do trigonometry, which some schools try to teach while others do not. Had we looked at these skills, we would probably have found more variation between the alumni of different schools. Conversely, we would have found that simply attending school affected these skills less often than it affected the basic skills taught in all schools. We have chosen to focus on verbal ability, reading, arithmetic, and general information because we believe these things are more important than things like French and trigonometry. Yet even the basic skills are far less important than many people imagine.

In analyzing the effects of schooling on basic cognitive skills, we will begin by trying to estimate the effect of staying in school as against dropping out. Subsequent sections will examine the effects of qualitative variations between schools and of curriculum differences within schools.

## The Effects of School Attendance

In order to assess the effects of school attendance on test scores, we must compare individuals who attended school at a given age to similar individuals who did not. This is relatively easy to do at the preschool level, where attendance is nothing like universal, and access is not yet defined as a matter of right. It is much more difficult at the elementary school level, since virtually all American children attend elementary school, and those who do not are deviant in many other respects. In order to assess the effects of elementary schooling we must rely on a few "natural experiments," in which children who would normally have attended school were denied this opportunity for some reason. Such situations are seldom adequately studied. At the secondary level, we can compare the eventual test scores of students who drop out to the eventual scores of students who remain in school, but it is hard to be sure that we have made the right adjustments for discrepancies in such students' initial ability and motivation.

Taken as a whole, evidence about the effects of school attendance on test scores is woefully inadequate. Such evidence as there is suggests that preschooling has few permanent effects, that elementary schooling is quite important to the development of the skills measured on standardized tests, and that secondary schooling and college also boost test scores to some extent. We will take up these three conclusions in turn.

### PRESCHOOL

The reinvention of preschool is a perennial phenomenon in American education.[71] The latest such cycle began in the early 1960s. Unfortunately, we have no surveys relating adult cognitive skills to preschool attendance. EEOS does, however, provide relevant data on children still in school.[72]

In northern urban elementary schools, four children in five said they had attended kindergarten. Once socio-economic differences were taken into account, there was a negligible difference in mean sixth grade achievement between schools with high proportions of kindergarten alumni and schools with low proportions.[73]

EEOS also asked students whether they had attended nursery school. Once socio-economic differences were taken into account, there were no significant differences in sixth grade achievement between those who said they had attended nursery school and those who said they had not. Given the probable inaccuracies in the data, this finding is hardly conclusive, but it is consistent with most other surveys and experimental research on preschooling.

Follow-ups of preschool alumni have a long history.[74] They fall into a predictable pattern. The majority show that children who attend preschool do quite a lot better on standardized tests at the end of their preschool year than children who did not attend preschool. But children who do not attend preschool usually catch up with children who do attend by the end of the first grade.[75] Only one or two small studies claim appreciable differences beyond first grade.[76]

The largest single follow-up of preschool alumni was the 1968 Westinghouse-Ohio survey of Head Start graduates.[77] This study concluded that neither year-round nor summer Head Start programs had a significant long-term effect on children's cognitive growth. When we reanalyzed this data, we found a few year-round centers in which the Head Start children's advantage over non-Head Start children persisted through first grade.[78] Beyond first grade, however, the picture was gloomy. Overall, the evidence strongly suggested that Head Start's effects on children's cognitive growth had been quite transitory.

This is not surprising. Unlike politicians and parents, Head Start teachers and directors have not been primarily concerned with raising children's test scores. They have favored "supportive, unstructured socialization programs rather than structured informational programs."[79] They have assumed that a child would get plenty of disciplined instruction when he reached first grade and that he would not do any better in first grade if he started such work a year or two early. The evidence suggests that the teachers and administrators were right.[80]

Even if preschooling could be shown to provide long-term cognitive advantages, this would probably not reduce cognitive inequality. Head Start now excludes the middle classes, but this is only politically practical because most middle-class parents do not want their children in preschools with poor children. No study has yet suggested that pre-school programs do more for disadvantaged than for advantaged children. Thus, we cannot expect universal preschooling to narrow the gap between rich and poor or between whites and blacks. Universal preschooling might even widen the gap.

ELEMENTARY SCHOOL

One way to estimate the effect of elementary schooling on cognitive skills is to look at situations in which schooling suddenly ceases to be available to a particular group for some reason. During World War II, for example, many elementary schools in Holland were closed. The IQ scores of children entering at least one secondary school after the end of the war appear to have dropped about 7 points as a result.[81] Also, the schools in Prince Edward County were closed by the local board of education during the early 1960s, in order to avoid integration. When schools were reopened, black children who had not attended school for several years scored substantially lower than most black children of their age.[82] So too, the New York City schools were closed for several months in the fall of 1968 as a result of a strike, and the city reported a drop in test scores the following spring. We have not been able to discover whether any of these losses were permanent.

Schools are also usually closed during the summer months. Both the folklore among teachers and the available evidence suggest that chil-dren's test scores increase more slowly over the summer than during the school year. In some cases children's scores actually drop over the summer. A study of New York City, for example, found that the average child's reading scores improved almost three times as fast dur-ing the school year as during the summer. The average black child's scores improved nearly as fast as the average white child's scores while school was in session, but they hardly improved at all over the summer. This particular study concluded that only half the achievement gap between black and white children in New York City was attribut-able to differential growth during the school year. The other half was explained by differential growth over the summer.[83] This highly sug-gestive study has not yet been replicated.[84]

These findings imply that if all elementary schools were closed down, so that growing up became an endless summer, white middle-class children might still learn much of what they now learn. Some of these children are taught to read before they enter school anyway, and some of them read a great deal at home, developing their skills without any help from school. But most poor black children would probably not learn to read without schools. The cognitive gap between rich and poor and between black and white would thus be far greater than it is now. Those who propose to abolish schools ought to ponder this possibility.

SECONDARY SCHOOL

An extra year of secondary schooling or college is usually associated with a 3 or 4 point advantage on adult aptitude and intelligence tests.[85] We cannot, however, conclude that schooling causes this advantage. Those who get a lot of schooling have higher test scores to begin with.[86] To a large extent, schools and colleges simply screen out students whose cognitive skills are below par, conferring diplomas on those with high initial scores.

Only 2 American studies have tried to separate the effects of initial ability from the effects of schooling. A study in New York City before World War II found that each additional year of school increased boys' IQ scores by about 2.5 points over the level expected on the basis of their earlier school achievement scores.[87] The sample was far from ideal, but several Swedish studies also yield results in this range.[88] The other American study found, however, that additional schooling had no consistent effect on Stanford-Binet scores.[89] If we synthesize data from diverse sources, our best estimate is that each extra year of schooling boosts an individual's adult IQ score about 1 point above the expected level.[90]

We are far from confident about the validity of these contradictory estimates. Surveys are likely to overestimate the actual effects of school attendance on test scores, because they seldom measure all the prior differences between those who stay in school and those who drop out.[91] No experimental evidence is available.

Despite our reservations, we tentatively conclude that if students leave school early in adolescence, their verbal and numerical skills do not develop as much as if they remain in school. We do not know whether this also applies to students who leave college or graduate school. We also infer that equalizing the amount of schooling people get might do quite a lot to equalize cognitive skills. This reflects the fact that although each extra year of schooling has only a modest effect on test scores, the benefits are now largely concentrated on those who are already advantaged. If everyone received the same schooling, the "double advantage" phenomenon in this area could be eliminated.[92]

CONCLUSIONS

The evidence we have reviewed supports three conclusions:

1. Preschools have little permanent effect on cognitive development.
2. Elementary schooling is helpful for middle-class children and crucial for lower-class children.
3. Secondary schools and colleges do less than elementary schools but more than most jobs or housework in developing the skills measured on standardized tests.

Perhaps the most astonishing feature of this whole inquiry is that virtually no research has been done on these issues, either by defenders of schools or by their critics. As a result, our conclusions are all based on problematic inferences of uncertain validity. The most we can claim is that such evidence is better than nothing.

## Differences between Schools

Nearly anything can happen in a place called a school. Some schools consist of a single room in which children of all ages are mixed with a barely literate teacher. Others are huge enterprises, with highly trained staffs from the world's leading universities. Some of these schools are run like prisons, with rigid routines that determine what every child is doing almost every minute of the day. Other schools are more like asylums, with constant battles to maintain order and no sequential activity that lasts more than a few minutes. A few schools are like permissive families, with children pretty much working out what they want to do, doing it on their own or in groups, and getting attention or help from adults only when they want it or when they "misbehave." Given this diversity, we did not expect all schools to have precisely the same effects on children's test scores. The differences are, however, surprisingly small. This suggests that public schools are more alike than parents and teachers think they are.

HIGH SCHOOLS

Let us look first at high schools. The best currently available evidence about high schools' effects on their students is found in survey data collected by Project Talent. The most relevant portion of this survey covered 5,000 students in 91 predominantly white comprehensive high schools. These students were given 49 different tests in 1960, when they were in ninth grade. They were given some of the same tests again in 1963, when they were in twelfth grade. We compared students' performance in ninth and twelfth grades on six of these tests: Vocabulary, Social Studies Information, Reading Comprehension, Abstract Reasoning, Mathematics, and Arithmetic Computation.

Predictably, ninth grade scores largely determine twelfth grade scores. Changes between ninth and twelfth grade have almost nothing to do with the school a student is in. If we look at vocabulary, for example, we find that all students' scores increase between ninth and twelfth grade. If we predict students' twelfth grade scores from their ninth grade scores, knowing nothing about their school, our predictions are never off by an average of more than 5 points for any school. In schools with enough students to yield stable estimates, the mean is always within 3 points of the expected level. Furthermore, the schools where students show unusual improvement on one test are not the same as the schools where students show unusual improvement on other tests.[93]

If we average schools' effects on several different tests, the average twelfth grader's overall performance is within 3 points of what we would expect on the basis of his ninth grade scores. Stating it slightly differently, we can say that if all high schools were equally effective (or ineffective) inequality between twelfth graders would fall less than one percent.[94] This picture is reinforced by the EEOS data on high schools. The average difference between a high school's mean twelfth grade scores and the twelfth grade mean predicted from its mean ninth grade scores was 3 points.[95]

ELEMENTARY SCHOOLS

Children's test scores change in less predictable ways during the early years of elementary school than later on. We therefore expected differences between schools to have somewhat more effect on young children than on older children. We have found some evidence to support this expectation.

There have been no national longitudinal surveys of elementary schools comparable to Project Talent. This means we cannot actually follow children through elementary school to see how much their growth depends on their initial characteristics and how much it depends on the school they attend. In the absence of longitudinal data, we turned again to EEOS.

EEOS elementary schools whose entering students had low scores were appreciably more likely to have high scoring graduates than EEOS high schools whose entering students had low scores.[96] This suggests that variations in school quality have more effect on young students than on older ones.

Nonetheless, the overall effect of elementary school quality on test scores appears rather modest. Suppose we rank schools in terms of their effects on test scores and then compare students who are in the most effective fifth of all elementary schools to students from apparently similar socio-economic and racial backgrounds who are in the least effective fifth of all schools. These students' sixth grade test scores will differ by about 10 points. This implies that 10 points is a maximum estimate of the average effect of attending an elementary school that ranks in the top rather than the bottom fifth. If we could compare sixth graders who resembled each other not only in terms of race and socio-economic background but in terms of initial ability, we suspect this estimate would be closer to 5 points than to 10. This implies that eliminating differences between elementary schools would reduce cognitive inequality by 3 percent or less.[97]

We do not know how much of this difference is really explained by variations in what schools do, how much is explained by inadequate adjustments for variations in initial ability and in neighborhood characteristics, and how much is due to various kinds of measurement error. One reason we suspect a lot of error is that schools' effects do not appear to be very stable from one year to the next. When we look at New York City elementary schools, for example, we find that in any given year there are some schools whose sixth graders do much better on reading tests than we would have predicted on the basis of the class's scores in earlier years. Each year there are also some schools whose sixth graders do worse than we would have expected on the basis of the class's performance in earlier years. This implies significant variation in schools' effectiveness. But on the average, schools which appear to have been unusually effective or ineffective with one class appear to have been only a third as effective (or ineffective) with the preceding and following classes. Perhaps these changes are real, reflecting mysterious changes in school "climate" from one year to the next. We suspect, however, that a lot of the apparent variation in these schools' effectiveness is due to measurement error.[98]

## CUMULATIVE EFFECTS OF ELEMENTARY AND SECONDARY SCHOOLS

Suppose that we define a school's "effectiveness" strictly in terms of its effect on students' test scores. The cumulative contribution of schooling to cognitive inequality will then depend on the extent to which students who start school with an advantage attend schools which are unusually effective, on the extent of variation in schools' annual effects, and on the extent to which students who attend "effective" schools in one year also attend effective schools in prior and subsequent years. If unusually talented students enter unusually effective elementary schools, if these elementary schools send their students to unusually effective high schools, and if these high schools then induce unusually large proportions of students to attend college, the cumulative impact of the educational system on an individual's test scores could be quite large, even though the effect in any one year is small. But if effective elementary schools send their students to ineffective high schools, and if high schools that are effective in boosting test scores do not send unusually high proportions of their students to college, the cumulative impact of the educational system on cognitive inequality will be much smaller.

Unfortunately, we do not have good data on cognitive "value added" for individual students in American elementary schools. We can, however, use EEOS to see whether elementary schools whose students "overachieve" relative to their socio-economic background feed into high schools whose students "overachieve" in these same terms. At least in the urban North, they do not. If we judge an elementary school's effectiveness by whether its sixth graders do better or worse than sixth graders in other schools with a similar socio-economic mix, and if we judge high schools in the same way, the correlation between an elementary school's effectiveness and the effectiveness of the high school into which it feeds is almost nil.[99] This means that a student who attends an elementary school which is good at boosting test scores is not especially likely to attend an equally effective high school. We suspect that this is because the observed differences between high schools are largely due to random measurement error.

We also estimated the effect of each northern urban EEOS high school on its students' chances of attending college. Students who attended an elementary school that seemed to boost their test scores were not especially likely to attend high schools that further improved their chances of attending college.[100]

As a further check on the contribution of differences between schools to cognitive inequality, we investigated whether students with high initial test scores were likely to attend schools that were unusually effective in boosting test scores. At the secondary level, the answer seems to be no. There is no correlation between the mean achievement scores of students entering the 91 Project Talent high schools we studied and their rate of cognitive growth between ninth and twelfth grade.[101]

Unfortunately, we do not have data suitable for answering this question at the elementary level.

CONCLUSIONS

Overall, the evidence shows that differences between high schools contribute almost nothing to the overall level of cognitive inequality. Differences between elementary schools may be somewhat more important, but evidence for this is still inconclusive. The average effect of attending the best rather than the worst fifth of all elementary schools is almost certainly no more than 10 points and probably no more than 5. The difference between, say, the top and bottom halves is even less.

Under these circumstances the reader should not be surprised to learn that it is very difficult to identify specific characteristics of schools that influence student achievement. The next section describes our futile attempt to identify resources that make one school more effective than another, and the following section summarizes our findings about the effects of a school's social composition on the achievement of various kinds of students.

## The Effects of School Resources

EXPENDITURES

When legislators talk about school resources, they mean money. Taxpayers have a similar bias. Once the overall level of expenditure has been set, professional educators have the dominant voice in determining what the money goes for. In deciding whether to raise expenditures, then, laymen must assume that the money will mostly be used to buy the same things that money is now used to buy: higher salaries, smaller classes, more specialized personnel, lighter teaching loads, newer textbooks, better facilities, and so forth. This means that the best way to appraise the likely effect of, say, doubling per pupil expenditures is to assume that schools now spending $400 per pupil will become like schools now spending $800, that schools now spending $800 will become like schools now spending $1,600, and so forth.

The evidence we have examined does not suggest that doubling expenditures would raise students' performance on standardized tests. A school's annual expenditure is, it is true, moderately related to the test scores of its alumni. But this is because affluent schools enroll students whose test scores are above average to begin with. When we compare schools with similar entering students, we do not find those with fat budgets turning out more skilled alumni than those with inadequate budgets.

In our analysis of Project Talent we found that when we compared an impoverished high school to one that spent twice as much, students in the rich school gained no more between ninth and twelfth grades than students in the poor school.[102] EEOS measured only district-wide expenditures, rather than expenditures in each high school. Nonetheless, if expenditures influenced achievement, we would expect affluent districts to outscore indigent ones. In fact, each extra $100 of per pupil expenditure was associated with an extra point on the EEOS tests, but this was only because high schools with high expenditures had high scoring students to begin with.[103] This finding is consistent with other studies of "value added" in high schools.[104]

When we turn to elementary schools, the data is less conclusive but equally discouraging. EEOS found no association of consequence between district-wide expenditures and mean achievement in elementary schools. Nor have other surveys found any consistent association between expenditures and elementary schools' effectiveness in raising test scores.[105]

In order to test the validity of inferences from survey research, it is useful to look at the effect of changes in expenditure on test scores in specific schools or for specific students. We know of no systematic efforts to evaluate the effects of increased state or local expenditures, but the failure of test scores to rise between 1960 and 1970 is discouraging, since expenditures rose sharply in those years.[106] The federal government has also made sporadic efforts to determine whether the "compensatory" programs established in 1965 under Title I of the Elementary and Secondary Education Act were actually raising children's test scores. These evaluations are generally discouraging. The evaluators usually had inadequate budgets, inadequate information, limited cooperation from the schools, and limited technical expertise. Nonetheless, if additional Title I funds were raising children's test scores by substantial amounts, the evaluations ought to show this more often than they show the opposite. In fact, the results of evaluations appear to be virtually random. Students in Title I programs do worse than comparison groups as often as they do better.[107]

There are two popular explanations for the fact that raising expenditures does not raise test scores.

1. Some critics argue that school administrators and teachers are not very interested in raising test scores. The way money is actually spent

partly supports this argument. A superintendent often wants a new gymnasium because the high school basketball team is popular in the community—or because he used to be a basketball coach himself. He wants more money for teachers' salaries because otherwise the teachers will strike—and he will get an ulcer. He wants smaller classes because teachers prefer small classes and because small classes make it easier to keep order. The superintendent usually hopes these expenditures will raise achievement scores too, but if they do not, he wants them anyway.

2. Other critics assume that school administrators and teachers want to raise achievement but have no idea how to go about it. This theory has two variants. One version holds that the problem is intrinsically insoluble, at least with present knowledge and technology. According to this view, demands that schools raise achievement scores are like the demands that hospitals cure senility. A second version of the theory holds that test scores can be raised if administrators and teachers use their resources wisely, but that they rarely do so.

We have not done any empirical research on what school administrators and teachers are really trying to do. We suspect that their primary objective is to teach children to behave themselves the way schools want them to behave. However, teaching the skills measured on standardized tests is probably a close second. We can see no evidence that either school administrators or educational experts know how to raise test scores, even when they have vast resources at their disposal. Certainly we do not know how to do so.

POLICIES AND RESOURCES

In hope of collecting some information that would help professional educators use their resources more efficiently, we have tried to identify schools that were unusually effective in boosting test scores, in order to see if they had any objective characteristics in common. We concentrated on school policies and resources that could be directly controlled by legislators, school boards, and administrators. This means we looked at things like physical facilities, libraries and library books, how much homework a school assigned, whether it had heterogeneous or homogeneous grouping, numbers and kinds of personnel, salaries, criteria for selecting teachers, and so forth. We did not look in any detail at things like morale, teacher expectations, school traditions, and school "climate." While these things may well be associated with unusually rapid or slow cognitive development, policy-makers cannot usually control them, social scientists cannot usually measure them, and no one can be sure whether they cause achievement or only result from it.

Survey data on the relationship of school policies and resources to student achievement has been gathered and analyzed by many different scholars.[108] The results of such studies have been contradictory. Resources which are associated with high scores in one city are not associated with high scores in another city. Resources which have a positive relationship to the achievement of one kind of student have a negative relationship for another kind of student. Resources that look helpful when the data is analyzed one way look unimportant when the data is analyzed another way.

In an attempt to clarify some of these problems, we have reanalyzed the original data from three of the largest and most comprehensive school surveys: EEOS, Project Talent, and the Plowden survey in England.[109] There has been a great deal of debate, often acrimonious, about the right way to analyze such surveys.[110] Nonetheless, two general conclusions seem justified.

First, no measurable school resource or policy shows a consistent relationship to schools' effectiveness in boosting student achievement. The specific school resources that have a "statistically significant" relationship to achievement change from one survey to the next, from one method of analysis to another, from one sort of school to another, and from one type of student to another. While it is always possible to invent explanations for all this after the fact, it is never possible to predict much about such differences in advance.

Second, the gains associated with any given resource are almost always small. In EEOS, for example, the presence of an important school resource is typically associated with a difference of no more than 2 to 4 months in mean sixth grade achievement. This is roughly equivalent to 2 to 4 IQ points. Thus, even if we were to persuade ourselves that resources had consistent effects, it would be hard to argue that they had pedagogically important effects.

Experimental studies of the relationship between student achievement and such things as school size, class size, ability grouping, and curriculum point to the same conclusion. Some show benefits, some show losses, and some show no effect either way.[111]

The most plausible explanation for these findings is that school resources have small inconsistent effects on achievement. Experienced teachers are more competent than average in some systems, less competent than average in other systems. Teachers with high verbal scores help certain students to develop their verbal skills but inhibit others.

Another complementary interpretation is that resource allocation responds to achievement in some communities but not others. Thus some communities allow experienced teachers to move to better schools, creating a spurious impression that experience causes high achievement.[112] Other systems do not allow experienced teachers to move, so there is no association between teacher experience and student achievement. Both these interpretations have the same practical implication. Legislators, school boards, and school superintendents cannot expect that any general policy which simply provides more school resources will raise children's test scores.

In concluding this discussion we must again emphasize one major limitation of our findings. We have only examined the effects of resource differences among existing public schools. This tells us that if schools continue to use their resources as they now do, giving them more resources will not change children's test scores. If schools used their resources differently, however, additional resources might conceivably have larger payoffs. If, for example, principals or parents had control over the school budget and could spend their money on whatever they thought their school needed most, extra resources might affect test scores more than they now do.[113] There is no way of testing this theory except by experimentation. Past history is discouraging, but the future is not always a rerun of the past.

## The Effects of Segregation

This section will deal with the effect of segregation on students' test scores. We will look first at how school segregation affects blacks, then at how it affects poor whites and students with low initial test scores, and finally at how it affects "advantaged" students. We will use the term "advantaged" throughout the discussion to designate students who have what the majority defines as desirable traits: e.g. white skin, affluent parents, or high initial test scores.

### EFFECTS ON BLACKS

The debate about racial segregation is by now so old that the theoretical arguments have all been made—and rebutted. In general they fall into four categories.

1. Advocates of desegregation say it gives black students access to school resources that were previously denied them: physics laboratories, small classes, experienced teachers, teachers who know their subject,

and so forth. Critics reply that desegregated schools spend only marginally more than all-black ones, and in some cities they spend less. In addition, as we have seen, neither expenditures in general nor the particular things schools buy with their money have any consistent effect on black students' cognitive development.[114]

2. Advocates of desegregation argue that it will put black children in contact with classmates who have certain kinds of knowledge (e.g. knowledge of "standard" grammar) that many black students lack. Critics answer that whether white schoolmates are a valuable resource to black students depends on how they actually relate to one another. If they become enemies or if their relations are mostly derisory, hostile, or violent, it is hard to see how either group will benefit.[115]

3. Advocates of desegregation often argue that teachers in desegregated schools expect more of black students than teachers in segregated schools and that black students learn more as a result. Unfortunately, we have no evidence on this point. Teachers in predominantly white schools often express distaste for black students,[116] but whether they expect more or less academically from black students we do not know.

4. Desegregation may convince a black student that he has a chance to make it in the larger society. This may make him work harder and learn more, even if the desegregated school is no better than a segregated one. But while the symbolism of desegregation may help convince a black student that he has a change of making it in the larger society, direct exposure to teachers and students who put him down seems likely to have the opposite effect.

Educators and social scientists who have thought carefully about desegregation have usually concluded that its effects are unpredictable, depending on exactly how desegregation is initiated and implemented and how the participants view the process. This leads some experts to distinguish "desegregation" from "integration." Desegregation is defined as having black and white students under the same roof. Integration is defined as knitting the two groups into a single social community. When desegregation leads to trouble or fails to raise test scores, this is attributed to the fact that there was no "genuine integration." When desegregation "works," by whatever criteria someone judges relevant, it is hailed as an example of "genuine integration."

This explanation has considerable heuristic value. It does not, however, tell us when desegregation will raise disadvantaged students' achievement scores, when it will lower their scores, or when it will leave them unchanged. In order to make predictions, we need some way of anticipating when desegregation will lead to integration and when it will not. No one has yet developed a method for doing this.[117]

The effects of desegregation on test scores have been studied in two ways. One approach has been to study "natural experiments." This has meant comparing the achievement of black students in all-black schools to the achievement of more or less comparable black students in desegregated schools. The difficulty with this approach is that the black student who enrolls in a desegregated school may differ in unknown ways from outwardly similar black students in segregated schools.

An alternative approach is therefore to study the effect of actually moving black students from all-black schools to desegregated schools. A number of northern cities have conducted such studies as part of desegregation efforts. Once again, it is hard to decide who the desegregated blacks should be compared to. Sometimes students' scores after a year or two of busing are compared to their scores before busing. Unfortunately, this requires that we distinguish the effects of getting older from the effects of desegregation, which is not always easy. Sometimes the desegregated students are compared to supposedly similar blacks in all-black schools. Desegregation is seldom completely random, however, so it is always hard to be sure how comparable the 2 groups really are. Elaborate statistical techniques have been developed for dealing with all these difficulties, but none is foolproof.

These methodological difficulties would be of little concern if studies of desegregation yielded consistent results. Unfortunately, they do not. Virtually all surveys of natural experiments show that black students in desegregated schools score above apparently similar blacks in all-black schools.[118] This pattern holds for a wide variety of tests and at all grade levels: But when black students are actually bused from segregated to desegregated schools, their test scores do not always improve.

Two alternative explanations for this apparent contradiction come to mind. Those who believe in desegregation often argue that the busing programs have not been operating long enough to produce social integration, and that this accounts for their uneven effect on test scores. Those who oppose desegregation argue that the high test scores of blacks in naturally integrated schools reflect the greater motivation or resources of black parents who put their children in desegregated schools.

Given the importance of the issue, a brief review of the best available studies may be helpful. The most famous survey of "naturally" desegregated schools is EEOS. James Coleman and his colleagues concluded from this survey that the socio-economic level of a student's school had more effect on his achievement than any other measurable factor except the socio-economic level of his home.[119] Effectively, this meant that both blacks and whites were better off in predominantly white schools, since these schools were much more likely to be middle class.

Most reanalyses have supported Coleman's original conclusion.[120] However, almost all these studies show that desegregation is associated with higher test scores only if it involves socio-economic as well as racial desegregation. There is little evidence that black test scores are any higher in schools where the whites are as poor as the blacks.[121]

The most serious objection to these analyses is that black students in different types of schools were matched only on their socio-economic level, not on initial ability. Further analysis of EEOS has shown that there were substantial differences in initial ability between black students entering segregated and desegregated northern urban elementary schools in 1965. When we took these differences into account, we found that black improvement between first and sixth grade appeared to have been greatest in schools that were predominantly but not overwhelmingly white. Black first graders in schools which were 25–50 percent black averaged 2 points below the northern urban black mean on the EEOS first grade tests. Black sixth graders in the same schools averaged 3 points above the northern urban black mean on the four sixth grade EEOS tests. The implied gain is 5 points. In 10–25 percent black schools, the pattern was reversed. Black first graders in these schools were 5 points above the northern urban black mean, while sixth grade blacks in the same schools were no better than the black mean. The implied loss was thus 5 points. Blacks in predominantly black schools were equally far below national norms on both the first and sixth grade EEOS tests.[122]

Like its predecessors, this analysis of EEOS has several major limitations, the most important of which is that there were only 126 black children in the first grades of the 10–25 percent black schools, and 549 in the first grades of the 25–50 percent black schools. Nonetheless, the fact that this analysis tries to take initial ability into account makes it slightly more persuasive than other analyses of EEOS data. In the absence of other evidence it would suggest that blacks benefited from elementary school desegregation so long as they were a large enough minority.

Reanalysis of the EEOS northern urban high school data shows that twelfth grade blacks in the 42 predominantly but not exclusively white high schools score 3 points higher than would be expected from looking at ninth grade blacks in the same school. Since many blacks drop out of school between ninth and twelfth grades, it would be dangerous to draw many conclusions from this finding.[123]

The theory that desegregation boosts black test scores more often than it lowers them is supported by a 1966 survey of black adults.[124] The survey covered 1,624 northern urban blacks born between 1921 and 1945. Half were educated in the South, half in the North. Of those educated in the North, half said they had attended desegregated schools, a quarter said they had attended segregated schools, and a quarter said they had attended both. Those who had attended desegregated schools scored 2 or 3 points higher on a short verbal test than those who had attended segregated schools. The two groups did not appear to differ in socio-economic background. We do not know whether they differed in terms of initial ability.

Most local surveys have also found that blacks in desegregated schools score higher than blacks in all-black schools. The two best studies are by Alan Wilson and Nancy St. John. Wilson conducted a survey in Contra Costa County, California, and found that black students' scores rose faster in desegregated than in segregated schools. This held true even when initial test scores were controlled. Like EEOS, Wilson found that blacks benefited only when they attended school with middle-class whites, not when they attended school with whites as poor as themselves. He also found that school racial mix affected test scores, while neighborhood racial mix did not. Racial mix had more effect in elementary than in secondary school.[125]

St. John conducted surveys of Pittsburgh ninth graders and Boston sixth graders. In Pittsburgh, black ninth graders did better in arithmetic, but no better in reading, if they were in desegregated schools.[126] The same thing appears to have been true in Boston.[127]

Taken together, these surveys suggest that black students educated in desegregated elementary schools score 2–3 points higher on standardized tests if they attend desegregated elementary schools than if they attend all-black elementary schools. If this estimate is realistic, we might also expect to find the following:

1. Black students in truly integrated schools, whatever they may be, might gain more than 3 points on standardized tests.[128]

2. Black students in schools which did not have meaningful social integration might not gain anything at all, or might even lose. This would be especially likely if desegregation was recent and had been accompanied by social dislocation and disruption of school routines. The same might hold for schools where blacks were a small minority.

3. Blacks from "good" all-black schools might gain nothing from desegregation. They might even lose if they moved into "bad" desegregated schools.

4. The benefits of desegregation might be confined to certain grade levels and to certain kinds of students, as well as to certain kinds of schools.[129]

If this is the way the world works, we would also expect busing experiments in diverse communities and grade levels involving small numbers of children to yield contradictory results. Some would show no gains whatever. Many would show gains so small they could reasonably be attributed to chance. A few would show losses. Such a mixed pattern would be particularly common when the "receiving" schools in busing studies were being desegregated for the first time. Studies that tried to identify changes in test scores after only one or two years of busing would also be likely to yield a lot of statistically insignificant differences, since short-term changes involve more random error.

The busing studies we have surveyed conform to these expectations. Some show inconsistent gains. Some show no difference. Very few show (or at least report) losses.

In Hartford, Connecticut, Project Concern randomly chooses classrooms of black children for busing to white suburbs. In 1970, children who had been in the program three years had reading scores 7 to 8 points above the average for the all-black schools they had left. Others showed less improvement. There are a multitude of problems with this study, but in general it is encouraging.[130] In Riverside, California, on the other hand, a massive intracity busing program seems to have had negligible effects on black students' test scores.[131] In Evanston, Illinois, desegregation seems to have improved blacks' scores slightly in the early grades but not in later grades.[132] This mixed bag of findings could be expanded.[133]

Taken in isolation, none of these studies proves very much. When they are taken together, they seem consistent with our conclusion that if desegregation continues over a fairly long period it usually raises black students' scores slightly. But the gains are usually small, and they depend on factors that nobody fully understands.

When we turn from racial to economic segregation, the picture is equally murky. Analysts who try to disentangle the effects of racial and economic segregation on blacks generally conclude that economic segregation is far more important than racial segregation. This implies that poor blacks would benefit as much from going to school with middle-class blacks as from going to school with middle-class whites. It also implies that blacks do not benefit from going to school with poor whites.

It seems reasonable to infer, although we have no direct evidence, that blacks also benefit primarily from going to school with students who have high test scores, not from going to school with students whose parents are merely affluent.

### EFFECTS ON POOR WHITES

The effects of desegregation on disadvantaged white students have not been widely studied. Coleman and his colleagues reported that white students' test scores were not much affected by the characteristics of their classmates.[134] This analysis was, however, flawed in several crucial respects.[135] Subsequent analyses of EEOS have implied that poor whites benefited from being in predominantly middle-class schools, but less than poor blacks. Unfortunately, the possibility that this was due to differences in initial ability was not ruled out.[136] But Wilson's study of Contra Costa County controlled initial scores and still found that working-class whites' scores rose more if they attended predominantly middle-class schools. Wilson also found that desegregation did not help whites as much as blacks, and that it only helped in elementary school.[137] In contrast, a study of Brookline, Massachusetts, found that economic segregation had no effect on test scores at the elementary school level.[138]

Project Talent shows that working-class whites gain as much between ninth and twelfth grades when they attend predominantly working-class high schools as when they attend predominantly middle-class high schools.[139] This is consistent with Wilson's study. A study of Nashville reached essentially the same conclusion.[140]

The weight of the evidence thus supports the assumption that poor white students benefit academically from desegregation at the elementary level but probably not at the secondary level. The evidence is not very weighty, however.

### EFFECTS ON ADVANTAGED STUDENTS

Advocates of desegregation are seldom very interested in its effects on advantaged students. Some actually hope that desegregation will depress advantaged students' achievement, so as to narrow the gap between them and the disadvantaged. Others expect desegregation to make advantaged students get along better with disadvantaged students. They assume that this is more important than academic gains or losses. Still others assume that advantaged students learn what they need to know at home, and that desegregation will not affect their test scores at all.

Opponents of desegregation naturally take a different view. Almost all the arguments usually advanced for believing that desegregation will help blacks or poor whites can be turned around to show that desegregation will also hurt middle-class whites:

1. Desegregation implies a more equitable distribution of scarce resources between the advantaged and the disadvantaged. If this raises the achievement of the disadvantaged, it may lower the achievement of the advantaged.

2. Desegregation implies that teachers will adapt their expectations to a new and more heterogeneous group of students. These new expectations are likely to be lower if the teachers are dealing with a mixed group of students than if they are dealing exclusively with advantaged students.

3. If desegregation leads to social integration, advantaged students will spend more time with disadvantaged students than before. This means advantaged students will spend less time with students who are likely to teach them the cognitive skills measured by standardized tests. (Disadvantaged students may well teach their advantaged friends other things of more value, but here we are concerned only with test scores.)

4. Desegregation may also lead to the creation of a new set of peer group norms, in which achievement may be less highly valued.[141]

5. If desegregation raises the self-esteem of disadvantaged students, it may also lower the self-esteem of advantaged students. Thus upper-middle class whites are fond of explaining poor whites' resistance to desegregation on the grounds that it leaves poor whites with nobody to look down on.

Advocates of desegregation have answers to all these arguments. They say that if students have the necessary advantages at home, they will achieve close to their maximum potential no matter what their school and schoolmates are like. They also say that teacher expectations and student culture are shaped by the modal style of the students, and that if a school is composed mostly of advantaged students, it can absorb a large minority of disadvantaged students without ill effects. This implies that there are "tipping points" below which desegregation does not affect advantaged students' scores, but above which it does.

Let us begin by asking what effect racial desegregation has on the average white student's test scores. The original analysis of EEOS appeared to show that whites were not much affected by desegregation, but this was due to the peculiar method of analysis and certain technical errors.[142] Subsequent analyses of this data have focused primarily on elementary schools. These analyses have also found that white sixth graders scored lower if they were in school with blacks.[143] But the reason for this seems to be that whites who are in school with blacks have lower scores when they enter. In predominantly black northern urban EEOS elementary schools, white first graders were as far below national norms as white sixth graders. In schools where blacks were a large minority (i.e. 25–50 percent of the sixth grade enrollment), white sixth graders scored about 3 points *higher* relative to national norms than white first graders.[144] Thus if desegregation has any effect on whites, EEOS suggests that it is positive rather than negative.

This tentative conclusion from EEOS is, however, contradicted by Wilson's California study. He found that whites who attended racially mixed elementary schools did worse than whites who attended all-white schools. He also found that the difference was not accounted for by his measures of initial ability or economic background. Fortunately, the size of the effect was generally small.[145]

None of the busing studies we reviewed reported that white students' scores had declined when their schools were desegregated. In several cases, however, these studies only involved busing blacks to previously white schools, not busing whites to previously black schools. In some studies, the white students were not even tested. Even when they were, it could be argued that there had not been enough time for desegregation to bring social integration. This means that white students' scores might decline later on.

The effects of racial desegregation on whites, if they exist at all, also seem to depend on the economic background of the blacks whose schools they attend. Racial composition has no independent effect on white students once the economic characteristics of the student body have been taken into account.[146] Thus, there is no reason to suppose that middle-class whites suffer from exposure to middle-class blacks.

The effects of economic desegregation on whites are unclear. Wilson found that whites' scores did not improve as fast in working-class elementary schools as in middle-class elementary schools. But our reanalysis of the Plowden survey in England did not show any difference in rates of improvement for initially similar students in working-class and middle-class schools.[147] Our study of Brookline, Massachusetts, also found no differences.[148]

At the high school level, neither the racial nor the economic composition of a school seems to have much effect on white students' scores once their initial ability is taken into account. Our analyses of Project Talent show that white high school students' scores are not affected one way or the other by the racial, economic, or academic composition of their high schools. We find the same thing when we define advantage in terms of initial test scores. Those who score high in ninth grade gain as much in working-class schools as in middle-class schools and as much in schools with high ninth grade scores as in schools with low ninth grade scores.[149] Wilson's California study also shows trivial effects at the high school level.[150]

All in all, there is little evidence that desegregation has appreciable effects on initially advantaged students. This is a deliberately evasive conclusion. We cannot say for sure that desegregation never lowers advantaged students' test scores. All we can say is that if desegregation affects these students' scores, the effect must be fairly small and inconsistent.

CONCLUSIONS

We have reached four overall conclusions about the potential effects of desegregation on cognitive inequality.

1. About 80 percent of all blacks were in predominantly black schools in 1965. They averaged 15 points below the white mean on standardized tests. Our best guess is that desegregation raises black scores by 2–3 points. Eliminating *all* predominantly black schools might therefore reduce the overall black-white gap from 15 to 12 or 13 points. Such a gain would not be completely trivial, but it would certainly not have much effect on the overall pattern of racial inequality in America.

2. Economic desegregation might raise poor whites' average test score by 1 or 2 points.

3. While desegregation would almost certainly reduce the overall amount of variation in test scores, the reduction would probably be quite small. Most cognitive inequality is within racial groups, within economic groups, and within schools. Desegregation will not affect these disparities much.

4. Finally, the case for or against desegregation should not be argued in terms of academic achievement. If we want a segregated society, we should have segregated schools. If we want a desegregated society, we should have desegregated schools. We suspect that most blacks, like most whites, want a mixture of the two, based on some degree of voluntarism at least among blacks. If this is so, we need a system of pupil assignment that reflects the preferences of individual black parents to some extent. The effects of segregation on test scores are certainly not large enough to justify overriding the preferences of parents and students.

## The Effects of Tracking

We have argued that differences between schools have very little effect on test scores. Achievement differences between schools are, however, relatively small compared to achievement differences within the same school. If we compare the top fifth of all northern urban elementary schools to the bottom fifth, for example, the difference in mean sixth grade verbal scores is only 2 years. But within the typical school, the top fifth of all sixth graders have verbal scores almost 4 years above the bottom fifth.[151] From this it follows that even in the best northern urban elementary schools, the bottom fifth of the students are well below the northern urban average. Conversely, even in the worst schools, the top fifth of the students are above the northern urban average.

This means that every elementary school is nearly a microcosm of the larger society as far as cognitive inequality is concerned. This is even more true at the high school level. A strategy for reducing cognitive inequality must therefore be primarily a strategy for equalizing students in the same school. The difficulty of this task is obvious. But pretending that the main problem is parity between schools will not make it any easier. If by some miracle we were able to equalize the achievement of all American schools, leaving only differences between students in the same school, we would have reduced cognitive inequality by only about 20 percent. If each school were able to eliminate inequalities among its students, leaving differences between them and students in other schools untouched, inequality would fall by about 40 percent.[152]

Aside from differences in initial ability, the most obvious explanation for test score differences among students in the same school is that schools do not try to teach everyone the same things. At the elementary level, many schools put slow learners in slow classes and fast learners in fast classes. At the secondary level, they also put students in separate curriculums. If these differences do not affect students' test scores, nothing else is likely to do so.

We began our studies of tracking and curriculum placement with mixed expectations. We were used to finding that school policies and programs had inconsistent and generally trivial effects on student achievement. Reasoning by analogy, some of us expected that tracking would have equally inconsequential effects. But we were also used to finding that segregation of advantaged and disadvantaged students into different schools increased cognitive inequality. Again reasoning by analogy, some of us expected that internal segregation would do the same. After an extensive review of previous research and reanalyses of four school surveys, we have concluded that if tracking affects test scores at all, the effect is too small to be pedagogically significant.

Research on tracking has a long history. The number of published studies boggles the mind. In 1968, the National Education Association reviewed what it regarded as the 50 best studies published in the previous 8 years. The results are shown in Table 3–1. As with school

TABLE 3-1

*Number of Studies Showing Various Effects of Ability
Grouping on Achievement*

| Ability Level of Students | Favorable Effects | Mixed Effects | Unfavorable or Insignificant Effects |
|---|---|---|---|
| Talented | 18 | 11 | 17 |
| Average | 11 | 12 | 10 |
| Slow | 12 | 10 | 17 |

Source: National Education Association, Research Division, *Ability Grouping,* Research Summary 1968-Se (Washington, D.C., 1968).

resources, we have to conclude that ability grouping sometimes helps disadvantaged students, sometimes hurts them, and sometimes has no effect. The same appears to be true of advantaged students. Nobody knows when tracking will produce one effect or another.

Unlike many previous researchers, we were not primarily interested in the average effect of tracking. We assumed it would be trivial. Our interest was in whether tracking affected the amount of variation in test scores. We thought it might well boost the scores of the students in fast classes, while lowering the scores of students in slow classes. Research of this kind poses serious methodological problems.[153] We did, however, find one excellent body of data on English primary schools, collected by the National Foundation for Educational Research between 1964 and 1967. This study tested students when they were 7 and again when they were 10, using the same tests. After correcting for unreliability in the initial tests, we found that students who were in fast streams ended up about 2 points ahead of initially similar students assigned to slow streams.[154] Like others before us, then, we concluded that elementary school tracking had little effect on cognitive inequality.

We also investigated the effects of high school curriculum placement. We looked at 91 predominantly white comprehensive high schools throughout the United States that had tested their students for Project Talent in the ninth grade and had retested them in the twelfth grade. We compared students with initially similar scores on six different tests, some of whom said they were in the college preparatory curriculum and some of whom said they were in other curricula. We found that students in the college preparatory curriculum averaged 1 point higher when tested in the twelfth grade than students who had been in other curriculums.[155] We also estimated the effects of curriculum placement on vocabulary and social studies information for students with both high and low initial scores. There was no difference between the two groups.[156]

These analyses have convinced us that desegregating schools internally would not have much effect on students' test scores. We continue to favor internal desegregation, for reasons given in Chapter 2, but we do not think it can be justified in terms of its effect on cognitive inequality.

## Conclusions about Cognitive Inequality

The available data suggest that:

1. If we could equalize everyone's genes, inequality in test scores would probably fall by 33 to 50 percent.
2. If we could equalize everyone's total environment, test score inequality would fall by 25 to 40 percent.
3. If we merely equalize everyone's economic status, test score inequality would fall by 6 percent or less.
4. Equalizing the amount of schooling people get might reduce cognitive inequality among adults by 5 to 15 percent, although this estimate is very rough.
5. Equalizing the quality of elementary schools would reduce cognitive inequality by 3 percent or less.
6. Equalizing the quality of high schools would reduce cognitive inequality by 1 percent or less.
7. Eliminating racial and socio-economic segregation in the schools might reduce the test score gap between black and white children and between rich and poor children by 10 to 20 percent.
8. Additional school expenditures are unlikely to increase achievement, and redistributing resources will not reduce test score inequality.[157]

Most differences in adult test scores are due to factors that schools do not control. It does not follow, however, that schools could not equalize people's test scores if they tried. They probably could. If, for example, we wanted everyone's reading scores to approximate the present national average, we could provide only 1 or 2 years of schooling to very bright youngsters, 6 years to youngsters who were a bit above average, 12 years to those who were a bit below average, and 18 or more years to the very slow learners. This would, we suspect, greatly reduce inequality of reading scores. We do not, however, favor such a solution. We think of "equal opportunity" as implying that everyone should get as much schooling as he wants. Equal opportunity, in this sense, guarantees unequal results.

If unequal performance on standardized tests were a principal cause of inequality in other realms, this traditional doctrine might need reexamination. The evidence discussed in Chapters 6 and 7 does not, however, suggest that variations in cognitive skill account for much of the inequality among American adults. There is nearly as much economic inequality among individuals with identical test scores as in the general population. Thus we can hardly suppose that making everyone's scores equal would appreciably reduce economic inequality in the general population.

While we reject the idea that schools should try to eliminate all variation in cognitive skill, it does not follow that schools need accept the present degree of cognitive inequality as inevitable. We have already argued that if people's cognitive skills are far below national norms they are likely to be at a significant disadvantage, not only economically but socially and psychologically. At least in a highly competitive society like ours, an individual who cannot read even simple instructions, or who cannot do enough arithmetic to tell whether he has been short-changed, is likely to be exploited in a variety of ways. Relatively few students leave school in this condition, but reducing their number still ought to be a high priority.

Unfortunately, few discussions of schooling and inequality focus on these extreme cases. When people talk about the schools' failure to prepare disadvantaged students for modern economic life, they are not usually talking about the handful of illiterates and innumerates, but about the much larger number of students who leave high school reading at the eighth or ninth grade level. As we shall see, these students are by no means unemployable. Nor are they automatically excluded from the main stream of American life. They are not likely to become physicians or physicists, but this would be true even if they were reading at the twelfth grade level. At least in economic terms, the cost of reading at eighth grade rather than twelfth grade level is quite small.

# NOTES

1. This issue is discussed in Chapters 6 and 7.
2. At the high school level, ETS reports a mean *KR*-20 reliability for the tests of about 0.84. Mayeske et al., in "Item Response Analyses," report a mean correlation between pairs of tests of 0.66. The estimated "true" correlations between tests average 0.79. The figures for sixth grade

are similar. For the first and third grades, both figures are lower. For details, see Jencks, "The Quality of the Data Collected."

3. After correcting for unreliability, the first principal component explained 86 percent of the variance in individual students' ninth grade scores and 81 percent of the variance in their twelfth grade scores (see Jencks, "The Quality of the Data Collected").

4. For some tests that approximate this criterion, see the Project Talent battery. Two examples are "Knowledge of Hunting" and "Clerical Checking." Intercorrelations among these tests are reported in Shaycoft, *The High School Years.*

5. Note, for example, that verbal aptitude scores typically predict success in math and science courses almost as well as quantitative aptitude scores, and vice versa. There is a long-standing controversy and a vast literature on the question of whether people really have one general ability and many special abilities, or simply many special abilities which tend to be correlated. See, for example, Burt, "Inheritance of General Intelligence," and Guilford, "The Structure of Intelligence," and the sources cited there.

6. Guilford, in "The Structure of Intelligence," provides a taxonomy of the diverse kinds of intelligent behavior that could usefully be tested, but seldom are.

7. The correlation between high school grades and scholastic achievement is usually between 0.4 and 0.6. See, for example, Sewell et al., "The Educational and Early Occupational Status," and Heyns, "Curriculum Assignment and Tracking Policies." There is considerable variation from one school to another.

8. See Bayley, "Consistency and Variability"; Bayley, "Research in Child Development"; and Anderson, "The Limitations of Infant and Preschool Tests." But compare Skodak and Skeels, "A Final Follow-Up Study of 100 Adopted Children."

9. See Bayley, "Consistency and Variability," and Bayley, "Research in Child Development."

10. See Honzik, "Developmental Studies," and Skodak and Skeels, "A Final Follow-Up Study of 100 Adopted Children."

11. See Honzik, "Developmental Studies," and Skodak and Skeels, "A Final Follow-Up Study of 100 Adopted Children."

12. See Bayley, "Consistency and Variability," and Honzik et al., "The Stability of Mental Test Performance." Bradway et al., in "Preschool IQ's after 25 Years," report 0.6, which is high. These correlations ought perhaps to be inflated by about 10 percent to take account of random measurement error. The correlation of preschool scores with scores at the age of nine to thirteen is higher than with scores in adulthood. Skodak and Skeels, in "A Final Follow-Up Study of 100 Adopted Children," report $r = 0.59$ using scores at 13 as a criterion. Payne, in "The Selection and Treatment of Data," reports $r = 0.68$ using scores at 11 as a criterion. Sontag et al., in "Mental Growth and Personality," report $r = 0.55$ using scores at age ten as a criterion. For a general review of this literature see Chapters 3 and 4 in Bloom, *Stability and Change.*

13. A correlation of 0.50 implies that a one standard deviation increase

in one variable is associated with a 0.50 standard deviation *average* increase in the other variable. Thus children with IQ scores 20 points (1.33 standard deviations) above the mean at age 4 will average $1.33 \times 0.5 = 0.67$ standard deviations (i.e. 10 IQ points) above the mean as adults.

14. See Bayley, "Consistency and Variability"; Honzik et al., "The Stability of Mental Test Performance"; the mimeographed Supplementary Tables for Douglas et al., *All Our Future;* and Terman and Oden, *The Gifted Group at Mid-Life.*

15. See Chapter 4 in Bloom, *Stability and Change.*

16. See Shaycoft, *The High School Years,* for full matrices using forty-nine tests from Project Talent. For conventional tests, the correlations are mostly between 0.65 and 0.75. In many cases, the correlations over 4 years approach the internal reliabilities. For tests of specialized knowledge, the correlations fall as low as 0.15. If several ninth grade scores are used to predict the same twelfth grade scores, the correlation approaches 0.85. For further analysis, see Jencks, "The Effects of High Schools on Their Students." For similar results, see Traxler, "Reading Growth." For parallel Scandinavian results, see Harnqvist, "Relative Changes."

17. Bradway and Thompson, in "Intelligence at Adulthood," reported on 111 individuals who were tested with the Stanford Binet in preschool, early adolescence, and adulthood, and also with the Wechsler Adult Intelligence Scale in adulthood. The time between the adolescent and adult tests was 15 years. The correlations were 0.80 to 0.85, depending on the test. Bayley, in "Consistency and Variability," reported on 40 unusually gifted individuals tested on the Wechsler Adult Intelligence Scale at 16 and 36. She reports correlations of 0.69 for women and 0.97 for men. Jones, in "Intelligence and Problem Solving," reported on 83 individuals tested at 17 and 33. He reported correlations of 0.84 for men and 0.90 for women. Owens, in "Age and Mental Abilities," reported a correlation of 0.77 between 127 Iowa State undergraduates' scores on Army Alpha in 1920 and their scores in 1950. This value would be in excess of 0.80 were it not for the relative uniformity of the initial scores.

One complication in interpreting the evidence on stability is that the individuals who are unavailable for retesting are likely to be the individuals whose environments changed the most and whose test scores ought therefore to be least stable.

18. If the observed correlation is 0.80, the standard error of the second score when estimated from the first is $(15)(\sqrt{1 - 0.80^2}) = 9$ points. If the observed correlation is 0.90, the standard error is 7 points. For estimates of the "true" correlations, see Appendix B.

19. If a 6 year old has an IQ of 85, his mental age will be $(0.85)(6) = 5.1$ years. If a 12 year old has an IQ of 85, his mental age will be $(0.85)(12) = 10.2$ years. For an 18 year old the figure will be $(0.85)(18) = 15.3$ years.

20. See, for example, Bloom, *Stability and Change in Human Characteristics.*

21. See Chapter 2 in Bloom, *Stability and Change in Human Characteristics.*

22. Super and Crites, in *Appraising Vocational Fitness,* report *AGCT*

correlated 0.90 with Army Alpha. This equals the reported test-retest reliability for *AGCT*. They report that *AGCT* correlated 0.83 with Otis IQ, 0.79 with the American Council on Education Psychological Examination, and 0.53 with reading comprehension. Wechsler, in *The Measurement of Adult Intelligence,* reports correlations of 0.83 to 0.86 between *AGCT* and Wechsler Bellevue IQ. For Army Alpha, Super and Crites report correlations of 0.70 with Otis IQ and 0.74 with Wechsler-Bellevue scores. Yerkes, in "Psychological Examining in the U.S. Army," reports correlations in excess of 0.80 between Army Alpha and the Stanford-Binet.

23. Tuddenham (see "Soldier Intelligence") gave Army Alpha to a representative sample of draftees in 1943. He obtained a mean score of 101.2 and a standard deviation of 46.0. His World War I comparison group was a large sample of white recruits, who had already been accepted in the army when tested and who were literate in English. Their mean score was about 69, with a standard deviation of about 40. The difference, then, was 0.7 to 0.8 standard deviations, depending on the reference point.

Before accepting these results, however, we must ask whether the samples were representative of the populations from which they were drawn. Tuddenham's World War II sample had a mean educational attainment of 10.0 years, with a standard deviation of 3.0 years. The mean for all men aged 25 to 34 in 1940 was 9.5 years with a standard deviation of 3.6 years, while the mean for all men aged 25 to 34 in 1950 was 10.5 years with a standard deviation of 3.5 years. Allowing for the effects of the GI bill on the second group, it seems clear that the mean educational attainment of the population from which World War II draftees came was pretty close to 10.0 years. In this respect, Tuddenham's World War II sample is representative. His sample did, however, have a somewhat smaller standard deviation for schooling than the general population. This is not surprising. Men who were very poorly educated were often not forwarded for examination, since it was expected that they would be rejected. Men who were well educated often became officers and were excluded from the sample.

Tuddenham's World War I comparison group had a mean educational attainment of 8.0 years, with a standard deviation of 2.6 years. The male population of comparable age had a mean of 7.8 years with a standard deviation of 3.8 years. Again, this is as expected. The World War I comparison group excluded both nonwhites and those who were not literate in English. In addition, some inept recruits must have been eliminated before the testing took place, and officers were not included.

Since the correlation between educational attainment and years of schooling was 0.74, we suspect that test score comparisons between army recruits and the entire male population would have yielded much the same results as our educational comparisons. We therefore accept the proposition that the mean score of the male population increased between 1917 and 1943. Since both samples are restricted in range, conclusions about changes in true standard deviations are risky. If the restriction in test score range for the two samples were comparable to the restriction in educational range, we would infer that the population standard deviation was $(40)(3.8)/(2.6) = 59$ Alpha points in 1917 and $(46)(3.6)/(3.0) = 55$ Alpha points in

1943. We put relatively little weight on the implied decline in the standard deviation. If the population standard deviation was roughly 56, however, the increase in the mean score from World War I to World War II was only 0.57 standard deviations, rather than 0.7 or 0.8 standard deviations.

24. Wheeler, in "A Comparative Study," reports an increase of 0.7 standard deviation in IQ for children of school age in Eastern Tennessee between 1930 and 1940, a period of rapid social change in that area.

25. Schrader, in "Test Data as Social Indicators," reports an 0.2 standard deviation increase in national norms between the mid-1950s and mid-1960s using a wide variety of school achievement tests, mostly for the middle years of school. See, also, Shane, "We Can be Proud of the Facts," and the National Education Association, "The Three R's Hold Their Own," for fragmentary data suggesting a similar trend in previous decades. Flanagan and Jung, in "Progress in Education," found no gain in the reading comprehension of eleventh graders between 1960 and 1970, using large representative national samples. But since low scoring students dropped out before eleventh grade more often in 1960 than in 1970, the results imply a small improvement in the performance of the total population. Peaker, in "Standards of Reading of 11-Year Olds," reports an increase of about two-thirds of a standard deviation in the reading scores of English 11 and 15 year olds between 1948 and 1964. But a more recent study (Start and Wells, "The Trend in Reading Standards") showed that the trend did not continue thereafter.

26. See Higgins et al., "Intelligence and Family Size," and Bajema, "Estimation of the Direction and Intensity of Natural Selection," as reworked by Falconer, in "Genetic Consequences."

27. On the effect of urbanization on test scores, see, for example, Klineberg, *Negro Intelligence and Selective Migration,* and McNemar, *The Revision of the Stanford-Binet Scale.*

28. See note 23.

29. Note, for example, that in World War I the army had to use a separate test, the Beta, to test the many recruits who were not literate in English. This was not thought necessary in World War II. See Yerkes, "Psychological Examining in the U.S. Army," for details.

30. See Jensen, "How Much Can We Boost IQ and Scholastic Achievement?" and Herrnstein, "IQ."

31. Here and throughout the text we assume a simple additive relationship between the effects of genes and the effects of environment. For arguments against this model see Smith, "Models of the Determination of Intelligence," and Light and Smith, "Social Allocation Models of Intelligence." While there are many logical reasons for rejecting additive models, there is not much empirical evidence that any other model works better. See Burt and Howard, "The Multifactorial Theory," and Jinks and Fulker, "Comparison of the Biometrical Genetical, MAVA, and Classical Approaches."

32. See Appendix A, p. 281.

33. See Appendix A, p. 299.

34. See Appendix A, pp. 288–289 and Table A–10.

35. See Appendix A, pp. 304–309 and Table A–10.

36. See Appendix A, pp. 309–314.

37. The total variance in test scores is $h^2 + 2hes + e^2$, where $h^2$ is the effect of genetic inequality, $e^2$ is the effect of environmental inequality, and $s$ is the correlation between genotype and environment. Appendix A shows that $2hes \cong 0.20$. Assume that $h^2 = 0.45 \pm 0.10$ and $e^2 = 0.35 \pm 0.10$. Reducing $e$ to zero makes $h^2 + 2hes + e^2 = 0.45 \pm 0.10$. The standard deviation of test scores would then be $\sqrt{0.45} \pm 0.10 = 59$ to 74 percent of the original standard deviation. The mean difference between random individuals would become $(17)(0.59) = 8.0$ to $(17)(0.74) = 12.6$ points. Note that this method again assumes an additive relationship between the effects of heredity and the effects of environment.

38. Calculated on the same assumptions as note 37. Doubling $e$ would raise the total variance to $h^2 + 4hes + 4e^2$. The final standard deviation will be between $\sqrt{0.55 + 0.40 + 1.00} = 140$ percent and $\sqrt{0.35 + 0.40 + 1.80} = 160$ percent of the original  standard deviation.

39. See Higgins et al., "Intelligence and Family Size," and Bajema, "Natural Selection in Relation to Human Intelligence." Both these studies deal with white, midwestern populations. Bajema's subjects had most of their children between World War I and World War II. The child-bearing years of Higgins et al.'s parents are not reported but appear to have covered a longer period. Both studies suggest that the genotypic variance probably increased slightly, but that the mean did not change much.

40. See Appendix A, pp. 271–273.

41. This estimate is based on the assumption that genes account directly or indirectly for $45 \pm 10$ percent of the variance in test scores and that covariance accounts for another 20 percent. This means that if genetic inequalities were eliminated, the variance of test scores would be reduced by $65 \pm 10$ percent. The standard deviation would then be 50 to 67 percent of its present level.

42. See Appendix A. About 20 percent of the total variance is apparently due to covariance between genotype and family background. Eliminating 20 percent of the variance reduces the standard deviation to $\sqrt{1 - 0.20} = 89$ percent of its prior level.

43. See Appendix A, pp. 315–316.

44. These estimates are derived from the contradictory data in Appendix A. The estimate in Appendix B is lower, first because it applies only to white nonfarm males, and second because it is constrained by the requirement that it predict the observed IQ correlation between brothers exactly, and ignores data on IQ correlations between unrelated children in the same home.

45. This estimate is derived from Appendix A on the assumption that the standardized regression coefficient of IQ score on family background ($i$ in Figure A–2) is 0.45, that families in the top fifth are 2.8 standard deviations above families in the bottom fifth, and that the difference in terms of test scores is, therefore, $(2.8)(0.45)(15) = 19$ IQ points. In Appendix B we estimate $i$ at 0.348, which implies that if we ignore covariance, family background accounts for $0.348^2 = 12$ percent of the IQ variance. The differ-

ence between the top and bottom fifths would then average 15 rather than 19 IQ points. The 15 point estimate is consistent with Jensen's heritability estimates in "How Much Can We Boost IQ?"

46. In EEOS, the correlation between sixth graders' test scores and their reports of their father's occupation averages around 0.30 for the verbal test and somewhat less for reading, math, and nonverbal ability. Correcting for measurement error, we estimate the "true" correlations at about 0.35 for the verbal test and about 0.30 or less for the other tests. The correlations are similar in the ninth and twelfth grades. The correlations for the ninth and twelfth grade general information test resemble those for the verbal test, while the correlations for reading and math are again lower. EEOS did not obtain estimates for parental income.

Flanagan and Cooley, in Appendix E of *Project Talent: One Year Follow-Up Studies,* report correlations between twelfth graders' scores on a variety of Project Talent tests and their reports of their father's occupation, their father's education, their mother's education, and their family income. As in EEOS, the general information test is more highly correlated with background than are the "skills" tests. As in EEOS, father's education, mother's education, and father's occupation correlate about equally well with any given test.

Flanagan and Cooley report correlations between family income and test scores about two-thirds as large as the correlations between the other background variables and test scores. This may reflect poor measurement of family income. But if this is the case, reporting errors in family income must be quite highly correlated with reporting errors in parental occupation and education, since the correlations between children's reports of their parents' education, occupational status, and income are very similar to the correlations in data obtained directly from parents (see Duncan et al., *Socioeconomic Background).* We infer that the true correlation between test scores and family income is less than the correlation between test scores and either parental education or father's occupation.

In multiple regression equations using Talent data, the coefficient of reported family income is generally trivial once father's occupation and education are controlled. The correlation of test scores with an index of economic status that gives equal weight to occupation and income is also lower than the correlation of these same test scores with occupation alone.

All these estimates are based on data obtained from children. Such data may contain a lot of random error. However, Sewell et al., in "The Educational and Early Occupational Status" obtained data on parental occupation and income from state tax returns for a representative sample of Wisconsin high school seniors. This data is presumably quite accurate. Using this information plus information on parental education, they extracted a first principal component which they then treated as an SES index. The correlation of this SES index with eleventh grade scores on the Henmon-Nelson group "intelligence" test was 0.288. We therefore reject the theory that measurement error produces an appreciable downward bias in the estimated correlation between test scores and status. But see also McNemar, *The Revision of the Stanford-Binet Scale,* for data implying a correlation of 0.36 between Stanford-Binet scores and father's occupation. See also Shaycoft "The High School Years" for evidence that a family background index which includes cultural and psychological measures (P-801) will correlate better than 0.35 with many tests.

47. Derived on the assumption that the top and bottom fifths differ by 2.8 standard deviations and that the true correlation between a father's occupational status and a child's test score is between 0.30 and 0.36.

48. See, for example, the appendix to Coleman et al., *Equality of Educational Opportunity,* and Appendix E in Flanagan and Cooley, *Project Talent.*

49. The best set of comparable data for different countries is found in the report on the international math study in Husen, *International Study.*

50. See Chase and Pugh, "Social Class and Performance," and the studies cited there. See also, Lesser et al., "Mental Abilities." In addition, see the sources cited in Stanley, "Predicting College Success."

51. See, for example, Stodolsky and Lesser, "Learning Patterns."

52. This argument is presented in, for example, Burt, "Ability and Income;" Young and Gibson, "Explanation of Social Mobility;" Eckland, "Genetics and Sociology;" Jensen, "How Much Can We Boost IQ and Scholastic Achievement?"; and Herrnstein, "IQ."

53. The relevant studies of natural parents and their adopted children are Skodak and Skeels, "A Final Follow-Up Study of 100 Adopted Children;" Burks, "The Relative Influence of Nature;" and Burt, "The Genetic Determination of Differences in Intelligence." Some of the data is shown in Appendix A, Table A–3. The results are not consistent.

Skodak and Skeels studied 100 children placed before 6 months of age. They found correlations of 0.31 to 0.38 between a natural mother's education and her child's Stanford-Binet scores 5 to 10 years after adoption. The correlation was higher after the children reached school age than before. Such correlations are as high as the usual correlations for mothers who raise their own children.

Burt reported on 53 pairs of English identical twins. One member of each pair was reared by its natural parents, while the other was not. Burt was kind enough to make this data available to CEPR before his death, and it has been further analyzed by Randall Weiss and Jencks. The correlation between the Binet score of the twin reared in his own home and the occupation of his natural father was 0.37. The correlation between the adopted twin's score and the occupational status of the natural father was 0.17. The correlation for adopted children was thus about half the correlation for children who were reared by their natural parents.

Burks reported a correlation of 0.07 between the occupational status (Barr scale) of natural fathers and the Binet scores of 91 children. This is 20 to 25 percent of the usual correlation when children are raised by their natural parents.

54. See Burks, "The Relative Influence of Nature;" Burt, "The Genetic Determination of Differences in Intelligence;" Leahy, "Nature-Nurture and Intelligence;" and Skodak and Skeels, "A Final Follow-Up Study of 100 Adopted Children." Again, the results are inconsistent.

Burks reported correlations averaging 0.09 between the adopting parents' education and the test scores of 194 children adopted before twelve months, compared to 0.27 for 102 control families. The disparity for income was much less.

Burt's data yields a correlation of 0.003 between an adopting father's occupation and a child's test score vs. 0.37 for natural fathers and the scores of their children when reared at home.

Leahy studied 194 children placed before the age of six months and 194 control children. She reported a correlation of 0.54 between the control parents' mean educational attainment and their children's Stanford-Binet scores, compared with a correlation of 0.24 between the adopting parents' mean attainment and their adopted children's scores.

Skodak and Skeels reported correlations ranging from 0.05 to 0.10 between the adopting mother's educational attainment and the Binet scores of 100 children adopted before six months.

55. See Skodak and Skeels, "A Final Follow-Up Study of 100 Adopted Children," and Burt, "The Genetic Determination of Differences in Intelligence."

56. See Burks, "The Relative Influence of Nature."

57. See Appendix B, Figure B–7. The "genetic" effect is $(0.144$ to $0.161)(0.707) \cong 0.106$. The "environmental" effect is $(0.700$ to $0.725)$ $(0.348) \cong 0.248$. The total effect is, thus, $0.106 + 0.248 = 0.354$.

58. Compare the estimated correlations between genotype and various status measures in Table B–3 of Appendix B.

59. Using the figures in note 57, the contribution of father's occupation to the total IQ variance consists of its "unique" environmental contribution of $0.248^2 = 6.2$ percent, and its contribution (via its correlation with genotype) to the covariance, i.e. $(2)(0.15)(0.707)(0.250) = 5.3$ percent. Its total contribution is thus about 11.5 percent, or 2.0 points out of 17. The figures are quite similar for an economic index that includes income as well as occupational status and for a full national sample. Cutting the variance by 11.5 percent would cut inequality (i.e. the standard deviation) by 6 percent. Controlling other background factors besides genes would almost certainly lower our estimate of the unique contribution of economic inequality to cognitive inequality.

60. This estimate is derived on the following assumptions: (1) the top fifth averages 1.4 standard deviations above the mean; (2) the correlation between economic background and test scores is 0.32; (3) the children of the top fifth therefore average $(1.4)(0.32) = 0.45$ standard deviations above the mean on tests; (4) the cutting point for the top fifth is 0.85 standard deviations above the mean; and (5) the standard deviation of the scores of the top fifth is $\sqrt{1 - 0.32^2} = 95$ percent of the overall standard deviation. In order to get into the top fifth, then, an upper-middle class child must be $(0.85 - 0.45)/0.95 = 0.42$ standard deviations above the mean for his class. Only 33.7 percent of a normally distributed population is more than 0.42 standard deviations above the mean.

61. Shuey, in *The Testing of Negro Intelligence*, provides a useful

bibliography of this research, although her summaries should be used with considerable caution and her conclusions are very one-sided.

62. See Coleman et al., *Equality of Educational Opportunity*, for summary data on EEOS tests. See Lesser et al., "Mental Abilities," for an elegant study of children about to enter school. This research shows distinctive patterns of mental ability for Negro, Puerto Rican, Chinese, and Jewish children. These patterns are the same for middle-class and lower-class children in each group. The Negro children are more disadvantaged on nonverbal than on verbal tests. See Stanley, "Predicting College Success" for a summary of the literature on the relationship between blacks' scores and their grades.

63. See Newman et al., *Twins: A Study of Heredity and Environment.*
64. See note 23.
65. See Wheeler, "A Comparative Study."
66. See Skodak and Skeels, "A Final Follow-Up Study of 100 Adopted Children," as well as the discussion on pp. 281–283.

67. Using EEOS data, the initial gap between blacks and whites is reduced by about a third when father's occupation and home items are controlled. Similarly, using 1962 CPS data, Duncan, in "Inheritance of Poverty," found that black male respondents aged 25 to 64 were 0.70 standard deviations below the white mean on education, 0.97 standard deviations below the white mean on occupational status, and 0.67 standard deviations below the white mean on income. (All three comparisons use white standard deviations rather than standard deviations for the total population.) If we take the intercorrelations of the status variables from Duncan and the correlations between test scores and status from Appendix E in Flanagan and Cooley, *Project Talent: One Year Follow-Up Studies,* we can estimate the coefficient of race in an equation predicting test scores from race, education, occupation, and income. Race has a coefficient of about 12 points, vs. 15 points with no controls. Adjusting for measurement error in the Flanagan and Cooley data lowers the gap to 10 or 11 points. Including only the environmental effects of status again raises the gap to around 12 points. We also obtained similar results using the Project Talent 5-year follow-up samples of ninth and eleventh graders, in which students are identified by race.

68. Mercer and Brown, in "Racial Differences in IQ," report a large study in Riverside, California, in which the entire test score gap between blacks and whites was explained by the following parental traits: Participation in Formal Organizations, Neighborhood Ethnic Mix, Cultural Contact with Whites, Socio-Economic Status, Urbanism, Home Ownership, Individualistic Achievement Values, and Family Structure.

69. See Chomsky, "The Fallacy of Richard Herrnstein's IQ."

70. Husen, in *Psychological Twin Research,* reports a correlation of 0.20 between IQ scores and height for Swedish males. He tries to show that this association is due to environmental factors. So far as we know, no other investigator has thought the point worth pursuing, despite evidence showing that initial salaries of B.A.s are as closely related to their height as to their grades (see Deck, "Buying Brains by the Inch").

71. For a history of this phenomenon, see Lazerson, "Social Reform," and more generally, Lazerson, *Origins of the Urban School.*

72. EEOS asked children whether they had attended both kindergarten and nursery school. While their answers were not always accurate, especially with respect to nursery school, the data are far from worthless. For details, see Coleman et al., *Equality of Educational Opportunity,* and Jencks, "The Quality of the Data Collected."

73. This analysis is reported in detail in Jencks, "The Coleman Report." Within any given school there were dramatic achievement differences between those children who had attended kindergarten and those who had not. Black sixth graders who said they had attended kindergarten scored ahead of black sixth graders who said they had not been in kindergarten. This was true on all the EEOS sixth grade tests, even after socio-economic differences between kindergarteners and nonkindergarteners had been taken into account. There was a similar gap between white kindergarten alumni and nonalumni on the verbal test, though the difference on the reading and math tests was much smaller. A kindergarten enthusiast might therefore argue that attending kindergarten was boosting test scores. If this were true, however, schools with high proportions of kindergarten alumni should have had higher average scores than schools with low proportions of kindergarten alumni. Since they did not, we infer that either (a) parents who fail to enroll their children in kindergarten differ in important but otherwise unmeasured ways from those who enroll their children, or (b) sixth graders with low verbal ability did not recognize the word "kindergarten" and were therefore more likely to say they had not attended.

74. In 1940, the National Society for the Study of Education devoted a whole section of its *Yearbook* to studies of preschool. Anyone who thinks that progress is possible in education should read this entire yearbook. Most of the issues of the 1960s were debated in the 1930s, and the same kind of evidence was presented in the 1940 *Yearbook* as we present in this book.

75. For summaries of the literature on preschool effects on test scores, see Bissell, "Cognitive Effects" and Stearns, "Effects of Preschool Programs".

76. See Weikart et al., "Longitudinal Results," and Gray and Klaus, "An Experimental Preschool Program."

77. See Westinghouse Learning Corporation/Ohio University, *The Impact of Head Start.*

78. See Smith and Bissell, "Report Analysis."

79. Boyd, "Project Head Start."

80. For an interesting analysis of these issues by a former advocate of structured preschooling, see Bereiter, "An Academic Preschool for Disadvantaged Children."

81. See DeGroot, "War and the Intelligence of Youth."

82. See Green et al., "Educational Status."

83. See Hayes and Grether, "The School Year and Vacations." It should be noted that this was a cross-sectional rather than a longitudinal study, based on school means rather than individual data.

84. Heyns is currently replicating this study in Atlanta using individual longitudinal data.

85. Reported correlations between adult test scores and adult attainment are reviewed in Appendix B, pp. 325–327. The correlations appear to have fallen slightly since World War II, but this may be explained by the declining standard deviation of schooling. Karpinos, in "Mental Test Qualifications," presents data from the 1960s indicating that an extra year of schooling was associated with 3.4 extra points on the $AFQT$ using an IQ metric. If we assume that the range of test scores in Tuddenham's World War II sample (see note 23) was restricted to exactly the same extent as the range of educational attainment in the sample, we can estimate the standard deviation of scores in the sample as $(15)(3.0)/(3.5) = 12.9$ points, again using an IQ metric. If this is correct, each extra year of schooling was associated with $(12.9)(0.74)/(3.0) = 3.2$ IQ points advantage during World War II. This calculation assumes that the population standard deviation was the same in World War II as in the 1960s. If it declined, the absolute increment associated with an extra year of school may have been constant.

Assuming our estimated standard deviation for the World War II sample is correct, the standard deviation for Tuddenham's the World War I sample was $(12.9)(40)/(46) = 11.2$ points. Since the reported correlation between education and Army Alpha in the World War I sample was 0.68 and the standard deviation of schooling in the sample was 2.6 years, an extra year of schooling implied an advantage of $(11.2)(0.68)/(2.6) = 2.9$ points.

86. See Appendix B, pp. 323–325.

87. The basic sample was the one described by Thorndike in "Prediction of Vocational Success." The follow-up is reported by Lorge, in "Schooling Makes a Difference." The retesting covered only males, and only 1 in 6 was located. While these men's initial test scores were representative of the larger sample, the correlation between their initial scores and their eventual years of schooling was only 0.36, compared to 0.42 in the larger sample of males, 0.50 for females, and 0.50 to 0.60 in other samples.

88. See Harnqvist, "Relative Changes," and Husen, "The Influence of Schooling on IQ."

89. See Bradway and Thompson, "Intelligence at Adulthood." The sample included 111 reasonably representative individuals originally tested as part of the 1937 Binet standardization.

90. Appendix B implies a path coefficient from years of schooling to $AFQT$ scores of 0.217 after correcting for measurement error. Since the standard deviation of years of schooling in the sample covered by Appendix B is 3.3 years, and since the standard deviation of IQ scores is defined as 15 points, the estimated effect of an extra year of schooling is $(15)(0.217)/(3.3) = 1.0$ points.

91. Differences in socio-economic status do not appear to have much independent effect on adolescent achievement once their relationship to initial scores is taken into account (see Harnqvist, "Relative Changes in Intelligence," and Jencks, "The Effects of High Schools on Their Stu-

dents"). Variations in students' attitudes and motivation may be more important, however. In addition, there may be variations in initial ability that are not measured by the early test, but which affect both the amount of schooling men receive and their subsequent performance on tests, such as the *AGCT* and *AFQT* tests.

Another source of bias in these estimates is the fact that they are based on reports of the "highest grade completed" by individuals, not on "years in attendance."

92. Using Figure B–7 of Appendix B, the implied contribution of education to the total variance is $(0.217)^2 + (2)(0.217)(0.798)r_{IQ, ED}$, where $r_{IQ, ED} = 0.580$. This comes to 24.8 percent of the total variance. Clearly, the covariance (0.201) is far more important than the unique variance (0.047) in creating cognitive inequality, and its elimination would be far more consequential. The standard error of these estimates is *very* high, which is why we have not included them in the text.

93. In order to estimate schools' effects on students' test scores, we first derived the average within-school regression equation for each of our six twelfth grade achievement tests, controlling scores on all six ninth grade tests, parents' socio-economic level, and how much education students expected to get when they were in ninth grade (hereafter designated "aspirations"). We then compared each student's predicted twelfth grade score to his actual twelfth grade score, obtaining a residual score for each student. Next, we averaged the residual scores of students in the same school. We did this separately for each test. This mean residual is a maximum estimate of each school's average effect on its students' performance on each test. Correlating the mean residuals for different tests gave us an estimate of the extent to which schools that boosted performance on one test boosted performance on other tests. These correlations range from 0.561 to −0.302. The first principal component explained 25 percent of the variance in the six residuals, which is only a little more than we expect by chance.

94. For the vocabulary test, 10.7 percent of the variance is between schools. Using the average within-school regression equations to predict individual scores, we find that only 14 percent of the between-school variance (1.5 percent of the total) is unexplained. There is virtually no correlation between schools' initial scores and their average gain score, so the elimination of the unexplained between-school variance reduces the overall variance by 1.5 percent. This cuts the standard deviation by less than 1 percent. Details of this analysis are reported by Jencks, in "The Effects of High Schools on Their Students."

95. Unfortunately, this data was all collected at the same time, so we cannot compare students' test scores when they entered ninth grade to their scores 4 years later. Instead, we have to compare twelfth graders' test scores in 1965 to the test scores of ninth graders in the same school in 1965. Such a comparison shows that incoming students are very much like graduating students. The correlation between schools' mean ninth and twelfth grade test scores is as high as the correlation between schools' mean ninth and twelfth grade socio-economic levels. For the nation as a whole, both corre-

lations exceed 0.90. For urban high schools, the test score correlation is 0.96. When we allow for the fact that ninth and twelfth grade means are not based on the same students, the implied correlation for a single cohort is 0.98 in urban schools. For details see Jencks, "The Effects of High Schools on Their Students." For a similar analysis, see Hauser, "Schools and the Stratification Process."

96. The correlation between an elementary school's average scores in first and sixth grades is about 0.81 in the urban North. The correlation between high schools' average scores in the ninth and twelfth grades is 0.88 in the urban North. For details, including size corrections, see Jencks, "The Quality of the Data Collected." Mayeske et al., in *A Study of Our Nation's Schools,* report a correlation between first and sixth grade means of only 0.68 for the nation as a whole. This contrasts with 0.93 between ninth and twelfth grade means for the nation as a whole.

97. Using the matrices in the Appendix of Coleman et al.'s *Equality of Educational Opportunity,* Smith, in "The Basic Findings Reconsidered" found that for whites in the North 12.77 percent of the variance in verbal scores was between schools. Of this, 54.2 percent was explained by an individual-level regression equation in which Coleman et al.'s six "objective" background measures are the independent variables. This leaves 45.8 percent of the between-school variance or 5.85 percent of the total variance unexplained. This variance is potentially attributable to "school effects." For blacks, similar calculations imply that 7.46 percent of the total variance is potentially due to "school effects." Using a more direct method of calculating the between-school variance, Coleman et al. reported 10.32 percent of the variance between schools for whites and 13.89 percent for blacks. This implies that 4.95 percent of the white variance and 8.73 percent of the black variance is between schools and unexplained. The standard deviation of school effects is thus between $\sqrt{0.0495} = 22$ and $\sqrt{0.0585} = 24$ percent of the individual standard deviation for whites, and between 27 and 29 percent of the individual standard deviation for blacks. Since the black standard deviation is slightly less than the white one, the absolute "effects" are quite similar for blacks and whites. The gap between the top and bottom fifths of all schools is between $(2.8)(15)(0.22) = 9.2$ points and $(2.8)(15)(0.24) = 10.1$ points for whites. It is slightly more for blacks. We will use a general estimate of 10 points.

Some may reject this approach to estimating school effects on the grounds that if schools' effects are highly correlated with an individual's socio-economic status, part of the variance we have attributed to socio-economic status may really be due to schools. But 80 percent of the variance explained by socio-economic status is *within* schools, so the regression coefficients of the status variables depend almost entirely on the within-school relationship. The between-school coefficients of the socio-economic variables cannot change much even if we introduce school quality measures into our analysis. It follows that the socio-economic measures must explain almost as much of the between-school variance as we have estimated, unless the within-school coefficients are biased.

If we had data on initial ability, our experience with the Project Talent high schools indicates that we could reduce the unexplained between-school variance to about half the level estimated when we control only socio-economic background. This implies that only 3 or 4 percent of the total elementary school variance is really between-schools and unexplained. Furthermore, since the socio-economic variables leave about 70 percent of the within-school variance unexplained and since EEOS schools average only 70 students per grade, we expect at least 70/70 = 1 percent of the variance to be unexplained and between-schools, even if there are no consistent school effects. Thus, school effects probably account for only 2 or 3 percent of the total variance. This implies that the standard deviation of school effects is unlikely to exceed $\sqrt{0.03} = 17$ percent of the individual standard deviation, or 2.6 points. The difference between the top and bottom fifths is thus likely to be $(2.8)(15)(0.17) = 7.1$ points or less.

If the unexplained between-school variance is 6 percent of the total, equalizing elementary schools reduces inequality to $\sqrt{1 - 0.06} = 97$ percent of its prior level. If the unexplained between-school variance is 2 percent of the total, equalizing elementary schools reduces inequality to $\sqrt{1 - 0.02} = 99$ percent of its present level.

98. The analysis of New York City is reported by Acland in "Effects of Schooling." Year-end school means for all New York City elementary schools on the Metropolitan Reading Test were available for grades 2 to 6 for 5 successive years. Scores in grade 2 for 1966 were used to predict scores in grade 3 of the same school in 1967, and so forth. Discrepancies between predicted and observed scores were then correlated for successive cohorts. When scores for grades 5 and 6 were predicted on the basis of scores for grades 2 and 3, the correlations between residuals for successive cohorts averaged 0.30.

This correlation is analogous to a reliability coefficient. A correlation of 0.30 suggests that 30 percent of the variance in observed "school effects" is stable and 70 percent is transitory. The 30 percent estimate should not, however, be applied to the estimate of schools' total effects in note 97.

First, the New York City results might not be typical of the rest of the country. There appears to be about twice as much between-school variance in New York City on the Metropolitan Reading test as in the urban North for the EEOS reading test. Perhaps there is more segregation by academic ability in New York City than elsewhere. Or perhaps the reported New York City means contain more error variance than the EEOS means. In any event, the standard errors of estimates based on means from prior years are higher in New York City, even though $R^2$ is also higher. This makes the apparent effects of schools look larger.

Second, the New York City calculations are based on school means, whereas the calculations in note 97 are based on individual scores. The use of school means to estimate school effects eliminates all effects that derive from the tendency of students in a given school to become more like the average student in their school, and leaves only those effects that involve an increase or decrease in the school mean relative to the mean predicted on the basis of previous means. The former effects are likely to be more stable from one year to the next than the latter. Thus the school's *total* effect in any one year is likely to correlate more than 0.30 with its effect the next year.

Finally, the New York City estimates are for less than 6 years of schooling, and involve both a pretest and a post-test. This should make them much more precise than the EEOS estimates, which involve only SES controls. Data estimating the unexplained between-school variance in individual scores for sequential years at the elementary level is badly needed.

99. Jencks, in "The Coleman Report," calculated residual verbal scores for 684 northern urban elementary schools returning adequate data to the EEOS. The correlation between verbal residuals for elementary schools feeding the same high school was 0.63, indicating that 37 percent of the variance in what might be thought of as elementary schools' effects was within high school districts. The correlation between the mean elementary school residual for a district and the high school residual was 0.05. High school residuals were derived by regressing the 148 high schools' mean total score for all five EEOS twelfth grade tests on both their mean total score for the ninth grade tests and their mean twelfth grade socio-economic status.

100. Using principals' reports to estimate the percentage of tenth graders who entered college, and regressing these estimates on mean ninth grade socio-economic status, we derived residual college entrance rates for 127 northern urban EEOS high schools. We then correlated these residuals with the mean residual verbal, reading, and math scores of the elementary schools feeding the high school. The correlations averaged 0.06.

101. We calculated the average within-school regression of individuals' twelfth grade scores on their ninth grade scores, controlling SES and aspirations. We then calculated the difference between each individual's predicted twelfth grade score and his actual twelfth grade score on each test. Averaging these residuals across schools yields an estimate of the average effect of a school on its students' scores on each test. The correlation of the mean residuals with the school's mean ninth grade score on the same test ranged from −0.22 (for reading comprehension) to +0.41 (for math). The average value was 0.01.

102. Talent measured both high school expenditure per pupil and system-wide expenditure per pupil. The correlations of these variables with the mean test score residuals were −0.03 and +0.01.

103. See the Supplemental Appendices in Coleman et al., *Equality of Educational Opportunity*. The correlations between per pupil expenditures and twelfth grade achievement for the total white population are 0.1016 for verbal, 0.0390 for reading, and 0.0466 for math. In the ninth grade they are 0.1092, 0.0732, and 0.0783. The correlations increase between ninth and twelfth grades only for blacks in the South. Jencks, in "The Effects of High Schools", also found that salary expenditures per pupil, plant age, textbook age, numbers of ancillary personnel, and availability of specialized facilities like a library and science laboratories had no consistent association with changes in test scores between ninth and twelfth grade.

104. See Burkhead, Fox, and Holland, *Input and Output in Large City High Schools,* on Atlanta high schools. See analyses of the Project Talent high school data that show an association between expenditures and output in Burrows, "Some Determinants of High School Educational Achievement," and the National Center for Educational Statistics, "Correlation and Regression Analysis." Neither of these studies controlled input. See Goodman, "The Assessment of School Quality," and Kiesling, "Measuring a Local Government Service," for analyses of New York State data that try to control initial ability and yield equivocal estimates of the relationship between district expenditures and value added. Additional expenditures are associated with gains for some students and with retardation for others. Other bodies of data which lack adequate measures of initial ability include the ETS data analyzed by Mollenkopf and Melville, in "Secondary School Characteristics," which found an association; the Connecticut data analyzed by Connecticut Citizens for the Public Schools, in "Factors Related to Academic Achievement," which found no association; and the Boston area data analyzed by Corrazzini et al., in "Study of Higher Education," which found an association. Those interested in surveying this field should also look at Benson et al., "State and Local Fiscal Relationships"; Bloom, "1955 Normative Study"; Burkhead et al., *Input and Output in Large City High Schools;* Davenport and Remmers, "Factors in State Characteristics"; Guthrie, "A Survey of School Effectiveness Studies"; Hanushek, "Teacher Characteristics"; Hauser, "Schools and the Stratification Process"; Husen, *International Study of Achievement in Mathematics;* Katzman, *The Political Economy of Urban Schools;* Kemp, "Attainments in Primary Schools"; Kiesling, "High School Size and Cost Factors"; Levin, "Cost-Effectiveness Analysis"; Mayeske et al., *A Study of Our Nation's Schools;* Peaker, "Regression Analysis"; Raymond, "Primary and Secondary Public Education"; Schutz, "Factor Analysis of Educational Development"; Thorndike, "Community Variables"; Tuckman, "High School Inputs"; Warburton, "Attainment and the School Environment"; Wiseman, "The Manchester Survey"; and the sources cited in the previous notes in this section. The unpublished literature also includes Crandall, "A Study of Academic Achievement"; Gawkoski, "Community Characteristics"; Lennon, "Prediction of Academic Achievement"; and Thomas, "Efficiency in Education."

105. The original EEOS findings are reported in Coleman et al., *Equality of Educational Opportunity.* A reanalysis by Armor, in "School and Family Effects," reached the same conclusions, as did an analysis of northern urban elementary schools by Jencks in "The Coleman Report." Boston elementary school data is reported by Katzman in "Distribution and Production" while New York elementary school data is reported in First National City Bank, "Public Education in New York City."

106. On changes in test scores between 1960 and 1970, see Flanagan and Jung, "Progress in Education" and the comments in note 25 above.

107. See e.g. Piccariello, "Evaluation of Title I" and McDavid, "Innovations in Education." These findings are not altogether surprising. These programs have often been poorly managed. Sometimes the funds have been misspent. Often they have been widely diffused. Their aims are typically

hard to pin down. Most announce improved reading or mathematics achievement as their principal goal, but many also seek to improve students' self-concept, eliminate truancy, prevent dropouts, improve school-community relations, increase parent involvement, or prevent falling arches. Very few of these programs have done anything radically new. Most assume that what disadvantaged children need is pretty much what they have been getting, only more: more teachers, more specialists, more books, more audiovisual devices, more trips to museums, and so forth. The quality of a child's experience is seldom changed, so we should not expect the results of change.

108. See sources cited in notes 104–107.

109. For other analyses of Project Talent, see Shaycoft, *The High School Years,* and her bibliography, as well as Burrows, "Some Determinants of High School Educational Achievement"; the National Center for Educational Statistics, "Correlational and Regression Analyses"; and Burkhead et al., *Input and Output in Large City High Schools.* On EEOS, see Coleman et al., *Equality of Educational Opportunity;* Mosteller and Moynihan, *On Equality of Educational Opportunity;* Mayeske et al., *A Study of Our Nation's Schools;* Bowles and Levin, "Determinants of Scholastic Achievement," and "More on Multicollinearity"; Hanushek, "The Education of Blacks and Whites"; Levin, "A New Model of School Effectiveness;" and Michelson, "Teacher Resourceness." On Plowden, see Peaker, "Regression Analysis," and "The Plowden Children Four Years Later," and Acland, "Social Determinants."

110. On the EEOS, see Bowles and Levin, "The Determinants of Scholastic Achievement," and "More on Multicollinearity"; Coleman, "Reply to Bowles and Levin," "The Evaluation of Equality of Educational Opportunity," and "Reply to Cain and Watts"; Cain and Watts, "Policy Inferences"; Hanushek and Kain, "Guide to Public Policy"; Jencks, "The Coleman Report and the Conventional Wisdom," and "The Quality of The Data Collected"; Smith, "The Basic Findings Reconsidered"; and Michelson, "Teacher Resourceness." On Plowden, see Cohen, "Children and Their Primary Schools," and Acland, "Social Determinants."

111. On school size, see Alkin and Benson, "Economy of Scale"; Cohn, "Economies of Scale"; Kreitlow, "Long Term Study" (1962, 1966); Riew, "Economies of Scale"; and Worbois, "Changes in Stanford-Binet IQ." On class size, see, for example, DeCecco, "Class Size"; Fleming, "Class Size"; Husen, *International Study;* Marklund, "Scholastic Attainments"; and Nachman and Opochinsky "Different Teaching Methods". On ability grouping, see, for example, Ekstrom, "Experimental Studies"; Goldberg et al., *The Effects of Ability Grouping;* Marklund, "Scholastic Attainments"; and Peaker, "Regression Analysis." On curriculum, see, for example, Chamberlin et al., "Follow-Up Study"; Morris, *Standards and Progress in Reading;* Pritchard et al., "The Course of Mental Development"; Reymert and Hinton, "The Effect of a Change"; Rice, "The Futility of the Spelling Grind"; and Thorndike, "Retest Changes." On teacher characteristics, see, for example, Rolfe, "The Measurement of Teaching Ability"; Rosteker, "The Measurement of Teaching Ability"; St. John, "Thirty-Six Teachers";

Rosenshine, "The Stability of Teacher Effects"; and the review in Domas and Friedman, "Teacher Competence." In general, see Gage, *Handbook of Research on Teaching.* See also the review in Averch et al., "How Effective is Schooling? " For an opposite interpretation of all this evidence, see Guthrie et al., *Schools and Inequality.*

112. See Jencks, "The Coleman Report," for data on this.

113. See Michelson, "Principal Power."

114. Some readers may wonder whether school resources might not have more effect on blacks than on students in general. We have found no evidence for this (see Mosteller and Moynihan, *On Equality of Educational Opportunity*).

115. See, for example, Katz and Greenbaum, "Effects of Anxiety."

116. The EEOS questionnaire data shows that teachers in white middle-class schools express a stronger preference for white, middle-class, academically talented students than teachers in black or lower-class white schools. It seems reasonable to assume that preference for whites is often accompanied by negative feelings about blacks.

117. Crain, in *The Politics of School Desegregation,* studied the process of desegregation in the North, but he did not try to predict when test scores would improve and when they would not.

118. See, for example, data from EEOS in Coleman et al., *Equality of Educational Opportunity*; Armor, "School and Family Effects"; and Jencks, "The Coleman Report." See also Jencks, "The Effects of Desegregated Elementary Schools."

119. See Coleman et al., *Equality of Educational Opportunity.*

120. See the U.S. Commission on Civil Rights, *Racial Isolation,* on northeastern urban high schools; Hanushek, "The Education of Blacks and Whites," on northeastern and midwestern urban elementary schools; McPartland, "The Segregated Student," on high school classrooms; Cohen et al., "Race and the Outcomes of Schooling," on both elementary and secondary schools; and Jencks, "The Coleman Report," on northern urban elementary schools. Smith, in "The Basic Findings Reconsidered" found that Coleman et al.'s conclusion was based on an analysis in which several variables were accidentally mixed-up, but the conclusion seems nonetheless to have been correct.

121. The one EEOS analysis that appears to show such benefits is the U.S. Commission on Civil Rights, *Racial Isolation.* Its findings appear to result from imprecise measurement of schools' socio-economic levels.

122. See Jencks, "The Effects of Desegregated Elementary Schools."

123. See Jencks, "The Effects of High Schools on Their Students."

124. See Crain, "School Desegregation."

125. See Wilson, "Educational Consequences."

126. See St. John and Smith, "School Racial Composition." The meaning of the findings is not entirely clear, since eighth grade IQ was controlled in all analyses. The finding seems to imply that desegregation raises achievement more than it raises IQ. Perhaps controlling IQ neutralizes gains in reading but not in math. Blacks scored higher the longer they had been desegregated. The social class of their white classmates was not crucial.

127. See St. John and Lewis, "The Influence of School Racial Context." Again, the "gains" in math but not reading may reflect the fact that the initial ability measure was more like the final reading test than like the final math test.

128. McPartland, in "The Segregated Student," and Cohen et al., in "Race and the Outcome of Schooling," found that where blacks were in the same high school classrooms as whites they scored slightly higher than when they were in the same schools but different classrooms. The direction of cause and effect is hard to determine, however.

129. For a review of the literature on such differences, see St. John, "Desegregation and Minority Group Performance."

130. See Mahan, "Project Concern."

131. See Gerard and Miller, "Factors Contributing to Adjustment and Achievement," and Purl and Dawson, "The Achievement of Pupils."

132. See Hsia, "Integration in Evanston."

133. For reviews of this literature, see St. John, "Desegregation and Minority Group Performance," and Weinberg, *Desegregation Research.* See also Armor, "The Evidence on Busing," for a very pessimistic appraisal.

134. See Coleman et al., *Equality of Educational Opportunity.*

135. See Smith, "The Basic Findings Reconsidered".

136. See Jencks, "The Coleman Report."

137. See Wilson, "Educational Consequences."

138. See Smith, "The Brookline Study". The data includes a measure of initial ability. No Brookline school is really poor by national standards.

139. See Jencks, "The Effects of High Schools on Their Students."

140. See Hauser, "Schools and the Stratification Process."

141. For evidence that achievement is not very highly valued, even in middle-class schools, see Coleman, *The Adolescent Society.*

142. See Smith, "The Basic Findings Reconsidered".

143. See Hanushek, "The Education of Blacks and Whites," Armor, "School and Family Effects," and Jencks, "The Coleman Report." These analyses did not control initial ability very adequately. Hanushek found no effect of desegregation on whites so long as they remained a majority.

144. See Jencks, "The Effects of Desegregated Elementary Schools."

145. See Wilson, "Educational Consequences."

146. See Wilson, "Educational Consequences"; Hanushek, "The Education of Blacks and Whites"; and Jencks, "The Coleman Report."

147. See Acland, "Social Determinants."

148. See Smith, "The Brookline Study."

149. See Jencks, "The Effects of High Schools on Their Students."

150. See Wilson, "Educational Consequences."

151. Estimated from the northern urban EEOS data, assuming that (1) the extreme fifths differ by 2.8 standard deviations, (2) 78 percent of the variance in verbal scores is within schools (estimated by Smith from original EEOS data), and (3) one standard deviation represents eighteen months of verbal growth in sixth grade (see Coleman et al., *Equality of Educational Opportunity*). From this we estimate the mean within-school difference between the top and bottom fifths at $(2.8)(\sqrt{0.78})(18) = 45$ months

and the mean difference between the top and bottom fifths of all schools at $(2.8)(\sqrt{1 - 0.78})(18) = 24$ months. Jencks found that in the urban North the within-school standard deviation had a coefficient of variation of 0.20, and was uncorrelated with the mean.

152. Estimated from Mayeske et al., *A Study of Our Nation's Schools*, who report that for the nation as a whole, using a composite achievement index based on all EEOS tests at a given grade level, an average of 35 percent of the total variance in test scores is between schools. Thus, the between-school standard deviation is $\sqrt{0.35} = 59$ percent of the overall standard deviation, while the within-school standard deviation is $\sqrt{0.65} = 81$ percent of the overall standard deviation. In our 91 Project Talent schools, from 9 to 15 percent of ninth grade variance was between schools, depending on the test and the sample.

153. For example, Acland, in "Social Determinants," studied English primary schools which returned satisfactory data to the 1964 Plowden survey. Students in these schools were followed up again in 1968. Students who had been in fast streams in 1964 were 3 to 6 points above students with comparable scores in 1964 who had been in slow streams. But Acland found that English primary schools assigned students to streams largely on the basis of test scores. A school's estimate of a student's true score was therefore at least as likely to be accurate as the Plowden survey estimate, which was based on a single reading test. Thus, if a student was in a fast stream but scored badly on the initial Plowden test, we have to assume that the test probably underestimated his overall ability. Conversely, if he was in a slow stream but scored high on the initial Plowden test, we have to assume that the test was usually overestimating his ability. The Plowden follow-up used different tests from the initial survey. Thus, if a student's overall ability was initially overestimated, he was likely to show an apparent loss, and vice versa. Students in high streams who score low on the initial Plowden test therefore tended to "improve," while students in low streams who scored high on the initial test tended to show "losses." This kind of initial measurement error could account for the entire difference in later test scores of students in different tracks.

154. The magnitude of the "effect" varied from 0 to 10 points depending on the subject matter and form of the test. Because the initial and final scores are on the same test, correcting the observed correlation matrix for unreliability yields a reasonable estimate of the true correlations between initial competence, final competence, and stream placement. In the Plowden survey, the tests cover different kinds of competence, and correction for unreliability is insufficient to eliminate bias. This research is reported in detail in Acland, "Streaming in British Junior Schools."

155. Details of this analysis are reported in Heyns, "Curriculum Assignment."

156. See Jencks, "The Effects of High Schools on Their Students."

157. The evidence supporting these generalizations is found in notes 37, 41, 59, 92, 94, and 97, and in the portions of the text that deal with the effects of desegregation and additional resources.

# CHAPTER FOUR

# A Note on Noncognitive Traits

Cognitive skills are not the only outcome of schooling. Educators claim schools teach virtues ranging from patriotism and punctuality to curiosity and creativity. Critics claim that schools teach an equally wide range of vices, ranging for competition and conformity to passivity and authoritarianism.[1] None of these traits is well measured by cognitive tests.

We would like to be able to give the factors influencing each of these traits as much attention as we gave cognitive skills, but we do not know enough to do this. We do not even have generally agreed upon names for these traits, much less a system for measuring them. Our discussion of them must therefore be largely conjectural.

Our tentative conclusions about noncognitive traits can best be explained by anticipating some of the findings of the next 3 chapters. Chapters 6 and 7 will show that neither parental status nor IQ scores explains most of the variation in occupational status and income. Yet we find it hard to believe that all of this variation is due to luck or chance. Experience suggests that there are personality differences between people who end up in high- and low-status occupations, and also between people who have high and low incomes. We believe, though we cannot prove, that these noncognitive traits explain part of the variation in adult success.[2]

Social scientists have written dozens of volumes trying to specify what these traits might be: "need achievement," "the Protestant ethic," "future orientation," "respect for authority," "empathy"—the list is almost endless. In each case, a prima facie case could be made for believing that schools developed the trait in question, and that good schools did this more effectively than bad schools. In order to test such theories we need to identify some readily measurable form of behavior which indicates the presence of the traits we are interested in.

One kind of behavior that seems logically to meet this requirement is staying in school. Staying in school predicts occupational status much better than test scores do, and it predicts income at least as well as test scores do. Some attribute the effect of staying in school entirely to the magical influence of the diploma or degree, but we suspect that people who stay in school also have a variety of noncognitive traits that make employers and professional associations prefer them to less educated workers. People who are ambitious and persistent, for example, are likely both to stay in school and to get good jobs. People who get into a lot of trouble with their superiors are likely to drop out of school, and since employers dislike "troublemakers," such people are also likely to end up in low-status occupations.

If staying in school is an indication that an individual has some of the noncognitive traits that employers value, we might infer that schools with low dropout rates and high college entrance rates were doing an unusually good job in developing these traits. As we shall see, however, differences between high schools have surprisingly little effect on whether students drop out or enter college. This suggests that differences between high schools do not have a dramatic effect on the noncognitive traits that employers value.

Such an argument is hardly airtight. Nonetheless, it does seem to put the burden of proof on those who claim that differences between schools contribute in some important way to adult economic inequality. We first assumed that good schools made for economic success by boosting cognitive skills. Confronted with evidence that this was rarely true, we fell back on the theory that good schools influenced noncognitive traits, which in turn increased an individual's chances of getting credentials. This theory has also turned out to be largely wrong. At this point we are inclined to believe that all schools have relatively uniform effects, at least on the personality characteristics that affect economic success. Those who think otherwise are under an obligation to produce contrary evidence.

This argument does not, of course, apply to all possible noncognitive traits. We have no doubt, for example, that a school with a lacrosse team will produce some lacrosse addicts, and that a school which lacks such a team will produce very few. This is also true of cognitive skills. More students learn French in schools that teach French than in schools that do not.

The character of schools' likely effects on noncognitive traits is illustrated by a comparison of public and parochial school alumni. In 1963–1964, the National Opinion Research Corporation conducted a survey of American Catholics, about half of whom had attended public schools and about half of whom had attended parochial schools.[3] Most of the respondents had attended school between 1912 and 1958.

Parochial schools differed from public schools in a wide variety of ways during these years. Indeed, it seems fair to assume that the average difference between parochial and public schools during these years was considerably greater than the difference between one public school and another.

The survey was designed to determine what effect attending parochial school had on a broad range of attitudes. Parochial and public school alumni turned out to have almost indistinguishable attitudes on most issues, particularly after socio-economic background had been controlled. This suggests that differences between parochial and public schools were much less consequential than most people assumed at the time. Or putting it slightly differently, it suggests that Americans' attitudes during those years were largely formed by social and cultural forces that did not depend on the school they attended.

It is important to note, however, that parochial school alumni were more conscientious than public school alumni about the ritual aspects of Catholicism, such as church attendance. We cannot be absolutely sure that this was a school effect. These Catholics may just have had more conscientious parents. Still, efforts were made to compare individuals who reported similar parental values, and those who had attended parochial schools were still more devout than those who had not. This suggests that differences between schools affect some attitudes more than others. It also suggests, though it certainly does not prove, that the effect is usually confined to things which are subject to conscious control and which schools explicitly try to promote or not to promote.[4] In areas where schools have the same avowed objectives, or where they have no explicit operational objectives at all, their effects are likely to be quite uniform. Most of the noncognitive traits that influence economic success probably fall into this latter category. We therefore doubt that differences between schools have much effect on the noncognitive determinants of economic success.[5]

This conclusion does not mean that school per se has no effect on noncognitive traits. Survey research has turned up a multitude of differences between educated and uneducated adults. People who have spent a great deal of time in school vote differently, have different political attitudes, and score differently on a wide variety of psychological tests. They tend to go to psychiatrists more than uneducated people and to go to jail less. Such findings support the notion that staying in school has an effect on these traits. The reader will recall, however, that we also found large differences in cognitive skill between educated and uneducated people. Further analysis indicated that this was primarily because schools selected on the basis of cognitive skills and only secondarily because staying in school affected such skills. Unfortunately, the methodology of attitude research is not sufficiently well developed for us to separate the effects of initial traits from the effects of schooling. In the absence of evidence, we are inclined to believe that the relationship between schooling and noncognitive traits is much like the relationship between schooling and cognitive traits. We believe, in other words, that noncognitive differences between the highly educated and the poorly educated derive primarily from selection. But we also assume that staying in school has a modest effect on many of the noncognitive traits that employers value.[6]

This chapter is, then, largely a confession of ignorance and a plea for rethinking our attitudes toward the schools. The evidence reviewed in Chapters 6 and 7 suggests that noncognitive attributes may play a larger role than cognitive skills in determining economic success or failure. The evidence of our senses tells us that noncognitive traits also contribute far more than cognitive skills to the quality of human life and the extent of human happiness. We therefore believe that the noncognitive effects of schooling are likely to be more important than the cognitive effects. But we do not know what these noncognitive effects are likely to be.

# NOTES

1. See, for example, Goodman, *Compulsory Mis-education,* and Illich, *Deschooling Society.* In a more sociological vein, see Dreeben, *On What Is Learned in Schools,* and Gintis, "Towards a Political Economy."

2. For a more detailed development of this argument, see Gintis, "Characteristics of Worker Productivity," and "Towards a Political Economy."

3. See Greeley and Rossi, *The Education of Catholic Americans.*

4. For some contrary evidence, see Coleman, *The Adolescent Society.*

5. The reader will discover in Chapter 6 that Catholics from Catholic schools ended up in higher status occupations than Catholics from public schools. This could be due to the academic selectivity of many Catholic high schools or to unmeasured social and psychological differences between Catholics who attend parochial rather than public schools. It could, however, also be a true "school effect."

6. For one suggestive study, see Trent and Medsker, *Beyond High School.*

# CHAPTER FIVE

# Inequality in Educational Attainment

We have argued that schools have rather modest effects on the degree of cognitive and noncognitive inequality among adults. Most people find this argument difficult to accept. Highly educated people differ from uneducated people in many important ways, and most people assume that schools must cause many of these differences. In response we have argued that people who stay in school and attend college would differ from people who now drop out even if they all had exactly the same amount of school. We have argued, in other words, that schools serve primarily as selection and certification agencies, whose job is to measure and label people, and only secondarily as socialization agencies, whose job is to change people. This implies that schools serve primarily to legitimize inequality, not to create it. With this in mind, we turn to the question of who gets educational credentials, and why.

Schools do not have to be certification agencies. Nor does certification have to depend on time spent in school. Certification could be done strictly by examinations. Such a system exists to some extent in many European countries, where schools prepare students for national examinations, and the results of these examinations determine certification. A student can often take the examinations without having attended school. Conversely, merely attending school is no guarantee that he will pass the examinations.

In America, however, there is no national certification system. Free enterprise fills the gap, with thousands of schools and colleges issuing their own separate diplomas and degrees. The primary criterion for certifying a student is usually the amount of time he has spent in school, not the skills he has learned. This arrangement guarantees the schools a captive audience. It also guarantees that young people will be kept out of the labor market. Imagine, for example, what would happen to high school enrollment if states allowed anyone, regardless of age, to take a high school equivalency examination. Most capable students would probably leave high school by the time they were

16. The only way to keep many of these students in school is to make continued school attendance the quickest route to certification.

A second reason schools have become certification agencies is that this serves the interests of a society that wants people sorted and graded but does not know precisely what standards it wants to use. If high school diplomas or other certificates of competence were given solely for passing examinations, there would have to be political agreement on what the examination should cover. This would be hard to get. Delegating the problem to the schools is a way of sweeping it under the rug. A third advantage of relying on schools to certify students is that employers are at least as interested in whether their workers behave properly and do what they are told as in the workers' cognitive skills. This means that employers need a certification system that includes some direct observation of an individual "at work." Schools can provide this. Examination boards cannot.

This chapter investigates the effects of turning certification over to the schools. It asks what kinds of people schools certify and what kinds of people they fail to certify. This is obviously a complex question. Schools and colleges issue an enormous variety of diplomas and degrees. In order to get an overall picture of the relationship between educational certification and other kinds of inequality, we will have to simplify the question by assuming that the value of any given credential depends solely on how long it takes to acquire. We will assume, in other words, that the value of an individual's credentials is proportional to the highest grade of school he has completed. We will call this "educational attainment."

This approach has at least two limitations. First, it treats each extra year of school or college as if it were exactly as valuable as the next. This is clearly an oversimplification. An extra year of college increases a man's earning power more than an extra year of high school. Completing the last year of either high school or college also brings more economic benefits than completing any of the three preceding years. Nonetheless, the differences are relatively modest. Assuming that one year of school or college is just like the next reduces our ability to explain adult economic success by only 3 to 5 percent, and it greatly simplifies our analysis.[1]

A second major limitation of our approach is that we make no qualitative distinctions between types of certification or types of institutions. A Master's degree in Engineering is harder to get than a Master's degree in Education, and it is more valuable economically. Similarly, a B.A. in English from an Ivy League college is harder to get than a B.A. in English from a state college, and the economic benefits are greater. Once again, however, the effects of these distinctions among types of B.A.s and higher degrees is rather modest.[2]

The remainder of this chapter examines the factors that determine how long people stay in school. The next 4 sections deal with the effects of economic background, race, family background, and academic aptitude on who gets academic credentials. We then turn to the effects of schools on their students' eventual attainment. We conclude by examining the policy implications of our findings.

In some respects, this discussion is an extension of Chapter 2, in which we examined the influence of economic background and race on the distribution of educational resources. There is a crucial difference, however. Chapter 2 viewed school attendance as a consumption item. This allowed us to talk about the absolute amount of inequality in the distribution of school resources. We assumed, for example, that since the best-educated fifth of the population used to get 10 years more schooling than the worst-educated fifth, but now gets only 8 years more, inequality had declined. This does not, however, mean that the distribution of credentials is necessarily more equal than in the past. If credentials measured skills that were only learned in school, equalizing the distribution of schooling would equalize the value of the credentials schools conferred. But educational credentials also measure traits that people acquire outside of school. Equalizing the amount or kind of schooling people receive cannot alter these traits. This means that an 8-year gap between the best- and worst-educated fifth today may be just as important as a 10-year gap used to be. We will not try to determine whether this, is really the case or not. We will look at credentials in strictly relative terms, assuming that they serve primarily to rank individuals rather than to certify absolute levels of competence. We will simply ask who ends up ranking high and who ends up ranking low.

A second difference between this discussion and the discussion in Chapter 2 is that we cannot use the same standards for evaluating the distribution of educational credentials as for evaluating the distribution of educational resources. In Chapter 2, we assumed that everyone had the same claim on public benefits, and that if people did not stay in school they ought to get alternative benefits instead. When we look at educational credentials, we cannot use such egalitarian logic. Credentials are by definition unequally distributed. Whether the distribution is just or unjust depends not on the degree of inequality, but on whether this inequality is necessary and useful. We cannot answer this question until we have examined not only the basis on which credentials are distributed, but also the uses to which Americans put these credentials. We will postpone these issues until Chapters 6 and 7.

## The Effects of Economic Background

One of the ways economically successful families try to help their children retain their privileges is by making sure that their children "get a good education." Such efforts are moderately successful. The correlation between a white child's educational attainment and his father's occupational status is almost 0.50.[3] Using a combined index of father's occupation and income would probably raise the correlation to about 0.55.[4] This correlation appears to have been stable throughout the first half of the twentieth century.[5]

A correlation of 0.55 means that if we define economic status strictly in terms of father's occupation and income, as we do in this book, and if we compare the educational attainment of children from different strata, the educational gap between the children will average 55 percent of the economic gap between their parents. Suppose, for example, that we call all families that rank in the top fifth of the economic hierarchy upper-middle class and all families in the bottom fifth lower class. Roughly half the children born into the upper-middle class will end up with what we might call upper-middle class educational credentials, i.e. with more schooling than 80 percent of their age-mates. Likewise, about half the children born into the lower class will end up with what we might call lower-class credentials, i.e. less schooling than 80 percent of their age-mates. Upper-middle class children will average 4 years more schooling than lower-class children.[6]

There are several possible reasons why children with economically successful parents get more credentials than children with unsuccessful parents. First, they are more likely to have a home environment in which they acquire the intellectual skills they need to do well in school. Second, they are more likely to have genes that facilitate success in school. Third, they seldom have to work or borrow money to attend college. Fourth, they may feel that they ought to stay in school, even if they have no special aptitude for academic work and dislike school life. Fifth, they may attend better schools, which induce them to go to college rather than to drop out.

Less than 10 percent of the overall effect of parental economic status on children's educational attainment appears to be explained by the fact that economically advantaged children have superior IQ genotypes.[7] Another 20–25 percent of the difference seems to be due to the fact that economically advantaged parents provide environments that nurture the cognitive skills that schools value. Overall, then, about a third of the discrepancy in educational attainment between economically advantaged and disadvantaged students is explained by differences in their test scores.[8]

We do not know how much direct effect money from home has on students' chances of staying in school. Considering the importance of the problem, good evidence is surprisingly hard to find. Dropouts often say they quit school or college because of money problems.[9] But we have no evidence that students who report money problems have appreciably less money than students who report no such problems. Students who report money problems may simply be students who have expensive tastes or who are unusually reluctant to go into debt to get a college degree. As far as we can discover, no one has compared the amount students actually receive from home with the amount of schooling they get. Students who have jobs in college are only 5 to 10 percent more likely to drop out than students who do not.[10]

We would be surprised if money per se explained more than 10 or 15 percent of the overall difference in attainment between students from different class backgrounds. This seems to leave at least half the gap unexplained. The usual response to this finding is to attribute the remaining difference to motivation. We are not sure, however, exactly what this means.

There is a popular theory among both educators and laymen that middle-class children work harder in school than poor children. We cannot find any good evidence that this is so. When we compare economically advantaged students to disadvantaged students with the same test scores, for example, we find that they get the same average high school grades.[11] We assume that diligence has more effect on school grades than on standardized test scores, and we therefore conclude that economically disadvantaged students probably work as hard as economically advantaged students with comparable aptitudes. More generally, we conclude that high school teachers reward a set of traits which, with the exception of academic aptitude, are not very class-related. This clearly contradicts most people's preconceptions. We suspect, though we certainly cannot prove, that these preconceptions are based on a misunderstanding of the dominant values of working-class families. While a few lower-class and working-class children behave in ways that schools find unacceptable and try to punish, the great majority evidently do not. The deviant minority seems, however, to shape middle-class stereotypes of working-class values and behavior.

Nonetheless, all school surveys show that children with affluent parents want more education than children with poor parents, even when we compare individuals with the same test scores and grades. This is apparent as early as the ninth grade. The correlation between socio-economic background and ninth grade aspirations is as high as the correlation between socio-economic background and eventual attainment.[12]

How are we to explain the relationship between educational aspirations and socio-economic background? Initially, we placed considerable emphasis on the theory that middle-class children found school life more agreeable than working-class children. But if this were the case, we would expect middle-class children to earn better grades than working-class children with similar test scores. Since they do not, the whole theory that school life is essentially middle class is called into question. While we cannot reject this traditional view on the basis of a single piece of evidence, we must at least consider alternative explanations.

One obvious possibility is that middle-class students have higher educational aspirations because they feel under more pressure from home to continue their education than students from working-class and lower-class homes. There is persuasive empirical evidence for this. Indeed, perceived pressure from home seems to explain most of the difference between working-class and middle-class students' educational aspirations.[13]

Another plausible explanation for the high level of educational aspirations among middle-class students is the fact that such students have higher occupational aspirations than working- and lower-class students.[14] Once again, however, we face a chicken-egg dilemma when we try to talk about causation. Occupational aspirations are highly correlated with educational aspirations, but which causes which? Some students certainly stay in school solely to qualify for a high-status occupation, but others seem first to decide how long they want to stay in school, and then adjust their occupational aspirations to fit their taste for schooling. Working-class children may, then, have lower occupational aspirations partly because they are more reluctant to stay in school, rather than the other way around.

Still another theory is that working-class students have lower aspirations because they "know" that they cannot go to college. This theory is essentially circular, however. Some working-class students go to college; some do not. Our question is what makes the difference. Test scores are one factor and money is another, but much is left unexplained. To say that those who do not want to attend are "just being realistic" does not add to our understanding.

Our final hypothesis was that middle-class students had higher aspirations and higher eventual attainment because they attended better schools. Our analysis of Project Talent, reported in more detail later in this chapter, does not support this view. It is true that students from affluent families attend high schools with slightly bigger budgets than average. It is also true that these affluent high schools have fewer dropouts and send more of their students to college than the average high school. But this is because they enroll students from high-status families with high initial aspirations.

Overall, the data lead us to three general conclusions. First, economic origins have a substantial influence on the amount of schooling people get. Second, the difference between rich and poor children is partly a matter of academic aptitude and partly a matter of money. Third, cultural attitudes, values, and taste for schooling play an even larger role than aptitude and money. Even if a middle-class child does not enjoy school, he evidently assumes that he will have to stay in school for a long time. Children with working-class parents or lower-class parents evidently assume that if they dislike school they can and should drop out. As we shall see, students who plan to drop out usually assume they will have to take low-status jobs.[15] But such jobs evidently seem more acceptable to working-class students than to most upper-middle class children. This suggests that if we want to equalize the educational attainment of children from different economic backgrounds, we will probably have to change not only their test scores and financial resources, but also their attitudes and values.

## The Effects of Race

Since 1900, the educational attainment of blacks has risen faster than that of whites. Blacks born at the turn of the century averaged 3 years less schooling than whites. Blacks born during World War II averaged 1 year less than whites.[16]

It is still too early to say how much effect the civil rights movement of the 1960s will have on black attainment. White colleges did not begin recruiting black students in a systematic and self-conscious way until 1965, and these efforts did not have a major effect on enrollment patterns for several years.[17] Even in 1968, more colleges favored whites over equally well-qualified blacks than vice versa.[18] Nonetheless, black enrollment rose considerably faster than white enrollment during the late 1960s.[19] It therefore seems reasonable to assume that the up-coming generation of blacks will get almost as much schooling as whites get.

The fact that the average young black now has only a year less schooling than the average white is quite surprising when we consider the handicaps with which blacks enter school. The average black child born during World War II, for example, had parents with 2 to 3 years less schooling than the average white. His parents also had worse jobs, less money, and more children. Even if skin color had been of no consequence in America, we would have expected children from such families to get at least a year less schooling than the national average.[20]

Furthermore, black children enter school at even more of a disadvantage than socio-economic statistics imply. On the basis of economic background, for example, we would expect black children to be about 5 points below white children on standardized tests when they enter school.[21] In fact, they average 15 points below the white mean. The typical white born during World War II who entered school with an IQ score of 85 apparently got about 10.6 years of school. Yet the typical black born in this period entered school with an IQ score of about 85 and got 11.0 years of schooling. This implies that blacks born during World War II got slightly more schooling than whites with comparable test scores. (This does not seem to have been true before World War II.) [22]

This inference is supported by comparisons between blacks and whites who score at the same level on the Armed Forces Qualification Test. On the average, blacks with low scores have had about a year more schooling than whites with similar scores. Blacks with high scores have had about the same amount of schooling as whites with high scores.[23] Likewise, black high school students who returned questionnaires to Project Talent's 5-year follow-up survey got more schooling than whites with comparable scores.[24]

Surveys have repeatedly found that blacks said they wanted more schooling than whites with comparable test scores and economic backgrounds. This is often presumed to mean that blacks have unrealistic expectations. This does not appear to be the case. Blacks not only want but get more schooling than whites with similar test scores.[25]

These findings suggest two conclusions. First, the overall difference between black and white educational attainment is much smaller than the difference between black and white test scores, occupational status, income, or almost anything else we can think of. Young blacks have nearly caught up with whites in terms of educational credentials. This has not enabled them to catch up in terms of other things, or at least not yet. Second, differences between black and white attainment can today be explained by differences in their test scores. The effects of test scores are, moreover, partially offset by the high level of black educational aspirations. Discrimination seems to have trivial effects.

## Overall Effects of Family Background

Having described the relationship between educational attainment, economic background, and race, we must now assess the overall influence of all aspects of family background on educational attainment. The reader should recall that we have defined "family background" as including all features of the environment that make brothers and sisters alike. Family background is not, then, a unitary concept with a consistent meaning in all contexts. The family characteristics that influence cognitive development, for example, may be quite different from those that influence educational attainment. Still, the concept is quite useful if its limitations and ambiguity are clearly recognized.

Estimating the effect of family background on educational attainment involves many uncertainties. We know the degree of resemblance between brothers, but such resemblance may be due either to genes, family background, or the direct influence of one brother on another. Appendix B deals with these problems in some detail. It shows that on almost any reasonable set of assumptions, family background explains nearly half the variation in educational attainment.[26] A family's economic status is, of course, a major determinant of its overall impact on its children. But noneconomic factors also account for a significant fraction of a family's overall effect on its children's attainment.[27]

## Academic Aptitude and Academic Credentials

There has always been a conflict in American education between the idea that academic credentials should measure competence and the idea that they should reward effort. The result has been a series of battles between those who want to maintain standards by failing students who do poor work and those who want to encourage academic effort by conferring diplomas and degrees on people who have tried to do academic work, regardless of whether they did it well or poorly.

Many schools and colleges have ended up awarding credentials primarily for effort rather than performance. Thus, high schools have largely abandoned the idea that students should have to know anything in particular in order to earn a diploma. The student who has spent 12 years in attendance is generally felt to have "earned" some kind of diploma, and it seems "unfair" to send him away empty handed. Colleges also flunk out fewer and fewer students. The same is true of graduate schools. In many institutions admission has become a virtual guarantee of graduation, at least for students who are willing to go through the required motions.

Yet the very fact that admission guarantees graduation has made colleges and professional schools more careful about whom they admit. Instead of letting in large numbers and failing the less competent, many institutions now have elaborate procedures for excluding in advance those whom they think unworthy of a degree. This spares the faculty the unpleasant task of flunking students whom they may know personally. Instead, they can simply send polite letters of rejection to the less promising applicants, saying there was not enough room for everyone, however well qualified. Arrangements of this kind have increased the apparent importance of aptitude test scores, which are often explicitly used in choosing among candidates for admissions. Grades, while still used along with test scores in making admissions decisions, are rarely used to deny a student the diploma or degree of the institution in which he is enrolled. This means that mastery of subject matter probably plays less of a role than it used to play in determining who gets certified.

Despite the apparently increasing importance of test scores, the correlation between elementary school test scores and eventual educational attainment seems to have hovered just under 0.60 for some decades. This is only a little higher than the correlation between educational attainment and economic background.[28]

It is not clear to what extent cognitive skills really cause differences in educational attainment and to what extent they are simply associated with coming from the right family. If we compare two groups of students born during World War II whose IQ scores in elementary school differed by 15 points, we estimate that the clever students ended up with about 1.6 years more of schooling than the slower students. If we compare individuals from similar economic backgrounds who differed by 15 points, their estimated educational attainment differs by about 1.25 years.[29] If we compare pairs of men raised in the same home whose scores differ by 15 points, our best guess is that their educational attainment will differ by less than a year.[30] This suggests that the actual effect of cognitive skills on educational attainment is around half the observed association. The other half of the association arises because high test scores are related to having the right parents.

If these estimates are even approximately correct, the effect of IQ genotype on educational attainment must be quite modest. Appendix B suggests that IQ genotype per se explains between 2 and 9 percent of the variation in eventual educational attainment.[31] If we compare the most genetically advantaged fifth of the population to the least genetically advantaged fifth, and hold everything else constant, their educational attainments will probably differ by about 2 years. The exact value is uncertain, however. It could be anywhere from 1 to 3 years.[32]

There is no evidence that the correlation between initial ability and eventual educational attainment is rising.[33] We must therefore reject the popular theory that education is growing more meritocratic, at least if IQ genotype or actual test scores are taken as the measure of "merit."

Even though academic aptitude causes only a modest fraction of the variation in educational attainment, it is still worth asking *how* it exercises its influence. We began by exploring the theory that test scores influenced attainment by influencing students' success in school. We assumed that students with low scores received low grades, that students with low grades were less likely to stay in school, and that schools were also less likely to want them to stay. About half the association between test scores and attainment seems explicable in these terms.[34]

Test scores also affect educational attainment by affecting school curriculum placement. Students with low scores are frequently placed in noncollege programs. This reduces their chance of attending college. Curriculum placement seems to explain between a third and a sixth of the relationship between test scores and a student's chances of entering college.[35]

Academic aptitude may also influence attainment by influencing colleges' and graduate schools' decisions to admit applicants and to retain them after admission. Unfortunately, it is not easy to separate the effects of institutional policy from the effects of individual choice. We can, however, report that 76 percent of the twelfth graders who said in 1963 that they expected to earn a B.A. were in 4-year colleges the following year. All other things being equal, a 15 point difference in such students' test scores was only associated with a 4 percent increase in their chances of entering college.[36] For students whose aspirations remain high, then, low test scores do not seem to be an insuperable barrier to staying in school.

We can sum up our conclusions about the effects of academic aptitude on educational attainment in the following generalizations:

1. Academic aptitude has slightly more influence than economic background on a student's chances of acquiring educational credentials.[37]

2. About a quarter of the correlation between test scores and attainment can be explained by the fact that students with high test scores tend to come from economically successful families.

3. Another quarter of the correlation can probably be explained by other subtler family background characteristics.

4. The factors influencing educational attainment are overwhelmingly social, not biological.

One final observation about the relationship between test scores and educational credentials is in order. Attending school increases most cognitive skills. This means that even if those who got a lot of schooling had the same aptitudes as everyone else when they started school, they would often have more information and more skills than other people by the time they had finished. The correlation between attainment and test scores in adulthood is therefore considerably higher than the correlation between attainment and scores in childhood. The skills measured on standardized tests, such as adult intelligence tests or the Armed Forces Qualification Test, correlate 0.60 to 0.70 with educational attainment.[38] This means that an employer who is looking for workers with high test scores can do moderately well if he recruits on the basis of educational attainment. Still, he could do considerably better if he simply gave a test himself.

## The Effects of School Quality on Educational Attainment

Chapter 3 showed that qualitative differences between schools had relatively little impact on students' test scores, especially at the high school level. This section shows that differences between schools also have relatively little effect on students' eventual educational attainment. We will look first at high schools, then at elementary schools, and finally at the cumulative impact of elementary and secondary schools together.

### HIGH SCHOOLS

Both Project Talent and EEOS provide some information on the educational attainment of students who attend different high schools. Just as with cognitive skills, there is much more inequality in the educational attainment of different students in the same high school than between the average student in one high school and the average student in another high school. If, for example, we rank ninth graders in the same high school according to how much education they eventually get, the top 20 percent typically get nearly 7 years more education than the bottom 20 percent. If we rank high schools in this same way, we estimate that ninth graders from the top fifth of all high schools get only 2 or 3 years more schooling than ninth graders from the bottom fifth.[39]

Another point that emerges from both Project Talent and EEOS is that differences between high schools can be largely explained by the characteristics of their entering students. In Project Talent, for example, differences in comprehensive high schools' effects on their students explain no more than 2 percent of the variation in the students' eventual educational attainment. If we compare students from typical socioeconomic backgrounds who have typical ninth grade aspirations and test scores, about 50 percent of those in the most effective fifth of all high schools go to college, compared to 30 percent of those in the least effective fifth of all schools. ("Effectiveness" here is defined solely in terms of keeping students in school and getting them to attend college.) Putting it slightly differently, attending a high school in the top fifth boosts the average student's eventual attainment about half a year above the expected level, while attending a high school in the bottom fifth lowers his probable attainment about half a year.[40]

ELEMENTARY SCHOOLS

No one has ever collected comparative data on the eventual educational attainment of children who attend different elementary schools. When we began our work on educational attainment, however, we assumed that if an elementary school did an unusually good job in raising verbal, reading, and math scores, its alumni would have an unusually good chance of earning good grades in junior high school, being placed in a college preparatory program, doing well on college entrance examinations, and eventually earning impressive educational credentials. Unfortunately, the scanty available data offer little support for this assumption.

In order to test our assumptions, we matched 127 northern urban high schools in EEOS with the elementary schools from which they normally received students. Then we ranked these elementary school feeder systems according to their effectiveness in boosting sixth grade verbal, reading, and math scores.[41] High schools drawing their students from the most effective fifth of all elementary feeder systems were sending 44.0 percent of their students to college, whereas high schools drawing their students from the least effective fifth of all elementary systems were sending 38 percent of their students to college.[42] This implies an eventual difference in mean educational attainment of about a tenth of a year.[43]

We do not have data on college entrance rates for the alumni of different elementary schools in the same high school.[44] There could be appreciable differences. We can be almost certain, however, that attending an elementary school that ranks in the top rather than the bottom fifth in terms of its effect on test scores will not increase the average student's eventual educational attainment more than 0.8 years, and our best guess is that the effect is far smaller.[45]

We have no evidence on the extent to which differences between elementary schools influence students' eventual appetite for more schooling.[46] Nor do we know whether elementary schools that raise aspirations are the same as those that boost test scores.[47] Our guess, however, is that elementary schools have very few permanent effects of this kind.

CUMULATIVE EFFECTS OF SCHOOLS

Conventional wisdom tells us that effective elementary schools are usually found in the same district as effective secondary schools. This is because effective schools are presumed to be those which have ample budgets and middle-class students. But the conventional wisdom is wrong. The next sections will show that there is no correlation between what a high school spends and its impact on students' attainment, nor is there any consistent correlation between a high school's social composition and its impact on attainment. Furthermore, elementary schools that boost achievement are not especially likely to be found in the same districts as secondary schools that boost educational attainment.[48] This means that an individual whose test scores rise as a result of attending a good elementary school is as likely to attend a high school that discourages college attendance as a high school that encourages it.

For these reasons, living in the "right" school district seems to make relatively little difference to an individual's educational attainment. Our best guess is that the cumulative impact of school quality alters the average student's educational attainment less than half a year.[49] Attending the right school may, of course, make an enormous difference to particular students. But the school that is right for one student seems very often to be wrong for another. The average effect of any given school is therefore small.

## The Effects of High School Resources

High schools with ample resources have slightly fewer dropouts and send slightly more students to college than high schools with scanty resources. But this is because high schools with ample resources enroll students with slightly more successful parents, higher test scores, and higher initial aspirations than the average high school. If students are alike in these respects, they end up with the same amount of schooling, regardless of how much their high school spends.

Our 91 Project Talent high schools reported their expenditures per pupil, the expenditures per pupil in the entire school system, the average salary of their teachers, and the number of teachers per student. If we compare ninth graders with similar aspirations, test scores, and economic backgrounds, we find that those who got the most education attended high schools which spent less money than average, had worse-paid teachers, and had larger classes.[50]

The reader should not, of course, jump to the conclusion that raising per pupil expenditures increases the dropout rate or lowers the proportion of students who attend college. A more plausible theory is that our 91 Project Talent schools are simply atypical. This view is supported by the fact that teacher salaries and class size are not associated with college entrance rates in the EEOS sample, once ninth graders' characteristics are taken into account.

None of the specific things high schools buy with their money seems to affect dropout rates or college entrance rates. Both Project Talent and EEOS sent long questionnaires to principals. EEOS also collected information from teachers. These questionnaires yield hundreds of different measures of school policies and resources. A few of these measures show nonrandom (i.e. statistically significant) relationships to the students' estimated educational attainment, even after controlling the students' characteristics when they entered a high school. But the length of the school day is the only policy or resource that has a statistically significant relation to attainment in both Project Talent and the EEOS national sample. Even in this case, there is no consistency between EEOS results for the North and the South, for urban and rural areas, or for blacks and whites.

Two additional examples should suffice to illustrate the general pattern. First, let us consider the impact of high school guidance counselors on educational attainment. In Project Talent, students in schools with one or more guidance counselor got about a fifth of a year less schooling than similar students in schools without counselors.[51] In the EEOS national sample, students from schools with counselors were less likely to go to college than students with similar ninth grade aspirations and socio-economic backgrounds who were in schools without counselors. These findings do not mean that counselors keep students out of college. They may mean that schools acquire more counselors when they have a dropout problem, or when they are not sending as many students to college as the school board thinks they should. In our EEOS regional and ethnic samples (urban North, rural North, white rural South, black rural South) the relationship between counselors and college entrance rates is entirely random.[52]

Another school characteristic that might reasonably be expected to influence the percentage of students going to college is the percentage of ninth graders whom a school assigns to the college preparatory curriculum. In both Project Talent and EEOS, however, the percentage of ninth graders who said they were in a college curriculum had no relationship whatever to the percentage who attended college, once the characteristics of entering students were taken into account. EEOS did find a consistent relationship between the percentage of twelfth graders who said they were in the college curriculum and the percentage who attended college. We suspect, however, that this derived from the fact that students who planned to attend college were likely to say they were in a college preparatory curriculum no matter what they were studying.

Examples of this kind could be enumerated more or less indefinitely. We can sum up the overall pattern by saying that while some schools are unusually effective both in preventing dropouts and in encouraging college attendance, none of the policies or resources about which surveys habitually obtain information has a consistent relationship to this kind of effectiveness. A high school's impact on individual students seems to depend on relatively subtle "climatic" conditions, not on the size of the budget or the presence of the resources professional educators claim are important.

We have tried to check this conclusion against the results of intervention programs designed to raise students' educational attainment. Unfortunately, such programs are rarely evaluated in a systematic way. Our impression, based on conversations with school administrators and reading of the educational press, is that such programs rarely make much difference. There are, however, a number of alleged exceptions.

The most impressive exception is Upward Bound, a federally funded by-product of the war on poverty. Upward Bound is aimed at "promising" but "disadvantaged" high school students from "disadvantaged" backgrounds who would not (it is said) normally go to college. The program tries to persuade these students that they ought to go to college and then helps them get there. It uses a wide range of techniques, including remedial instruction, counseling, and direct exposure to colleges during the high school years.

Upward Bound students typically score just below the national average on standardized tests when they enter the program. This means they are well below the average for college students. Their scores do not improve as a result of being in the program. Nonetheless, 62–72 percent of Upward Bound alumni attend college, as compared to 39–48 percent of their older brothers and sisters. As a result, Upward Bound alumni end up with 0.3 to 0.4 years more schooling than their siblings.[53]

By design, of course, Upward Bound is selecting the most talented members of disadvantaged families. We have already seen, however, that in the normal course of events siblings end up quite similar in terms of educational attainment. It would take considerable ingenuity to select students so as to get intrafamily differences as large as those Upward Bound reports. We therefore suspect that the program is making a real difference.

Upward Bound's apparent success may, however, be an exception that proves the general rule about high school resources not affecting students' college chances. Upward Bound programs are not run by high schools. They take students who seem to be on their way out of the school system, and they show these students how to survive in high school and how to get into college. They reject many of the schools' traditional values and practices, and they encourage students to look at themselves and the world in a different way. Pouring more money into existing high schools seldom has any of these results.

## The Effects of Segregation

We turn next to the effects of economic and racial segregation on students' chances of earning educational credentials. Once again, the evidence comes mostly from high schools and is generally discouraging.

### ECONOMIC SEGREGATION

Research on the relationship between a high school's socio-economic composition and its students' college plans became a minor sociological industry during the 1960s. Most investigators found that students in predominantly middle-class high schools had higher aspirations than students in predominantly working-class high schools.[54] These differences persisted even after various statistical adjustments had been made to take account of initial differences between the students entering middle-class and working-class schools. In recent years, however, sociologists have gathered better data and have become more sophisticated in their use of statistics. The best recent studies have concluded that the socio-economic composition of a high school has virtually no effect on students' aspirations.[55]

Our own research has followed this same course. We began by looking at aspirations. We first investigated whether students in different EEOS high schools said they wanted to attend college and whether they had taken steps to implement their hopes (like writing for a college catalogue). We found that students in middle-class high schools were much more likely to plan to attend college than students with similar test scores and socio-economic backgrounds in working-class high schools.[56] EEOS was not a longitudinal study, however, so we could not rule out the possibility that students who attended middle-class high schools had higher aspirations before they entered these schools.

We therefore turned to the 91 white comprehensive Project Talent high schools discussed elsewhere in this book. Instead of looking at high school seniors' plans, we looked at whether students actually entered college the year after high school. When we compared the 18 schools with the most middle-class students to the 18 schools with the fewest, we found that the former sent 38 percent of their tenth graders to college, while the latter sent 15 percent.[57] We then compared the educational attainment of students with the same ninth grade test scores, aspirations, and economic background. To our surprise, students in the middle-class schools were *less* likely to finish high school and enter college than similar students in the working-class schools.[58]

How are we to explain this? We assumed that students made new friends in high school. We therefore expected students who attended high schools where most of the other students planned to attend college to acquire friends who planned to attend college also. Both common sense and quantitative social science suggest that friends have some influence on one another's college plans.[59] We therefore expected that attending a school where other students went to college would encourage an ambivalent student to attend. Yet this did not happen.

The most plausible explanation of our findings is that middle-class high schools have two contradictory effects on students. On the one hand, they increase a student's chances of making college-oriented friends. This raises the probability that the student will go to college. On the other hand, middle-class high schools have higher academic standards than working-class high schools. This means that if a student at any given ability level enters a middle-class school, he is likely to rank lower in his class than if he enters a working-class school. He is likely to find this discouraging. The college of his choice may also hold it against him.

If this explanation were correct, we would expect a student's chances of attending college to be greatest if he attended a high school where the other students had high aspirations but low test scores. We would expect his chances to be lowest in a high school where the other students had high test scores but low aspirations. We would not expect his chances of attending college to be affected much either way if he entered a high school where the other students had both high test scores and high aspirations, or where they had both low test scores and low aspirations. Since most schools fall into one of the two latter categories, we would not expect social composition to have much impact in most cases.

The data from our 91 Project Talent high schools are consistent with this theory. When we examined the effect of classmates' aspirations and test scores on individual students, we found that classmates with high aspirations seemed to raise the average student's eventual attainment, while classmates with high test scores seemed to lower it.[60] In an analysis of this complexity, a sample of only 91 schools might yield such results entirely by chance. The Educational Testing Service has, however, conducted a much larger study of 35,330 students in 518 schools, which also tried to disentangle the effects of academic and socio-economic context on aspirations. The results were consistent with ours.[61] College students' chances of attending graduate school also seem to be lowered if they attend academically selective colleges.[62]

All in all, the evidence indicates that a white student with a given test score and family background is no more likely to end up with impressive educational credentials if he attends a middle-class high school than if he attends a working-class high school. Neither is he any more likely to end up with high test scores.[63]

RACIAL SEGREGATION

When we turn from economic to racial segregation, our conclusions have to be more tentative. Very little of the research on aspirations discussed earlier in this chapter covered high schools with appreciable numbers of black students.[64] Project Talent did not collect information on students' race until 1965, and it has never managed to locate most of the blacks who were presumably in the 1960 sample. EEOS provides information on blacks and whites in both segregated and desegregated high schools, but it provides no data on whether their aspirations changed between ninth and twelfth grade.[65]

Despite these limitations, we have reanalyzed EEOS data on aspirations, and our findings require brief comment. The reader will recall that when we compared twelfth graders who had similar test scores and socio-economic backgrounds, those in predominantly middle-class schools had substantially higher aspirations than those in working-class schools. Since middle-class schools tend to be predominantly white, and since black schools tend to be predominantly working class, we expected to find a relationship between a school's racial composition and twelfth graders' aspirations. Surprisingly, the relationship turned out to be nil. When we compared individuals with similar family backgrounds and test scores, those in predominantly black schools had the same aspirations as those in predominantly white schools.[66]

This finding probably reflects the "big fish in a small pond" phenomenon described earlier. Blacks at any given economic level have lower test scores than whites. This means that a student at any given ability level will rank higher in his class if he attends a predominantly black school than if he attends a predominantly white school. In addition, blacks have higher aspirations than whites of similar ability and economic origins. This means that students are more likely to have friends who want to attend college if they attend predominantly black schools than if they attend academically and economically similar white schools.[67] Thus while aspirations are lower in working-class than in middle-class schools, they are higher in black working-class than in white working-class schools.

Having found that the racial composition of a high school did not seem to affect students' aspirations, we still suspected that students in predominantly white high schools might find it easier to realize their aspirations than students in predominantly black high schools. EEOS data did not support this suspicion. Once the aspirations, socio-economic status, and test scores of the ninth graders had been taken into account, the racial composition of a high school had no relationship to the percentage of students whom the principal said dropped out before graduating, or to the percentage he said entered college. The principals of these schools were also specifically asked how many blacks attended college. Principals in predominantly black schools reported slightly more blacks attending college than principals in predominantly white schools.[68]

These 1965 findings are hard to reconcile with survey data on blacks who attended desegregated schools prior to 1960. Among blacks brought up in the North, those who attended racially mixed elementary and secondary schools came from the same economic and educational backgrounds as those who attended all-black schools. But those who attended racially mixed schools ended up with half a year more schooling than those who attended all-black schools.[69] Perhaps desegregation at the elementary level increases attainment, whereas desegregation at the secondary level does not. Or perhaps attending a desegregated high school was more of an asset to a black prior to 1960 than in 1965. Neither explanation seems fully convincing.

The foregoing comparisons all deal with northern schools that were desegregated because blacks and whites lived in the same area. Such "natural experiments" may or may not be relevant to the current controversy over busing. We know only one study of such a situation. The study deals with black students who were voluntarily bused from Boston to predominantly white suburban high schools outside Boston. These students were somewhat more likely to attend college than their older siblings.[70] This is, however, a highly publicized program, and the mere fact of being in it may increase a student's chances of getting into college.

Taking all the evidence together, we can find no convincing evidence that racial desegregation affects students' eventual educational attainment one way or the other. This holds for both blacks and whites. Admittedly, the evidence is not good enough to be regarded as final. There is still a real need for studies of districts where high schools have been desegregated by court order or by deliberate administrative changes in attendance patterns. In addition, we do not know whether desegregating elementary schools affects either students' aspirations or their ability to cope with the demands made by high schools and colleges. Still, the most reasonable assumption at present is that desegregation makes little or no difference to students' college prospects.

CONCLUSIONS ABOUT DESEGREGATION

Chapter 3 showed that high school segregation had no effect on students' test scores and that elementary school segregation probably had a very small effect. Now we have seen that high school segregation probably has no effect on students' chances of earning educational credentials. These findings may convince some readers that segregation is not so bad after all, and that reformers should devote themselves to other causes.

We must therefore emphasize once again that the outcomes of schooling discussed in this book are not all-embracing. Test scores and credentials may be the two products of schooling most likely to influence economic success, but even this is not certain. We must also emphasize that the most important effects of school desegregation may be on adults, not on students. School desegregation can be seen as part of an effort to make blacks and whites rethink their historic relationship to one another. If blacks and whites attend the same schools, then perhaps they will feel more of a stake in each other's well-being than they have in the past. If that does not happen—if blacks and whites emerge from desegregated schools as alien from one another as before—the struggle will have been in vain. This will be so even if the racial disparity in test scores and educational credentials is slightly reduced in the process —which is far from certain. The question, then, is how desegregation affects the attitudes of children and of adults. It is easy to construct theories showing either that desegregation will make things better or that it will make them worse. Past experience can also be cited to support either view. Our own prejudice is that in most contexts desegregation will probably increase tension in the short run and reduce it in the long run. But we have no real evidence for this. All we have is a conviction that the debate over desegregation ought to focus on this issue, not on test scores and college entrance rates.

## The Effects of Curriculum Placement

We have already noted that there is far more variation in educational attainment between different students in the same school than between the average student in one school and the average student in another school. Almost every high school has some dropouts, some students who take a diploma but do not attend college, and some students who enter college. Nationally, the ratio of these groups to one another is now about 20–40–40. Relatively few high schools deviate dramatically from these norms. Most fall between 40–40–20 and 10–30–60. This makes the reasons for unequal attainment within any given school considerably more important than the reasons for disparities between schools.

In general, we expect students to remain in school and enter college if they are good at doing the things schools value and reward. We expect them to drop out of school if they are bad at doing these things. Of course, we also expect exceptions. Some students will drop out even though they have done very well in school, both socially and intellectually. Others stay in school and attend college despite poor grades, conflict with the school authorities, or both. In general, however, we view persistence in school and college as a measure of how agreeable a student finds life in these institutions, and we believe most students find school life agreeable if they are good at the tasks schools set. We also think that different American schools set quite similar tasks.

Ideally, we would like to be able to evaluate the impact of all sorts of rewards and punishments on students' persistence in school. In practice, we do not have enough data to do this. We know, for example, that students are less likely to finish high school or enter college if they receive low grades. But we do not know whether low grades actually *cause* attrition. We do not know of any controlled experiments in which schools or teachers have given out grades randomly and then tried to assess the results. We suspect that if poor students are given higher grades than they deserve, their subsequent performance improves. Classical pedagogic theory predicts the opposite, and habitual cynicism predicts no significant change of any sort.

Neither do we know much about the effects of tracking. We suspect that if students of comparable ability and personality are assigned to different tracks in elementary school, those in the fast track are more likely to end up in the college curriculum in high school, more likely to earn a diploma, and more likely to enter college. We would need controlled experiments to test this theory. Simply comparing the fate of students with similar test scores in different tracks tells us relatively little, since there are probably noncognitive differences between students who get assigned to different tracks.

The same problem arises when we try to assess the impact of high school curriculum assignment on college entrance rates. Project Talent shows, for example, that about 60 percent of the ninth graders who were in college preparatory curriculums in 1960 entered college in 1964, compared to 18 percent of those in other curriculums. But students in the college curriculum came from more affluent families and had higher grades, test scores, and educational aspirations in the ninth grade than those in noncollege curriculums. If we compare students who were at national norms in all these respects, about 44 percent of those who said they were in the college curriculum in ninth grade entered college, compared to 32 percent of those who said they were in other curriculums.[71]

Viewing the issue in a different way, we can divide students into those who would go to college regardless of what curriculum they ended up in, those who would not go regardless of curriculum, and those whose fate depends on which curriculum they enter. The latter group apparently constitutes something like 12 percent of the total high school population, though the exact figure could be anywhere from 5 to 20 percent. This way of formulating our results makes it clear that curriculum assignment is not the main explanation for differences in educational attainment among students in the same high school. Nonetheless, the effect is not trivial. It is similar for both high and low aptitude students.[72]

In light of these findings, one might reasonably expect schools with large college curriculums to send more students to college than schools with similar students and smaller college curriculums. This does not seem to be the case.[73]

Thus it is hard to argue that curriculum assignment influences educational attainment by preparing students for college academically. If that were the case, trying to teach algebra and history to more students ought to increase the proportion who went to college. Nor can we argue that curriculum assignment affects the distribution of school resources. If that were the case, providing the entire school with more resources should make more students attend college.[74] Our findings require a "zero-sum" theory, in which assigning an individual to the college curriculum gives him an advantage relative to his classmates, but assigning more students to the college curriculum does not increase the overall level of well-being. The most plausible theory is that assigning a student to the college curriculum is like giving him a high grade: it tells the student that he is going to go farther than his classmates, but it does not tell him how far. Schools cannot convince all their students that they will "get ahead," because teachers cannot believe this and neither can the students. Students can, however, believe that they are going to get ahead if they can see that someone else is going to get left behind. This means that if a few students are assigned to a college curriculum they see themselves as an elite and react accordingly. If more students are assigned to the college curriculum, the significance of the distinction diminishes. If everyone is assigned to the college curriculum, the distinction loses its meaning entirely, as an "A" loses its meaning when everyone gets one.

## Conclusions about Educational Attainment

This chapter has investigated the reasons why some people end up with more impressive educational credentials than others. We have shown that the most important determinant of educational attainment is family background. The impact of family background is accounted for partly by measurable economic differences between families and partly by more elusive noneconomic differences. Except for family background, the most important determinant of educational attainment is probably cognitive skill. The precise effect of cognitive skill is hard to determine, however, since we do not know to what extent test scores are a proxy for unmeasured, noncognitive differences between home environments. Race now seems to affect educational attainment almost entirely by affecting test scores and aspirations.

Qualitative differences between high schools seem to explain about 2 percent of the variation in students' educational attainment. Unfortunately, we cannot say what qualities of a high school boost its college entrance rates and what qualities lower it. School resources do not appear to influence students' educational attainments at all. Attending high school with bright, highly motivated classmates seems to have both positive and negative effects on a student's chances of attending college. The curriculum to which a student is assigned is the one measurable factor that influences attainment, and it explains differences within rather than between schools.

What are the policy implications of all this? The answer is not that "nothing matters." It is true that making high schools more alike would have a negligible effect on the distribution of credentials. But if colleges altered their criteria for admitting students and awarding degrees, some groups would gain and some would lose. This is why there is now so much political pressure to alter admissions procedures in various ways.

Suppose, for example, that America adopted a certification system based entirely on standardized tests of the kind now used in college admissions. Such a system would benefit white working-class children and reduce the advantage now enjoyed by white middle-class children by about a third.[75] But while such a system would benefit poor whites, it would not benefit blacks. Blacks now seem to get slightly more education than whites with comparable test scores. They would lose this advantage if test scores were the sole basis for awarding diplomas and degrees.[76]

A system in which credentials were distributed entirely on the basis of grades, and in which standardized tests played no part, would improve the position of working-class students and reduce the advantage of the middle classes even more than a system based entirely on test scores.[77] This may be one reason why admission to public colleges has traditionally depended largely on high school grades, while private colleges have usually weighted grades and test scores about equally.

A system in which all students end up with as much education as they think they can stand would have less predictable effects. Suppose all education were free and no institution had admission or graduation requirements. If we judge by the amount of schooling people now say they would like, the relative advantage of middle-class over working-class students would not decline at all.[78] A system which gave everyone as much education as he wanted would, however, slightly reduce the correlation between educational attainment and cognitive skill.[79] If aspirations remained unchanged, then, and credentials remained equally valuable, such a system would create an elite no less hereditary, but slightly less clever than the present elite. If aspirations *did* change, the consequences might be more appealing.

Without some evidence about the way in which society would operate if credentials were distributed on a different basis, we cannot really choose among these alternatives. If cognitive skills are important for on-the-job success, for example, a credentialing system which ignores cognitive skills will not work. If competence depends mainly on non-cognitive traits, a drastic change in the present system may be more feasible. We turn to these issues in the next chapter.

# NOTES

1. In technical terms, we are assuming that the effects of educational attainment are linear. In the NORC veterans sample, the correlation between education and income for whites aged 25 to 34 is 0.387, while *eta* is 0.416, using 8 categories of educational attainment. For education and occupational status, $r = 0.609$ and *eta* is 0.649. Blau and Duncan, in *The American Occupational Structure,* also investigated nonlinearity in the relationship between years of schooling and occupational status. They found minor deviations. Census data on the relationship between education and income also shows rather small deviations from linearity. The estimated reduction of efficiency in prediction cited in the text is based on the difference between $0.649^2$ and $0.609^2$, and between $0.416^2$ and $0.387^2$.

2. For some relevant data on colleges see Havemann and West, *They Went to College,* and Daniere, "Social Class Competition." Reed and Miller, in "Variation in Earnings," using Census data on earnings, found that field of specialization explained 4.0 percent of the variance in a B.A.s earnings and 7.2 percent of the variance in earnings for men with graduate degrees, with-

out IQ controls. With IQ controls, it would be slightly less. Similarly, they found that an index of college academic selectivity derived from Project Talent explained 4.2 percent of the variance in earnings among B.A.s and 4.8 percent among men with higher degrees. Again, we must assume that the relationship would be weaker if we controlled individual IQ or some equivalent. Qualitative differences among high schools seem unlikely to have much direct effect on earnings, over and above effects on test scores and college entrance rates. Overall, then, differences in institutional prestige and program probably explain less than 4 percent of the earnings variance.

3. Appendix B estimates the true correlation for white, nonfarm males at 0.485. Including blacks and farm-born whites raises the observed correlation by about 0.02. We do not have data on father's occupation and the educational attainment of daughters. The correlation between father's occupation (very poorly classified) and a ninth grader's chance of entering college is 0.30 for males and 0.32 for females, using our sample of 95 white and nonwhite Project Talent schools. This suggests that the overall correlation for daughters is very close to that for sons. Claudy, in "Educational Outcomes," also found almost identical relationships between educational attainment and Project Talent's global measure of family background for girls and boys. In contrast, Table 12 in the U.S. Bureau of the Census, "Factors Related to College Attendance: 1960," implies correlations between father's occupation and a twelfth grader's chances of attending college of about 0.28 for males and 0.40 for females. (This estimate is based on a dichotomous, white-collar/blue-collar status measure.) This implies a higher overall correlation for daughters than for sons. Since the bulk of the evidence suggests very minor differences in correlations between the sexes, we will use 0.49 for whites of both sexes.

4. Tables 7 and 8 of the U.S. Bureau of the Census, "Factors Related to High School Graduation: 1967," suggest that the observed correlation between parental income (as reported by the parents) and a child's chances of attending college is very close to the observed correlation between father's education (as reported by the parents) and a child's college chances. Since self-reports on income are slightly less reliable than self-reports on education, we assume the true correlation between parental income and a child's educational attainment is slightly higher than the true correlation between father's education and a child's education. We will use a value of 0.44 for the correlation between parental income and white, nonfarm males' educational attainment ($r = 0.426$ for fathers' and sons' education, as shown in Appendix B, Table B–2). The estimated true correlation between fathers' occupation and sons' attainment for white, nonfarm males is 0.485 (see Appendix B, Table B–2). The observed correlation between occupational status and self-reports of individual income is also about 0.44 for men of parental age (see p. 51 of Duncan et al., *Socioeconomic Background*). Correcting for measurement error, we obtain a true correlation between occupation and individual income of 0.485. The correlation between a man's occupation and his family income is likely to be lower—let us say 0.40. The multiple correlation between a child's educational attainment and the family's economic status then turns out to be 0.55 for white, nonfarm males. The

value might be slightly higher if we included farm-born males, nonwhites, and females.

5. See Blau and Duncan, *The American Occupational Structure.* Their data covers only father's occupation and father's education, not parental income. But since the influences of father's occupation and education are stable, the same is likely to be true of parental income.

6. We assume that the extreme fifths average 1.4 standard deviations from the mean on our economic index. A correlation of 0.55 implies that the children average $(1.4)(0.55) = 0.77$ standard deviations from the mean on educational attainment. This is the seventy-ninth or twenty-second percentile. It implies that the extreme fifths average $(0.77)(2.80) = 2.16$ years from the mean.

7. The paths in Appendix B, Figure B–7, imply that the genetic impact of a father's occupation on a son's IQ is between $(0.707)(0.161)$ and $(0.707)(0.144)$, i.e. about 0.107. Since the correlation is taken to be 0.357, about $0.107/0.357 = 30$ percent is genetic. Since 30 percent of the overall relationship between parental status and a son's attainment is due to IQ, and since 30 percent of this is genetic, 9 percent of the total is genetic. These calculations ignore the possible effects of other unmeasured background factors. A comparison of Figure B–2 and Figure B–7 (Appendix B) shows that including unmeasured background characteristics in an analytic model lowers the implied effect of IQ on educational attainment. This in turn lowers the implied effect of genes on attainment.

8. Using a 3 variable model in which a father's occupation influences both his son's IQ and his son's educational attainment, and in which a son's IQ also influences his educational attainment directly, we can decompose the effect of IQ on attainment into "direct" and "indirect" effects. The indirect effects are those that operate through IQ. Using the correlations in Appendix B, Table B–2, the total effect is 0.485, the direct effect is 0.319, and the indirect effect is 0.166. Project Talent's 1-year follow-up data yields lower correlations but a similar ratio of direct to indirect effects. Including income as well as father's occupation raises the direct effects more than the indirect effects. The Wisconsin data presented by Sewell et al. in "Educational and Early Occupational Status" suggests that test scores explain 28 percent of the gap between upper-middle and lower-class twelfth graders' eventual levels of attainment.

9. See, for example, Panos and Astin, "Attrition Among College Students." In this study, about a fifth of the college dropouts said they could not afford to continue. This is fairly typical. The precise percentage varies from one study to another, according to the sample and how the question is phrased.

10. The relationship between family income and attainment was discussed in the text and in note 4, but family income is not a good measure of a student's financial resources. Lansing et al., in *How People Pay for College,* found that family income correlated only 0.3 with what parents spent on their children's college education. The data on students with jobs were estimated from Tables B–1 to B–4 of Astin's "College Dropouts." Astin found that whether students dropped out was only sporadically related to whether

they said that their parents were their principal source of support. Holding a job had a more consistent negative effect. In both cases, the correlations were 0.10 or less. Parental income had no effect.

The effect of parental income on high school attrition seems to be small. (See U.S. Bureau of the Census, "Factors Related to High School Graduation: 1967.") The direct effect of parental income on college entrance rates is probably larger.

11. See Sewell et al., "Educational and Early Occupational Status." The data cover a large representative sample of 1957 Wisconsin high school seniors. The correlation between aptitude and grades is 0.59. The correlation between aptitude and father's economic status is 0.29. The correlation between grades and father's economic status is 0.19. This means that if 2 students have the same test scores and differ by 1 standard deviation in background, their grades will differ by 0.03 standard deviations. In Project Talent, where students reported their own grades, the correlation between grades and SES, after controlling test scores, is zero. Heyns, in "Curriculum Assignment," obtained similar results in northern urban EEOS high schools.

12. In our 91 Project Talent schools, the Project Talent composite measure of an individual's socio-economic background correlates 0.456 with the amount of education an individual expects to get in ninth grade, 0.442 with educational attainment at age 23, and 0.432 with projected eventual attainment. While Project Talent did not ask students how much schooling they wanted, EEOS did. Heyns, in "'Curriculum Assignment," found a correlation of 0.307 between father's education (as distinct from overall socio-economic status) and the amount of education twelfth graders *wanted* in 48 northern urban EEOS high schools. She found a correlation of 0.339 between father's education and the amount of education twelfth graders *expected* to get in northern urban Project Talent high schools. The two variables also have almost identical correlations with verbal ability (0.464 *v.* 0.471). We will therefore treat preferences and expectations as interchangeable, and will use the general term "aspirations" for both.

13. See Sewell et al., "Educational and Early Occupational Status." Unfortunately, we do not know how much relationship there is between students' perceptions of what their parents want and what the parents actually want. To some unknown extent, students' perceptions of what their parents want are probably projections of what they themselves want, for whatever reasons. Working-class parents' hopes for their children may well be higher than their children say they are.

14. See Sewell et al., "Educational and Early Occupational Status," and sources cited there. See also Chapter 6 of this volume.

15. See "The Effects of Educational Credentials" in Chapter 6.

16. This improvement is partly attributable to the fact that educational inequality in general has diminished. But even in relative terms, blacks are better off than they used to be. Table 2–1 (in this volume) shows that the average black born at the turn of the century ended up 0.75 standard deviations below the national average, whereas the average black born during World War II ended up 0.43 standard deviations below the national average.

It should be noted that because of the large percentage of both blacks and whites who have exactly 8 or 12 years of education, percentile comparisons between the 2 distributions can be very misleading. Among blacks born at the turn of the century, for example, 14.9 percent exceeded the white median (i.e. 8 years). Among those born during World War II, 15.7 percent exceeded the white median (i.e. 12 years). This suggests little improvement. But in the later period another 40.1 percent of all blacks were just below the white median since they had 12 years of schooling and the median was 12.6. This was not true in the earlier period.

These caveats also apply to differences between medians. Table 2–1 (Chapter 2) shows that the behavior of the median was not parallel to the behavior of the mean. Because large numbers of individuals received exactly 8 years of schooling in the earlier period and exactly 12 years of schooling in the later period, large increases in mean attainment often did not alter the median much.

Interpretation of Census education statistics would be greatly facilitated by the publication of means as well as medians—a practice recently adopted for Census income statistics.

17. The U.S. Bureau of the Census, in "The Social and Economic Status of Negroes: 1970," estimates that in 1965 there were more blacks in predominantly black colleges than in predominantly white colleges. By 1968, blacks in predominantly white colleges outnumbered blacks in predominantly black colleges 2 to 1. By 1970, the ratio was almost 3 to 1. This was due to an increase in black enrollment in traditionally white colleges, not to a decline in black enrollment in black colleges.

18. Walster et al., in "Effect of Race and Sex," created a series of imaginary applicants, who differed only on race and sex. They sent applications from these students to 240 representative colleges in 1969. Applicants were turned down slightly more often when they were described as black than when they were described as white, everything else being equal. This was as true in the North as in the South. The probability of the observed difference occuring by chance in a sample of 240 colleges was 0.06.

19. The U.S. Bureau of the Census, in "School Enrollment: 1970," shows that the proportion of blacks between the ages of 18 and 24 who were enrolled in colleges rose from 10 percent in 1965 to 16 percent in 1970. For whites the comparable percentages were 26 in 1965 and 27 in 1970. This improvement in black college enrollment was partly a matter of blacks spending longer in school and college. But at least half the improvement was simply a matter of their moving through school and college more rapidly. There was, for example, no net increase between 1965 and 1970 in the percentage of black 18 and 19 year olds who were in some kind of school. There was simply a decline in the percentage who were in high school and an increase in the percentage who were in college. This may imply an extension of automatic promotion to the college level.

20. Duncan, in "Discrimination against Negroes," shows that for males born between 1925 and 1935, the expected gap on the basis of background differences was 0.9 to 1.2 years, while the actual gap was 2.0 years. Including women, as we do in Table 2–1 of Chapter 2, would not appreciably

alter the expected gap, but it lowers the actual gap. Moving forward to the cohort born between 1940 and 1944 reduces the expected gap a little, but it reduces the observed gap much more. The U.S. Bureau of the Census, in "Educational Attainment: 1969," shows that mean educational attainment for blacks born between 1915 and 1924 was 8.7 years, versus 11.1 for whites. Because of fertility differences, the mean difference between black and white parents was even larger. This difference is, thus, at least 0.75 standard deviations. Assuming those born between 1915 and 1924 are similar to the parents of those born between 1940 and 1944, the expected difference in attainment for the latter group is about $(0.4)(0.75) = 0.30$ standard deviations, or $(0.30)(2.8) = 0.84$ years. Including other background variables would raise this to at least a year.

21. See Chapter 3, "The Effects of Race."

22. Duncan, in "Inheritance of Poverty," found that black men born between 1897 and 1936 received 2.3 years less education than white men born in the same period. He estimated that whites born in these years, with economic backgrounds and test scores comparable to the average black, ended up 2.1 years below the white mean. Duncan inferred that whites had received 0.2 years more schooling than blacks with comparable test scores and family backgrounds. He did not, however, stratify this sample of blacks by age. Black attainment rose faster during the first half of the twentieth century than we would have expected on the basis of changes in parental status or children's test scores. Thus, for males and females born between 1940 and 1944, the observed gap between blacks and whites was only 1.2 years. The predicted gap was, however, still about 2.1 years on the basis of Duncan's regression estimates and Census data on black-white background differences for those born in the 1930s and early 1940s. This suggests that blacks get a year more education than comparable whites.

23. Karpinos, in "Mental Qualification," tabulated educational attainment by $AFQT$ score for national samples of blacks and whites, using Defense Department records. Cutright, in "Achievement, Military Service, and Earnings," also tabulated educational attainment by $AFQT$, using Selective Service System Records for a slightly older cohort. Transforming their percentage distributions into means, we find some discrepancy between the two data sets. Nonetheless, the findings reported in the text hold true in both studies. Karpinos' data is probably more representative. His tables imply that blacks in the lowest 10 percentiles on the $AFQT$ averaged 7.0 years of schooling, while whites who scored at this level averaged 5.8 years. Among men who scored between the tenth and thirtieth percentiles, the blacks averaged 10.2 years, while the whites averaged 9.6 years. For men scoring above the sixty-fifth percentile, the situation was reversed, with whites averaging 12.3 years, while blacks averaged 11.8. But the average black above the sixty-fifth percentile has a lower $AFQT$ score than the average white. Cutright's sample shows the same pattern below the $AFQT$ mean. It includes too few blacks above the mean to make reliable black-white comparisons.

Since these tests are usually administered after school is completed, the differences could theoretically be caused by differences in what blacks and whites learn from the same amount of schooling. The evidence in Chapter 3 suggests, however, that blacks learn about the same amount per year as whites with similar initial scores.

24. The estimates in the text are based on the 91 predominantly white and 4 predominantly black comprehensive Project Talent high schools which returned adequate ninth grade data in 1960 and were retested in 1963. The race of individual students was not determined in either of these surveys, but it was determined in the 1968 5-year follow-up. Only 3.8 percent of the 1968 respondents were black. Blacks were, however, somewhat more adequately represented in a special follow-up of a subsample of initial nonrespondents. After appropriate weighting of these special follow-up cases, blacks constituted 6.2 percent of the sample. This is still inadequate, but less egregiously so. In the unweighted sample, blacks got 1.1 years less schooling than whites; in the weighted sample the gap was 0.96 years. In the unweighted sample blacks got 0.6 years more schooling than whites with similar test scores; in the weighted sample they got 1.2 years more schooling. This suggests that nonresponse leads to an underestimate of blacks' advantage over comparable whites, not to an overestimate. Controlling socio-economic background, family size, region, urbanism, and sex did not appreciably alter these estimates. Controlling the amount of education ninth graders said they expected to get cut the difference to 0.23 years in the unweighted sample and 0.49 years in the weighted sample. Controlling the amount of education twelfth graders expected to get cut the difference to 0.01 years in the unweighted sample and 0.18 years in the weighted sample. This suggests that differences in test scores and aspirations account for almost all the difference in educational attainment between blacks and whites, but that their effects partly cancel each other. There is no evidence that explicitly racial discrimination by colleges either lowers or raises black attainment to an appreciable extent, since race has an insignificant coefficient once scores and aspirations are controlled.

These inferences were also tested on eleventh graders in these same 95 schools. In this cohort, blacks constituted 2.5 percent of the unweighted sample and 6.9 percent of the weighted sample. The students in question graduated from high school in 1961 rather than 1963, and were resurveyed in 1966. This means their educational attainment was not appreciably influenced by colleges' recruitment of blacks during the late 1960s. In the unweighted sample, blacks got 1.2 years less schooling than whites; in the weighted sample, they got 1.0 years less schooling than whites. But blacks then got 0.3 years more schooling than whites with comparable test scores, in both the unweighted and weighted samples. Controlling socio-economic background increased the apparent advantage of these blacks, in a way that it did not for those born two years later. The difference between the samples could, however, be due to chance. Controlling the amount of education students expected to receive when they were in the eleventh grade reduced the blacks' advantage to 0.18 years in the weighted sample and 0.05 years in the unweighted sample. These differences are so small they could easily occur by chance. We again conclude that aspirations and test scores account for the entire observed difference between black and white attainment.

There does not seem to be any evidence that explicitly racial discrimination affected black attainment at the college level even in the early 1960s. It may, of course, have affected the kinds of colleges blacks attended.

25. On black aspirations see, for example, Wilson, "Educational Consequences," Armor, "Racial Composition," and Heyns, "Curriculum Assignment." On the relationship of black aspirations to attainment, see note 24. If blacks "overaspired," the coefficient of race would be negative once aspirations and test scores were controlled. It is not.

26. The estimate is derived from Appendix B, Figure B–7. The variance explained by *EF-ED* and *EF-IQ* is $q^2 + 2qmip + i^2p^2$. This takes on values ranging from 0.466 if $m = 1$ to 0.423 if $m = 0.50$.

27. See Appendix B, Figure B–7. Father's occupation "explains" between $0.595^2 = 35$ percent and $0.669^2 = 45$ percent of the variance in the effects of family background (*EF-ED*). Income explains perhaps another 15 percent. This leaves 40 to 50 percent unexplained.

28. See Appendix B, Table B–2. These estimates are corrected for measurement error. Using Project Talent's weighted ninth grade sample for 95 schools, a composite measure of socio-economic background correlated 0.45 with attainment 8 years later while a composite achievement score correlated 0.58. The correlations for eleventh graders in the same schools, followed up 6 years later, were 0.40 for socio-economic status and 0.50 for a slightly different achievement score composite.

29. Approximated by comparing the correlation between *IQ-11* and *ED* in Appendix B, Table B–2, to the path coefficient from *IQ-11* to *ED* in Appendix B, Figure B–2. (The effect of controlling father's education in Figure B–2 is roughly comparable to the effect of controlling family income —see note 4.) The data from both Project Talent and Sewell et al., in "Educational and Early Occupational Status," imply that controlling economic status reduces the apparent effect of test scores by about 25 percent.

30. See Appendix B, Figure B–7. The path from *IQ-11* to *ED* ranges from 0.227 to 0.415. Since the standard deviation of attainment for this cohort is 2.8 years, the expected difference between brothers (i.e. the difference holding *EF-ED* constant) is between $(2.8)(0.227) = 0.64$ years and $(2.8)(0.415) = 1.16$ years.

31. See Appendix B, Figure B–7. The explained variance is $h^2p^2$, which has values between 0.026 and 0.086.

32. Derived from Appendix B, Figure B–7, on the following assumptions: (1) the standard deviation of educational attainment is now about 2.80 years, and (2) the gap between the most genetically advantaged fifth and the most genetically disadvantaged fifth is 2.8 standard deviations. This yields estimated differences in attainment of $(2.80)(0.707)(0.227)(2.8) = 1.3$ to $(2.80)(0.707)(0.415)(2.8) = 2.3$ years. If we have overestimated $h$ in Figure B–7, the difference could be even less. If we have underestimated $h$, the difference could be more.

33. Appendix B, Table B–2, estimates the true correlation at 0.58. The pre-World War II local studies cited in Appendix B yield correlations between 0.50 and 0.60 for elementary school scores and attainment. In Project Talent, for a national sample of 1960 ninth graders, the observed value

of the weighted multiple correlation of scores on vocabulary, social studies, reading, and arithmetic with attainment 5 years after high school was 0.58. The correlation with sixth grade scores is unknown. The correlation with twelfth grade scores is identical to that with ninth grade scores once dropouts are eliminated.

Sewell et al., in "The Educational and Early Occupational Status," report an observed correlation of 0.49 between eleventh grade Henmon-Nelson IQ scores and educational attainment of 1957 Wisconsin high school graduates. Had they included nongraduates in their sample, their "true" correlation would probably also have approached 0.58.

34. Using the correlation matrices in Sewell et al., "Educational and Early Occupational Status," the correlation between test scores and attainment is 0.486, while the standardized partial regression coefficient after controlling grades is 0.261. The partial regression coefficient of test scores controlling SES is 0.399. This falls to 0.184 when grades are also controlled.

35. There are two alternative causal models for estimating the effects of curriculum placement. Model I assumes that placement is causally prior to aspirations. Applying this model to our 91 white Project Talent high schools, we regress twelfth grade curriculum on ninth grade test scores, SES, region, urbanism, family size, and sex, and obtain a path of 0.382 from test scores to curriculum. We then regress a student's chances of entering a 4-year college on his or her twelfth grade curriculum, ninth grade test scores, SES, region, urbanism, family size, and sex. The path from curriculum to college chances is 0.401. The compound path from test scores to college chances via curriculum is thus $(0.382)(0.401) = 0.153$. The zero-order correlation is 0.477, so curriculum assignment explains $0.153/0.477 = 32$ percent of the relationship.

Model II assumes that ninth grade scores influence aspirations, which then influence placement. In this model we therefore control ninth grade aspirations in estimating the relevant paths. The path from achievement to twelfth grade curriculum is then 0.232, while the path from curriculum to college chances is 0.338. The compound path is thus $(0.338)(0.232)/0.477 = 16.4$ percent of the observed correlation.

36. Based on tabulations from our 91 Project Talent high schools. The control variables were SES, region, sex, curriculum assignment, and whether the student also wanted a graduate degree. The deficiencies in the Project Talent follow-up make the absolute percentages unreliable and may slightly bias the estimated differences.

37. The estimates presented in this chapter are based on true correlations of 0.55 for attainment and economic status and 0.58 for attainment and test scores. The difference when we use observed correlations is even larger (see Claudy, "Educational Outcomes," on the Project Talent 5-year follow-up of ninth graders; Sewell et al., "Educational and Early Occupational Status," on the Wisconsin longitudinal study; and Jencks, "The Effects of High Schools on Their Students," on the Project Talent follow-up of ninth graders). In Project Talent, the measures of parental economic status probably contain more error than the measures of academic aptitude. This is less likely in Sewell et al., "Educational and

Early Occupational Status." It would, however, also be easy to construct an a priori argument for believing that economic inequality had less effect on college attendance in Wisconsin than in, say, Massachusetts or Mississippi.

38. See Appendix B, pp. 325–327.

39. The U.S. Bureau of the Census, in "Educational Attainment:1969," shows that for those born between 1940 and 1944, *who entered high school,* the standard deviation of educational attainment was 2.54 years. For reasons given below, we assume that about 12 percent of the variance is between schools. The standard deviation of high school means is thus about $(2.54)\sqrt{0.12} = 0.88$ years, while the within-school standard deviation is about $(2.54)\sqrt{0.88} = 2.38$ years. The difference between top and bottom fifths is taken as 2.8 standard deviations.

The 12 percent estimate for attainment variance between high school is a compromise between several sources. First, we looked at principals' reports of dropout and college entrance rates. Both Project Talent and EEOS asked principals the percentage of their tenth graders who eventually graduated from high school and the percentage of their graduates who entered college. We combined these two items to create a single index of the percentage of tenth graders who entered college. For our supposedly representative subsample of 95 Project Talent high schools, the weighted mean was 30.1 percent. The standard deviation of this percentage is 14.7. Five years later EEOS obtained a weighted mean of 40.6 percent with a standard deviation of 18.5 percent. Since this is a dichotomous variable, we can also infer the individual level standard deviations from the weighted mean, i.e. $\sqrt{(0.301)(1-0.301)} = 0.458$ for Project Talent, and approximately $\sqrt{(0.406)(1-0.406)} = 0.492$ for EEOS. The Project Talent figures thus imply that $(0.147^2/0.458^2) = 10.3$ percent of the variance between schools, while EEOS figures imply 14.1 percent.

To check these estimates, we also calculated the percentage of variance between schools in individual reports of actual attainment. Using Project Talent's 1-year follow-up data, we found 10.1 percent of the variance in educational attainment between high schools. The percentage was similar using unweighted 5-year follow-up data. Using weighted 5-year follow-up data, the percentage of variance between schools rose to about 20 percent. This appears, however, to be an artifact of the highly unequal weights and the fact that many Project Talent high schools were very small.

40. In both Project Talent and EEOS, we first estimated mean educational attainment for each school from principals' reports of dropout rates, entrance rates for 4-year colleges, and entrance rates for other kinds of postsecondary school training programs. In EEOS, 14.1 percent of the total variance is between schools. A regression equation based on the socio-economic composition of the school, the mean educational aspirations of the ninth graders, and region explains 45.6 percent of the between-school variance. Mean test score in ninth grade added almost nothing. The unexplained between-school variance in EEOS is thus 7.7 percent of the total. In Project Talent, 10.3 percent of the variance is between schools, and a similar regression equation explains 45.0 percent of the between-school

variance. This leaves 5.7 percent of the total variance unexplained and between schools.

We suspected, however, that there was probably a good deal of measurement error in principals' responses. We therefore turned to data obtained by Project Talent directly from students 1 year after they would normally have finished high school. In the 91 Project Talent high schools which (1) retested ninth graders in the twelfth grade, (2) were not vocational schools, and (3) were more than 75 percent white, 10.1 percent of the variance was between schools. Each student's eventual educational attainment was predicted on the basis of the average within school regression equation, using ninth grade test scores, aspirations, socio-economic background, sex, and family size as independent variables. The difference between each student's predicted and actual attainment was then calculated and averaged across schools. The variance of the mean residuals was 3.4 percent of the variance of individual educational attainment. (This is roughly equivalent to saying that the mean within-school regression of educational attainment on ninth grade test scores, aspirations, and socio-economic status explained 66.3 percent of the between-school variance in attainment.) The difference between this and the 45.0 percent, explained when we used principals' responses, is presumably due to random error in principals' responses.

"School effects" cannot, then, increase the total variance more than 3.4 percent. Furthermore, some of these "school effects" are almost certainly due to random fluctuations from one year to the next in the percentage of students staying in school and entering college. We estimated the magnitude of such random fluctuations in two ways.

One way to estimate random fluctuations is to note that the within-school regression equation explained only 41.4 percent of the variance in individual attainment, and that the average school enrolled only 45 students with follow-up data. We therefore expect roughly $(100-41.4)/45 = 1.3$ percent of the total variance to be between schools, simply as a result of chance. This suggests that only $3.4 - 1.3 = 2.1$ percent of the total variance is between schools and nonrandom.

Another way of estimating the amount of random error is to examine the correlation between residuals for different subgroups within a school. We computed such correlations for males and females, for students with high and low ninth grade test scores, for students with high and low grades in eighth grade, for students with high and low aspirations, for students in college and noncollege programs, and for students from high- and low-status homes. The correlations between residuals for nonoverlapping groups range from 0.500 to 0.296. The mean correlation is 0.375. There is no evidence of systematic interactions. We can therefore treat this as a split-half correlation and make the usual Spearman-Brown correction. The implied reliability of the mean residual for all students is then $(2)(0.375)/(1 + 0.375) = 0.545$. This is the estimated correlation between mean residuals in successive years for these schools, assuming no change in the character of the schools or the population served. It implies that 54.5 percent of the unexplained between-school variance is nonrandom. This amounts to $(0.545)$

(3.4) = 1.9 percent of the total. This is slightly less than the 2.1 percent estimate using our alternative method.

There are several possible technical explanations for the discrepancy between our two methods of estimating the nonrandom, unexplained between-school variance. The actual size of the discrepancy is trivial, however. As a compromise, we will assume that "high school effects" explain 2.0 percent of the total attainment variance. The standard deviation of high school effects is thus $\sqrt{0.02} = 14.1$ percent of the individual standard deviation. This is $(.141)(2.56) = 0.36$ years for students who enter high school. The difference between top and bottom quintiles is, then, $(2.8)(0.36) = 1.0$ years.

Since 38 percent of Project Talent ninth graders who returned questionnaires 4 years later say they are in college, the standard deviation of college chances is $\sqrt{(0.38)(1 - 0.38)} = 0.485$. The standard deviation of school effects on college chances is thus $(0.141)(0.485) = 6.8$ percent. Given a random sample of entrants, the most effective fifth of all high schools would send about $38 + (1.4)(6.8) = 48$ percent of its students to college, while the least effective fifth would send 28 percent. For reasons explained in more detail by Jencks in "The Effects of High Schools," this is likely to be an overestimate of the actual difference.

41. These rankings were based on the difference between observed mean test scores and predicted mean score, using the percent white, the mean socio-economic level of sixth graders, and region as independent variables. For a detailed description of the sample and the predictive equations see Jencks, "The Coleman Report."

42. The mean percentage of tenth graders entering college from these schools was 40.9 with a standard deviation of 20.4, using unweighted data. The mean attainment residuals for verbal, reading, and math scores in the associated sixth grades explained 1.2 percent of the variance in college entrance rates. No controls altered this coefficient. The coefficient is based on math residuals. The reading and verbal residuals do not enter the equation. None of the relationships is statistically significant. The estimated disparity between the most and least effective fifths is $(2.8)(\sqrt{0.012})(20.4) = 6.3$ percent. This would be smaller if we weighted by school size.

43. If 12 percent of the variance in attainment for those who reach ninth grade is between high schools, and if elementary schools explain 1.2 percent of the between-high school variance, then elementary schools explain 0.144 percent of the total variance. The standard deviation of elementary school effects is, then, $\sqrt{0.00144} = 3.8$ percent of the overall standard deviation, i.e. $(0.038)(2.56) = 0.10$ years.

44. In the EEOS data just described, 61 percent of the variance in mean verbal score residuals was between high school feeder systems. This leaves 39 percent of the variance in elementary school effects within the same high school.

45. Assume that the standard deviation of educational attainment for elementary school graduates is 2.8 years (see Chapter 2, Table 2–1). Assume that the effect of attending the top fifth of all elementary schools is to raise test scores 0.33 to 0.67 standard deviations higher than if one attends the

bottom fifth (see Chapter 3, "Differences between Schools"). Assume that the path from sixth grade test scores to educational attainment is between 0.415 and 0.227 (see Appendix B, Figure B–7). The maximum attainment gap between the top and bottom fifths of elementary schools is, then, $(0.67)(0.415)(2.8) = 0.78$ years, while the minimum gap is $(0.33)(0.227)$ $(2.8) = 0.21$ years. The gap could, of course, be larger if elementary schools that boosted test scores also boosted motivation and aspirations. This is not the case with high schools, however. In Project Talent, the correlation between mean residual attainment and mean residual tests scores average 0.00. The correlation between test score gains for individual students between ninth and twelfth grades and students' eventual attainment is also 0.00. In EEOS, the correlation between test score and attainment residuals for schools is 0.25 in the urban North.

46. EEOS collected data on sixth graders' educational aspirations, but we have no basis for estimating the stability or meaning of the responses.

47. In EEOS, the correlation between mean sixth grade achievement scores and mean sixth grade aspirations is almost entirely explained by their both being correlated with mean socio-economic composition.

48. See Chapter 3, note 100.

49. Note 45 estimates a difference of 0.78 to 0.21 years between the top and the bottom fifths of elementary schools, implying a standard deviation of school effects between $0.78/2.8 = 0.28$ and $0.21/2.8 = 0.08$ years. Note 40 estimates the standard deviation of high school effects at 0.36 years. If the two are uncorrelated, the maximum overall standard deviation is $\sqrt{0.28^2 + 0.36^2} = 0.46$ years.

50. The educational attainment residuals (see note 40) correlate $-0.192$ with system-wide expenditure per pupil, $-0.203$ with high school expenditure per pupil, $-0.121$ with average teacher salary, and 0.215 with class size. The correlations are based on a sample of 91 schools and 4,208 pupils, with each school weighted by the number of pupils. Simple tests of statistical significance are inapplicable to weighted samples. Using an unweighted sample, however, the correlations are even larger. The negative correlation with expenditure per pupil is significant at the 0.01 level in the unweighted sample. Nonetheless, we assume it is spurious.

51. The correlation between the mean residual for educational attainment (see note 40) and the presence of one or more counselors is $-0.148$. After eliminating measurement error in the residual, this correlation becomes roughly $-0.148/\sqrt{0.545} = -0.200$. The standard deviation of this dichotomous counselor variable is 0.326. The presumed standard deviation of high schools' effects on attainment is 0.36 years (see note 40). The effect of having a counselor is thus $(-0.200)(0.36)/(0.326) = -0.23$ years. (The observed effect is less, since the observed standard deviation was only 1.46 years at the time of the 1-year follow-up.) No other school characteristics were controlled, since the observed relationships between school characteristics and attainment all seemed random anyway.

52. Details of this analysis are reported in Jencks, "The Effects of High Schools on Their Students."

53. Estimated from Garms, "A Benefit-Cost Analysis."

54. On college aspirations see, for example, Wilson, "Residential Segregation"; Haller and Butterworth, "Peer Influences"; Rogoff, "Local Social Structure"; Michael, "High School Climates"; McDill and Coleman, "High School Social Status"; Herriott, "Social Determinants"; Alexander and Campbell, "Peer Influences"; Turner, *The Social Context of Ambition;* Krauss, "Sources of Educational Aspirations"; Boyle, "The Effect of the High School;" McDill et al., "Institutional Effects"; and McPartland, "The Segregated Student." On high school dropouts see Rhodes, "Dropouts," but compare Nam et al., "School Rentention."

55. See Sewell and Armer," "Neighborhood Context," and Hauser, "Stratification Process," See also, the controversy generated by Sewell and Armer's work in the October 1966 issue of the *American Sociological Review.*

56. See Riley and Cohen, "Comparison or Conformity."

57. College entrance rates were estimated from principals' reports. The socio-economic classification was based on data supplied by ninth grade students.

58. In an unweighted analysis of our 91 high schools, the mean educational attainment residual (see note 40) correlated $-0.17$ with the mean socio-economic status of ninth graders (based on Project Talent's composite index of socio-economic status). In weighted analyses, the correlation drops to $-0.10$ or $-0.06$, depending on the weights used. The weighted correlations are probably statistically insignificant. The unweighted correlation approaches significance.

59. For empirical evidence to support this assumption, see Campbell and Alexander, "Structural Effects"; Erickson, "Normative Influence"; and Duncan et al., "Peer Influences."

60. When the mean educational attainment residual (see note 40) is used as a dependent variable, the standardized regression coefficient of mean aspirations is 0.258, controlling mean vocabulary. The standardized regression coefficient of mean vocabulary in this same equation is $-0.382$. When we estimate the coefficients for mean vocabulary and mean SES, they are even larger ($-0.553$ and $0.397$ respectively, in an equation using these 2 variables to predict the mean educational attainment residual). These coefficients have very high standard errors, however, and they fluctuate a great deal when the weighting system is changed. The analysis is, therefore, only suggestive.

61. See Meyer, "High School Effects."

62. See Davis, "The Campus As a Frog Pond." Davis is responsible for the introduction of the "frog pond" metaphor into this line of research. It is interesting to speculate about why sociologists talk about frog ponds, when the metaphor in common usage involves big *fish* in little ponds, and vice versa. We are inclined to favor the fish metaphor, since the variance in the size of both fish and fish ponds is greater than that for frogs. This should produce more reliable estimates. As far as we know, however, no empirical studies of this have been done. The results might be different if we compared fish only to other fish of their own species, rather than to fish in general. It is possible that the coefficient of variation for the size of, say,

small-mouth bass is less than that for frogs. Additional research seems needed here, since regional interactions may be important.

63. See Chapter 3, "The Effects of Segregation."

64. See, however, Lindsay and Gottlieb, "High School Racial Composition," and St. John and Smith, "School Racial Composition."

65. For analyses of EEOS data on aspirations, see Armor, "Racial Composition of Schools," and McPartland, "The Segregated Student."

66. See Riley and Cohen, "Comparison or Conformity," for a summary of the results in the text. Armor, also using EEOS data, found that lower-class black males had higher aspirations in white than in black schools, but that black females often had lower aspirations. McPartland concentrated on the effects of racially-mixed classrooms. This makes his findings hard to interpret, since blacks with high aspirations are more likely to be in fast classes of various kinds, and these in turn are likely to have disproportionately large numbers of whites in them.

67. For data supporting these generalizations, see Chapter 3, "The Effects of Race," as well as the section on "The Effects of Race" in this chapter, and Heyns, "Curriculum Assignment."

68. This may, of course, only mean that principals in predominantly black schools overstate the percentage of blacks attending college, while principals in predominantly white schools understate it.

69. See Crain, "School Integration and Academic Achievement."

70. See Armor, "The Evidence on Busing." Armor's data cover only 32 bused and 16 control students, so it would be a mistake to draw any general conclusions from it. Recent newspaper reports indicate that the advantage of bused students over their siblings has persisted for subsequent cohorts, but no details are available.

71. Of the ninth graders who were located 4 years later, 38.3 percent had entered a 4-year college. We regressed a dichotomous variable (enrolled in a 4-year college in 1964 or not enrolled) on 7 independent variables: region, sex, a family background index, ninth grade test scores, grades in eighth grade, educational aspirations in ninth grade, and a dichotomous variable representing whether the student had said he was in a college preparatory curriculum or some other curriculum in the ninth grade. The unstandardized coefficient of the curriculum variable was 0.120. A similar analysis of students who were in junior high schools in ninth grade yielded a coefficient of 0.09 for the curriculum they said they were in. Students' descriptions of their curriculum may simply be another measure of whether they plan to attend college.

Thus, we cannot be sure whether the 12 percent difference is really caused by being in the college curriculum. The true effect could be less, if curriculum reports are a proxy for unmeasured differences in aspirations, or it could be an underestimate, if curriculum assignment had influenced aspirations. If we do not control aspirations, the coefficient of ninth grade curriculum rises to 0.217. This corresponds to a 21.7 percent difference in the proportions of college entrants from the two sorts of curriculum, other things being equal.

72. Jencks, in "The Effects of High Schools," conducted separate analyses

for students with high and low ninth grade scores and for students from high- and low-status families. The coefficient for curriculum assignment did not show statistically significant variations from one analysis to another.

73. In Project Talent, the correlation between the mean educational attainment residual and the percentage of ninth graders who said they were in the college curriculum was −0.03. In an EEOS national sample of 584 high schools, the partial correlation between the percentage of ninth graders who said they were in the college curriculum and the estimated educational attainment of the students was 0.02 after controlling mean ninth grade socio-economic status, and −0.02 after adding mean ninth grade aspirations and region (see Jencks, "The Effects of High Schools on Their Students").

74. Thus Heyns, in "Curriculum Assignment," shows that students in the college curriculum see counselors more than other students. Yet we have already cited evidence that schools with more counselors do not send more students to college. We must therefore reject the theory that extra counseling time raises college chances in the college curriculum.

75. The section on "The Effects of Economic Background" shows that the multiple correlation between economic status and educational attainment is about 0.55. In Chapter 3, our best estimate was that father's occupation correlated about 0.36 with a child's test scores, and that father's income added almost nothing to the accuracy of our estimates of a child's test scores. The multiple correlation of the two economic measures with test scores is therefore close to 0.36. This means that if educational attainment was based solely on test scores, the correlation between economic background and attainment would fall from 0.55 to around 0.36. This would be a 35 percent reduction.

76. See the section in this chapter on "The Effects of Race" for data on this point.

77. See note 11.

78. See the data in note 12.

79. In the unweighted Project Talent sample, ninth grade test scores correlate 0.546 with attainment at age 23, 0.469 with twelfth grade aspirations, and 0.481 with ninth grade aspirations. This same pattern holds for the Project Talent 5-year follow-up of eleventh graders. In the Wisconsin sample, eleventh grade test scores correlate 0.486 with educational attainment 7 years after high school and 0.418 with educational aspirations in the last year of high school.

# CHAPTER SIX

# Inequality
# in Occupational Status

When we began our research on inequality, we assumed that almost everyone wanted a high-status job, both as an end in itself and as a means to other ends, like wealth, power, and happiness. Our research has forced us to question this assumption. Surveys of high school students do not indicate that the majority want to enter high-status occupations. Perhaps this is because, as we shall see in Chapters 7 and 8, entering a high-status occupation is no guarantee of job satisfaction or even high income. Nonetheless, it is still important to understand why some people end up in high-status occupations while others do not. This chapter will describe the little we know about that question.

Some of the evidence supports traditional liberal assumptions about America. There is a great deal of occupational mobility from one generation to the next. Men who get a lot of education are likely to end up in high-status occupations, even if their fathers worked in low-status occupations. But since family background influences a son's educational attainment, it also influences his occupational status to some extent.

Before describing this evidence in more detail, we will briefly describe what social scientists mean by occupational status, and how they measure it. We will then describe the extent of social mobility, and evaluate the role of educational attainment, test scores, genes, school quality, and race in determining men's eventual occupations. Finally, we will discuss the policy implications of our findings.

## Measuring Occupational Status

An occupation's prestige, relative to other occupations, can be determined from opinion surveys. In 1947, for example, the National Opinion Research Center asked people to look at a list of job titles and say whether they felt that the "general standing" of the occupation was "excellent," "good," "average," "somewhat below average," or "poor." Others have asked the question in other ways, obtaining very similar results.[1]

Ratings derived from such surveys reflect the average person's perceptions and values about occupations. Such perceptions are remarkably uniform throughout American society. Men's judgments are almost indistinguishable from women's; white people's judgments are the same as blacks'; Northerners are the same as Southerners. City residents have pretty much the same ideas as country residents, the educated have the same ideas as the uneducated, the rich have the same ideas as the poor, and the young have the same ideas as the old.[2] People tend to overestimate the prestige of their own occupation, but not by very much.[3] Americans rank occupations in pretty much the same order as people in other industrial societies, although there is more difference between countries than between different groups within the United States.[4] Occupational rankings are also very stable over time. Americans rank the same occupations high and low today as when they were first polled on the question in 1925.[5]

Although different groups rate occupations in much the same way, different individuals often disagree quite sharply about the standing of particular occupations. In the 1947 NORC survey, for example, the percentage distributions of responses for five fairly typical occupations were as follows:

| | Response | | | | | |
|---|---|---|---|---|---|---|
| Occupation | Excellent | Good | Average | Below Average | Poor | Don't Know |
| Physician | 67 | 30 | 3 | 0 | 0 | 0 |
| Author of Novels | 32 | 44 | 19 | 3 | 2 | 9 |
| Undertaker | 14 | 43 | 36 | 5 | 2 | 2 |
| Mail Carrier | 8 | 26 | 54 | 10 | 2 | 0 |
| Bartender | 1 | 6 | 35 | 36 | 31 | 2 |

Using any sensible method for scoring these responses, the five occupations rank in the order shown above. Except for physicians, however, there is considerable disagreement about each occupation.[6] What consensus there is about an occupation's prestige derives largely from two facts. First, most people rank an occupation high if it attracts highly educated workers. Second, most people rank an occupation high if it pays well.[7] People's judgments about an occupation also seem to be influenced by the percentages of blacks and women in it. But these considerations are less important than education and income.[8] Since prestige seems to depend on income and education, social scientists usually estimate an occupation's prestige from Census data on educational requirements and economic rewards, rather than from survey data on prestige itself. We will refer to estimates obtained from Census data as "status" rankings. An occupation's "status" and its prestige are very highly correlated, but they are not identical. Insofar as they differ, occupational status seems to be more important than prestige.[9]

There is no obvious "natural" unit for measuring status, any more than for measuring cognitive skill. The classic measure of occupational status is the "Duncan scale." Duncan used a metric in which the highest score turned out to be 96 points and the lowest was zero. When he calculated status scores for all male workers, he found that the mean was about 40 and that the standard deviation was about 25. The meaning of such a standard deviation is probably easiest to grasp if we compare specific occupations. The distance between an engineer and a librarian, for example, is 25 points. The distance between a doctor and a policeman is 50 points, or two standard deviations. The distance from the top to the bottom is four standard deviations.[10]

We do not know for sure whether status disparities between occupations are increasing, decreasing, or remaining the same. The best way to answer this question is probably to see if the degree of consensus about the prestige of different occupations is increasing or decreasing. If status disparities are declining, we would expect less and less agreement between raters. If status disparities are growing, we would expect more agreement between raters today than in the past. Unfortunately, we do not have exactly comparable data from different points in time, but such data as we do have suggest little change, at least since 1947.[11]

One limitation on our definition of occupational status is that it refers only to occupations, not to the specific jobs which individuals hold. Some of these individual jobs are much more attractive and rewarding than others, even though they are classified together in a single occupation.[12] We do not know to what extent the prestige of a particular man's work depends on the unique attributes of his job and to what extent it depends on the prestige of the occupation with which he is identified. Do all real estate brokers have high prestige—even when they are poorly educated and make little money—simply because the majority of real estate brokers are relatively well educated and make a good deal of money? Do all taxi drivers have low prestige, simply because the majority are poorly educated and make little money? Or does the exceptional taxi driver who is well educated or who makes a great deal of money have higher prestige? We do not know the answers to these questions. In the absence of answers, we will assume that the status of a man's job is largely determined by the status of his occupation.

## The Inheritance of Status

The role of a father's family background in determining his son's status is surprisingly small, at least compared to most people's preconceptions. The correlation between a father's occupational status and his son's status is less than 0.50.[13] If two fathers' statuses differ by, say, 20 points, their sons' statuses will differ by an average of 10 points.[14] Fathers thus pass on half their occupational advantage or disadvantage to their sons. Stating it another way, 42 percent of the men whose fathers are in the top fifth of the occupational hierarchy end up there themselves.[15]

If we extend this analysis over several generations, the relationship between a man's status and his ancestors' statuses grows progressively weaker. Thus if two men have statuses that differ by 20 points, their sons' statuses will differ by an average of 10 points, their grandsons' statuses will differ by about 5 points, and so forth. It follows that the amount of occupational mobility in American society (or any other) depends on the time span we consider. If we look at a single generation, we will find a lot of "short distance" mobility, but relatively little mobility from the very bottom to the very top, or from the very top to the very bottom. If we look at changes over two generations, we will find many more rags-to-riches and riches-to-rags stories.

When we turn from the effect of a father's occupation to the overall effect of family background on a son's occupation, the relationship is stronger, but by no means decisive. One way to estimate the overall effect of family background is to compare the occupational statuses of brothers. If we compare random individuals, their statuses differ by an average of 28 points. If we compare fathers and sons, their statuses differ by an average of about 20 points. If we compare brothers, their statuses differ by an average of 23 points.[16] Thus there is nearly as much variation in status between brothers as in the larger population. Family background is not, then, the primary determinant of status. Still, we must ask how parental status exercises its influence.

We can try to answer this question by comparing white, nonfarm men in the top and bottom fifths of the occupational hierarchy. These men's status scores differ by an average of 60–65 points. We expect their sons' statuses to differ by about 31 points. Differences in IQ genotype explain

5 to 10 percent of this gap. Differences in their cognitive skills due to their home environments account for another 10 to 20 percent. Differences in educational attainment that have nothing to do with cognitive skills account for 40 to 50 percent. School quality seems to explain very little. Thus about 35 percent of the gap has nothing to do with either education or cognitive skills.[17]

If test scores and educational attainment explain 65 percent of the eventual occupational difference between children with high- and low-status fathers, how are we to explain the other 35 percent? In some cases, occupational status is literally inherited. A father who passes his business along to his son also passes his status along. A farmer does the same, and so does an electrician who gets his son into the union. High-status parents may also inculcate values and habits that help their sons to get high-status jobs. If we could measure all such non-cognitive differences, we might well find that they played an even larger role than cognitive skills. They probably influence how much schooling people get, and they probably have some direct effect on status, over and above their effect on educational attainment.

Whatever the explanation, the pattern has been remarkably stable, at least since the end of World War I.[18] The rate of social mobility has not increased as a result of political reforms, nor has it decreased as a result of the end of immigration or technological changes. This does not, of course, mean that the rate of social mobility is immutable. It is higher in Australia than in America, for example.[19] The rate of mobility does not, however, seem to respond to most of the things social theorists expect it will respond to.

## The Effects of Educational Credentials

Occupations that require a lot of schooling generally have higher prestige than occupations that require very little schooling. This being so, a positive correlation between educational attainment and occupational status is inevitable. This does not imply that we are measuring status the wrong way, or that the correlation would disappear if we had a different status measure. It implies that Americans are impressed by educational credentials and that credentials confer status in the same way that indulgences confer grace. Trying to invent a status index that does not take education into account is like trying to invent a standard of living index that does not include income.[20]

This makes it difficult to talk about the extent to which education gives a man access to high-prestige occupations. To some significant degree, occupations acquire prestige because educated people choose them. Occupations like preaching and teaching, which pay badly but attract educated people, have as much prestige as occupations that pay much better but attract uneducated people.[21] Indeed, occupations frequently try to raise their status by raising the amount of schooling required for entry.[22]

Nonetheless, occupations recruit on the basis of a number of criteria, of which schooling is only one. Furthermore, people choose jobs on the basis of a number of criteria, of which status is only one. The educational attainment of workers in the same occupation therefore varies. The correlation between a man's educational attainment and his occupational status is around 0.65.[23] This tells us that men with the same amount of education have occupations that are even more alike than men who have the same parents.[24]

An extra year of schooling confers a status advantage of about 6 points.[25] That is the difference between a chemical and an electrical engineer, or between a construction foreman and a plumber. Four extra years of schooling confer roughly four times as much advantage, i.e. the difference between a doctor and an accountant, or between the manager of a clothing store and the manager of an auto repair shop.

Three overlapping explanations for the correlation between educational attainment and occupational status come to mind:

1. People with different amounts of education prefer different occupations.
2. Everyone prefers the same occupations, but people who get a lot of education have cognitive skills or noncognitive traits that make them more competent at high-status jobs.
3. Everyone prefers the same occupations, and everyone is more or less equally qualified to work in most occupations, so high-status occupations use arbitrary educational requirements to ration access to desirable jobs.

First, let us consider the occupational preferences of people with different amounts of education. Suppose that everyone got as much schooling as he wanted and then was able to enter whatever occupation he wanted. We would expect people who liked school to get a lot of it. We would also expect people who liked school to prefer different jobs from people who hated school and quit early. Other things being equal, we would expect highly educated workers to want jobs that involved sitting still and thinking. We would expect many dropouts to prefer jobs that were active rather than cognitive. If the range of choices among people at the same educational level were 24 percent narrower than the range for all workers, and if occupations that attracted educated people automatically acquired high status on that account, the correlation between education and status would be 0.65.

This is not, of course, an adequate description of modern America. We know that some high-status occupations exclude people who lack educational credentials. We also know that some individuals stay in school not because they enjoy school, but in order to enter high-status occupations. Nonetheless, much of the correlation between occupational status and educational attainment is certainly attributable to the fact that those who enjoy school prefer cognitively oriented jobs, while those who hate school prefer other kinds of work. Indeed, as we shall see, peoples' educational and occupational preferences at 17 or 18 are even more highly correlated than their actual education and their actual occupation in adulthood.

What about employers? There is abundant evidence that employers prefer workers with more education to workers with less. Professional associations have even stronger prejudices and usually establish elaborate educational requirements for becoming a practitioner. This may reflect real differences between people with a great deal of schooling and people with less schooling, or it may be an essentially arbitrary rationing system, whose primary function is to keep the number of people trying to enter high-status occupations in balance with the number of places. There is something to be said for both theories and very little evidence that allows us to choose between them.

The strongest reason for supposing that employers' preference for educated workers is capricious rather than rational is that once people enter a particular occupation, those with additional education do not make appreciably more money than others in the occupation. Within any given occupation, an extra year of school or college is associated with an average salary advantage of only 2 or 3 percent.[26] This difference seems, moreover, largely to reflect differences in cognitive skill between those with more and less schooling. If we compare men who not only are in the same occupations but also have similar test scores, there seems to be virtually no relationship between schooling and earnings.[27] This suggests that men with extra education make more money largely because they enter lucrative occupations, not because education enhances their earning power thereafter. This makes intuitive sense. A man trying to get his first job has nothing to offer but educational credentials. Once an individual has entered a field, his prior performance can be evaluated. If performance is only marginally related to schooling, the correlation between schooling and income will be negligible. If schooling were poorly related to performance, the correlation between schooling and status would fall as men got older. It does.[28]

It would be tempting to conclude that employers who favor educated applicants are simply being arbitrary. Despite spending vast sums on personnel offices, most employers make no systematic effort to see whether hiring educated workers rather than uneducated ones really pays off.[29] This suggests that they may have noneconomic reasons for wanting highly educated employees. Perhaps both large employers and professional associations feel that their prestige is enhanced by excluding the uneducated and by recruiting people with impressive credentials. Or perhaps they just find highly educated workers easier to manage.

There is, however, an alternative explanation of the data. Highly educated workers may be slightly more productive on the average than less educated workers. But employers may show just the right degree of prejudice in favor of educated applicants. Thus when two workers with different amounts of education end up in the same job, the less educated of the two may normally have other compensating virtues. Were this the case, we would not expect to find any relationship between education and productivity when we compared workers in the same occupation or on the same job.

The data do not, then, allow us to say whether employers' preference for educated workers is rational or irrational. We suspect, however, that employers would favor educated applicants even if such applicants were not especially productive. Employers need a legitimate device for rationing privilege. Credentials are widely accepted as one of the fairest systems available for doing this. (Unions, for example, generally take the view that privilege should be based primarily on seniority, secondarily on credentials, and not at all on judgments about on-the-job performance.) Employers could, of course, also solve the problem by manipulating pay scales so that no job was more attractive to the average worker than any other. But so long as some jobs are more desirable than others, rationing is needed, and credentials serve this purpose quite well.

Credentials make a good rationing device because many adolescents dislike school. The fact that high-status occupations are believed to require a lot of schooling deters many young people from trying to enter these occupations. As a result, the distribution of occupational aspirations among high school students is surprisingly congruent with the distribution of actual opportunities. Were this not the case, the whole fabric of American society might begin to unravel.

The best data we have been able to find on occupational aspirations comes from a random sample of Wisconsin high school seniors who reported in 1957 on the occupations they hoped to enter. Seven years later, these same individuals were working in occupations whose average status was only 4 points lower than the ones to which they had aspired.[30] This is the difference between chemical and industrial engineers, or between municipal and private policemen. By now, the future professional workers in the sample have gotten their degrees, and the disparity between high school aspirations and actual careers is probably even smaller than it was 7 years after high school.

The mechanism by which occupational aspirations are kept from outstripping the available opportunities becomes clear when we compare these Wisconsin students' occupational aspirations to their educational plans. The correlation between the two was far higher than the correlation between actual educational attainment and actual status in the adult population.[31] The myth that schooling is synonymous with status is thus even more widespread than the reality. Men who do not plan on getting a lot of schooling rarely have high occupational aspirations, and men who plan to quit school usually have low occupational aspirations.

The congruence between high school aspirations and actual opportunities is not, of course, perfect. EEOS found, for example, that about 40 percent of all ninth graders and 41 percent of all twelfth graders wanted to enter a professional or technical occupation. No more than half these students are likely to realize their ambition.[32] Schooling probably plays a crucial, if negative, role in redirecting many of these students' interests. EEOS also found that only 6 percent of all high school students said they wanted to become managers, officials, or proprietors. More than twice that percentage will actually do so.[33] Most of these managers will probably be people who initially said they wanted to be professionals. In many cases, they will probably be college dropouts or B.A.s who switch because they find they do not want as much schooling as they would need to enter the profession they found attractive in high school. Shifts from professional to managerial occupations involve some reduction in status. But shifting from a professional to a managerial occupation does not usually mean a loss of income.[34] This means we cannot say that the loss of status is necessarily accompanied by a feeling of frustration or defeat.

When we look at individual cases rather than averages, we find a surprisingly weak relationship between high school aspirations and eventual status. When we compared Wisconsin high school students' mean aspirations to their average status 7 years later, we found an overall difference of only 4 points. But when we look at specific individuals, the absolute difference between aspirations and actual status

7 years later is typically about 21 points.[35] These shifts are almost as likely to be upward as downward. If we ignore the minority who ended exactly where they intended, roughly 42 percent of these Wisconsin seniors entered occupations that ranked above the one to which they aspired, while 58 percent entered occupations that ranked below the one to which they had aspired.[36] This disparity should decline slightly as these men get older.

None of this suggests that America is a nation filled with upwardly mobile youngsters whose dreams are frustrated by employers' insistence that they acquire credentials. Rather, it seems that many (perhaps most) young people have very little idea what they want to do, change their aspirations easily and often, and follow the course of least resistance into whatever slots the economy makes available. Those who enjoy school and want to attend college say they want to enter a profession, because this provides a rationale for doing what they want to do anyway, namely stay in school. Conversely, those who dislike school and do not want to attend college say they want a lower-status job, because they assume they cannot enter a profession without staying in school. The fact that high-status occupations are believed to require extensive schooling thus serves as a way of limiting the number of would-be entrants, keeping the distribution of aspirations in balance with the distribution of actual opportunities.

## The Effects of Cognitive Skills

Since the correlation between educational attainment and adult test scores is between 0.60 and 0.70, and since educational attainment is one of the prime determinants of occupational status, there is inevitably a correlation between test scores and occupational status. The exact magnitude of this correlation depends on the type of test, the age of the workers, and the range of occupations covered. After eliminating measurement errors, the correlation for white, nonfarm men probably averages around 0.50.[37] This does not suggest that everyone entering a high-status occupation has high scores, or that low-status occupations get uniformly low-scoring workers. Indeed, the correlation between a man's occupational status and his test scores is about the same as the correlation between his status and his father's status. It is considerably lower than the correlation between his status and his educational attainment.

The relationship between test scores and status is not quite as simple as this description makes it sound. Men with very low scores rarely end up in very high-status jobs. But men with high test scores quite often end up in low-status occupations.[38] Presumably, many high-scoring men lack some other trait needed for success in high-status occupations.

There is no evidence that this correlation has changed much over the past 50 years. When the Army administered the first group "intelligence" tests to military recruits in 1917 and 1918, the pattern of occupational differences was very similar to what it is today.[39] The correlation between educational attainment and occupational status has also been stable since the turn of the century, as has the correlation between educational attainment and test scores.[40] There is no evidence that occupational selection is getting more "meritocratic," at least if credentials and test scores measure merit.

We can test the theory that educational requirements account for the correlation between occupation and test scores by looking at the fate of men with similar amounts of schooling but different test scores. In general, if we compare two men whose test scores differ by 15 points, their occupational statuses will typically differ by about 12.5 points. If they have the same amount of education and the same family background, their statuses will differ by only about 2.5 points.[41] This suggests that while cognitive skills may help a man get through school, they do not help him obtain a high-status job if for some reason he does not get through school.

This argument gains further support from looking at the relationship of test scores to success on the job. If two men in the same occupation have IQ scores that differ by 15 points, their incomes will differ by an average of 5 or 10 percent.[42] If we compare men with the same amount of education but different grades, income differences are again trivial. Men who receive high grades in college and in professional schools earn no more in business than men who receive poor grades in the same institutions.[43] The same is true in engineering.[44] Most studies of the relationship between high school grades and economic success have also found negligible correlations, even when occupation was not held constant.[45]

The modest relationship between test scores and wages in most occupations seems to reflect the fact that test scores have only a modest effect on actual competence in most lines of work. Supervisors' ratings have an average correlation of about 0.30 with workers' IQ scores in most occupations.[46] There is enormous variation from one employer to another, and in many settings the correlation is actually negative.[47]

We have not located much research on the relationship between test scores and competence in either managerial or professional work.[48]

We have, however, located a number of studies relating professional competence to college grades. Among elementary and secondary school teachers, the correlation between college grades and observers' (or supervisors') ratings has averaged between 0.2 and 0.3.[49] Supervisors' ratings of medical interns are not correlated with either undergraduate grades or grades in the preclinical years of medical school. They correlate about 0.3 with grades in the clinical years.[50] Trained observers' evaluations of young practicing physicians also show a small positive correlation with medical school grades, but as physicians get older the correlation disappears.[51]

Studies of doctors and scientific researchers obviously deal with men whose test scores are almost all well above average. Low correlations do not, therefore, prove that "anyone" can be a doctor or a theoretical physicist. They do, however, suggest that the relationship between grades and success in these fields is much weaker than most people suppose. Even in these highly technical fields, the difference between good and bad work seems to be more a matter of habits, values, attitudes, and outlook than of knowing the right answers to written or oral questions.

All the evidence we have reviewed points in the same direction. Most jobs require a wide variety of skills. Standardized tests measure only a very limited number of these skills. If an individual with low scores has the necessary noncognitive skills, and if he can get into an occupation, his performance on the job will not usually be appreciably below the norm for the occupation. Entering many high-status occupations does, however, depend on having met formal or informal educational requirements, and meeting these requirements is extremely difficult for people with low test scores. Thus, an individual with low scores has considerably less chance of getting into a high-status occupation than if he had high scores.

We can quantify these conclusions by considering the life chances of two brothers whose IQ scores differ by 15 points. We expect their educational attainment to differ by 0.6 to 1.2 years.[52] We expect their statuses to differ by 5 to 7 points.[53] If for some reason these two brothers get the same amount of schooling, their occupational statuses will probably differ by less than 3 points.

Such findings do not support the theory that if schools and colleges placed less emphasis on academic standards and cognitive skills, employers would fall back on tests to measure these skills. They suggest that if schools and colleges placed less emphasis on cognitive skills, the correlation between test scores and status might just fall.

Nor do these findings support the theory that occupational success depends heavily on the genes that influence IQ. Our best estimate is that, all other things being equal, men who rank in the top fifth of the genetic distribution end up with occupational statuses 5 to 8 points above the mean, while those whose IQ genotypes are in the bottom fifth end up 5 to 8 points below the mean.[54] Differences of this magnitude are relatively small. Fourteen points is the difference between a dentist and a newspaper reporter or between a locomotive engineer and a fireman.

## The Effects of School Quality

Since educational credentials seem to be related to occupational status, it seems reasonable to ask whether status also depends on the quality of the school one has attended. Those who believe that attending the right school affects a person's chances of getting a good job do not always say how they think this comes about, but four mechanisms are frequently named:

1. Some schools may be better than others at teaching cognitive skills.
2. Some schools may be better than others at developing noncognitive habits, values, and attitudes required by high-status occupations.
3. Some schools may be better than others at getting students to attend college and acquire credentials.
4. Some schools may provide students with information and contacts that lead directly to good jobs.

We have already discussed the effects of school characteristics on cognitive development. These effects appear relatively small. When translated into occupational terms, they look even smaller. We speculated in Chapter 3 that if students attended the most effective fifth of all elementary schools, whatever these may be, their achievement test scores might be 5 to 10 points higher than if they attended the least effective fifth of all elementary schools. If this gain were permanent, it might lead to an eventual status difference of 2 to 5 points.[55] As we have seen, this is a pretty small difference.

The character of a high school may also affect a student's status. The potential effect of high schools on status is, however, more likely to derive from the school's effect on whether its students go to college than from its effect on test scores. We estimated that a student who attended a high school that ranked in the most effective fifth might get a year more schooling than if he had attended a high school that ranked among the least effective fifth. This in turn implies that he might end up in an occupation whose status was 5 points higher than it would have been if he had attended a high school in the bottom fifth.[56]

Theoretically, then, a student who attended the best elementary and secondary public schools might gain a 10 point occupational advantage over a student who attended the worst public schools. Chapter 3 showed, however, that elementary schools which boosted test scores were not especially likely to be in the same districts as secondary schools that boosted college entrance rates. Such schools are, moreover, hard to identify. Expenditures and other educational resources seem to be irrelevant. The social composition of elementary schools may make a difference, but the composition of secondary schools has very unpredictable effects. The parent who wants his children to have "the best" will therefore need to do a great deal of careful research to be sure they are getting it. Under these circumstances, the idea that parents preserve their children's status by sending them to the right public schools does not seem very plausible.

All this evidence is indirect, but we also have two bits of direct evidence on the relationship between schooling and status. In the mid-1960s, northern blacks who had attended desegregated schools were more likely than northern blacks from segregated schools to be working in occupations with relatively few other blacks. As a result, their occupational status was about 3 points higher than that of blacks from apparently similar backgrounds who had attended segregated schools.[57] We cannot be absolutely certain that attending school with whites actually caused the observed differences. Still, the data does not support any obvious alternative explanation. We therefore assume that desegregation has had some occupational value for blacks. The average black's occupational status was, however, 24 points below the average white at the time of this survey, so while desegregation probably helped close the gap, it did not help very much.

Comparisons between Catholics who attended public schools and those who attended parochial schools also show a modest difference in later occupational status. In this case, however, the alumni of "segregated" (i.e. Catholic) schools appear to have been at an advantage rather than disadvantage.[58] This advantage persisted even after controlling parental status. Whether it would still persist if we could control all the other unmeasured differences between parochial and public schools students is more problematic.[59] Parochial schools often attract students whose parents are mobility conscious. They also weed out students with serious academic and behavioral problems. Many Catholic high schools are explicitly "academic" in orientation, so Catholics who do not plan to attend college are likely to transfer to a public high school.[60] Still, the evidence suggests that segregation may have been a slight asset to Catholics, just as it was a slight liability to blacks.

If differences between parochial and public schools, and between black and predominantly white public schools, have such small and contradictory effects on later occupational status, it is hard to imagine that the difference between one white public school and another has a large effect. We therefore conclude that school quality usually affects children's later status by only a couple of points.

## The Effects of Race

In 1962, before the civil rights movement had had any appreciable impact on employment patterns, the average black was in an occupation that ranked 24 points below the national average, i.e. below about 84 percent of all whites.[61] This is roughly the difference between a doctor and a schoolteacher, between a schoolteacher and a telephone repairman, between a telephone repairman and a baker, or between a baker and an unskilled laborer.

Many people assumed in 1962, and some still assume today, that blacks were concentrated in low-status occupations primarily because they were the victims of a "vicious circle of poverty." According to this theory, blacks had low-status parents, and therefore had less than equal opportunities. This meant they ended up in low-status jobs themselves. But this does not seem to explain much of the difference between blacks' and whites' occupations. Among whites, lowly origins do not result in equally low destinations. Millions of white men have had parents with as little education and as low-status occupations as the average black man's parents. On the average, however, these poor whites ended up in occupations only 7 points below the white mean. This meant they were 17 points above the black mean.[62] Had blacks been as successful as most poor whites in overcoming their initial socio-economic handicaps, they would have been only a third as disadvantaged as they actually were in 1962.

The cost of being black is perhaps clearest if we look at the fate of men born into the black middle class. If a black man had a father in the same occupation and with as much education as the average white, and a family as small as the average white, he still ended up in an occupation 19 points below the average white—only 5 points above the average black.[63] What this implies is that, so far as white employers in 1962 were concerned, "all blacks looked alike." A few blacks had middle-level or even high-level jobs in 1962, but they had been picked more or less randomly. Having the right parents had been of very little value. Even having additional education had been of limited value.[64] Apparently a black middle-class parent could do relatively little to pass his hard-won position along to his children. This may well have made many talented blacks feel that the sacrifices required to enter the black bourgeoisie were not worth the cost.

Many people also assume that blacks get lower-status jobs because they are short on the cognitive skills measured by standardized tests. Like low-status parents, however, low test scores explain only a small fraction of the status gap. Whites with IQ scores of 85 are likely to end up in occupations about 12 points below the white mean. Blacks with similar scores end up 24 points below the white mean—or did in 1962. At most, then, cognitive differences accounted for half the occupational gap between blacks and whites at that time.

Unfortunately, we do not have good data on developments since 1962. One thing is clear, however. If the occupational status of blacks has improved, this has been because of direct efforts to eliminate discrimination and compensate for past discrimination. It has not been because blacks' test scores have risen or because they have appreciably more educational credentials than they did a decade ago.

## Conclusions about Occupational Inequality

Our first general conclusion is that occupational status is strongly related to educational attainment. Americans are impressed by people with a lot of schooling, and they are deferential toward occupations that require extensive schooling. Thus, if one's ambition is to be impressive and to win deference, getting a lot of schooling is a good idea.

Our second conclusion is that schooling seems to be important in and of itself, not as a proxy for cognitive skills or family background. Both family background and cognitive skills help a man get through school, but beyond that they have very little direct influence on status. Years of schooling, in contrast, have a substantial influence, even when we compare individuals from identical backgrounds and with identical cognitive skills.

Our third major conclusion is that while occupational status is more closely related to educational attainment than to anything else we can measure, there are still enormous status differences among people with the same amount of education. This remains true when we compare people who have not only the same amount of schooling, but the same family background and the same test scores. Anyone who thinks that a man's family background, test scores, and educational credentials are the only things that determine the kind of work he can do in America is fooling himself. At most, these characteristics explain about half the variation in men's occupational statuses.[65] This leaves at least half the variation in men's occupational statuses to be explained by factors that have nothing to do with family background, test scores, or educational attainment.

Some of this unexplained variation seems to be variation in the status of the same individual at different times in his life. Published data on the stability of a man's status over time is both scarce and contradictory, but what we have suggests that people move up and down quite a lot, especially in their twenties and thirties.[66]

Some of this unexplained variation is presumably due to unmeasured character traits, like alcoholism, mental health, and drive to succeed, but we doubt if these explain very much.[67] Much of the variation is probably due to chance (one steelworker gets laid off and takes a temporary job as a painter, while another keeps his job because his plant happens to be busier). Some is due to choice (a businessman decides to give up making underwear and becomes a clergyman).

Both social theorists and social scientists are heirs to the rationalist tradition. We tend to believe that if only we had better analytic models and better measurements, we would be able to predict human behavior perfectly. This may be true at some very theoretical level, but it is plainly untrue in any practical sense. Predicting a man's occupational status is like predicting his life expectancy: certain measurable factors make a difference, but they are by no means decisive.

What does this imply about public policy? The answer depends on your objectives. Some people are interested in reducing occupational inequality. Others assume that occupational inequality will persist no matter what we do, and that the only practical objective is to give everyone an equal opportunity to rise to the top—or sink to the bottom. We will discuss this latter objective first.

POLICIES FOR INCREASING MOBILITY

The most important implication of the research we have discussed is that neither credentials nor examination scores predict performance in most lines of work very accurately. This means that the use of credentials or test scores to exclude "have-not" groups from desirable jobs can be viewed in the same light as any other arbitrary form of discrimination. The Supreme Court reached this same conclusion in

1971 in the *Griggs* decision. The Court held that the use of test scores and credentials to select employees was a violation of Title VII of the 1964 Civil Rights Act when (1) this selection system resulted in underrepresentation of minorities, and (2) the employer could not show a relationship between test scores or credentials and performance on the job.[68]

Virtually any system of tests and most systems based on degrees and diplomas will result in some underrepresentation of minorities, especially blacks. Our inquiry suggests that neither tests nor diplomas are likely to correlate very well with job performance, although there will certainly be some exceptions. We doubt that the present Court will pursue this logic to its revolutionary conclusion. Nonetheless, we can certainly anticipate a series of test cases challenging the use of tests and credentials in a variety of contexts. Some of these are likely to be successful. If they are, the correlation between educational attainment and occupational status might begin to decline. Before applauding this development, however, we need to ask what the alternative is likely to be.

The most obvious alternative to a system which rations access to high-status occupations on the basis of objective criteria like test scores and credentials is a system which rations access on the basis of subjective criteria, like the impression a man makes in an interview or the rating his supervisor gives him after a few weeks on the job. Such criteria will not necessarily work to the advantage of currently disadvantaged groups. They could easily have effects even more discriminatory than credentials and tests. In England, for example, education authorities that use teacher ratings as the basis for allocating 11 year olds to grammar schools admit fewer working-class children than those that use test scores.[69] We suspect that if American employers stopped relying on diplomas and used only interviews to pick job applicants, upwardly mobile men from low-status homes would find themselves at more of a disadvantage than they do now.

Another possible alternative to educational credentials, however, is objective examinations covering material that is supposedly relevant to doing a good job. Success on such examinations usually depends on some combination of aptitude and cramming. The results should show about the same correlation with class background as school grades. The evidence we have reviewed suggests that using such exams would increase the proportion of whites from low-status families entering high-status occupations. This judgment is based on the fact that parental status has more influence on a son's educational attainment than on his aptitude test scores, and more influence on his aptitude scores than on his grades. But such a change in policy might well reduce the proportion of blacks in high-status jobs. This reflects the fact that race has more influence on test scores than on educational attainment. (Unfortunately, we do not have good data on the relationship between race and grades.) Conversely, policy changes like "open enrollment," which seek to reduce the correlation between test scores and educational attainment, will benefit blacks at the expense of both poor and middle-class whites.

What would be the best way to reduce the correlation between a father's status and a son's status (i.e. to increase the amount of social mobility)? The most effective strategy is obviously reverse discrimination. If all employers always favored job applicants with low-status fathers, regardless of their other attributes, the correlation between fathers' and sons' statuses could eventually fall to −1.00. This version of "shirtsleeves to shirtsleeves in three generations" is not likely to have much political appeal, however. Efforts to increase occupational mobility generally have to be pursued under some other guise, such as providing opportunity for the talented or rewarding virtue. This means rationing access to high-status jobs on some basis other than parental status.

*All* the rationing systems we have examined would result in high-status sons obtaining somewhat more than their share of the high-status jobs. Some systems are, however, significantly more discriminatory than others. In general, low-status boys will rise furthest if high-status occupations select on the basis of grades or test scores. They will be worse off if high-status occupations select on the basis of educational attainment, as they now do. They will be only a little better off if they select on the basis of motivation and aspirations. The Wisconsin survey to which we alluded earlier obtained the following correlations between a son's characteristics and his father's status, making no corrections for measurement error:

| Son's Characteristic | Correlation with Father's Status |
|---|---|
| Grades | 0.194 |
| Test Scores | 0.288 |
| *Actual Occupational Status at Age 25* | *0.331* |
| Occupational Aspirations in Twelfth Grade | 0.366 |
| Educational Aspirations in Twelfth Grade | 0.380 |
| Educational Attainment | 0.417 |

These correlations tell us three things. First, if high-status occupations were open exclusively to people with high test scores and if all people with high test scores chose to enter the highest-status occupation open to them, the correlation between fathers' and sons' statuses would be slightly less than it is now (0.288 rather than 0.331). If high-status occupations went exclusively to students with high grades, the correlation between fathers' and sons' statuses would fall even further (0.331 to 0.194). Second, if high-status occupations were open only to people with educational credentials, and if people with educational credentials all chose to enter high-status occupations, the correlation between fathers' and sons' statuses would be stronger than it is now (0.417 rather than 0.331). Third, if everyone entered the occupation he wanted to enter when he was a high school senior, the correlation between fathers' and sons' statuses would change very little.[70]

This implies that a system which allocates status on the basis of cognitive skills is likely to result in more social mobility than any of the obvious alternatives. Perhaps that is why America does not have such a system.

Yet, as we have already noted, a system which emphasizes cognitive skills would be far less satisfactory for blacks than for poor whites. For blacks, the ideal system is one which discounts test scores and emphasizes aspirations. Failing this, a system that emphasizes credentials is better for blacks than one that emphasizes test scores. The right policy thus depends on whose opportunities you want to equalize.

Confronted with such a difficult decision, the reader may begin to share our suspicion that maximizing social mobility is the wrong objective. We would like to see a society in which everyone could enter the occupation of his choice and perform competently in it. America is not such a society today. But if it were, there is no reason to suppose that the rate of social mobility would be higher than it is now. So long as the degree of occupational inequality remains fixed, high-status children are likely to have higher status aspirations than low-status children, just as they do today. Thus even if everyone were able to do exactly what he wanted, the rate of mobility might not be very different from what it now is. Certainly that is the implication of the Wisconsin survey cited above.

POLICIES FOR INCREASING EQUALITY

Increasing social mobility is a policy for reducing inequality between groups (the initially advantaged and the initially disadvantaged) without reducing inequality between individuals. It assumes that the economic, social, and psychological distance between occupations is fixed, and tries to tinker with the factors determining success and failure.

We can see no great virtue in such a policy. We do not want to randomize inequality; we want to reduce it. Merely ensuring that every group is proportionately represented in high-status occupations would not achieve this, even if we knew how to do it.

Equalizing opportunity and equalizing results may, of course, be related politically. One way to reduce status disparities between occupations may be to fill high-status occupations with what have previously been regarded as low-status people, and to fill low-status occupations with what have previously been regarded as high-status people. Furthermore, if children with successful parents have the same chance as everyone else of falling into very low-status occupations, high-status adults may take more interest than they now do in policies designed to improve conditions in low-status occupations. Policies which increase mobility may thus help create a climate in which people also want to reduce inequality. Nonetheless, it seems important to distinguish between promoting social mobility as a tactic aimed at making people worry more about equality and promoting social mobility as an end in itself.

Unfortunately, the evidence discussed in this chapter does not provide much guidance for those who want to reduce status disparities between occupations. Economists argue, and we tend to agree, that the only way to make all occupations equally attractive in a competitive labor market is to eliminate systematic differences in the value employers place on different workers' services. If all workers were equally attractive to prospective employers, high-status occupations would presumably be inundated with qualified applicants. Wages and other perquisites in these occupations would therefore fall. Conversely, low-status occupations would have to raise wages and perquisites in order to get enough workers. If every worker had a genuine choice between all occupations, all jobs would have to be made equally attractive in order to get the work done. All jobs would not, of course, have to be equally attractive to everyone. But every job would have to have some combination of characteristics that made it the best of all jobs for at least one individual. Prestige differences between occupations might persist in such a society, but occupations with low prestige would have to compensate for this with high wages, good working conditions, and the like. Inequalities in occupational status would cease to be of much social or moral consequence.

If people's bargaining power remains unequal, a free labor market is bound to produce status disparities between occupations. Certain skills and behavior patterns will be widely regarded as desirable, and employers will compete to hire workers with these traits. Occupations which require these traits or skills will have to offer more perquisites, either monetary or nonmonetary, than occupations which require skills that virtually every worker has. This could only be prevented if we abandoned the notion that an individual's wages and working conditions should depend solely on his value to his employer.

Some progress can often be made in this direction if the perquisites of different jobs are determined by collective rather than individual bargaining. The wage differential between mechanics and sweepers may, for example, be 2 to 1 on the open market. But if union solidarity limits the degree of inequality the union can tolerate among its members, it may insist on a differential of only 1.5 to 1. Employers may accept this because it is cheaper than a strike. Considerations of this kind can also limit inequality within an organization even when wages and working conditions are negotiated individually. An employer may feel that he cannot pay workers highly unequal wages, even though he places very different values on their services, because the workers in question will view this as unfair.

Unfortunately, union contracts and informal norms are mainly useful in promoting occupational equality within organizations, not between them. Furthermore, so long as we have a competitive labor market, any organization that moves too far toward internal equality runs the risk of losing its most valuable employees, since they will be able to do better for themselves elsewhere. If a corporation does not pay professional workers what they are worth, because this would create bad feelings within the organization, the workers in question may start their own firm and sell their services to the corporation at their market value. Unless the state restricts these options, egalitarian pressures within organizations can have only limited impact on overall inequality between occupations.

Reducing occupational inequality probably requires national (or perhaps even international) restrictions on the extent to which unusually valuable workers can gain special privileges. Such restrictions on an individual's freedom to pursue his private advantage are generally regarded as un-American.

Egalitarians therefore tend to fall back on trying to equalize individual bargaining power. The evidence reviewed in this chapter does not provide much guidance for doing this. It seems clear that equalizing the cognitive skills measured by standardized tests would not be very helpful, even if we knew how to do it. There is almost as much variation in the status of individuals with equal test scores as in the overall population.[71] Equalizing the distribution of certain noncognitive virtues might do more to equalize workers' competence and usefulness than equalizing their test scores. But we cannot prove this, because we do not know which specific noncognitive virtues make workers unusually valuable. Furthermore, the traits employers value may not be accepted as virtues by all potential employees. This would make it peculiarly difficult to ensure that everyone had his share of them.

One need not, of course, know which specific virtues make one worker more valuable than another in order to devise a strategy for reducing disparities. Many people assume, for example, that equalizing the distribution of schooling would help equalize the distribution of the virtues employers value. They make this assumption even though they admit uncertainty about precisely what schools do and what employers value. The conclusion depends, however, on the assumption that exposure to schooling actually changes people. If, as we suspect, the relationship between educational attainment and occupational status derives primarily from the fact that schools certify people who were different to begin with, then giving everyone the same amount of schooling and the same credentials would not make them more alike or equalize their bargaining power when they sought jobs.

Suppose, for example, that educational reformers succeeded in creating a society in which everyone ended up with a B.A. If workers still differed drastically in terms of competence or desirability, employers would resort to other devices for identifying the people they wanted to hire. They might, for example, favor people who had attended what they regarded as "good" colleges,[72] people who had earned high grades, people who came from the "right" families, or people who made a good impression in interviews.

Equalizing the way children are treated at home would do more than equalizing the schools to produce a labor force in which people's bargaining power was equal. Yet even this strategy has rather limited potential, and it is extraordinarily difficult to implement. We have already indicated that status inequality between brothers is about 82 percent of status inequality in general. It does not necessarily follow that brothers differ drastically in terms of competence and productivity. They may be quite similar but may choose occupations of differing status for idiosyncratic reasons. Nonetheless, the existence of large status disparities between brothers puts the burden of proof with those who claim that equalizing home environments would make adults significantly more equal.

We conclude, then, with a series of caveats. Strategies designed to increase social mobility must be evaluated with great caution, since getting rid of one obstacle to mobility may lead to the creation of a new system which is even less favorable to mobility. In a competitive economy, strategies for equalizing the status of different occupations cannot work very well unless they equalize the value employers place on different employees. This cannot be done by equalizing the quality of the schools people attend. We doubt if much can be done by equalizing the amount of schooling people get. Even equalizing home environments would probably have rather modest effects. We suspect, in short, that there is no practical way to equalize either competence or the other traits that make some workers more valuable than others. This means that if we want to equalize the status of different occupations, we will have to move away from a competitive economy toward a more highly regulated system, in which equality is an explicit objective of public policy.

# NOTES

1. See the literature discussed by Reiss, in *Occupations and Social Status,* and Siegel, in "American Occupational Structure."

2. See Reiss, *Occupations and Social Status,* and Siegel, "American Occupational Structure." A few occupations are rated quite differently by different groups, but the overall pattern is strikingly similar for every group. Different groups' rankings of the same jobs correlate better than 0.90, and often better than 0.95.

3. Ibid.

4. See Hodge et al., "A Comparative Study."

5. See Hodge et al., "Occupational Prestige." Estimates at different points in time correlate 0.93 to 0.99 with one another.

6. Paul Siegel, in correspondence, reports that in the most recent NORC survey data, the ratings provided by 918 respondents for 100-odd occupations have an average correlation of 0.694 with the mean ratings derived from these same respondents. Table II–9 of Reiss, in *Occupations and Social Status,* also gives data on the distribution of respondent rankings for 90 occupations. About half the response variance is within occupational categories, and about half is between. The analysis of variance approach is potentially misleading, however, since if 2 raters rank occupations in the same order but one ranks all occupational categories higher than the other, this inflates the intraoccupation variance. Nevertheless, both methods yield similar results, i.e. about half the response variance is within occupations.

7. See Duncan, "Properties and Characteristics." Among males in a

given occupation in 1950, the percentage of high school graduates correlated 0.85 with the mean prestige ranking assigned by NORC respondents in 1947. The percentage of men earning $3,500 or more correlated 0.84 with the mean prestige ranking. These two predictors correlated 0.72 with one another; together they correlated 0.91 with mean prestige. This NORC data covers less than fifty occupations. Duncan et al., in *Socioeconomic Background,* estimate the correlation between prestige and Duncan scores for all occupations at 0.86.

8. For an analysis of these issues, see Hodge and Siegel, *Occupational Prestige.*

9. Duncan et al., in *Socioeconomic Background,* show that the correlation between father's and son's status, measured on the Duncan scale, is appreciably higher than the correlation of father's and son's prestige ratings, using NORC prestige rankings. Indeed, the partial correlation of father's prestige with son's prestige, after controlling status, appears to be nil.

10. For status rankings of all occupations, see Duncan, "Properties and Characteristics." For means and standard deviations, see Duncan et al., *Socioeconomic Background.*

11. See the data cited in note 6. Siegel's data are from the mid-1960s, while Reiss's are from 1947.

12. The range of earnings within an occupation (using the 435 Census categories) is about 85 percent of the range for the nation as a whole. Appendix B estimates the correlation between individual white men's incomes and their occupational statuses at 0.44. Since an occupation's status correlated 0.93 with the percentage of males earning more than $3,500 in 1949, it must have correlated close to 0.90 with mean income in 1949. The correlation between individual income and mean income for an occupation was thus about $0.44/0.90 = 0.49$ in 1949. This implies that about 24 percent of the variance in income was between occupational groups and that about 76 percent was within. The standard deviation for income is thus about 87 percent ($\sqrt{0.76}$) of the overall standard deviation. The figure for earnings would probably be slightly lower, i.e. around 85 percent.

13. Blau and Duncan, in *The American Occupational Structure* (Table 5–1), report an observed correlation of 0.405 for men between the ages of 25 and 64 in 1962. If we correct for measurement error using the reliabilities in Appendix B, an observed correlation of 0.405 implies a true correlation of 0.483. The value in Appendix B is slightly lower since it only covers white, nonfarm men, and is averaged within age groups.

14. If fathers' statuses were as unequal as sons', the discrepancy would be $(0.48)(20) = 9.6$ points. However, fathers are bunched at the lower end of the status hierarchy, due to differential fertility, and are thus more equal than their sons. So a correlation of 0.48 implies a ratio of differences slightly in excess of 0.5.

15. If the top fifth averages 1.4 standard deviations above the mean, its sons will average $(1.4)(0.48) = 0.67$ standard deviations above the mean. The standard error of this estimate will be roughly $\sqrt{1 - 0.48^2} = 87$ percent

of the overall standard deviation. The top fifth includes only men who are more than 0.84 standard deviations above the population mean. Roughly 42 percent of any normally distributed group will end up at least $(0.84 - 0.67)/0.87 = 0.20$ standard deviations above the norm for their group.

16. The estimated product-moment correlation between fathers and sons is 0.48 (see note 13). If we treat intergenerational changes in mean status as spurious, on the grounds that the absolute supply of status cannot change over time, and if we assume constant variances, the product-moment correlation is equivalent to the intraclass correlation between these pairs of individuals. This implies that 48 percent of the total variance is between pairs, while 52 percent is within pairs. The intrapair standard deviation is thus $\sqrt{0.52} = 72$ percent of the population standard deviation. The mean intrapair difference is presumed to equal the intrapair standard deviation times 1.13. The estimated mean difference is thus $(25)(0.72)(1.13) = 20$ points.

The estimated correlation between brothers' statuses is 0.32 (see Appendix B). This means that 32 percent of the status variance is between pairs of brothers, and that the mean difference between brothers is $(25)(\sqrt{1 - 0.32})(1.13) = 23$ points.

17. These estimates are derived from Appendix B, Figure B–7, in the following manner. The overall correlation between father's occupation and son's occupation is 0.440. The compound paths via IQ genotype sum to between 0.020 (assuming $m = 1$ and $v = 0$) and 0.035 (assuming $m = 0.50$ and $v = 0.107$), which is between 4.5 and 8.0 percent of the correlation. The compound paths via *EF-IQ* sum to between 0.048 and 0.088, which is between 10.9 and 20.0 percent of the correlation. The compound paths via *EF-ED* sum to between 0.212 and 0.176, which is between 48.2 and 40.0 percent of the correlation. The direct path from father's occupation to son's occupation is 0.158, which is 35.9 percent of the correlation. The gap between fathers in the top and bottom fifths is roughly $(2.8)(25) = 70$ points. The gap between the sons is roughly $(0.44)(70) = 31$ points.

18. See the data in Blau and Duncan, *The American Occupational Structure,* on 10-year cohorts born between 1897 and 1936, and the data on test scores in Appendix B.

19. See Jones, "Occupational Achievement." For more general international comparisons, see Cutright, "Occupational Inheritance," and the sources cited there, as well as Fox and Miller, "Social Determinants of Mobility."

20. Some have argued that the inclusion of educational attainment in Duncan's status index introduces a spurious correlation between individual education and individual status. Blau and Duncan, in *The American Occupational Structure,* show, however, that an occupational status index based on income and white-collar status yields much the same results as an index based on income and education. This is not surprising, inasmuch as the two indices are very highly correlated. For evidence that educational attainment is, in fact, a crucial dimension of status, see Klatsky and Hodge, "Canonical Correlation," who demonstrate that the likelihood of a man whose father had a given occupation ending up in another specified occupa-

tion is as well predicted by knowing the average educational attainment of the two occupations as by knowing both average education and average income.

21. For details, see Duncan, "Properties and Characteristics," and "Socioeconomic Index."

22. Raising educational requirements may also be a device for creating an artificial labor shortage and thus boosting the income of people in the occupation. But this is not always the primary motive. An occupation that merely wants to exclude people can do so by establishing examinations and then manipulating the percentage who pass. Architects, for example, keep their numbers down by failing most of those who take the registration exam. Doctors use medical school admissions to achieve the same goal. If medical schooling took 4 weeks instead of 4 years, there would still be a shortage of doctors, because the medical schools would still exclude most applicants as incompetents. Educators, in contrast, have gone to great lengths to ensure that everyone will be able to meet the requirements for entering teaching. Education courses and teachers' colleges have been widely available and virtually free. Academic standards are minimal. Requiring teachers to have 16 or 17 years of schooling does not seem to be a device for keeping down the supply of teachers or for driving up salaries. It seems to be a device for raising the status of teachers by making them better educated.

23. See Appendix B for an estimate covering white, nonfarm males. See Siegel and Hodge, "A Causal Approach," for a national estimate corrected for measurement error.

24. The correlation of 0.65 implies that education explains about 42 percent of the variance in status. Family background explains 32 percent.

25. The current standard deviation of attainment is 2.8 years (see Chapter 2, Table 2–1). The correlation between attainment and status is taken to be 0.65. The standard deviation of status is 25 points. A one-year increase in attainment thus implies an increase of $(25)(0.65)/2.8 = 5.8$ points.

26. See Duncan et al., *Socioeconomic Background*. In equations for 4 different age groups predicting a son's income from parental characteristics, a son's education, and a son's occupational status, the standardized regression coefficient of a son's education averaged 0.10. This means that with background and occupation held constant, men who were one standard deviation above the mean on education were 0.10 standard deviations above the mean in terms of income. A one-year increase in education represented 0.30 standard deviations in this population and was associated with a $(0.10)(0.30) = 0.03$ standard deviation increase in income. The observed standard deviation of income averages $5,708 within age cohorts. This translates into $($5,708$)(0.03) = $171$ for each year of school. At the mean of $7,090, a $171 increase in income is 2.4 percent. Plausible corrections for measurement error reduce these apparent returns even further (see Appendix B).

One possible objection to these analyses is that they involve controlling for occupational status, not for mean earnings of the occupation. The Duncan status scale is based on both education and income. This means that if two occupations have the same status, the occupation with better-educated workers must, by definition, have worse-paid workers. The negative correlation between mean education and mean income among occupations at the same status level implies that whatever the correlation between education and income within specific occupations, the correlation within status groups will be lower. On both theoretical and empirical grounds, however, we expect this bias to be very small.

Miller, in *Income Distribution,* provides data on the relationship between education and income within a number of specific occupations. Four extra years of schooling yield an average income increase of 14 to 15 percent, so one year yields about 3 percent. This difference would be reduced slightly if family background were controlled.

27. See Appendix B. Controlling *AFQT* scores and occupational status and correcting for measurement error reduces the direct path from education to income to zero. The correction for measurement error is uncertain, however, so the true path might be 0.05 or so. The observed path in the NORC veterans sample is 0.15. This would be lower if we corrected for the fact that men with very low *AFQT* scores do nct become veterans. Still, we must be cautious in our interpretation of the "corrected" matrices in Appendix B.

28. See the cohort data in Blau and Duncan, *The American Occupational Structure,* and the discussion in Appendix B of this volume.

29. See Berg, *Education and Jobs.*

30. See Sewell et al., "Educational and Early Occupational Status."

31. Sewell et al., "Educational and Early Occupational Status," report a correlation of 0.77 between high school students' educational and occupational aspirations. They report a correlation of 0.62 between educational attainment and occupational status seven years later, which matches the correlation in national samples quite closely.

32. See Mayeske et al., "Item Response Analyses." The estimates in the text include both males and females. Some of the females will not be employed at all. The estimates make no attempt to allocate the students who either said they did not know what they wanted to do, or who did not answer the question. These students constituted 34 percent of the ninth grade respondents and 24 percent of the twelfth grade respondents. The U.S. Bureau of the Census, in "Income in 1970," shows that in 1970 about 18 percent of the experienced civilian labor force between the ages of 25 and 44 was engaged in professional, technical, or kindred occupations. This percentage will presumably rise slightly by the time the EEOS respondents are 25 to 44.

33. See the sources cited in note 32.

34. See Chapter 7, Table 7–5.

35. This estimate is based on the Wisconsin data reported by Sewell et al., in "Educational and Early Occupational Status." The mean level of occupational aspiration is 44.7, while the mean level of attainment seven years later is 40.4. The variance in initial aspirations is $26.2^2$, while the variance in actual statuses is $23.7^2$. This yields a mean difference of 4.3. The product-moment correlation between initial aspirations and actual attainment is 0.48,

so the variance within pairs of observations on the same individual is $4.3^2 + (26.2)(1-.48)(23.7) = 18.5^2$. The mean difference is then $(1.13)(18.5) = 21.0$ points. This estimate is obviously rough since the distribution of status scores is not normal, but the order of magnitude is about right.

36. See the data in note 35. A correlation of 0.48 implies a standard error of $(23.7)(\sqrt{1 - 0.48^2}) = 20.8$ points. If the distribution of residuals were normal, 42 percent of them would fall $(4.3/20.8) = 0.207$ or more standard errors below the mean. The remaining 58 percent would be above this cutting point.

37. See Appendix B, Table B–2.

38. See, for example, the distributions in Stewart, "AGCT Scores." Compare, also, Yerkes, "Psychological Examining," and Harrell and Harrell, "Army General Classification." The same pattern is also found in the NORC veterans survey. The findings in these surveys can be summarized by saying that the standard deviation of status rises as mean $AFQT$ score rises. In the NORC survey, for example, men who scored above the ninety-third percentile on the $AFQT$ had a mean status of 54.8, with a standard deviation of 23.4. Men in the tenth to twentieth percentiles on the $AFQT$ had a mean of 25.3 and a standard deviation of 16.4. Others were in between. The overall standard deviation in this sample was 22.9.

39. For data on occupational differences in World War I, see Yerkes, "Psychological Examining." For a comparison of occupational medians for World War I and World War II recruits, see Stewart, "AGCT Scores." While the correlation between World War I and World War II rankings is very high, the absolute level of competence appears to have risen across the board (see Chapter 3, "Historical Changes in Americans' Test Scores").

40. See Appendix B.

41. Derived from Appendix B, Figure B–7. The correlation between $AFQT$ scores and a son's status is 0.502, so a 1 standard deviation $AFQT$ difference leads to a $(25)(0.502) = 12.5$ point status difference. The direct path is 0.099, which implies a $(0.099)(25) = 2.5$ point difference.

42. A 4 percent estimate was derived by Jencks directly from the 1964 NORC veterans survey. Mean earnings were \$6,360 for all veterans with complete data. A 15 point $AFQT$ difference led to a \$253 difference in 1963 earnings after controlling status of father, schooling, occupational status, race, farm origins, whether the individual was head of a household, and whether he was in school. Mean earnings were \$6,360, so the difference is 4 percent of the mean. After correcting for measurement error, the equation predicting income from family background, respondent's education, respondent's occupation, and $AFQT$ score yields a standardized regression coefficient of 0.152 for $AFQT$ in Appendix B. Using a coefficient of variation of 0.70 (see note 9, Chapter 7), this implies a difference of $(0.152)(0.70) = 10.6$ percent. The discrepancy between these two estimates derives from the fact that the observed coefficient of variation is only 0.38 for the NORC sample, versus 0.70 for a fuller sample.

43. Hoyt, in "College Grades and Adult Achievement," reviewed seven such studies. Only two, both dealing with AT&T, showed statistically significant correlations.

44. See Hoyt, "College Grades and Adult Achievement."

45. See Clem and Dodge, "High School Leadership and Scholarship"; Dugan, "Follow-Up Study"; Lorge, "Prediction of Vocational Success"; Martin and Morgan, "Education and Income"; Shannon, "Post-School Careers"; and Shannon and Farmer, "Correlation of High School Scholastic Success." For studies showing positive relationships, see Crowley, "High School Backgrounds"; Leech, "Scholarship and Success"; and Thornhill and Landis, "Extra-Curricular Activity."

46. This summary of an extensive literature relies largely on Ghiselli, "The Validity of Commonly Employed Occupational Tests." For a more recent review see Super and Crites, *Appraising Vocational Fitness*.

47. See Ghiselli, "The Validity of Commonly Employed Occupational Tests."

48. On managerial success, see Thompson, "Selecting Executives."

49. See Hoyt, "College Grades and Adult Achievement," and the sources cited there. The validity of supervisors' ratings is itself problematic. For analyses of EEOS that relate teachers' test scores to student scores, see Coleman et al., *Equality of Educational Opportunity*; Hanushek, "The Education of Blacks and Whites"; Levin, "Cost-Effectiveness Analysis"; Michelson, "Teacher Resourceness"; Armor, "School and Family Effects"; Jencks, "The Coleman Report"; and Smith, "The Basic Findings Reconsidered."

50. See Richards et al., "Medical Intern Performance."

51. See Peterson et al., "Analytical Study." This excellent study covered a carefully chosen sample of 88 North Carolina physicians.

52. The paths from early IQ to educational attainment in Appendix B range from 0.227 to 0.415. The standard deviation of educational attainment is today about 2.8 years for white males. Hence, the effect of a 1 standard deviation difference is between $(2.8)(0.227) = 0.6$ and $(2.8)(0.415) = 1.2$ years.

53. See Appendix B, Figure B–7. The sum of the compound paths from *IQ-11* to occupational status is between 0.198 and 0.297.

54. Derived from Appendix B, Table B–5, assuming a 1.4 standard deviation gap between the extreme fifths and the mean and a 25 point standard deviation for status. The compound paths from IQ genotype to occupational status range from 0.140 to 0.218, so the effect is between $(1.4)(0.140)(25) = 4.95$ and $(1.4)(0.218)(25) = 7.63$ points.

55. The compound paths from *IQ-11* to occupational status in Appendix B, Figure B–7, sum to between 0.198 and 0.297. Increasing test scores by 10 points (0.667 standard deviations) thus increases status by $(0.667)(0.198) = 0.132$ to $(0.667)(0.297) = 0.198$ standard deviations, or 3.3 to 5.0 points.

56. See Appendix B, Figure B–7. A year of school today represents a 0.36 standard deviation advantage. The compound paths from education to occupational status sum to 0.526, so a 1 year increase means an effect of $(0.36)(0.526)(25) = 4.7$ points of occupational status.

57. See Crain, "School Integration and Occupational Achievement."

58. See Greeley and Rossi, *The Education of Catholic Americans*. The difference appears to be about 0.9 deciles, which is about 9 points, with no

background controls. With backgrounds controls, the difference appears to be about 6 points.

59. Greeley and Rossi use an analytic technique (*gamma*) which makes fewer assumptions about linearity and interaction, but which does not allow simultaneous controls for large numbers of variables. The status difference between Catholics from public and parochial schools might have disappeared in an analysis controlling more of the parental characteristics measured in their survey.

60. We do not have any national data on test scores of Catholic high school students, but we have seen local newspaper reports indicating 5 or 10 point differences between Catholic and public high schools. A 10 point test score difference would explain the status difference found by Greeley and Rossi.

61. These estimates are derived from Duncan, "Inheritance of Poverty." The percentile rank of the average black is very rough, since the distribution of status scores is skewed (see Duncan, "Properties and Characteristics").

62. See Duncan, "Inheritance of Poverty."

63. This estimate is derived from Duncan, "Inheritance of Poverty," in the following way. First, we estimated the educational attainment of blacks whose father's education, father's occupation, and family size equaled the white mean. We did this by substituting the white means into a regression equation that predicted black educational attainment. We then estimated the occupational status of blacks whose father's occupation, father's education, and family size equaled the white mean. We did this by substituting the white means for the background variables, plus the newly derived mean for the educational attainment of blacks from backgrounds comparable to the average white, into a regression that predicted black status. The estimated status of blacks whose father's education, father's occupation, and family size equaled the white mean was 25.0. The mean status of all blacks was 19.7. The mean status of all whites was 43.5. The white standard deviation was 24.6. The black standard deviation was 16.9.

This method of estimation differs from that used by Duncan to estimate the effects of discrimination. Duncan assumed that equalizing the black and white means would also equalize the black and white regression equations. He therefore estimated the effects of discrimination by substituting black means into the white equation. This produced a lower estimate of the effects of discrimination than our procedure of substituting white means into the black equation. It seems to us that disparities between the black and white equations should be reckoned as a key part of discrimination.

64. Equalizing educational attainment as well as family background in the equations described in note 63 reduced the status gap by less than 1 point.

65. See Appendix B. After correcting for measurement error, the variables in the text account for 44.3 percent of the variance in status for white, nonfarm males. Nonadditive interactions and nonlinearities might raise the total to 50 percent. Blau and Duncan, in *The American Occupational Structure*, using multiple classification analysis on a full national

sample, explained about 40.77 percent of the variance in a son's status with variables that embodied ethnicity, geographic mobility, family size, ordinal position in the family, father's education, father's occupation, and son's education, but not test scores or aspirations. The data in Appendix B indicates that test scores explain another 1 percent. Reanalysis of the correlation matrices in Sewell et al., "Early Occupational Status," shows that, in their twelfth grade Wisconsin sample, parental status, test scores, and educational attainment explain 39.4 percent of the variance in status at age 25. Occupational aspirations at age 18 raise the explained variance by only 0.8 percent.

66. See Duncan and Hodge, "Education and Occupational Mobility," for Chicago data, and Hochbaum et al., "Socioeconomic Variables," for Minneapolis data. Both obtained correlations between occupational status in 1950 and status in 1940. The Chicago study obtained detailed work histories and found that, for men between the ages of 55 and 64, the correlation $r_{60,50}$ was 0.87. For men between the ages of 45 and 54, $r_{50,40}$ was 0.77. For men between the ages of 35 and 44, $r_{40,30}$ was 0.55. The Minneapolis study obtained a single retrospective report on status 10 years prior to the survey, and found $r_{60,50} = 0.96$, $r_{50,40} = 0.91$, $r_{40,30} = 0.83$. The Chicago values seem likely to be lower than those for a national sample because (1) there was, probably, more occupational mobility during World War II than at most times, and (2) there are probably more mobile people in Chicago than in most places. However, the Minneapolis values seem improbably high, since the estimated interview-reinterview reliability of reports on occupational status is only 0.91. We infer that failure to obtain detailed work histories led to an exaggerated picture of occupational stability in Minneapolis.

We can generate a correlation matrix between statuses at ages 30, 40, 50, and 60, using the correlations reported in note 67 and assuming that $r_{30,50} = r_{30,40} \, r_{40,50}$, that $r_{30,60} = r_{30,40} \, r_{40,50} \, r_{50,60}$, and that $r_{40,60} = r_{40,50} \, r_{50,60}$. (These assumptions are likely to underestimate the true value of $r_{30,50}$, $r_{30,60}$, and $r_{40,60}$.) The first principal component derived from such a matrix explains 72 percent of the variance in the Chicago data and 88 percent in the Minneapolis data. Thus, 12 to 28 percent of the variance in adult status is variance within a single lifetime.

67. Duncan and Featherman, in "Psychological and Cultural Factors," explore those issues in more detail. For an earlier and simpler version, see Duncan et al., *Socioeconomic Background*.

68. See *Griggs v. Duke Power Company*, 91 S. Ct. 849 (March 8, 1971).

69. See Floud and Halsey, "Intelligence Tests."

70. The correlations are taken from Sewell et al., "Educational and Early Occupational Status." They are not corrected for attenuation and do not cover students (12 percent of the total Wisconsin population) who had dropped out before twelfth grade. The values are very similar to those obtained from Project Talent for a national sample.

71. See note 38. On the average, inequality among men with identical scores is $\sqrt{1 - 0.50^2} = 87$ percent of the overall level.

72. Daniere, in "Social Class Competition," argues that college quality

is already replacing years of schooling as the primary basis for determining status and income. Once inputs are controlled, however, college quality has rather small effects on test scores (see Astin, "Undergraduate Achievement") and on the percentage of students earning Ph.D.s (see Astin "Undergraduate Institutions"). We therefore suspect that differences in the characteristics of entering students account for most status and income differences between alumni of different colleges. For additional data on the effects of qualitative differences between colleges, see Chapter 5, note 2.

# CHAPTER SEVEN

# Income Inequality

Why are some men rich and others poor? The question has baffled philosophers for centuries, and modern economics has not taken us very far towards an answer either. Still, we have learned something. It seems reasonably clear that neither men's genes nor the quality of their schooling explains much of the variation in their incomes. Family background explains a bit more, as does overall cognitive skill. Educational credentials also have a modest effect. But even when men are identical on all these factors, they *still* end up with very unequal incomes.

Our discussion will first describe the extent of income inequality and the trend in inequality over the past 40 years. Next, we take up the relationship between an individual's income and his socio-economic, racial, and family background. We then look at the relationship between test scores, education, and income, and at income differences between men in different occupations. Finally, we will draw some conclusions, the most important of which is that if we want to equalize incomes, we must do so directly, rather than equalizing something else and hoping this will redistribute income.

## The Extent of Income Inequality

Table 7–1 shows the degree of inequality in family income from 1929 to 1970. The table shows, for example, that in 1970 the top fifth of all families had incomes that averaged 223 percent of the national average, while the bottom fifth had incomes 28 percent of the average.[1] There are a number of minor defects in the data, and the exact percentages should not be taken too literally.[2] The basic trends are almost certainly real, however. There seems to have been some reduction in income inequality during the Depression, and there seems to have been a further reduction during World War II. The degree of inequality did not change much from 1946 to 1960. There was a slight decline in inequality from 1960 to 1968 and a reversal of the 1960–1968 trend between 1968 and 1970.

The major conclusion to be drawn from this data seems to be that it takes a cataclysm like the Great Depression or World War II to alter

Table 7-1

*Pretax Incomes of Families and Individuals in Each Quintile as
a Percentage of National Mean: 1929–1968*

| | 1929 [a] | 1935–1936 [b] | 1941 [b] | 1946 [b] | 1960 [c] | 1968 [d] | 1970 [d] |
|---|---|---|---|---|---|---|---|
| Poorest Fifth | 20 | 21 | 21 | 25 | 25 | 29 | 28 |
| Fourth Fifth | 45 | 46 | 48 | 56 | 55 | 57 | 55 |
| Middle Fifth | 70 | 71 | 77 | 80 | 80 | 80 | 79 |
| Second Fifth | 95 | 105 | 112 | 109 | 115 | 115 | 115 |
| Top Fifth | 270 | 259 | 244 | 231 | 225 | 218 | 223 |
| Top 5 Percent [e] | 600 | 530 | 480 | 426 | 400 | 334 | 344 |
| Mean (Current Dollars) | $2,340 | $1,630 | $2,210 | $3,940 | $6,820 | $8,840 | $10,100 |
| (1968 Dollars) | $5,210 | $4,340 | $5,380 | $6,620 | $7,860 | $8,840 | $9,040 |
| Coefficient of Variation [f] | 1.23 | 1.09 | 0.98 | 0.87 | 0.83 | 0.72 | 0.75 |

Note: Definitions of income differ from those used elsewhere in this chapter so that distributions are not precisely comparable, even for 1968.

[a] U.S. Bureau of the Census, *Historical Statistics of the United States; Colonial Times to 1957* (1965), p. 166.

[b] Goldsmith et al., "Size Distribution of Income."

[c] U.S. Department of Commerce, *Survey of Current Business* (April 1964), pp. 5–8.

[d] Table 14 in the U.S. Bureau of the Census, "Income in 1970," corrected for comparability to Office of Business Economics data used in Column 5. Correction assumes constant underreporting of income to Current Population Survey during 1960–1970 period. For evidence supporting this assumption see Herriott and Miller, "Who Paid Taxes in 1968?" and Miller, *Income Distribution*. The 1960 OBE/CPS ratio for each fifth was used to inflate or deflate the 1968 and 1970 CPS data for each fifth. The trends from 1947 to 1970 were, also, calculated directly from CPS data. The absolute degree of inequality is less in the CPS series, but the trend is the same.

[e] Excludes capital gains. For discussion of this issue see Goldsmith, "Size Distribution," Kolko, *Wealth and Power,* and Herriott and Miller, "Who Paid Taxes in 1968?". Omission of capital gains probably reduces share going to the top 5 percent more in recent years than in the past. Inclusion of undistributed corporate profits (i.e. realizable capital gains) would raise the 1968 income of the top 5 percent from 334 percent of national average to 375 percent. Inclusion of capital gains from real estate might add another 10 percent.

[f] Calculated from grouped data shown in this table in order to maintain comparability between years. Collapsing detailed categories results in a reduction in coefficients for all years. The reduction averages 10–20 percent.

the distribution of income significantly. Political shifts, such as the election of a liberal or a conservative President, seem to have quite minor effects, except on the very rich and the very poor. The fact that the top and bottom fifths receive almost the same fraction of the nation's income today as in 1946 does, however, conceal two important changes.

First, everyone's income has risen. Second, the absolute gap between the rich and the poor has increased. In 1946, for example, the bottom fifth averaged about $1,650, and the top fifth averaged about $15,300 (in 1968 dollars). The gap was thus $13,650. During the next 22 years real income per family increased about 33 percent. Had this increase been evenly distributed, all families would have received an extra $2,200. The bottom fifth would have ended up with $3,850 a year and the top fifth with $17,500 (still using 1968 dollars). But this is not what happened. The incomes of the bottom fifth rose about $1,000 while the incomes of the top fifth rose about $4,000. The gap had increased by $3,000.

Trends such as those shown in Table 7–1 depend on three factors: the degree of inequality in individual incomes, differences between families in the number of people with incomes, and the correlation between the incomes of different people in the same family.

The average number of earners per family has increased over the past 20 years, and it has probably increased even more over the past 40 years.[3] Forty percent of all wives now work, compared to only 15 percent in 1940.[4] This increase in working wives has been only partially offset by a decline in the number of working children and other relatives. (Children tend to stay in school longer and begin working later. When they do start work, they are more likely to move out of their parent's house, leaving their parents and younger siblings to fend for themselves economically.)

Working wives equalize the distribution of income slightly. Wives are slightly more likely to work if their husbands have below-average incomes.[5] As a result, some families end up in the middle-income brackets, even though neither earner is well paid. If all wives worked, the distribution of income would probably be more equal than it is now. This is because the elimination of nonearners would make the distribution of income between wives more equal than it is now. In addition, husbands with high incomes would often have wives with low incomes, and vice versa.[6]

Unfortunately, while the average family has more earners than in the past, and this promotes equality, there are also more families with no earners at all, which leads to inequality. Before 1929, America spent virtually nothing on welfare or old-age pensions. Nonearners had to live on savings, live with earners, or starve. Today, social security and welfare enable many nonearners to live on their own, albeit at desperately inadequate levels. Increased longevity and rising divorce rates make such families more common every year. These families without earners are almost always poor. The ironic result is that if nothing else changes, improving the welfare system makes the distribution of pretax family income look increasingly unequal, simply because it allows more poor people to maintain separate families.[7]

The degree of inequality in family income is, then, determined by both family structure and the degree of inequality in individual incomes. We have not investigated the factors influencing family structure, although several of the authors are now exploring these issues in more detail. The remainder of this chapter will concentrate on the factors that account for variation in individual incomes.

Earnings (wages, salaries, and most income from self-employment) today provide about 75 percent of disposable income in the United States.[8] Table 7–2 shows the distribution of earnings for full-time, year-round workers in America in 1968. These figures exclude individuals who did not work all year and individuals who worked less than full-time. They also exclude "unearned" income (i.e. dividends, interest, rent, welfare, social security, etc.). Table 7–2 therefore gives a fairly good indication of the degree of inequality in weekly wages. The disparity between the best- and worst-paid workers is striking. The best-paid fifth earned twice the national weekly average, while the worst-paid fifth earned only 38 percent of the national weekly average. Because men with low weekly earnings are more likely to be unemployed and less likely to have large unearned incomes, there is slightly more inequality in annual incomes than in weekly earnings.[9]

Property income (e.g. dividends, interest, and rent) accounts for another 15–20 percent of disposable income. Transfer payments (e.g. private pensions, social security, unemployment insurance, and welfare) account for about 8 percent.[10] Unfortunately, we know relatively little about the factors influencing people's ability to accumulate either property income or transfer payments. Property income depends to some extent on inherited wealth, but as we shall see, this is not the main factor. Transfer payments seem to depend largely on age and absence of earnings.

Most survey respondents seriously underreport both their property and transfer incomes, so reported income is even more dominated by earnings than actual income.[11] The discussion which follows will therefore treat earnings and individual income as almost interchangeable concepts. It will also concentrate on the factors influencing male incomes. This is because we know very little about the factors influencing women's incomes.[12] More work on this problem is badly needed.

Table 7–2
*Annual Earnings of Full-Time Year-Round Workers in 1968*

| Amount | Males | Females | All Workers |
|---|---|---|---|
| $0–1,999 | 4.7 | 10.4 | 6.2 |
| $2,000–3,999 | 8.2 | 30.9 | 14.8 |
| $4,000–5,999 | 17.1 | 34.2 | 22.0 |
| $6,000–7,999 | 24.4 | 16.6 | 22.1 |
| $8,000–9,999 | 17.9 | 4.8 | 14.1 |
| $10,000–14,999 | 19.5 | 2.5 | 14.6 |
| $15,000–24,999 | 6.3 | 0.3 | 4.6 |
| $25,000 and over | 1.9 | 0.1 | 1.4 |
| Total | 100.0 | 99.8 | 99.8 |
| Mean Earnings | $8,440 | $4,580 | $7,320 |
| Standard Deviation | $5,508 | $2,645 | $5,290 |
| Coefficient of Variation | 0.65 | 0.58 | 0.72 |
| Mean for Top Fifth | $15,940 | $8,410 | $15,010 |
| Mean for Bottom Fifth | $3,120 | $1,640 | $2,780 |
| Number of Workers | 37,068,000 | 15,013,000 | 52,081,000 |

Source: Table 48 in the U.S. Bureau of the Census "Income in 1968." Means for intervals approximated from Table 1 of the same source. Workers without earnings excluded.

## The Effects of Socio-Economic Background

Socio-economic background has less effect on individual incomes than many people imagine, but the effect is still substantial. Suppose, for example, that we rank families on the basis of the father's occupation and the father's educational attainment. Suppose we then compare sons who come from the most privileged fifth of all families to sons who come from the least privileged fifth. For convenience, let us call the first group of families "upper-middle class" and the second group "lower class." The best available data suggests that men with upper-middle class parents earn about 28 percent more per year than the national average, while those with lower-class parents earn about 28 percent less.[13] These estimates suggest that, on the average, upper-middle class sons can expect to make about 75 percent more money than lower-class sons. This difference probably declined somewhat between 1929 and 1945, but not much after that.[14]

One obvious objection to this conclusion is that we have defined the class into which an individual is born entirely in terms of the father's educational attainment and occupational status, not in terms of the parents' actual income. We do not believe, however, that the results would be appreciably different if we also included income in our definition of class. Chapters 3 and 5 suggested that parental income had virtually no independent effect on a child's cognitive skills, and that it had a rather modest independent effect on his educational attainment, once parental education and occupation had been taken into account. Except in the atypical case where the son takes over the father's farm or business, we find it hard to imagine that father's income has much independent effect on the job a son gets, once the father's education and occupation and the son's education and test scores have been taken into account.

Parental income could have a big independent effect on a son's income if large number of parents passed along capital assets to their children, but this seems to be relatively rare. The best data on inheritances comes from a 1960 survey of 3,000 American families. Four-fifths of these families reported that they had not inherited anything. Another 14 percent reported having inherited less than $10,000. This meant that, at normal interest rates, their inherited capital increased their incomes by less than $1,000 per year, and often by less than $500. Two percent of all families reported having inherited between $10,000 and $25,000. Inheritances of this size should increase annual income by $500 to $2,500. Only 1 percent of all families reported inheriting more than $25,000. These "large" inheritances boosted the recipients' incomes by an average of $2,900.[15] Even among the top 1 percent, then, inherited capital accounts for a very small fraction of the recipient's total income. Probably no more than one family in a thousand gets more income from inheritance than from earnings.[16]

These arguments suggest that knowing how much money a man's parents made would not enable us to predict his eventual income much better than simply knowing his father's occupation and education. We therefore think that our estimates of income differences between children born into different social classes would hold up fairly well even if parental income were included in our definition of who is upper-middle and lower class. At most, we would expect the estimated income of upper-middle class sons to be 135 or 140 percent of the mean, instead of the 128 percent estimated earlier.

The fact that men born into the upper-middle class make 75 percent more than men born into the lower class implies a large absolute gap, but the difference is not large relative to the difference between the rich and poor in general. The richest fifth of all men made at least 650 percent more than the poorest fifth.[17] The disparity between the sons of upper-middle and lower-class families is trivial in comparison.

This means that eliminating differences in social-class background (or neutralizing their effects) would not take us very far toward eliminating income inequality. Suppose, for example, that we compare individuals whose fathers had the same occupational status and the same amount of education. Our best estimate is that within such a group the best-paid fifth earns about 550 percent more than the worst-paid fifth.[18] This means there is almost as much income inequality among men from the same socio-economic background as among men in general.

Our next question was *how* family background exercised its influence on a son's income. Table 7–3 decomposes the overall income disparity between upper-middle and lower-class sons into discrete causes, each of which contributes something to the overall gap. Three conclusions seem warranted.

First, genes account for no more than 10 percent of the difference. As usual, biological explanations for the inheritance of privilege do not take us very far.

Second, the theory that the upper-middle class maintains its priv-

Table 7–3

*Estimated Importance of Various Factors Contributing to the Cumulative Income Advantage of Men With High-Status Fathers*

| Source | Percent |
|---|---|
| 1. IQ Genotype | 7–9 |
| 2. IQ Advantage Due to Superior Home Environment | 16–20 |
| 3. Extra Schooling for Those with Equal IQs | 24–29 |
| 4. Higher-status Occupations for Those with Equal Schooling and Equal IQs | 18 |
| 5. Higher Incomes for Those with Equal-status Occupations, Equal Schooling, and Equal IQs | 30 |
| Total | 100 |

Source: Appendix B, Figure B–7.

Derivation: The overall correlation between father's occupation and son's income is 0.287 (see Appendix B, Figure B–7). This correlation can be decomposed by summing the compound paths from *POPOC* to *INC* in Figure B–7. Thus, for line 4 above, we calculate $(0.158)(0.327)/0.287 = 0.18$. Due to underreporting of property income to the CPS, line 5 is probably underestimated.

ileged economic position by ensuring that its children get more education than other people is closer to the mark than the theory that the upper-middle class is biologically superior. Educational advantages per se seem to account for about a quarter of the income advantage enjoyed by men from upper-middle class backgrounds. If we also include educational advantages deriving from differences in test scores, we can explain another 10 percent of the gap.[19] If we had information on the quality of the colleges individuals had attended, we might explain another 5 to 15 percent, i.e. 40 or 50 percent of the total gap.[20]

Third, the biggest single source of income differences seems to be the fact that men from high-status families have higher incomes than men from low-status families, even when they enter the same occupation, have the same amount of education, and have the same test scores.[21]

Nonetheless, our strongest overall impression is that there does not seem to be *any* mechanism available to most upper-middle class parents for maintaining their children's privileged economic position. Insofar as incomes are relative rather than absolute, most upper-middle class children simply end up worse off than their parents. Among men born into the most affluent fifth of the population, for example, we estimate that less than half will be part of this same elite when they grow up.[22] Of course, it is also true that very few will be in the bottom fifth. Rich parents can at least guarantee their children that much. Yet if we follow families over several generations, even this will not hold true. Affluent families often have at least one relatively indigent grandparent in the background, and poor families, unless they are black or relatively recent immigrants, have often had at least one prosperous grandparent. This is particularly true of maternal grandparents, since affluent families seem to have a harder time guaranteeing their daughters a good marriage than guaranteeing their sons a good job.[23]

## The Effects of Race

In 1970, white men who worked full-time and year-round earned an average of $200 a week. Black men who worked full-time and year-round averaged about $130, while black women averaged about $90.[24] The ratio of black to white wages rose during World War II, held fairly steady for the next 20 years, then rose again in the late 1960s.[25]

The absolute gap between black and white workers (i.e. the absolute difference in their purchasing power) also declined between 1968 and 1970. But over the long haul the absolute difference has tended to increase. In this respect, the situation of blacks has been like that of the poor in general, namely that their relative position has improved somewhat, but not fast enough to narrow the absolute gap between them and the rich.[26]

The ratio of black to white earnings seems to depend on political and economic conditions. World War II and northward migration of blacks helped a great deal. Full employment during the middle 1960s may also have helped, but improvement continued even during the economic doldrums of 1968–1970, presumably because of the delayed influence of the civil rights movement. The main beneficiaries of improvement were young blacks just entering the labor market. Thus even if recent trends were to continue, which hardly seems certain in the present political climate, it would be a generation before black and white hourly earnings approached equality.[27]

Blacks not only earn less than whites on a weekly basis, they are also more likely to be unemployed or underemployed.[28] In addition, blacks have less unearned income than whites. This means that blacks' annual incomes lag somewhat further behind the white norm than their weekly wages. Black wives are, however, more likely to work than white wives, so black family incomes lag less than their individual incomes. Furthermore, at least in the North, young black families with working husbands and wives report incomes as high as comparable white families. Nonetheless, the overall disparity between black and white family incomes did not change much during the 1960s. The reason was that while black husband-wife families improved their position dramatically during the 1960s, the proportion of black families with both a husband and a wife declined. Black families headed by women not only grew more numerous but remained desperately poor, keeping overall black family income low.[29]

How are we to account for the persistent lag in individual black incomes? The best information on the factors influencing blacks' incomes was collected in 1962 and may be quite outdated by now. Nonetheless, the situation at that time is of considerable interest. Black males who were not born on farms and were in the experienced civilian labor force reported 1961 incomes averaging just under half the mean for similar whites. Blacks who had the same number of brothers and sisters as the average white, and whose fathers had the same amount of education and the same occupational status as the average white, received almost as much education as the average white. As a result, their incomes averaged 57 percent of the white norm instead of 46 percent. Those blacks who not only had the same amount of education as the average white, but also entered an occupation of the same status as the average white, had incomes 63 percent of the white mean.[30]

We do not have test score data for this particular group of blacks. Another large study of black earnings in the early 1960s found, however, that blacks who scored at the same level as the average white earned only 25 percent more than those who scored at the black norm.[31] We therefore conclude that at least half the income gap between blacks and whites in 1962 was probably due to discrimination or to unmeasured cultural differences. We suspect that discrimination was more important, but the two are hard to distinguish empirically.

This conclusion is based on a comparison between the average white and blacks who had similar advantages. It is also useful to compare the average black to whites with similar disadvantages. Suppose, for example, that we compare blacks' incomes to those of whites who are in occupations of the same status as the average black, who have as little education as the average black, who do as poorly on standardized tests as the average black, and who come from equally disadvantaged families. We find that, in 1961, the average black male had about 25 percent less income than comparable whites.[32] This means that employers paid relatively uneducated blacks in unskilled and semiskilled jobs about 25 percent less than similar whites. They paid blacks with average amounts of education in middle-level jobs about 35 percent less than similar whites. Blacks in professional and managerial jobs may have been even more discriminated against.

Since most blacks were at the bottom of the economic ladder, it could be argued that discrimination had a relatively modest effect. We suspect, however, that one reason blacks remained at the bottom of the ladder was that the economic rewards to climbing were so slight. Since blacks were treated alike, regardless of their family background, educational attainment, or occupation, there was no incentive to self-sacrifice. We therefore think that the degree of discrimination in top jobs is a better index of the overall effects of discrimination than the degree of discrimination at the bottom.

Since 1965, there has been an observable rush to hire qualified blacks, and this has driven up their wages relative to whites. In 1968, for example, black male college graduates had incomes 64 percent of the average for white college graduates. By 1970, they had incomes 69 percent of the white average.[33] The incomes of black men who had only finished elementary school fell during this same period from 77 to 75 percent of the average for comparable whites. If this trend continues, we can look forward to a situation where educated blacks are no more discriminated against than uneducated blacks. This will make the economic payoffs from education as great for blacks as for whites. We suspect that blacks with high test scores may also be improving their position relative to blacks with low test scores, but we know of no evidence for this. Thus, while educational attainment and cognitive skills did not explain an appreciable fraction of the income difference between whites and blacks in the early 1960s, we may be moving towards a situation where they will be considerably more important.

What does this imply about future income trends? Black educational attainment is rapidly approaching that of whites. Reducing differences in parental education and income may reduce the test score difference between black and white children by a few points.[34] Cultural differences between blacks and whites are likely to persist, however. Since cultural rather than economic differences now seem to account for the bulk of the black-white test score gap, we must assume that part of this gap will persist for some time to come. This need not, however, imply any significant amount of economic inequality. If the average black child scored 10–12 points below national norms, but was otherwise indistinguishable from the average white child, we would expect him to end up with an income about 88 percent of the white average.[35] If blacks continue to get more education than whites with comparable scores, the anticipated income gap would be even smaller. If the average black man was earning 88 percent of what the average white earned, and if black women continued to work more than white women, black family incomes would end up almost equal to white family incomes. If that happened, the whole issue of racial inequality would probably recede into the background in much the same way that controversy over other kinds of ethnic discrimination has receded into the background. In the interim, it seems wiser to concentrate on eliminating racial discrimination, which is both practical and effective, than to concentrate on equalizing black and white test scores, which is much harder and far less effective.

## The Effects of Family Background

Our best estimate is that family background explains around 15 percent of the variation in incomes. This is only a little more than we can explain in terms of social-class background alone. If this estimate is even approximately correct, it means that brothers raised in the same home end up with very different standards of living. In 1968, for example, if we had compared random pairs of individuals, we would have found that their earnings differed by an average of about $6,200. If we had had data on brothers, our best guess is that they would have differed by at least $5,600.[36]

This implies that even if America could reduce inequalities in opportunity to the point where they were no greater than those that now arise between one brother and another, the best-paid fifth of all male workers would still be making 500 percent more than the worst-paid fifth.[37] We cannot, then, hope to eliminate, or even substantially reduce, income inequality in America simply by providing children from all walks of life with equal opportunity. When people have had relatively equal opportunity, as brothers usually have, they still end up with very unequal incomes. If we want to prevent this, we will have to establish floors below which nobody's income is allowed to fall and ceilings above which it is not allowed to rise. We will return to this theme later.

## The Effects of Cognitive Skills

"If you're so smart, why aren't you rich?" The wryness with which the question is habitually asked suggests that most people see the connection between cognitive skill and economic success as rather problematic. This skepticism is well founded. While cognitive skill does have some effect on adult income, it is certainly not decisive.

If we make our usual comparison between those who score above the eightieth percentile and those who score below the twentieth percentile on the Armed Forces Qualification Test, we estimate that men in the first group have personal incomes 34 percent above the national average, while men in the second group have incomes about 34 percent below the average. The first group is thus making about twice as much as the second. This is roughly the same gap as we found between men whose parents were in the top and bottom fifths of the socio-economic distribution.[38] It is also roughly the same as the gap between the best- and worst-educated fifths of the population.

If we compare men with IQ genotypes above the eightieth percentile to men with genotypes below the twentieth percentile, the estimated difference is much smaller. The most genetically advantaged fifth of all men appear to have incomes about 35 to 40 percent higher than the most genetically disadvantaged fifth.[39] In a society where the best-paid fifth of all men earn 600 percent more income than the worst-paid fifth, disparities of this magnitude are not very significant. The point is even clearer if we estimate the degree of income inequality between individuals with exactly the same IQ genotype. Our best estimate is that we would find only about 3 percent less income inequality in genetically homogenous subpopulations than in the entire American population.[40]

The fact that high test scores are associated with slightly higher incomes does not mean that high test scores cause high incomes or that cognitive skills are essential for holding down a well-paid job. Men with high test scores tend to come from economically and socially advantaged families, and this accounts for part of their income advantage when they grow up. In addition, men with high test scores tend to get more than their share of educational credentials, and this helps them get into high-status occupations. Still, about half the observed relationship between test scores and income persists when we compare individuals who have the same family background and the same amount of schooling.[41]

The relationship between test scores and income is thus quite different from the relationship between test scores and occupational status. On the one hand, men with high test scores are more likely to enter high-status occupations than to have high incomes.[42] On the other hand, the effect of test scores on income seems to be more genuine than their effect on status, in that more of it persists after we control family background and credentials.[43] In neither case, however, is the direct effect of cognitive skill very large.

## The Effects of Credentials

"Everyone" knows that staying in school is important for "getting ahead," and most people assume that "getting ahead" includes making money. This idea has led to a vast amount of research which purports to show that attending school and college increases a man's earning power. (Less is usually said about the effect of schooling on women's earnings.)

In the 1950s and early 1960s, when schooling was being promoted as the solution to virtually all problems, it was fashionable to compare, say, the earnings of high school graduates and high school dropouts and impute the difference to the possession of a high school diploma.[44] Table 7–4 illustrates the results obtained in such studies. It gives the 1968 incomes of full-time, year-round workers with varying amounts of schooling as a percentage of the national average.[45] It shows considerable inequality between the best- and worst-educated workers.

Those who had done some graduate work were making 2.7 times as much as those who had not finished elementary school.[46]

It takes no great imagination to realize that comparisons of this kind can be very misleading. To infer, for example, that elementary school dropouts would have earned 171 percent of the national average instead of 64 percent if they had gone to graduate school seems clearly mistaken. In order to treble their incomes, they would not only have needed educational credentials, but all the other characteristics that differentiate graduate students from elementary school dropouts. When we compare individuals who come from similar family backgrounds and have similar initial test scores, the income difference between the highly educated and the poorly educated diminishes by about 40 percent.[47] If we compared individuals who were also similar in all other ways, except for schooling and its consequences, the apparent effect of schooling would be even further reduced.

What does this mean? Table 7–4 indicates that each extra year of elementary or secondary school is associated with a 6 percent income increase. Each year of college is associated with a 12 percent increase. A year of graduate school is associated with a 7 percent increase.[48] If 40 percent of these increases is due to the association between schooling, initial ability, and family background, an extra year of elementary

Table 7–4

*Incomes of Full-Time, Year-Round Workers over 25 With Different Amounts of Schooling, as a Percentage of the 1968 Average*

| Amount of Schooling | Males | Females | Total |
|---|---|---|---|
| Didn't Finish Elementary School | 70% | 40% | 64% |
| Finished Elementary School, No High School | 85% | 47% | 76% |
| Entered High School, Didn't Finish | 96% | 51% | 84% |
| Finished High School, No College | 111% | 61% | 95% |
| Entered College, Didn't Finish | 129% | 71% | 115% |
| Finished College, No Graduate School | 170% | 84% | 150% |
| At Least 1 Year of Graduate Work | 188% | 106% | 171% |
| All Individuals | 114% | 62% | 100% |
| Grand Mean | | | $7,995 |
| Number of Individuals in 1,000s | 34,432 | 12,575 | 47,008 |

Source: Table 41 in the U.S. Bureau of the Census, "Income in 1968." "Elementary School" includes the first 8 years of schooling. "High School" includes grades 9–12. "Finished College" means a 4-year college. "No High School," "No College," and "No Graduate School" includes individuals who entered these institutions but did not complete the first year.

or secondary schooling really boosts future income less than 4 percent, an extra year of college boosts it about 7 percent, and a year of graduate school boosts it about 4 percent.[49]

These figures are averages, and they obviously do not apply to each specific case. An extra year of graduate school is worth more for medical students and less for education students. An extra year of schooling also seems to do about twice as much for a student from a middle-class background as for a student from a working-class background.[50] It is more valuable for whites than for blacks, although as we noted earlier, this disparity is declining.[51]

We also expected to find that schooling paid off more for men who had high test scores than for men with low scores. This, after all, is the classic rationale for admitting only talented students to college. Conversely, we expected high scores to be more valuable to men who had had a lot of schooling than to men with relatively little schooling. We found no evidence for this in our large national samples, but these were composed entirely of men in their twenties and thirties. Smaller local studies of older men do show the anticipated pattern, although not in very dramatic form.[52]

Why should educational credentials be more valuable to white middle-class students than to others? One plausible theory is that middle-class students attend high-prestige colleges, whose diplomas impress employers more than the diplomas acquired by working-class students. But middle-class men also appear to benefit more from a high school diploma. This is hard to explain. There is enormous overlap between the high schools attended by middle-class and working-class whites. Furthermore, middle-class students get more income from extra schooling even when they have the same test scores as working-class students. We cannot, then, impute the difference to the fact that middle-class students are smarter or learn more in school or college. We have considered a variety of alternative explanations, but none seems entirely convincing. Since the evidence for a difference comes from a single, imperfectly representative sample, we think it wiser to make sure the pattern is real before inventing elaborate explanations.

Now, suppose that we define the "cost" of education as the student's out-of-pocket expenditures plus the earnings he loses by not working while in school. Suppose we define the "benefits" as his additional earnings that result from extra schooling. In addition, let us assume that the entire income difference between the well educated and the poorly educated is due to schooling. On these simplified assumptions, the "rate of return" on an individual's "investment" in schooling appears to be very high in elementary school, since the costs are trivial. For high school, the rate of return still averages 16 to 20 percent for white males. For college, it averages 7 to 12 percent for white males.[53] Taking differences in family background and cognitive skill into account would probably lower these estimates by about 40 percent, to 10 or 12 percent for high school and 4 to 7 percent for college.[54] The rates of return appear to be appreciably higher for white middle-class males and somewhat lower for white working-class males, black males, and females of all classes and colors.[55]

These averages do not tell us much about whether individual students should stay in school or drop out. The relatively high rate of return to high school, for example, reflects the low wages usually available to teenagers who are not in school. But if a student knows he can get a good job when he drops out, it may make economic sense for him to do so, even though it would not make sense for the hypothetical "average student." Conversely, the low rate of return to higher education reflects the assumption that college-age individuals can make fairly good wages if they are not in school, plus the assumption that their out-of-pocket costs are higher than high school students' costs. But if a student can get money from his parents to attend college but not to do anything else, his rate of return is much higher.

Rate-of-return estimates do tell us that efforts to keep everyone in school longer make little economic sense. The average rate of return for postsecondary education is quite low. For the kinds of students who are not now in college, it is even lower. For working-class whites, blacks, and women, dropping out seems in many cases to be the most economically rational decision. Efforts to get everyone to finish high school and attend college must, therefore, be justified primarily on noneconomic grounds. Otherwise, they probably cannot be justified at all.

This conclusion seems particularly persuasive when we recall that the financial return to extra schooling derives almost exclusively from the fact that schooling provides men with access to highly paid occupations, not from the fact that it enables men in a given occupation to earn more. Giving everyone more credentials cannot provide everyone with access to the best-paid occupations. It can only raise earnings if it makes people more productive within various occupations. There is little evidence that it will do this.[56]

If this argument is correct, equalizing everyone's educational attainment would have virtually no effect on income inequality.[57] At most, equalizing educational attainment might help demystify professional and managerial work, making the public more skeptical about monopolistic arrangements which now keep elite salaries high. If this happened, income differences between occupations might decline. This would somewhat reduce overall inequality in the distribution of income. As we shall see in the next section, however, even the complete elimination of income differences between occupations would make a rather modest dent on the overall pattern of income inequality, since most inequality is *within* occupations.

## The Effects of Occupation

The Census Bureau groups the labor force into 11 broad occupational categories. The relative earnings of full-time, year-round workers in these groups are shown in Table 7–5. While their earnings are certainly not equal, the differences are quite small compared to the differences between individual workers. The most affluent are the self-employed

Table 7–5

*Mean 1970 Earnings of Workers by Occupational Category*

| Occupations (% of Labor Force) | Earnings of Full-Time, Year-Round Workers as Percentage of Mean for All Full-Time, Year-Round Workers * | |
|---|---|---|
| | Male | Female |
| Professional | | |
| Salaried | 146.0 | 91.8 |
| Self-employed | 258.4 | — |
| Managers | | |
| Salaried | 162.3 | 84.3 |
| Self-employed | 105.0 | 59.4 |
| Clerical | 102.3 | 66.5 |
| Sales | 126.4 | 52.3 |
| Craftsmen | 108.5 | 59.3 |
| Operatives | 89.6 | 52.4 |
| Private Household | — | 25.0 |
| Service Workers | 84.4 | 46.8 |
| Laborers | 74.2 | 54.0 |
| Farmers | 58.6 | — |
| Farm Laborers | 44.0 | — |
| All Occupations | 114.7 | 65.6 |
| Mean Earnings | $9,918 | $5,675 |
| Number with Earnings | 36,132 | 15,476 |

Source: Table 55 in the U.S. Bureau of the Census, "Income in 1970."
* Mean for all male and female full-time, year-round workers was $8,645.

male professionals, who earned 258 percent of the national average in 1970. Only 2 relatively small groups, the "Private Household Workers" (i.e. domestic servants) and the "Farm Laborers and Foremen," earned less than half the national average when they worked regularly.

The occupational categories in Table 7–5 are, of course, extremely broad. "Service Workers," for example, include both firemen, who made about 140 percent of the national average, and janitors, who made about 70 percent.[58] But even when we divide the labor force into 435 detailed occupational categories, we still find very few occupations that deviate dramatically from the national average. Only 7 percent of all men and 19 percent of all women were in detailed occupational categories in which the average rate of pay was less than half the national average in 1959. Conversely, only 5 percent of all men and 0.6 percent of women workers were in detailed categories with earnings more than twice the national average.[59] There is no reason to suppose that further refining our occupational classification would carry us much further towards an understanding of why some people earn so little while others earn so much.[60]

The earnings of men in the same occupations are almost as unequal as the earnings of random individuals. Suppose, for example, that we were to equalize the average earnings of all occupations. Suppose, however, that we could not reduce the disparities among people in the same occupation. This would reduce inequality in earnings by perhaps a fifth.[61] Now suppose that we left economic inequality between occupations untouched, but that we found a way to eliminate inequality within occupations. This would reduce inequality by more than 40 percent.[62] A reform strategy which concentrates on access to different occupations may, then, be less promising than a strategy aimed at bringing everyone close to the average for his or her occupation.

## Conclusions about Income Distribution

Neither family background, cognitive skill, educational attainment, nor occupational status explains much of the variation in men's incomes. Indeed, when we compare men who are identical in all these respects, we find only 12 to 15 percent less inequality than among random individuals.[63] How are we to explain these variations among men who seem to be similarly situated?

One obvious possibility is that some men value money more than others, and that these men make unusual sacrifices to get it. One man may, for example, take a second job while another does not, or he may take a more dangerous job that pays better while another man turns it down. At least among the young, however, those who say that high income is their primary job objective earn no more than those who say income is not a major concern.[64] This may only prove that once men succeed in getting a well-paid job they start worrying about other objectives. Still, we know no empirical evidence suggesting that caring about money has a significant effect on income.

Incomes may also depend on varieties of competence that have very little relation to family background, educational attainment, or cognitive skill: the ability to hit a ball thrown at high speed, the ability to type a letter quickly and accurately, the ability to persuade a customer that he wants a larger car than he thought he wanted, the ability to look a man in the eye without seeming to stare, and so forth. We have no way of saying how much of the variation in people's incomes depends on characteristics of this kind, but it could be substantial.

Income also depends on luck: chance acquaintances who steer you to one line of work rather than another, the range of jobs that happen to be available in a particular community when you are job hunting, the amount of overtime work in your particular plant, whether bad weather destroys your strawberry crop, whether the new superhighway has an exit near your restaurant, and a hundred other unpredictable accidents. Those who are lucky tend, of course, to impute their success to skill, while those who are inept believe that they are merely unlucky. If one man makes money speculating in real estate while another loses it, the former will credit his success to good judgment while the latter will blame his failure on bad luck. So, too, if a worker's firm expands rapidly and promotes him, he will assume this is a tribute to his foresight in picking the right firm and his talent on the job. If his firm goes broke and leaves him with an unmarketable set of specialized skills, he will seldom blame himself. In general, we think luck has far more influence on income than successful people admit.

If this argument is correct, it is not surprising that family background, schooling, test scores, and occupation explain relatively little of the variation in income. If the argument is correct, however, it seems clear that strategies for reducing economic inequality by equalizing opportunity will not work very well. Such strategies seldom involve direct efforts at equalizing men's competence in their work, and they never deal with inequalities due to accidents over which an individual has no control.

Direct efforts to equalize competence would have to focus on the specific skills needed on actual jobs. Most organizations now run in such a way as to magnify initial differences in competence rather than reduce them. Those who have a skill are given opportunities to develop it. They acquire more power, and this encourages them to develop new skills. Those who do not have a skill are rarely encouraged to develop it. Deliberate efforts to reorganize work so that everyone has to develop a variety of skills and take some degree of responsibility are unusual. If America were really anxious to equalize competence, and if it were willing to pay something for this, such arrangements could be made more common. If, for example, the government were to offer substantial incentives to employers for rotating workers among jobs, and if employers actually began to do this to a significant extent, those who held power at any given time would be under real pressure to make sure that others were also competent to do their job. This would entail spending more time on training. Those who held power would also be under pressure to make other jobs more responsible, since they might soon hold these jobs themselves. In the long run, job rotation would discourage hierarchical organization and probably reduce disparities in competence. Israel's experience with the kibbutz suggests that a considerable amount of job rotation is possible without reducing efficiency. But experience with the kibbutz also suggests that significant disparities in competence persist even in the face of stringent efforts to eliminate them.

Since we suspect that luck has at least as much effect as competence on income, we have also given some thought to strategies for reducing its effect. The usual method for reducing the effects of luck is insurance. While income insurance is probably not politically practical, the idea is not completely absurd either.

Suppose that the federal government were to draw up actuarial tables which estimated every worker's probable income in future years. These estimates would be based on a worker's family background, educational attainment, test scores, occupational specialty, and any other criteria that proved relevant. The actuarial table would give the estimated mean income of all individuals with a specific set of characteristics, and would include some kind of escalator clause for inflation and rises in productivity. If the table were reasonably sophisticated, it would estimate an individual's probable future income almost as accurately as he could estimate it himself. (This would not mean it had to be very accurate.) If a worker decided to take out income insurance, the government would guarantee him an annual payment equal to half his predicted income in that year. In return, the individual would have to pay half his actual income in that year to the government. Anyone who earned less than his predicted income would thus have half his loss wiped out. Anyone who earned more than his predicted income would have half his gain wiped out. Anyone who decided not to work would receive half as much as he would have if he had worked.

One objection to this scheme is that it might reduce people's incentive to work. Experience with progressive income taxes does not, however, suggest that people lose interest in increasing their incomes if they have to pay half the increment to the Internal Revenue Service.[65] There is no obvious reason to suppose that people would feel differently if they were paying half their earnings to an insurance scheme.

A more serious objection to this approach is that large numbers of workers, especially males, would probably not buy such insurance. Some optimists would assume that they could do better than the government's actuarial tables predicted. Given the uncertainties of income prediction, they might well be right. Furthermore, even those who felt the actuarial tables were realistic "on the average" might prefer to take their chances on doing very badly in the hope of doing very well. Americans have a passion for insurance, but they also have a passion for gambling. Given an opportunity to either double their money or lose it by flipping a coin, many people will flip the coin.

A third objection to such a system is that it does nothing to eliminate predictable differences in income, even when these are based on characteristics like family background and IQ for which an individual deserves no real credit. Thus even a 100 percent insurance scheme that eliminated all income variation among people with similar family backgrounds, educational attainments, test scores, and occupations would leave income inequality at around 50 percent of its present level. A 50 percent insurance scheme such as the one discussed above would only reduce the overall level of inequality by about 30 percent.[66]

A more serious practical objection to income insurance is that a realistic system for predicting incomes would be politically unacceptable. A realistic system would have to take account of race and sex discrimination, for example. Otherwise, it could not offer white males enough benefits to be financially attractive. Yet a system that guaranteed blacks less than equally well-qualified whites would clearly be unacceptable. This suggests a more general problem, namely that nobody knows how nonparticipation might affect the viability of such a system, or how the existence of the system might affect future incomes. Our reason for suggesting the idea is not, then, that we think it could be put into practice. It does, however, clarify the character of income inequality and some of the obstacles to eliminating it.

Ironically, the best way to overcome many of the practical objections to income insurance would be to make it compulsory instead of voluntary. The result would be a system of highly progressive income taxes, coupled with income maintenance for families with low incomes from other sources. Suppose, for example, that every family earning more than the national average in a given year had to pay half the difference to the government, while every family earning less than the national average received a check for half the difference. Such a system would be self-financing. Unlike voluntary insurance, a compulsory redistribution system of this kind could reduce not only income inequalities based on luck and unpredictable differences in competence, but also inequalities based on factors like family background, cognitive skill, education, and occupation. Such a system would guarantee every family an income at least half the national average, which we argued was enough to stay above the poverty line. It would also reduce the overall level of income inequality by 50 percent.

The principal objection to this strategy is not economic but political. Americans have a strong feeling that once they have "earned" a sum of money, it is theirs to do with as they please. They view taxes as a necessary evil, not as an instrument for making the distribution of income more equitable. As a result, the effective rate of taxation on the rich is only slightly higher than on the poor.[67] We can see no obvious way to change this without changing a great many other things first.

This suggests that egalitarians should concentrate on making the distribution of pretax wages more equal, rather than trying to use taxation as a major instrument for redistribution. Equalizing the distribution of initial wages takes money from those with unusual luck or skill before they have formed a precise idea of what they really "deserve." Likewise, it allocates extra money to those with bad luck or little skill before others have decided they are not "worth" it. Such changes can be brought about either by direct legislation or by indirect incentives.

Direct legislative control over wages has generally been anathema both to laissez-faire economists and American labor unions. Nonetheless, its long-term effect is likely to be egalitarian. In its most limited form, such control might be nothing more than a combination of minimum and maximum wages, allowing great flexibility in the middle. A comprehensive incomes policy would, however, establish wages for all sorts of jobs. We have already done this for government employees, and the resulting distribution of wages is appreciably more equal than the distribution in the private sector. Were it not for the fact that the government must compete with private enterprise for certain kinds of employees, we suspect that the logic of "one man one vote" politics would make civil service wages even more equal than they are now.

Holding up the civil service as a model for private enterprise is not, of course, a convincing argument in a country where most people assume that the government is far less efficient than private enterprise. We suspect, however, that the efficiency of private enterprise derives largely from the fact that it seldom has a guaranteed market. If nobody wants buggy whips anymore, buggy-whip factories close. This is not always true of government agencies. Where both government and private enterprise try to provide the same service, private enterprise does not seem to be significantly more efficient. Comparisons of public and private utilities, for example, do not suggest that private enterprise is necessarily more efficient. Likewise, recent experience with performance contracting in the schools does not suggest that private enterprise can usually run a school more cheaply or better than a civil service.

We have not been able to find any evidence that big wage differentials contribute significantly to efficiency. The kibbutz, with no wage differentials whatever, has had a higher rate of economic growth than the rest of the Israeli economy, which has hardly been stagnating.[68] Japan, with the highest rate of economic growth in the world, also seems to have the most equal distribution of wages.[69] Closer to home, casual observation suggests that high-level civil servants work as hard for $25,000 a year as high-level business executives receiving five or ten times as much. Likewise, low-level civil servants seem to work at least as hard as their unionized counterparts in the private sector. High wage differentials may lead to a more efficient allocation of labor, e.g. by making it look sensible to hire another secretary to save a $300,000-a-year executive an hour a week. Unfortunately, it is not always obvious that such "efficiencies" are real. Nor is it clear that they should be encouraged, even if they are real.

Those who find direct government control over wages unattractive may prefer indirect methods of achieving the same end. The government could, for example, offer economic incentives to private employers for equalizing wages. One way to do this would be to make incentive payments to employers whose pay scales were relatively uniform, or to levy special taxes on those with highly unequal wage distributions. This would encourage employers to equalize the distribution of initial wages so long as the loss in efficiency was modest, while allowing them to keep an unequal distribution if this was highly efficient.[70]

Any scheme for equalizing the distribution of income should also deal with income from stocks, bonds, and rental property. Such income does not constitute a major fraction of the total, but it does exacerbate inequality quite a lot. One approach to this problem would be to impose progressive taxes on capital assets. Estate taxes levied when an individual dies are already progressive, but they are full of loopholes, and in any event we are also concerned with the effects of capital accumulated in a single lifetime. Progressive annual taxes on an individual's capital assets would significantly reduce the incentive to accumulate large amounts of capital and might help equalize the distribution of political power as well as income.

Unfortunately, none of these innovations could command widespread political support at the present time. Income inequality is not yet perceived as a major social problem, much less as a cause of other social ills. Most Americans seem to accept the existing distribution of income as legitimate. When Lee Rainwater asked a random sample of individuals to set wages for various types of workers, for example, he found that they proposed wage differentials almost exactly equal to those that actually prevailed in 1970.[71] The first step toward redistributing income is not, then, devising ingenious machinery for taking money from the rich and giving it to the poor, but convincing large numbers of people that this is a desirable objective.

# NOTES

1. For those who think in terms of income "shares," these figures imply that the top quintile received $223/5 = 44.6$ percent of all income, while the bottom quintile received $28/5 = 5.6$ percent. Other definitions and estimation procedures yield slightly different results. For discussions of various methods of measuring income and distribution trends, see, for example, Budd and Radner, "The OBE Size Distribution"; Friedman, *Consumption Function;* Garvey, "Inequality of Income"; Goldsmith et al., "Size Distribution"; Goldsmith, "Changes in the Size Distribution"; Hanna, "The Accounting Period"; Henson, "Trends in the Income of Familes"; Herriott and Miller, "Who Paid Taxes in 1968?"; Kolko, *Wealth and Power in America;* Kravis, *The Structure of Income;* Kuznets, *Shares of Upper Income;* Miller, *Income Distribution,* and "New Evidence"; Morgan and Smith, "Measures of Economic Well-Offness"; Orshansky, "Counting the Poor"; Pechman, "The Rich, The Poor"; Shutz, "Income Inequality"; and Summers, "Econometric Investigation." We have used coefficients of variation rather than Gini coefficients to measure inequality because they are

easier to manipulate statistically. The two measures yield very similar results when data is available for reasonably detailed categories, as it is here.

2. We have tried a wide variety of alternative approaches to measuring inequality, including the use of permanent rather than annual income, the use of per capita family income instead of total family income, the use of posttax rather than pretax income, and the use of adjustments that include capital gains. Each change makes sense in its own terms, but taken together they yield a picture quite similar to Table 7–1. The data in Table 7–1 has the great advantage of allowing comparisons over time and has been used for that reason. We do not have enough data to calculate changes over time in most other distributions.

3. Table 12, in the U.S. Bureau of the Census, "Income in 1970," shows an increase in mean earners per family from 1.47 in 1950 to 1.68 in 1970.

4. See p. 212 in the U.S. Bureau of the Census, *Statistical Abstract* (1972).

5. See Morgan et al., *Income and Welfare,* on the determinants of female labor force participation. Labor force participation seems to be inversely related to the husband's earnings, but directly related to the wife's potential earnings. For more recent data, see Table 31 in the U.S. Bureau of the Census, "Income in 1970."

6. The effect of working wives on the distribution of income depends on the mean and standard deviation for husbands ($\overline{H}$ and $S_H$), the mean and standard deviation for wives ($\overline{W}$ and $S_W$), and the correlation between husbands' and wives' incomes ($r_{HW}$). The coefficient of variation for the pooled earnings of husbands and wives is $(\sqrt{S^2_H + S^2_W + 2S_H S_W r_{HW}})/(\overline{H} + \overline{W})$. If no wife works, the variance in wives' earnings is zero and the inequality in total earnings reduces to $S_H/\overline{H}$. If some wives work, those who do not work must also be included in the analysis as having zero earnings, and the variance of wives' earnings may be larger than the variance of husbands' earnings. As the percentage of working wives approaches 100, the variance in wives' earnings is likely to fall. If all wives work, the variance in their earnings is likely to be less than the variance for husbands (see Table 7–2).

If the coefficients of variation for husbands and wives separately are approximately equal, the coefficient for their pooled earnings will invariably be smaller than for either separately. Thus if we assume completely nondiscriminatory employment, so that $\overline{H} = \overline{W}$ and $S_H = S_W$, the coefficient of variation for pooled incomes will be $(\sqrt{(1 + r_{HW})/2})(S_H/\overline{H})$. This has a value less than $S_H/\overline{H}$ except when $r_{HW} = 1$. Using the 1/1000 Census income data for northeastern families in 1959, we found that when both husband and wife worked full-time and year-round, the correlation between their earnings was only 0.19. We can see no reason to expect a higher correlation if all wives worked. This implies that if all wives worked and their earnings were equal to men's, the coefficient of variation would be $\sqrt{(1 + 0.19)/2} = 77$ percent as great as if only husbands worked. At present, when less than half of all wives work, their equalizing effect is very slight.

7. The statistically minded reader may find it helpful to think of the variance in family income as depending on the variance in individual earnings, the variance in earners per family, the correlation between the earnings of different individuals in the same family, and the correlation between mean earnings and the number of earners. The variance in earners per family increased appreciably between 1950 and 1970 (see Table 12 in the U.S. Bureau of the Census, "Income in 1970").

8. See, for example, p. 316 in the U.S. Bureau of the Census, *Statistical Abstract* (1970). The exact figure depends on (a) the fraction of income from self-employment defined as earnings," and (b) whether the effective tax rate on earnings is higher, lower, or the same as that on income from other sources.

9. The observed coefficient of variation for the 1961 incomes of native white nonfarm males of similar ages and in the experienced labor force averaged 0.81 (see p. 51 in Duncan et al., *Socioeconomic Background*). The coefficient for earnings of full-time, year-round workers is about 20 percent less than this. The coefficient for all individuals is, however, inflated by the inclusion of students, men who entered or left the labor force during the year, men who prefer to work part-time, and men who entered or left the armed forces during the year.

These coefficients are also biased by measurement error. Reported income is only about 88 percent of all income (see Miller, *Income Distribution*). In addition, about 10.4 percent of the observed variance is apparently due to random error (see Appendix B, Table B–2). If we eliminate these biases, we get a coefficient of variation equal to $(0.81)(1 - 0.104)(0.88) = 0.64$. However, since underreporting is more common in high-income brackets, this may be something of an underestimate. We will use 0.70 as a reasonable approximation. The coefficient declined slightly from 1961 to 1968, but the long-term trend is unclear (see, for example, Miller, *Income Distribution*).

10. See sources and caveats in note 8.

11. On underreporting see, for example, Herriott and Miller, "Who Paid Taxes in 1968?".

12. But see Morgan et al., *Income and Welfare*.

13. Appendix B, Table B–2, allows us to calculate the multiple correlation of personal income with father's education and father's occupation. It was 0.292 for white nonfarm males in 1962. The distribution of income is skewed, but the distribution of the effects of background variables is not, at least among the young. (In the NORC veterans survey, for example, income correlates 0.270 with father's occupation and 0.221 with father's education for white heads of household between the ages of 25 and 34 and not in school. The logarithm of income correlates 0.265 with father's occupation and 0.209 with father's education for this same sample.) This suggests that it is safe to assume that the children of the top quintile are about $(1.4)(0.292) = 0.409$ standard deviations above the mean, while the children of the bottom quintile are 0.409 standard deviations below the mean. Note 9 indicates that the true coefficient of variation is probably about 0.70.

Sons of the top quintile would thus get $(0.70)(0.409) = 28.1$ percent more than the mean, while sons of the bottom quintile would get 28.1 percent less. The disparities are greater for those at the peak of their earning power and less for the young and the old. Using permanent rather than annual income would increase the correlations but would reduce the coefficient of variation, leaving the estimates in the text unchanged. (Random errors in a dependent variable do not bias estimates of regression coefficients.)

14. We have no pre-1962 data on correlations between background and income, but the cohort data in Duncan et al., *Socioeconomic Background,* shows no consistent trends by age. The percentage differentials also depend on the coefficient of variation for earnings, which shows a downward trend from 1929 to 1945, but little change after that.

15. All data is from p. 89 of Morgan et al., *Income and Welfare.* The estimate for the $25,000-and-over group is based on the multiple regression equation. Two percent of the respondents failed to answer the question about inheritance, but the incomes of these nonrespondents were below average, so it seems unlikely that they had much inherited wealth. The rich may have underreported their inheritances, but there is no evidence for this.

16. Mean family earnings in 1962 were about $7,000. Those with large inheritances presumably had earnings in excess of the average: let us say at least $10,000. It takes an inheritance of around $200,000 to yield $10,000-a-year income. Fewer than 1,000 individuals left estates in excess of $200,000 in 1962 (p. 333 in the U.S. Bureau of the Census, *Statistical Abstract, 1970*). Some of this money went to taxes and some to charity. The rest was usually divided between several children, so many of the $200,000 estates probably did not yield $200,000 to any one individual. On the other hand, some large estates were divided into several portions before death, in order to avoid estate taxes. Some families also received several large bequests, and some very large estates yielded $200,000 for several individuals. A reasonable guess is therefore that somewhere between 500 and 2,000 families inherited $200,000 or more in 1962. Assuming that a generation is 30 years, it would follow that between 15,000 and 60,000 families inherit $200,000 or more at some point in their lives. There were close to 60,000,000 families and unrelated individuals in the United States in 1962, so families with more than $10,000 a year from inheritance probably constituted between 1/1,000 and 1/4,000 of the population. The latter figure seems more realistic than the former in light of the survey data cited in note 15.

17. Table 45 in the U.S. Bureau of the Census, "Income in 1970," gives income data for 1970 by age, race, and sex. For white males between the ages of 25 and 64, the coefficient of variation is 0.65. The income of the top fifth of all earners was 1.52 standard deviations above the mean, while the bottom fifth was 1.04 standard deviations below the mean. The ratio of the top to the bottom fifth was 6.2 to 1. The overall coefficient of inequality in this data is considerably lower than in Duncan et al.'s data for 1961, where it is 0.83. This is partly because of sample differences, partly because of grouping, and perhaps partly because of real changes. For consistency, we will use the value derived from Duncan et al. (see note 9).

However, we will use the Census tabulation to estimate the number of standard deviations separating the extreme quintiles from the mean. Using 0.70 as the coefficient of variation, the estimated ratio of the top to the bottom quintile is $[1 + (0.70)(1.52)] : [1 - (0.70)(1.52)] = 206$ to 27 or 7.7 to 1. The estimated ratio derived directly from grouped Census data on all males between the ages of 25 and 64 with income in 1961 is 207 to 23, or 9 to 1. Note that these ratios are highly sensitive to small changes in the income share of the bottom fifth. Comparing ratios derived from different sources is therefore often misleading.

18. For white nonfarm males, our two background measures explain $(0.292)^2 = 8.5$ percent of the variance in income. Allowing for minor nonlinearities, the true figure might be 9 or 10 percent. This leaves at least 90 percent of the variance within groups that are similar in terms of background. The standard deviation of income within such groups would then be about $\sqrt{0.90} = 95$ percent of the original standard deviation, and the coefficient of variation would also be 95 percent of the original coefficient, i.e. $(0.95)(0.70) = 0.665$. Again, we assume that the bottom quintile averages about 1.04 standard deviations below the mean, while the top quintile averages 1.52 standard deviations above the mean (see note 17). Reducing the coefficient of inequality by 5 percent will not alter the skewness much, but it will reduce the gap between the extreme quintiles and the mean by about 5 percent. Thus, the top fifth would get $(0.665)(1.52) = 101$ percent more than the mean, while the bottom fifth would get $(0.665)(1.04) = 69.2$ percent less. The income ratio would, thus, be about 201 to 30.8 or 6.5 to 1.

19. The compound paths from education to income can be derived from Appendix B, Figure B–7, as $(0.217)(0.099)(0.327) + (0.217)(0.152) + (0.504)(0.327) = 0.205$. Since the correlation between father's occupation and son's education is 0.485, the compound paths from father's occupation to son's income via son's education sum to $(0.485)(0.205) = 0.099$. This is 34 percent of the overall correlation between father's occupation and son's income (0.287).

20. See Chapter 5, note 2.

21. Part of this is probably due to the fact that high-status sons attend prestige colleges which give them an advantage in some occupations. However, this is probably offset by underreporting of property income. Our inference that inherited property income is seriously underreported is supported by the fact that the direct path from father's status to son's reported income does not rise with age. See p. 54 in Duncan et al., *Socioeconomic Background.*

22. This estimate assumes that the correlation between parents' permanent incomes and their sons' permanent incomes is roughly equal to the estimated true correlation of father's occupation and education with son's income, i.e. 0.292. We will use 0.30 as a rounded estimate. At least in regression models, the exact percentage who remain in the top quintile depends on the skewness of the distribution. Table 7–1 suggests that the top quintile was 1.38 standard deviations above the mean in 1929, 1.47 standard deviations above in 1941, and 1.64 standard deviations above in 1970. (This does not mean

inequality increased. It means skewness decreased.) A correlation of 0.30 implies that the children of the top quintile will be between $(0.30)(1.64) = 0.49$ and $(0.30)(1.38) = 0.41$ standard deviations above the mean. The cutoff point for the top quintile is 0.84 standard deviations above the population mean, or 0.35 to 0.43 standard deviations above the mean for sons born into the top quintile. The NORC veterans survey data shows that the standard deviaton of earnings for heads of households, between the ages of 25 and 35 and not in schools, is 18 percent larger for men with white-collar fathers than for all men together. Using this figure for sons from the top quintile, the estimated proportion of top quintile sons who remain in the top quintile would be roughly equal to the fraction of the normal distribution that falls more than $0.35/1.18 = 0.30$ to $0.43/1.18 = 0.36$ standard deviations above the mean. This would include 36 to 38 percent of all individuals. This is, obviously, a very rough estimate. Hence, the guarded language in the text.

23. Appendix H in Blau and Duncan, *The American Occupational Structure,* reports that a father's occupation explains 15.05 percent of the variance in a son's occupation and 9.35 percent of the variance in a son-in-law's occupation. Thus, if a daughter's position depends on her husband's position, we can say that daughters are more mobile, both up and down, than sons. If this is true of occupation, it is very likely to be true of income as well. One potentially complicating factor is the possibility that women whose husbands earn less than their fathers may be more likely to work in order to maintain the life-style in which they grew up. We know no data suitable for testing this theory.

24. Table 52 in the U.S. Bureau of the Census, "Income in 1970," shows that white male year-round, full-time workers earned an average of $10,218 in 1970. Black males earned $6,643, and black females earned $4,839.

25. Using figures for full-time, year-round workers in 1970, black males averaged 65 percent of the white male mean, while black females averaged 48 percent of the white male mean. In 1968, black males made 62 percent of the white male mean and black females made 42 percent of the white male mean. Unfortunately, we do not have means for earlier years. Using medians, the ratios for black males were 69 percent in 1970, 67 percent in 1968, and 62 percent in 1956. For black females, they were 48 percent in 1970, 44 percent in 1968, and 34 percent in 1956. (The 1956 figures include all nonwhites.) If we confine ourselves to wage and salary income, we can push the comparison back to 1939. For such income, the ratio of the nonwhite male median to the white male median was 70 percent in 1970 and 45 percent in 1939. The ratio of the nonwhite female median to the white male median was 50 percent in 1970 and 23 percent in 1939. Black female earnings have improved faster relative to white female earnings than relative to white male earnings. This is because the position of white females has deteriorated relative to that of white males. (For details, see Tables 52 and 59, in the U.S. Bureau of the Census, "Income in 1970," and Table 48 in the U.S. Bureau of the Census, "Income in 1968.") For a detailed analysis of changes prior to 1966, see Ashenfelter, "Changes in

Labor Market Discrimination." His data show little improvement for black males from 1950 to 1966. The effects of the civil rights movement on wages were apparently not felt until the late 1960s.

26. Note 25 shows that the dollar gap between white males and black males was $3,575 in 1970, while Table 48 in the U.S. Bureau of the Census, "Income in 1968" shows that it was $3,312 in 1968. Since the purchasing power of the dollar fell by 10 percent in the interval, the constant dollar gap declined a few dollars. The 1970 gap between white males and black females was $5,379, whereas the 1968 gap was $5,112. Allowing for 10 percent inflation, the real gap was again smaller in 1970 than 1968. It should be kept in mind, however, that inflation probably has an uneven impact on different income groups, so that a simple adjustment for changes in the value of the dollar may be misleading. Comparing median 1970 wage and salary incomes, we find a difference of $2,775 between white and black males and a difference of $4,699 between white males and black females. For 1939, using 1970 dollars, we find a difference of $2,110 between white and black males and $2,960 between white males and black females. Over the long haul, then, the absolute gap has increased.

27. The difference between white males and black males declined by 25 percentage points between 1939 and 1970. The gap for black females declined 27 percentage points. The residual gap was about 30 percent for males and 50 percent for females. Much of the decline was due to migration. This cannot continue indefinitely. Reducing the gap within regions is likely to be harder. See Bergman and Lyle, "Occupational Standing," for evidence that the black-white gap is more closely associated with the strength of the Wallace vote in a state than with "objective" economic factors.

28. See Table 52 in the U.S. Bureau of the Census, "Income in 1970."

29. U.S. Bureau of the Census, "Differences between Incomes," Table 1, shows that in the North, median black family income was 70.5 percent of median white family income in 1959, and 73.6 percent in 1970. For northern families with both a husband and a wife, the black median was 76.0 percent of the white median in 1959 and 88.3 percent in 1970. For northern husband-wife families with a husband aged 25–34, black income was 77.6 percent of white in 1959 and 94.3 percent in 1970, For northern families with a husband aged 25–34 and both husband and wife working, black income was 83.1 percent of white in 1959 and 98.2 percent in 1970. The pattern of improvement was similar in the South, but the absolute difference between blacks and whites remained much larger. For evidence that the whites' advantage is likely to increase as they get older, see the same source, and also Blum and Coleman, "Longitudinal Effects," While black husband-wife families improved their status relative to whites, they constituted a declining fraction of all black families (down from 75 percent in 1960 to 66 percent in 1971, according to these same Census statistics). For additional discussion, see Moynihan, "Schism in Black America."

30. We estimated the effect of family background on black incomes from Duncan, "Inheritance of Poverty," by inserting the white means in the black regression equation. Substituting the white means for father's occupation, father's education, and number of siblings into the black equation raises

the predicted level of educational attainment from 9.4 years to 11.3 years. This is just 0.4 years short of the observed white mean. This, in turn, boosts estimated income from the observed mean of $3,280 to $4,000. This is still $3,070 short of the white mean. Duncan, in "Discrimination Against Negroes," obtained lower estimates of the educational attainment of blacks whose family background was equal to that of whites when he calculated separate regression equations for each age group.

31. See Cutright, "Military Service." Black men in the lowest 10 percent of the *AFQT* distribution earned 86 percent of what similar whites earned. Blacks in the ninth to twenty-ninth percentiles earned 78 percent of what similar whites earned. Blacks above the thirtieth percentile earned 69 percent of what whites in the thirtieth to forty-ninth percentiles earned. The correlation between *AFQT* scores and income in Cutright's black sample averaged 0.11 in 1962–1964. Blacks who scored at the white mean had estimated 1964 earnings of $4,300, compared to $6,077 for whites and $3,481 for all blacks.

32. This estimate is derived from Table 4–4, in Duncan, "Inheritance of Poverty." Duncan shows that a white who scored at the black mean on background variables, educational attainment, test scores, and occupational status had a predicted income of $5,000, whereas the average black in the sample had an income of $3,600 to $3,800. Cutright's data shows a slightly smaller gap for young men.

33. For other trend comparisons, see Weiss and Williamson, "Black Education."

34. See Chapter 3, "The Effects of Economic Background," for estimates of the test score difference between blacks and whites whose parents have similar occupations, educational attainment, and incomes. Roughly speaking, the difference is 10 to 12 points, compared to 15 points for the general population. Reducing but not completely eliminating the socio-economic gap would presumably reduce the test score gap less than 5 points.

35. Estimated from Appendix B, Figure B–7. The compound paths from IQ score at age 11 to income are between 0.194 and 0.232 depending on the presumed values of $m$ and $p$ in Figure B–7. The coefficient of inequality for income is taken as 0.70 (see note 9). Individuals who score 0.8 standard deviations below the mean on IQ tests at age 11 are thus expected to be between $(0.194)(0.8)(0.70) = 10.9$ percent and $(0.232)(0.8)(0.70) = 13.0$ percent below the mean.

36. Father's occupational status and educational attainment explain 8.5 to 10 percent of the variance in sons' incomes. The analytic model in Appendix B, Figure B–7, which assumes that the overall effect of family background on income is entirely mediated through test scores, educational attainment, and occupational status, plus the direct effect of father's occupation on income, implies a correlation between brothers' incomes of 0.119 to 0.130. Including parental income in the model might raise the implied correlation slightly. Our best guess is that the observed value would be about 0.15. It is certainly no more than 0.20.

Even if family background explains 20 percent of the income variance, the within-family standard deviation will be $\sqrt{1 - 0.20} = 90$ percent of the population standard deviation. Table 7–2 shows the population standard deviation for 1968 as $5,508, so the difference between random individuals is roughly $(1.13)($5,508) = $6,224$, and the difference between brothers is about $(0.90)(1.13)($5,508) = $5,602$. If family background explains only 15 percent of the variance, the difference between brothers will be about $5,714.

37. If the intraclass correlation between brothers' annual incomes were 0.15, the standard deviation of annual incomes within pairs of brothers would be $\sqrt{.85} = 92$ percent of the overall standard deviation. Using the same logic as in note 18, the expected gap between the top fifth and the mean would fall from 1.54 to $(1.54)(.92) = 1.42$ standard deviations. The expected gap between the bottom fifth and the mean would fall from 1.04 to 0.96 standard deviations. Since the coefficient of variation is taken to be 0.70, the top fifth gets $1 + (0.70)(1.42) = 199$ percent of the mean, while the bottom fifth gets $1 - (0.70)(0.96) = 32.8$ percent of the mean. The ratio is, thus, 199 to 32.8 or 6.1 to 1. If the coefficient of variation changes, the ratio in the text changes, but the argument remains valid.

38. The estimated difference is derived from Appendix B, Table B–2. The presumed correlation between true *AFQT* scores and true income is 0.349. The distribution of test score effects on income appears to be normal. (The correlation of test scores with white male earnings in the NORC veterans survey, uncorrected for attenuation and restriction of range, is 0.241. The correlation of test score with the log of earnings is 0.208.) Note 9 gives the coefficient of variation for white male income at 0.70. We therefore infer that the income of those in the top test score quintile exceeds the mean by $(1.4)(0.349)(0.70) = 34$ percent, and that those in the bottom quintile are 34 percent below the mean. The top fifth is thus getting 134 percent of the mean, while the bottom fifth is getting 66 percent.

39. This estimate is based on Appendix B, Table B–5. The compound paths from IQ genotype to income fall between 0.137 and 0.179. Taking 0.16 as a compromise, and taking the coefficient of variation for white male income as 0.70, we estimate the incomes of the most genetically advantaged fifth at $(1.4)(0.70)(0.16) = 16$ percent more than the mean. The incomes of the bottom fifth are correspondingly less. The ratio is thus 116:84, or about 1.38 to 1.

40. The contribution of IQ genotype to income variance is equal to the square of the compound paths from genotype to income (i.e. $0.137^2$ to $0.179^2$, as shown in Appendix B, Table B–5), plus twice the covariance caused by the correlation of genotype with family background. The covariance terms have a maximum value of 0.012 (see Appendix B, Figure B–7), so the total variance attributable to genotype has a maximum value of $0.179^2 + (2)(0.012) = 0.055$. This means that if individuals have equal IQ genotypes, the variance in their incomes should be about 94.5 percent of the population variance, and the coefficient of variation for their incomes should be $\sqrt{0.945} = 97$ percent of the population coefficient. This estimate should be checked against income statistics for identical twins reared in random environments, but no such statistics have ever been collected.

41. Appendix B, Figure B–7, shows that the compound paths from *AFQT* to income, holding educational attainment and family background constant, sum to 0.184. This is just over half the observed correlation of 0.349 (see Appendix B, Table B–2). If we had information on the test scores and incomes of brothers, we could obtain a more direct and trustworthy estimate of the effect of cognitive skills on income, holding family background constant.

42. The correlation between *AFQT* scores and occupational status is 0.502, whereas the correlation between *AFQT* scores and income is 0.349 (see Appendix B, Table B–2).

43. Appendix B, Figure B–7, shows a compound path from *AFQT* to income of 0.184, holding family background and credentials constant. The path from *AFQT* to occupational status is only 0.099, holding family background and credentials constant.

44. For a summary of such data see, for example, Miller, *Income Distribution.*

45. For reasons best known to itself, the Current Population Survey does not tabulate earnings for groups with differing educational attainment. The use of income rather than earnings does not appreciably alter the results, however, so long as part-time and part-year workers are excluded. Earnings constituted 96.1 percent of all income reported by full-time, year-round workers in 1968. (See Tables 47 and 48, in the U.S. Bureau of the Census, "Income in 1968.")

46. This is an extreme comparison. If we make our usual comparison between the top and bottom fifths, we find that the best-educated fifth of all men make about twice as much as the worst-educated fifth. The relationship between educational attainment and income is, then, almost identical to the relationship between *AFQT* scores and income (see Appendix B, Table B–2).

47. The correlation between educational attainment and income is estimated at 0.353 in Appendix B, Table B–2. The paths from educational attainment to income in Appendix B, Figure B–7, including the effect of additional education on adult test scores, sum to 0.205, or 58 percent of 0.353. Controlling parental income would presumably reduce the direct path a little more. The only direct evidence relevant to these estimates is found in Gorseline, *The Effects of Schooling,* and is analyzed in Becker, *Human Capital.* Controlling family background but not test scores apparently reduced the pre-1940 effect of a year of schooling by about a third.

48. The average individual who did not finish elementary school had about 5 years of schooling (see Table 172 in the U.S. Bureau of the Census, *U.S. Census of Population: 1960*). The difference between those who did not finish elementary school and those who finished elementary school but did not enter high school was thus 3 years. This 3-year increment in years of schooling was associated with an income increase of $(76.0 - 63.3)/63.3 = 20.1$ percent, which implies an increase of 6.3 percent for each additional year of schooling. (The annual increases must be compounded to get an aggregate increase for 3 years.) A similar computation for high school implies a 5.9 percent increase per year of high school. The estimate for

college was derived in the same way as the estimates for elementary and secondary school. The estimate for graduate school is approximate, because no exact data are available on the number of years of graduate school completed by those reporting at least 1 year. Since a large fraction of these individuals are teachers who completed only 1 year of graduate work, the average is probably around 2 years. A figure of 2.0 was used in estimating the increase per year. For a roughly similar conclusion about the relative value of graduate and undergraduate education, using data for males only, see Hanoch, "An Economic Analysis."

Note that the use of absolute increases would create a different impression from the use of percentage increases. A year of graduate school, for example, increased absolute income more than a year of elementary school. But the increase was relative to a larger base, so that in percentage terms the effects were similar.

49. In the NORC veterans survey, the payoffs to schooling are lower than those estimated in the text, because the men are younger, but they follow the same pattern. Controlling *AFQT* and family background leads to proportional reductions in the coefficients for high school and college. There are not enough cases to say much about graduate school.

50. This conclusion must be somewhat tentative, since it is based on only one somewhat unrepresentative sample, namely, the 1964 NORC veterans survey. We examined white heads of household between the ages of 25 and 34 who were not in school and reported earnings in 1963. We analyzed the data separately for white men who reported father's occupations with Duncan status scores above and below 38.5. Controlling father's education and father's occupation, each extra year of elementary or secondary school was associated with an extra $371 in annual earnings for middle-class sons, and $165 for blue-collar sons. Each extra year of college increased annual earnings by $419 for middle-class sons and $208 for working-class sons. Controlling *AFQT* scores did not alter these ratios. Controlling the son's occupational status made the ratios even less favorable to blue-collar sons. The differences are statistically significant at the 0.01 level. Unfortunately, we have not had access to any other data which would allow us to check this finding. We did not find other significant differences between the equations for middle-class and working-class sons.

51. Duncan, in "Ability and Achievement," reports a correlation of 0.30 between educational attainment and income for blacks, compared to 0.31 for whites. The standard deviation of black income in this sample of non-farm males in the civilian labor force was only $2,000, compared to $5,700 for whites, and the standard deviation of black educational attainment was 3.5 years, compared to 3.3 for whites. A 1-year increase in educational attainment was therefore associated with a $170 income increase for blacks and a $535 increase for whites. Controlling family background reduces both coefficients by about a sixth. Miller, in *Income Distribution,* reports similar but less dramatic differences between blacks and whites, using data from the early 1960s.

Weiss and Williamson, in "Black Education," report much smaller racial disparities in the payoff from credentials in the late 1960s. Table 49, in the U.S. Bureau of the Census, "Income in 1970," shows that white high school graduates made 52 percent more than white elementary school graduates in 1970, whereas black high school graduates made 40 percent more than black elementary school graduates. In absolute terms, the white high school graduates were getting an extra $3,246, while the black high school graduates were getting an extra $1,890. The payoffs to college in 1970 showed a similar pattern. White B.A.s averaged $5,251 more than white high school graduates, while black B.A.s averaged $3,632 more than black high school graduates. These differences are large, but they are much less than those implied by Duncan's 1961 data. They imply that the percentage increase in income for blacks with an extra year of schooling was about the same as for whites, even though the absolute increase was less for blacks. Unfortunately, we have no data on changes in the relative value of credentials for middle-class and working-class whites.

52. In the 1964 NORC veterans sample, using white heads of household between the ages of 25 and 34 and not in school, we did not find statistically significant nonadditive interactions between *AFQT* scores and years of schooling. We tested this interaction both using multiplicative terms in regression equations and using dummy variables. Analysis of cross tabulations also showed no consistent pattern of interaction. Cutright, in "Military Service," shows no interaction in his sample of draftees followed up about 10 years later.

We also tested for interaction between family background and cognitive skills in the NORC veterans survey, but found no evidence for it.

Studies of older workers do, however, show interactions between education and IQ. Wolfle and Smith, in "Occupational Value," show positive interaction between the effects of test scores and college attendance, and Taubman and Wales found the same thing when they reanalyzed this data in "Effects of Education." Rogers, in "Private Rates of Return," also reported a positive interaction for older men, and this recurs in Hause's reanalysis of Rogers' data reported in "Ability and Schooling."

53. See Hanoch, "Economic Analysis." For other similar studies see, for example, Hansen, "Private Rates" and Becker, *Human Capital*. But compare Martin and Morgan, "Education and Income" and Weisbrod and Karpoff, "Monetary Returns."

54. The correction is based on NORC data for men between the ages of 25 and 34, and may be inexact for older men. Compare Becker, *Human Capital*.

55. We have not tried to estimate rates of return for blacks, or for middle-class and working-class whites separately. If the estimates in note 50 are correct, and if two-thirds of all sons are working-class, the rates of return for middle-class sons could be as much as 50 percent higher than the overall rate, while those for working-class sons could be 25 percent lower. The exact figure depends on differences in potential earnings of middle-class and working-class teenagers and on differences in their out-of-pocket spending for education. Rates of return for females are extremely low, since the

wage differential for education is lower among females than males, and many highly educated women have no earnings at all. Rates of return for blacks have historically been low (see Hanoch, "Economic Analysis" and Fogel, "Low Educational Attainment"), but may be rising.

56. For additional discussion, see Chapter 6, "The Effects of Educational Credentials." There is a vast inconclusive literature on the relationship between education and economic growth. See, for example, Schultz, "Education and Economic Growth" and Denison, "Why Growth Rates Differ."

57. See Thurow and Lucas, "The American Distribution of Income," for further discussion of recent experience.

58. Estimates are for 1959. See Table 208 in the U.S. Bureau of the Census, *U.S. Census of Population: 1960*. On the stability of relative earnings over time, see Hodge, "Status Consistency."

59. See the U.S. Bureau of the Census, "Subject Reports." The data are for 435 categories and are based on medians, since the 1960 Census did not publish means. The distribution of earnings within occupations is close to normal, so comparisons among medians yield much the same results as comparisons among means.

60. Table 43, in the U.S. Bureau of the Census, "Income in 1968," shows that the 11 broad occupational categories explained 19 percent of the variance in earnings for male workers in 1968. Chapter 6, note 12, estimates that the 435 detailed occupational categories explain about 25 percent of the variance for male workers. It is hard to believe that further refinements in the occupational classification would raise the explained variance much further, unless, of course, occupations were subdivided according to earnings.

61. The 11 broad occupational categories explain 26 percent of the earnings variance for males and females together, compared with 19 percent for males alone. (This reflects the fact that much of the inequality between males and females is associated with differences in their occupations.) Since 435 broad categories explain about 25 percent of the variance for males, we might expect them to explain about 34 percent for males and females together. (We have not calculated this figure, however.) This would leave 66 percent of the variance in earnings within occupational categories. The standard deviation of earnings in the average occupation would, then, be 81 percent of the standard deviation for all workers.

62. If 34 percent of the variance in earnings were between occupational categories, the standard deviation of occupational means would be 58 percent of the standard deviation for individual earnings. Thus, if everyone earned the mean for his or her occupation, the standard deviation would fall by 42 percent. It may seem paradoxical that eliminating inequality within occupations should reduce overall inequality by 42 percent, that eliminating inequality between occupations should reduce it 19 percent, and that eliminating both should, nonetheless, reduce inequality by 100 percent. The reason is that standard deviations are not additive; only their squares (i.e. the variances) are additive. Thus, reducing inequality by 42 percent would reduce the variance by $1 - 0.58^2 = 66$ percent, and reducing inequality by 19 percent would reduce the variance by $1 - 0.81^2 = 34$ percent. Together,

these two changes would reduce both inequality and the variance by 100 percent.

63. After correcting for measurement error, Appendix B, Figure B–7, explains 22.2 percent of the variance in white nonfarm workers' incomes. The coefficient of variation for the residuals is, thus, $\sqrt{1 - 0.222} = 88.4$ percent of the original coefficient. As noted on pp. 225–226, a more detailed occupational classification, based exclusively on mean income, would slightly increase the explained variance. Inclusion of women would raise both the explained variance and the coefficient of variation.

An analysis based on "permanent" instead of annual income yields similar results. (We take "permanent" income to be income averaged over several years, i.e. the income level that determines living standards.) The correlation between incomes in sequential years averages about 0.83 (see data in Friedman, *Consumption Function*, on family incomes, and data in Cutright, "Military Service," on young male individual incomes). These fluctuations are likely to be related to changes in occupation, but probably not to changes in family background, educational attainment, or *AFQT* scores, which are quite stable. Since family background, educational attainment, *AFQT* scores, and occupational status explain 22.2 percent of the variance in annual income, they should explain about $0.222/0.83 = 26.8$ percent of the variance in permanent income. This would leave 73.2 percent within categories, making the average standard deviation of permanent income within categories 86 percent of the overall standard deviation.

Estimates for lifetime income would be more complicated, since we do not know the correlation of permanent income with lifetime income. Nor is it clear why we should care about lifetime income as against permanent income. If living standards really change sharply in a single lifetime (i.e. if permanent income is not well correlated with lifetime income), the resulting inequality is real, not illusory.

64. The NORC veterans survey of men aged 25–34 collected data on the priority given to income as against other occupational goals by each respondent. Using income as a dependent variable, this variable never had a statistically significant coefficient in our analyses. It might be more important in an older sample.

65. See Break, "Income Taxes."

66. Appendix B, Figure B–7, indicates that family background, test scores, educational attainment, and occupational status explain 22 percent of the variance in white nonfarm male incomes. Allowing for nonlinearities and interactions and using a more detailed occupational classification might raise this to 30 percent. The coefficient of variation for those whose incomes were at the predicted level would then be $\sqrt{0.30} = 55$ percent of its present level. This would leave 70 percent of the income variance within categories. If the insurance scheme covered half of all income, it would reduce deviations from the predicted value by 50 percent. This would reduce the variance within categories to 25 percent of its present level. The total variance would then be $0.30 + (0.25)(0.70) = 47.5$ percent of its present level, making the coefficient of variation $\sqrt{0.475} = 69$ percent of its present level.

67. See Pechman, "The Rich, The Poor," and Herriott and Miller, "Who Paid Taxes in 1968?"

68. See Barkai, "The Kibbutz."

69. See Thurow and Lucas, "The American Distribution of Income."

70. This approach is discussed by Thurow and Lucas in "The American Distribution of Income."

71. See Rainwater, *It's a Living.*

# CHAPTER EIGHT

# Inequality in Job Satisfaction

We know very little about the factors that influence people's satisfaction with their jobs. We do not know, for example, how much of the variation in people's job satisfaction is explained by objective differences between their jobs and how much is explained by subjective differences between individuals who hold similar jobs.[1] We do, however, know something about the relationship between job satisfaction and the status of the occupation in which a job is classified. We also know something about the relationship between job satisfaction and how much a job pays. Finally, we know something about the relationship between an individual's educational attainment and his job satisfaction. In all three cases, the relationships are surprisingly weak.

The most comprehensive national survey of job satisfaction was conducted by the Survey Research Center (SRC) at the University of Michigan in 1969. The results of this survey have not yet been fully analyzed, and we have not analyzed the original data ourselves. Nonetheless, preliminary tabulations clearly show that job satisfaction had very little connection with either occupational prestige or education.[2]

The SRC survey asked workers eight questions designed to get an overall estimate of whether they liked their jobs or disliked them. These were questions such as whether the worker would recommend his present job to a friend (63 percent would), whether he would have any hesitation about taking the same job if he had it to do over again (27 percent would hesitate and 9 percent would not take it), whether he planned to look for a new job within the next year (30 percent said they might), and what he would do if he could have any job he wanted (49 percent would choose their present jobs). The eight items were combined into a general index of job satisfaction.[3] The overall correlation between occupational status and job satisfaction was 0.20.[4] This means that people who hold high-status jobs are only slightly more satisfied than people who hold low-status jobs.

When jobs were classified by type of work rather than status, the average professional or managerial worker ranked at the sixtieth percentile on the satisfaction measure. The average service worker ranked at the thirty-fifth percentile. The other seven major occupational categories all had the same average level of satisfaction.[5] This means that 40 percent of the professionals and managers were less satisfied than the national average.

Since most earlier studies of job satisfaction had reported substantial differences in satisfaction between high- and low-status occupations, we found the SRC data surprising. When we looked at the earlier studies more carefully, however, we found their findings quite consistent with the SRC findings. The only difference was that they had stressed the importance of small differences between occupations, while the SRC results were tabulated in a way which made the small differences between occupations look less important and made the huge variations within occupations look more important.[6]

One reason professionals and managers might be more satisfied is that they earn more. Yet the correlation between general satisfaction and satisfaction with one's earnings was only 0.38 in the SRC survey. Furthermore, a group's satisfaction with its earnings was only partly explained by its actual earnings. Professional and managerial workers were more satisfied with their earnings than most groups, and they also earned more. But "bench workers" were as satisfied as professionals and managers, and they earned much less. Perhaps they compared themselves to other blue-collar workers and felt satisfied because they earned more than most such workers.

The SRC survey also asked workers whether they found 20 other specific features of their work satisfactory or unsatisfactory. The pattern of answers to these questions implied the existence of four distinct areas of satisfaction or dissatisfaction: whether the job was challenging; whether the worker had a chance to do the job right; whether the worker had good relations with his fellow workers; and whether the job was comfortable in various ways.[7] Contrary to what many claim, workers reported that having a challenging job was more important than anything else. Workers who found their jobs sufficiently challenging were also more likely to be satisfied than workers who were satisfied with other aspects of the job.[8]

The SRC used seven questions to determine whether people found their jobs challenging. The questions dealt with whether the worker found his job was interesting, whether he had a great deal of freedom to decide how to do his work, whether he had enough authority to do the job right, whether he could see the results of his work, whether the problems were hard enough, whether he had a chance to develop his special abilities, and whether he had a chance to do the things he did best. Whether a worker found his job challenging correlated 0.28 with the status of his occupation. The average professional or managerial worker was at the sixty-first percentile of the national distribution on this index. Workers in farming, forestry, and fishing were equally high. The average service worker was at the thirty-fourth percentile of the national distribution. Other major occupational groups were all just about at the national norm.[9] The other three areas of satisfaction showed virtually no relation to occupational status, type of work, or industry.[10]

Satisfaction has even less relation to educational attainment than to occupational status. Overall job satisfaction (as measured by whether one would take the same job again, and similar questions) correlated only 0.12 with years of schooling in the SRC survey. Only workers with graduate degrees differed appreciably from the national average, and, even in this group, 37 percent were below the national average.[11] Also, educated workers did not find their jobs appreciably more challenging than uneducated workers. Nor were they appreciably more satisfied with their pay.[12]

We can imagine several possible interpretations of these findings. One possibility is that job satisfaction depends largely on the subjective characteristics of the worker, not the objective characteristics of the job. "Some people are easily satisfied; other people are never satisfied." Everyday experience suggests that this is partly true—but only partly.

Another explanation is that people evaluate a job by comparing it with other jobs they have had and with jobs their friends have, not by comparing it with some hypothetical national norm. If this theory were correct, we would not expect executives to be much more satisfied than unskilled laborers. Executives would compare themselves to other executives, laborers would compare themselves to other laborers, and the norm for the two groups would be similar. Unsuccessful executives would be more dissatisfied than steadily employed, well-paid laborers, and vice versa.

Such a theory would also explain the negligible correlation between job satisfaction and educational attainment. If educated people compare themselves to other people with similar amounts of education, the educated and the uneducated will inevitably turn out equally satisfied—or dissatisfied. The more education an individual has had, the more he expects from his job. If his expectations improve as fast as his options, he ends up no more satisfied than before.

We have not been able to test this theory empirically. It is, however, consistent with research on relative deprivation and reference groups. We are therefore inclined to assume that it is correct. If so, it has profound implications for public policy. If people's satisfaction depends largely on where they stand relative to their friends, eliminating differences *between* groups will do almost nothing to eliminate dissatisfaction. Instead, the primary need is to eliminate inequality *within* groups.

This conclusion is consistent with many of our other findings in this book. We have argued, for example, that it is more important to eliminate inequality within schools than to eliminate inequality between one school and another. The general implication of our work may therefore be that reformers should concentrate more attention on the internal workings of institutions and less on the relationships between institutions. Perhaps what America needs is more radical innovation in what might be called micro-politics and less concern with what might be called macro-politics.

# NOTES

1. Empirically, this question could be answered by surveying workers in a variety of essentially identical jobs. While no two jobs are exactly alike, many jobs in large organizations are similar enough so that they could be treated as identical. The ratio of the variance in satisfaction among workers holding identical jobs to the total variance is a minimum estimate of the percentage of the total variance explained by the psychological characteristics of the worker as against objective characteristics of the job.

2. The preliminary tabulations on which we based this judgment are reported in Quinn, "Working Conditions."

3. This index of job satisfaction included the following questions:

1. "Before we talk about your present job, I'd like to have some idea of the job you'd *most* like to have. If you were free to go into any type of job you wanted, what would your choice be?"
2. "All in all, how satisfied would you say you are with your job?"
3. "How often do you get so wrapped up in your work that you lose track of the time?"
4. "If a good friend of yours told you he/she was interested in working in a job like yours for your employer, what would you tell him/her?"
5. "Knowing what you know now, if you had to decide all over again whether to take the job you now have, what would you decide?"

6. "How often do you leave work with a good feeling that you've done something particularly well?"
7. "Taking everything into consideration, how likely is it that you will make a genuine effort to find a new job with another employer within the next year?"
8. "In general, how well would you say that your job measures up to the sort of job you wanted when you took it?"

No intercorrelations were published, but Quinn, "Working Conditions," reports that they were high. The split-half reliability of 0.80 for the 8-item scale supports this claim.

4. This correlation was computed using a 1-digit version of the Duncan scale scores for detailed Census categories.

5. The other occupational categories include "Farming, Forestry, and Fisheries," "Processing," "Machine Trades," "Bench Work," "Structural Work," "Clerical and Sales Work," and "Miscellaneous." The *eta* for all nine categories was 0.21. An occupational classification based on industry was less related to overall job satisfaction (*eta* = 0.16).

6. Heron, in *Why Men Work*, reported a *Fortune* survey showing 92 percent satisfaction among professional and executive workers, 72 percent among salaried white-collar workers, and 54 percent among factory workers. This suggests an *eta* of about 0.3. Centers, in *Social Classes*, using a general measure of job satisfaction, found 14 percent of the middle-class and 21 percent of the working-class dissatisfied. This is equivalent to an *eta* of less than 0.2. Kornhauser, in *Detroit as the People See It,* reported equally small differences in general satisfaction. Gurin et al., in *Americans View Their Mental Health,* reported that 31 percent of professional and managerial workers, 16 percent of farmers, 43 percent of skilled manual workers, 45 percent of semiskilled manual workers, 43 percent of unskilled manual workers, and 58 percent of clerical workers would prefer another job. This again suggests a low *eta*. In Detroit, where the general level of dissatisfaction seems to be above the national norm, Kornhauser found somewhat larger differences between skilled, semiskilled, and repetitive semiskilled jobs. For additional data, see Blauner, "Work Satisfaction," Wilensky, "Work Experience," and Morse and Weiss, "Meaning of Work."

Our conclusions from these findings differ in emphasis from those of most other analysts because we have emphasized measures of overall association rather than percentages. The potentially misleading character of percentages is illustrated by Centers' data. If 14 percent of the middle-class and 21 percent of the working-class are dissatisfied, radicals can tell themselves that the working-class is 50 percent more dissatisfied then the middle-class. Conservatives need only turn the percentages around to reach opposite conclusions. Since 86 percent of the middle-class and 79 percent of the working-class are satisfied, the working-class is only 8 percent less satisfied than the middle-class. Measures of association are not subject to such vagaries. They simultaneously show both the degree of difference and the degree of overlap between groups. In all these studies, the overlap is much greater than the differences.

7. The four areas described in the text, plus a fifth area labeled "pay," were derived by factor analyzing answers to 23 questions about specific areas of satisfaction and dissatisfaction. Quinn did not report the inter-correlations of the 23 items in "Working Conditions," but the split-half reliabilities of the indices were between 0.7 and 0.8, whereas the inter-correlations between the indices were between 0.26 and 0.56. The groupings, therefore, appear fairly reliable.

8. The overall measure of satisfaction (see note 3) correlated 0.49 with the "challenge" index, 0.31 with the "comfort" index, 0.23 with the "co-worker reactions" index, and 0.30 with the "resources" index.

9. Occupational groupings explained 6.8 percent of the variance in how challenging people found their work. The classification system was the same as that described in note 5. Industry groupings explained 2.6 percent of the variance.

10. All *eta's* were less than 0.12, and 5 out of 9 were statistically insignificant.

11. Workers with graduate degrees were 0.33 standard deviations above the national average.

12. Years of schooling correlated 0.13 with satisfaction about pay, 0.06 with satisfaction about challenge, −0.06 with satisfaction about comfort, −0.04 with satisfaction about coworker relations, and −0.08 with satisfaction about resources.

# CHAPTER NINE

# What Is To Be Done?

We have seen that educational opportunities, cognitive skills, educational credentials, occupational status, income, and job satisfaction are all unequally distributed. We have not, however, been very successful in explaining most of these inequalities. The association between one variety of inequality and another is usually quite weak, which means that equalizing one thing is unlikely to have much effect on the degree of inequality in other areas. We must therefore ask whether attempts to produce equality by more direct methods would be more effective, or whether the status quo is essentially unalterable. Before trying to answer this question, however, a recapitulation of our findings may be helpful.

We began by looking at the distribution of educational opportunity. We found that access to school resources was quite unequal. Schools in some districts and neighborhoods spend far more than schools in other districts and neighborhoods. We also found that utilization of school resources was even more unequal than access to them, at least after the age of 16. Middle-class students have access to slightly more than their share of the nation's educational resources, and they utilize substantially more than their share. Access to white middle-class classmates is also quite unequal, in the sense that schools are somewhat segregated by class and quite segregated by race. It is hard to tell how much of this segregation would disappear if everyone had a chance to attend the school of his choice. Within schools, we found that most students were in the curriculum of their choice, but that a significant minority was not.

We next turned to the distribution of the cognitive skills measured by standardized tests. We found that both genetic and environmental inequality played a major role in producing cognitive inequality. We also found that those who started life with genetic advantages tended to get environmental advantages as well, and that this exacerbated inequality. We argued that genes influenced test scores both by influencing the way children were treated and by influencing how much children

**253**

learned when they were treated in exactly the same way, but we could not assess the relative importance of these two processes. We found no evidence that differences between schools contributed significantly to cognitive inequality, nor were we very successful in identifying other specific genetic or environmental determinants of test performance.

We then examined the distribution of educational credentials. We found that family background had much more influence than IQ genotype on an individual's educational attainment. The family's influence depended partly on its socio-economic status and partly on cultural and psychological characteristics that were independent of socio-economic level. The effect of cognitive skill on educational attainment proved difficult to estimate, but it was clearly significant. We found no evidence that the role of family background was declining or that the role of cognitive skill was increasing. Qualitative differences between schools played a very minor role in determining how much schooling people eventually got.

Men's occupational statuses turned out to be quite closely tied to their educational attainment. Yet there was a great deal of variation in the status of men with exactly the same amount of education, and this variation did not seem to be explained by any other readily identified characteristic. Both family background and cognitive skill influenced occupational status, but they did this largely by influencing the amount of schooling men got, not by influencing the status of men who had completed their education. Since educational attainment is only partly determined by family background, and since occupational status is only partly determined by educational attainment, family background ends up exerting a moderate influence on a man's eventual occupation. We confirmed this judgment by comparing the statuses of brothers raised in the same family, which often differed substantially.

Variation in men's incomes proved even harder to explain than variation in their occupational statuses. Educational credentials influence the occupations men enter, but credentials do not have much effect on earnings within any given occupation, so their overall effect on income is moderate. Family background and cognitive skills have some effect on a man's occupation, and some effect on his income even after he has entered a given occupation, but their overall influence is also moderate. The genes that influence IQ scores appear to have relatively little influence on income. As a result, we estimate that there is nearly as much income variation among men who come from similar families, have similar credentials, and have similar test scores, as among men in general. This suggests either that competence does not depend primarily on family background, schooling, and test scores, or else that income does not depend on competence.

Job satisfaction proved even less explicable than other things. It is only marginally related to educational attainment, occupational status, or earnings.

These findings have important implications for both educators and social reformers. We will take up their implications for educators first.

None of the evidence we have reviewed suggests that school reform can be expected to bring about significant social changes outside the schools. More specifically, the evidence suggests that equalizing educational opportunity would do very little to make adults more equal. If all elementary schools were equally effective, cognitive inequality among sixth graders would decline less than 3 percent.[1] If all high schools were equally effective, cognitive inequality among twelfth graders would hardly decline at all, and disparities in their eventual attainment would decline less than 1 percent.[2] Eliminating all economic and academic obstacles to college attendance might somewhat reduce disparities in educational attainment, but the change would not be large. Furthermore, the experience of the past 25 years suggests that even fairly substantial reductions in the range of educational attainments do not appreciably reduce economic inequality among adults.

The schools, of course, could move beyond equal opportunity, establishing a system of compensatory opportunity in which the best schooling was reserved for those who were disadvantaged in other respects. The evidence suggests, however, that educational compensation is usually of marginal value to the recipients. Neither the overall level of educational resources nor any specific, easily identifiable school policy has much effect on the test scores or educational attainment of students who start out at a disadvantage. Thus even if we reorganized the schools so that their primary concern was for the students who most needed help, there is no reason to suppose that adults would end up appreciably more equal as a result.

There seem to be three reasons why school reform cannot make adults more equal. First, children seem to be far more influenced by what happens at home than by what happens in school. They may also be more influenced by what happens on the streets and by what they see on television. Second, reformers have very little control over those aspects of school life that affect children. Reallocating resources, reassigning pupils, and rewriting the curriculum seldom change the way teachers and students actually treat each other minute by minute. Third, even when a school exerts an unusual influence on children, the resulting changes are not likely to persist into adulthood. It takes a huge change in elementary school test scores, for example, to alter adult income by a significant amount.

These arguments suggest that the "factory" model which pervades both lay and professional thinking about schools probably ought to be abandoned. It is true that schools have "inputs" and "outputs," and that one of their nominal purposes is to take human "raw material" (i.e. children) and convert it into something more "valuable" (i.e. employable adults). Our research suggests, however, that the character of a school's output depends largely on a single input, namely the characteristics of the entering children. Everything else—the school budget, its policies, the characteristics of the teachers—is either secondary or completely irrelevant.

Instead of evaluating schools in terms of long-term effects on their alumni, which appear to be relatively uniform, we think it wiser to evaluate schools in terms of their immediate effects on teachers and students, which appear much more variable. Some schools are dull, depressing, even terrifying places, while others are lively, comfortable, and reassuring. If we think of school life as an end in itself rather than a means to some other end, such differences are enormously important. Eliminating these differences would not do much to make adults more equal, but it would do a great deal to make the quality of children's (and teachers') lives more equal. Since children are in school for a fifth of their lives, this would be a significant accomplishment.

Looking at schooling as an end in itself rather than a means to some other end suggests that we ought to describe schools in a language appropriate to a family rather than to a factory. This implies that we will have to accept diverse standards for judging schools, just as we do for judging families. Indeed, we can even say that diversity should be an explicit objective of schools and school systems. No single home-away-from-home can be ideal for all children. A school system that provides only one variety of schooling, no matter how good, must almost invariably seem unsatisfactory to many parents and children. The ideal system is one that provides as many varieties of schooling as its children and parents want and finds ways of matching children to schools that suit them. Since the character of an individual's schooling appears to have relatively little long-term effect on his development, society as a whole rarely has a compelling interest in limiting the range of educational choices open to parents and students. Likewise, since professional educators do not seem to understand the long-term effects of schooling any better than parents do, there is no compelling reason why the profession should be empowered to rule out alternatives that appeal to parents, even if they seem educationally "unsound."

The argument that school life is largely an end in itself rather than a means to some other end does not mean we believe schools should be run like mediocre summer camps, where children are merely kept out of trouble. We doubt that a school can be enjoyable for either adults or children unless the children feel they are doing something purposeful. One good way to give children a sense of purpose is to give them activities that contribute to their becoming more like grownups. Our findings suggest that a school's choice of objectives has rather little long-term effect on what kinds of grownups the children become. That is determined by outside influences. But since we value ideas and the life of the mind, we favor schools that value these things too. Others, who favor discipline and competitive excellence, may prefer schools that value high reading and math scores. Still others, more concerned with teaching children to behave properly, will prefer schools that try to do this. The list of competing objectives is nearly endless, which is why we favor diversity and choice.

But even if school systems do not try to diversify their educational programs, parents and children will usually assume that some schools are better than others. Most parents will assume, for example, that a school in a white upper-middle-class neighborhood is better than one in a poor black neighborhood, even if the formal curriculums are identical. Under these circumstances equity seems to require that every family have a free choice as to which schools its children attend. The mechanics of this were discussed in Chapter 2. The basic principle is simply that every child in a district should have the same claim on every school, regardless of where he happens to live. This means, for example, that if a poor black mother wants her children in a predominantly white school, and if such a school exists in her district, she should be free to enroll them, and the district should transport them there. It does not mean that if she wants white children in her neighborhood school, the district must compel white students to enroll there.

Even if everyone had equal access to all the schools in their district, the problem of disparities between districts would remain. In principle, we can see no reason why students should not be free to attend schools outside their district, but this is not likely to become widespread unless the Supreme Court upholds busing across district lines to achieve racial balance. The Court may, however, require states to eliminate, or at least drastically reduce, expenditure differentials between districts. Even if it does not, legislatures can perhaps be pushed in this direction. In addition, the federal government could easily do more to reduce expenditure differences between states.

Many conservatives have opposed such changes, on the grounds that equalizing resources would mean more central financing, and that more central financing would mean more central control. Central control is, in turn, often said to make schools less responsive to local needs. Experience suggests, however, that while central control may make the schools less responsive to the local establishment, whatever that may be, it often makes schools more responsive to other local groups. (Blacks in the South are an obvious case in point.) We therefore tend to favor central financing, both as a means of equalizing expenditures and as a way of making local schools somewhat more responsive to groups they have traditionally ignored.

Finally, there is the problem of equalizing access to higher education. It would be relatively simple to design a system in which access to higher education no longer depended on getting money from home. Indeed, the Higher Education Act of 1972 contains the outlines of such a system, even though it will not fully achieve this objective. It is somewhat more difficult to design a system in which access no longer depends on test scores or other imperfect predictors of academic success. Open admission is a step in this direction, since it makes continued access depend on actual performance in college rather than performance in high school or on an aptitude test. Open admission does not, however, solve the problem of the student who persists in trying to learn subjects for which he has relatively little aptitude. That would require not only open admission, but open readmission.

The foregoing reforms are all aimed at equalizing people's claims on a public resource, namely schooling. If we try to move beyond equal access and ensure equal use of educational resources, the problem becomes far more complex. It is relatively simple, for example, to guarantee working-class families the same opportunity as middle-class families to send their children to schools in middle-class neighborhoods. But it is not easy to make them use this opportunity. They may think such schools inconvenient, or they may fear that their children will be out of place and unhappy with classmates more affluent than themselves.

The same is also true of blacks, who can and should be guaranteed the right to attend predominantly white schools, but cannot always be persuaded to exercise this right. The problem is particularly difficult in the rural South, where the white community has often put enormous pressure on black families who tried to send their children to previously white schools. In such settings, judicial coercion and mandatory busing may be the only way to break the tradition of segregation. Once the tradition of complete segregation has been broken, however, mandatory busing makes less sense. If attending a desegregated school had significant long-term benefits for students, one could make a case against allowing parents to send their children to segregated schools even if they wanted to do so. The evidence we have reviewed suggests, however, that the long-term effects of segregation on individual students are quite small. This makes us favor a system in which black parents are free to decide for themselves whether they want their children in segregated or desegregated schools. For this to be a genuine choice, the school system must provide transportation, must give blacks access to nearby white schools, even if this makes them overcrowded, and must make sure that every parent is aware of having a choice. If this were done, experience with programs like Project Concern in Hartford suggests that most black parents would choose a desegregated school. But that should be their option, not a decision imposed by others for their alleged benefit.

Just as giving everyone access to every school may not lead to complete desegregation, so too giving everyone access to higher education will not persuade everyone to earn a doctorate, or even a B.A. We have already eliminated virtually all economic and academic obstacles to earning a high school diploma, and one student in five still drops out. This percentage is likely to keep falling. But the same considerations that lead students to quit high school will continue to operate in college, even if colleges are open to everyone and money is available to cover the costs.

We are not enthusiastic about coercion as a device for keeping reluctant students in school. Experience suggests that students who do not want to be in school rarely learn a great deal while they are there and that they often make schools extremely unpleasant for everyone else. Since keeping people in school the same length of time is not likely to make them significantly more equal in any other respect, we can see nothing to be said for it.

If we assume that higher education, like concerts and football games, will be used unequally, we must decide how to finance it. A system that makes students dependent on money from home, which many cannot get, is clearly unacceptable. But a system which finances higher education out of general tax revenues and then allows individual students to use their education for private gain also seems unacceptable. It is hard to see why, for example, an auto worker should pay taxes to send his cousin to law school and should then have to pay his cousin fat fees to obtain legal services. One alternative would be to equalize adult incomes. If the educated and the uneducated ended up with equal incomes, we could assume that the economic benefits of higher education were being more or less equally distributed. It would then seem reasonable that the costs also be equally distributed, coming out of general tax revenues.

In a society where individuals are free to retain most of the economic benefits of their education for themselves, it seems reasonable to ask them to pay most of the costs. The most equitable way to do this, in our judgment, would be to provide every student with free tuition and a living stipend, and then impose an income tax surcharge on those who had had these benefits. These surcharges should be large enough so that the average student repaid the cost of his schooling. Those who earned high incomes would repay more than their share, while those who earned low incomes would repay relatively little. Those who did not attend would pay nothing at all toward the cost of higher education.

These proposals would make educational opportunities more equal and educational finance more equitable. We believe these to be important and legitimate objectives, even though they would not have much effect on adult society. We suspect, however, that many readers will not feel this way. As Ivan Illich has argued, many people view schools as secular churches, through which they hope to improve not themselves but their descendants. This helps explain why schools are so often disagreeable: one cannot abolish original sin through self-indulgence. It also helps explain why educators' claims for the schools are so often extravagant: a religion which promises anything less than salvation wins few converts. In school, as in church, we deal with the world that we wish existed, trying to inspire our descendants with ideals we ourselves have failed to live up to. We assume, for example, that there is no chance of making adults live together in desegregated neighborhoods, so we try to impose this ideal on children by inventing elaborate school busing plans. If, as we argue in this book, intellectual and moral experiments on children have little effect on adult life, many people are likely to lose interest in schools. Children per se do not interest them very much.

For social reformers whose primary concern is adult inequality, our findings have more negative than positive implications. We have shown, for example, that different varieties of inequality are very loosely related to one another. This means that no single general strategy will eliminate all sorts of inequality. Instead, there must be a variety of specific strategies for dealing with specific kinds of inequality. Furthermore, since reducing inequality in one area has very limited effects on inequality in other areas, it is important to set priorities. The reader should by now have gathered that our primary concern is with equalizing the distribution of income, but it may be useful to review the reasons why we feel this way.

Chapter 3 discussed strategies for equalizing the cognitive skills measured by standardized tests. Given our limited knowledge of the genetic and environmental determinants of test performance, none of these strategies seemed very promising. But even if we knew how to equalize test performance, we would not want to make this a primary objective of social policy. Test score differences do not account for much of the variation in people's incomes, and we doubt if they account for much of the variation in their general well-being. We argued in Chapter 1 that nobody should be allowed to fall too far below the norm for his community, since this could lead to serious social problems. But there is no reason why people need to keep up with their most intellectual neighbors. Very few people need or want Shakespeare's verbal facility or Evelyn Wood's reading speed. Equalizing knowledge and cognitive skill is not, then, a very sensible objective, even though there is a strong case for not letting anyone fall too far below the national average. How this can be done remains unclear.

The distribution of educational credentials poses even more complicated problems. Chapter 2 showed that the distribution of schooling was becoming more equal. This reflects the fact that the percentage of students finishing high school and entering college is rising much faster than the percentage finishing college or entering graduate school. This trend seems to result from two facts. First, the demand for education has increased steadily. Second, the cost of education, in terms of both the income foregone by the student and the cost of instruction, rises precipitously as students get older. This means that the absolute number of students is rising faster at lower levels than at higher levels. Had this not happened, the cost of education to society would have risen even faster than it has, since even larger numbers of potentially productive individuals would have been kept out of the labor force.

The egalitarian trend in education has not made the distribution of income or status appreciably more equal over the past 25 years. We do not know whether the demand for schooling has been getting more equal, or whether consumption is becoming more equal only because of the economic constraints just discussed. Unless demand is equal, which it clearly is not, we cannot see much reason to view an equal distribution of schooling as an important end in itself. Nor is there much evidence that equalizing the amount of time people spend in school is an effective way of equalizing anything else.

When we turn from cognitive skills and educational credentials to occupational status, the case for equality becomes much more cogent. We argued in Chapter 1 that on the average people in low-status occupations would get more satisfaction from an improvement in their position than people in high-status occupations. These same arguments also apply to income. On the average, an extra dollar is likely to buy more satisfaction for those who have very little money than for those who have a great deal. These arguments imply that if the supply of status and income were fixed, the best distribution would be completely equal. Since strategies for equalizing the status of different occupations are likely to equalize individual incomes, and vice versa, we will treat these two problems together.

The data examined in this book shows that neither genetic inequality nor disparities in family background dictate anything like the degree of economic inequality now found in American society. It is true that genetic diversity almost inevitably leads to considerable variation in people's cognitive skills. But variation in cognitive skill need not result in any significant degree in income inequality, even in a society where income depends to a large extent on competitive advantage. We estimated, for example, that when all other things were equal, the most genetically advantaged fifth of all men earned only 35–40 percent more than the most genetically disadvantaged fifth. The difference would be even less if we included women. It is true that these estimates cover only those genetic advantages that influence test scores and that genes may also influence income in other ways. Genes may, for example, influence certain personality traits, and these may influence a man's earning power. To date, however, no one has provided convincing evidence that genes influence income in this way. We therefore conclude that if all the nongenetic causes of inequality were eliminated, and if America still placed the same value it now places on various kinds of skill, the income gap between the top and the bottom fifths of all male workers would fall from around 7 to 1 to around 1.4 to 1. If these estimates are even approximately correct, the existence of genetic differences should not cause economic egalitarians to despair.

Nor is inequality among parents a major obstacle to equality among their children. Family background has more influence than IQ genotype on an individual's educational attainment, occupational status, and income.[3] Nonetheless, if we could eliminate all the factors that make brothers' incomes unequal—or if we required all brothers and sisters to pool their incomes—we could reduce inequality to 35 or 45 percent of its present level.[4]

These conclusions do not tell us much about the actual causes of economic inequality, much less about the best way to reduce it. Most explanations of economic inequality emphasize the fact that some people are more competent than others. They also tend to assume that competence depends to a significant extent on an individual's upbringing, his schooling, and his cognitive skills. The evidence we have examined shows that neither family background, schooling, nor cognitive skill explains much of the variation in men's incomes. This seems to imply that family background, schooling, and test scores do not explain much of the variation in men's vocational competence. An alternative theory, however, is that competence does not explain much of the variation in income. We suspect that both statements are partly true. If so, equalizing competence remains important, even though none of the obvious devices for doing so looks very promising.

We have argued that the best way to equalize competence is to make this an explicit objective of social policy and to encourage employers to reorganize work with this objective in mind. Job development and job rotation could probably help equalize some varieties of competence. Nonetheless, kibbutz experience suggests that some disparities will also persist, even in a society that deliberately tries to reduce them.

If we want to equalize the distribution of income, then, we need a more direct approach. We explored a variety of mechanisms for doing this, ranging from progressive taxation and income maintenance to direct government regulation of wages or tax incentives to employers for equalizing wages. We argued for concentrating on the distribution of initial wages, on the ground that this was most likely to be politically acceptable over the long run.

As this is written, however, the selection of a suitable mechanism for equalizing incomes is an interesting but politically irrelevant exercise. The crucial problem today is that relatively few people view income inequality as a serious problem. Indeed, the Nixon administration apparently convinced itself that income was too equally distributed in 1968, and that the rich needed additional incentives to get even richer. The Kennedy and Johnson administrations were only marginally better. Neither made any explicit effort to equalize incomes. The subject was hardly discussed. Instead, reformers focused on equalizing opportunity. As we have seen, this is a very different objective and is likely to have different results.

If egalitarians want to mobilize popular support for income redistribution, their first aim should be to convince people that the distribution of income is a legitimate political issue. Americans now tend to assume that incomes are determined by private decisions in a largely unregulated economy and that there is no realistic way to alter the resulting distribution. Until they come to believe that the distribution of income is a political issue, subject to popular regulation and control, very little is likely to change. In this connection it is worth noting that until a generation ago, Americans also believed that the rate of economic growth depended on private decisions and that it could not be controlled by the government. Today, virtually everyone assumes that the federal government is responsible for the state of the economy. If private decisions are producing undesirable results, it is up to the government to find a remedy. The time may now be ripe for a similar change in attitudes toward income inequality. We need to establish the idea that the federal government is responsible not only for the total amount of the national income, but for its distribution. If private decisions make the distribution too unequal, the government must be held responsible for improving the situation.

Simply establishing public responsibility for something is not sufficient to change it, but it is a beginning. Americans are by no means universally committed to economic equality, but we doubt that most of them think the richest 5 percent of all families should have incomes 25 times as large as the poorest 5 percent. If income distribution were a political issue, and if Congress were forced to make explicit decisions about the degree of income inequality it wanted, some redistribution would probably take place.

Nonetheless, if we want substantial redistribution, we will not only have to politicize the question of income inequality but alter people's basic assumptions about the extent to which they are responsible for their neighbors and their neighbors for them. This will inevitably be a long, slow process, stretched over decades rather than years. Nonetheless, an official commitment to equalizing incomes is a good way to begin this process. Official rhetoric cannot create a world without selfishness or a world where no one uses competitive advantage for personal gain. It can, however, often help create a world where people feel ashamed of such behavior. Popular assumptions about the extent to which unusual talent or good fortune entitle an individual to economic privileges are not an invariant by-product of human nature. They vary from time to time and culture to culture. We suspect, moreover, that they can be altered by deliberate efforts of the state, just as Supreme

Court decisions and federal intervention altered attitudes toward racial inequality during the 1960s.

A successful campaign for reducing economic inequality probably requires two things. First, those with low incomes must cease to accept their condition as inevitable and just. Instead of assuming, like unsuccessful gamblers, that their numbers will eventually come up or that their children's numbers will, they must demand changes in the rules of the game. Second, some of those with high incomes, and especially the children of those with high incomes, must begin to feel ashamed of economic inequality. If these things were to happen, significant institutional changes in the machinery of income distribution would become politically feasible.

The long-term direction of such progress seems clear. In America, as elsewhere, the general trend over the past 200 years has been toward equality. In the economic realm, however, the contribution of public policy to this drift has been slight. As long as egalitarians assume that public policy cannot contribute to economic equality directly but must proceed by ingenious manipulations of marginal institutions like the schools, progress will remain glacial. If we want to move beyond this tradition, we will have to establish political control over the economic institutions that shape our society. This is what other countries usually call socialism. Anything less will end in the same disappointment as the reforms of the 1960s.

# NOTES

1. See Chapter 3, note 97.

2. Chapter 3, note 93 summarized our findings on the effects of high schools on test scores. Chapter 5, note 40 estimates the unexplained between-school variance in educational attainment at 2 percent of the total. Eliminating this would reduce the coefficient of variation for attainment by 1 percent.

3. See Appendix B, Table B-5 and Figure B-7.

4. Chapter 7, note 36 estimates that 10 to 20 percent of the individual income variance is between pairs of brothers. If we were to look at family income rather than individual income and if we were to include sisters as well as brothers, the percentage would be even lower. This means that if there were no variance within groups of siblings, the coefficient of inequality would be between $\sqrt{0.10} = 32$ percent and $\sqrt{0.20} = 45$ percent of the present level.

# APPENDIX A

## Estimating the Heritability of IQ Scores

Chapter 3 described the concept of "heritability" and suggested in general terms how heritability could be estimated from correlations among relatives. This Appendix describes the sources of the data on which we based the estimates presented in Chapter 3 and the methods used to reconcile conflicts between these sources.

Following Wright, "Path Coefficients," and Li, *Population Genetics,* we have relied heavily on path analysis to estimate heritability. Path diagrams make both the nature and the limitations of some analyses clearer than the conventional analysis of variance (for which see any standard text, such as Falconer, *Quantitative Genetics,* or Li, *Population Genetics*). Mathematically, the two methods are equivalent.

Our models assume that the relationship between genotype and environment is always additive. This is a major theoretical limitation. There are a variety of plausible situations in which we expect genes and environment to have nonadditive effects on test scores. Empirically, however, we have not found evidence that nonadditive interactions are important. If they were important, we would expect additive models which included no interaction terms to explain less than 100 percent of the variance in test scores. In fact, additive models in which the parameters are estimated independently usually explain more than 100 percent of the variance in test scores. While this "overexplanation" is a serious defect in the additive model, it suggests that nonadditive relationships are of limited importance.

Our model does allow us to consider the effects of dominant and recessive genes. We will not consider "epistasis" (nonadditive interaction between genes at different loci) in any detail, since there does not appear to be any good way to distinguish the effects of epistasis from the effects of dominance.

We will try to estimate the relative importance of genes and environment for white Americans. Where studies cover a restricted range of environments, we will try to adjust the results to simulate what might reasonably be expected for a national sample.

We will use the following notation throughout this appendix:

$F$ = Father (or husband)
$M$ = Mother (or wife)
$P$ = Parent (either sex)
$\overline{P}$ = Mean for both father and mother
$AP$ = Adoptive parent
$NP$ = Natural parent

**266**

    $C$ = Child of either sex
$NC = N$ = Natural child
$AC = A$ = Adopted child
    $G$ = Genotype
    $E$ = Environmental factors that influence IQ scores *but that are not influenced by G*
  $EU$ = All prenatal environmental factors shared by twins
  $EF$ = All environmental factors that are shared by children raised in the same family
  $ER$ = All environmental factors not shared by children born and raised together
  $MZ$ = Identical (monozygotic) twins
  $DZ$ = Fraternal (dizygotic) twins
 $SIB$ = Siblings
  $UN$ = Unrelated children
    $T$ = Children reared together (as in $MZT$ or $UNT$)
    $S$ = Children reared separately (as in $SIBS$ or $MZS$)
  $IQ$ = Score on a standard IQ test. Scores are on individually administered Stanford-Binet tests unless otherwise indicated. Most of the data comes from studies using the 1916 Revision.·

We will denote the traits of a particular individual by an appropriate subscript. Thus $G_F$ is the father's genotype. When writing correlations, we will combine the trait and the subscript on a single line. Thus, $r_{GF,GM}$ is the correlation between the father's genotype and the mother's genotype.

The first section will estimate the effect of environment ($E$) and genotype ($G$) on IQ scores ($IQ$) by looking at correlations between parents and children ($r_{PC}$).

The second section will consider relationships between children reared together.

The third section will consider relationships between children reared apart.

Each section will begin by postulating a basic model of how correlations arise between certain sorts of relatives. These models are shown in Figures A–1, A–2, and A–3. We will use these models to derive equations which express the correlations between relatives in terms of the path coefficients in the analytic model. We will then review the available empirical data to obtain estimates of the actual correlations between relatives. This will allow us to solve our equations for the unknown path coefficients. We will be particularly interested in the path from genotype to IQ scores, which we will designate as $h$. We will define the square of this path coefficient ($h^2$) as the heritability of IQ scores.[1] If our model is correctly specified, $h^2$ should indicate the amount of variance in IQ scores among individuals with random genes and identical environments. If $h^2 = 0.45$, for example, the variance in IQ scores among random individuals raised in identical environments should be 45 percent of the variance in the general population. We will obtain several independent estimates of $h^2$. These estimates will not agree closely with one another. Our final estimates will therefore be a compromise.

## Studies of Parents and Children

This section considers 3 kinds of relationships between parents and children:

1. The correlation between children and parents when the children are reared by their natural parents ($r_{IQNP,IQNC}$ or simply, $r_{IQP,IQC}$).

2. The correlation between children and their natural mother or natural father when the child has been adopted by another family at an early age ($r_{IQNP,IQAC}$).

3. The correlation between children and their adoptive mother or adoptive father when the child has been adopted at an early age ($r_{IQAP,IQAC}$).

Figure A–1 shows the analytic model we will use to explain resemblance

### FIGURE A–1
*Sources of Correlation between Parents' and Children's IQ Scores*

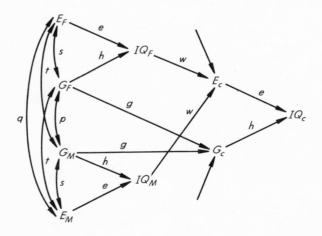

between the IQ scores of parents and children. The model has been deliberately simplified by omitting certain paths which might theoretically be expected to have at least modest importance. There is, for example, no direct path from $E_F$ or $E_M$ to $E_C$. The connection between parental environment and a child's IQ is presumed to operate entirely by way of parental cognitive skills, as measured by parental IQ. Inclusion of additional paths might make the model more adequate but would also make it impossible to estimate any of the path coefficients.

Rather than denoting the path coefficients in the model by subscripts, we have (we hope) simplified the reader's task by using lower case letters for each path. The correlation between fathers' and mothers' genotypes due to assortative mating will always be denoted as $p$. The path from a parent's genotype ($GP$) to a child's genotype ($GC$) will always be denoted as $g$. The path from genotype to $IQ$ will always be $h$. As noted above, $h^2$ is the fraction of the present IQ variance that would persist if all environmental variation (except that caused by genes) were eliminated. The fraction of the present IQ variance that would persist if all genetic variance were eliminated is $e^2$. The correlation between $G$ and $E$ will always be $s$.

We will assume that the heritability of adult scores is the same as the heritability of children's scores, even though Appendix B raises some questions about this assumption. The heritability of adult scores has seldom been estimated empirically. The heritability of young children's scores (i.e. under 5 or 6) appears to be lower than the heritability of later scores (see Honzik, "Developmental Studies"). We will ignore young children's scores in this analysis.

The reader should keep in mind that $E$ does not include any environmental influences that are directly influenced by, or responsive to, the child's genotype. The implications of this definition are discussed at length in Chapter 3. Here it is simply important to note that the correlation between $G$ and $E$ derives not from the *effect* of $G$ on $E$, but from the fact that children with favorable genotypes tend to be born (or to a lesser extent adopted) into environments that are above average for all children, regardless of genotype. The reasons for this will be discussed shortly. If we were to define $E$ as including *all* aspects of the environment, including those affected by $G$, we would need quite different models. The correlation between $G$ and $E$ would rise sharply. Such models cannot, however, be estimated empirically.

We will define $G$ and $E$ as completely determining $IQ$. This means that we assume all random measurement error is eliminated and that our estimates are based on "true" correlations, corrected for attenuation. (The problems involved in such corrections are discussed at length in Appendix B, and will not be discussed here.)

This definition implies certain mathematical tautologies. Just as in any multiple regression equation, the basic formula for computing the variance in $IQ$ explained by $G$ and $E$ is:

$$R^2_{IQ.G,E} = hr_{IQ,G} + er_{IQ,E} \tag{1}$$

But $R^2 = 1.00$ by definition, $r_{IQ,G}$ can be decomposed into $h + se$, and $r_{IQ,E}$ can be decomposed into $e + sh$. We therefore have:

$$1 = h(h + se) + e(e + sh) \tag{1a}$$

This can be transformed into:

$$1 = h^2 + 2hes + e^2 \tag{1b}$$

Equation (1b) is a tautology describing the sources of variance in IQ scores. The $h^2$ term represents variance due to genes, the $e^2$ term represents variance due to environment, and $2hes$ represents covariance due to the correlation between $G$ and $E$.

We are ultimately interested in the values of $h$, $e$, and $s$ in Figure A–1. In order to estimate them, we must first estimate the values of $p$, $q$, $t$, $g$, and $w$. The value of $g$ depends on the extent of dominance and epistasis. The values of $p$, $q$, and $t$ depend on the extent and character of assortative mating. The value of $w$ depends on the effect of parental cognitive skills on a child's environment. We will first discuss dominance and epistasis, then assortative mating, and then the effect of parental cognitive skills on children's environments.

DOMINANCE

Many popular discussions of the inheritance of IQ assume that the genetic correlation between two individuals is equal to the proportion of genes they have in common with one another. Since children receive half their genes from their mother and half from their father, the genetic correlation between a parent and a child, or between two siblings, is presumed to be 0.50. Unfortunately, this reasoning only holds if genes interact with one another in an extremely simple way, i.e. if their effects are completely independent and additive. This is unlikely.

At the risk of some oversimplification, we can describe the mechanism by which genes control biological development in the following manner. On any given chromosome there are a large number of genetic loci, each of which may have some influence on how an individual develops. At each locus there are typically two alleles. One of these alleles is identical to one of the mother's two alleles at the same locus. The other allele is identical to one of the father's two alleles at the same locus.

The simplest assumption is that when a child receives different alleles from its two parents, each allele exerts an equal effect. If, for example, a child has one allele leading to brown eyes and one leading to blue eyes, this theory leads us to expect that the child's eyes will be partly blue and partly brown, i.e. what is usually called "hazel." Similarly, if individuals who receive two alleles of type $A$ normally have IQ scores of 106, while those who have two alleles of type $a$ normally have IQ scores of 98, the simple theory leads us to expect that individuals with one $A$ allele and one $a$ allele will have IQ scores of 102.

In practice, IQ scores are influenced by many genetic loci. Again, however, the simplified theory is that the effects of different loci simply average out. Thus if an $Aa$ combination at one locus leads to an IQ of 102, everything else being equal, and a $BB$ combination at another locus leads to an IQ of 96, everything else being equal, we expect the two together to lead to an IQ score of 99, everything else being equal.

In some cases, however, both alleles and loci may interact in a more complicated way. Let us first consider different alleles at the same locus. In some cases, one is completely dominant and one recessive. This means that if a trait is controlled by a single locus, an individual who has a dominant and a recessive allele has the same expected trait value as an individual who has two dominant alleles. Only individuals with two recessive alleles differ from the norm. In the IQ example given above, if allele $A$ were completely dominant over allele $a$, individuals with $AA$ and $Aa$ combinations would all have expected IQs of 106. Only $aa$'s would have a different expected IQ, namely 98.

In some cases, there may be only partial dominance. If allele $A$ were partially dominant over allele $a$ in our IQ example, we might expect

*AA*'s to have IQs averaging 106, *Aa*'s to have IQs averaging 105, and *aa*'s to have IQs averaging 98.

The interaction between genes at different loci may be thought of in the same way as the interaction of alleles at the same locus. In the simple additive case, the effects on a given trait of a favorable and an unfavorable gene will simply be the average of their separate effects on that trait. This kind of additive relationship is often known as "blending." In some cases, however, the effects of genes may not average out in this way. The development of a desirable trait may, for example, depend on two different genes both being favorable. When an individual has only one favorable gene, it may have no observable effect. However, when two occur together, they may make a major difference. This kind of nonadditive interaction is known as epistasis. Analytically, its effects are almost impossible to distinguish from the effects of dominance.

The combination of genes required to produce an unusually favorable or unfavorable genotype is more specific when there is dominance or epistasis than when all genes blend. Both dominance and epistasis therefore reduce the likelihood that genetically favored parents will have genetically favored children. This increases the likelihood that a child's IQ will be close to the population mean even if its parents are at one of the extremes. Conversely, the likelihood that a child with an unusually high IQ will have parents with high IQs is lower. The correlation of a parent's IQ with a child's IQ therefore falls.[2]

The value of *g*, the path from parents' genotype to child's genotype, cannot be estimated directly from data on parents and children. All we can do is calculate a series of alternative values for *h*, *e*, and *s*, assuming different values of *g*. Using these estimates we can then predict the probable correlation between various kinds of children reared together. We will see in the next two sections that our predictions are more accurate if we assume that *g* is between 0.30 and 0.40 than if we assume higher or lower values. This implies a substantial amount of dominance or epistasis.

### ASSORTATIVE MATING

The existence of assortative mating is also frequently ignored in estimating the heritability of IQ scores. This is equivalent to assuming that *p*, the correlation of mother's genotype and father's genotype, *q*, the correlation of mother's and father's environment, and *t*, the correlation of one parent's genotype with the other's environment, are all zero. This is a serious error.

Table A–1 summarizes the literature on correlations between fathers' and mothers' test scores. Given the diversity of the communities covered, the diversity of the results is not surprising. We hardly expect the same amount of assortative mating with respect to vocabulary and similar skills in all kinds of communities. Nonetheless, all but two of the reported values fall between 0.40 and 0.61. The two extreme values are, moreover, suspect on theoretical grounds.[3]

The intraclass correlation between spouses is the ratio of the between-pair variance minus the within-pair variance to the total variance. Thus, $r_{FM} = (V_{BFM} - V_{WFM})/(V_{WFM} + V_{BFM})$, where $r_{FM}$ is the correlation be-

## TABLE A-1

### Observed Correlations between Husbands' and Wives' Test Scores in U.S. Studies

| Source | Location | Test | Pairs of Parents | Observed Correlation |
|--------|----------|------|------------------|----------------------|
| 1. Burks, "Nature and Nurture," Parents Raising Their Own Children | California | Stanford-Binet | 174 | 0.55 |
| 2. Burks, "Nature and Nurture," Parents Raising Adopted Children | California | Stanford-Binet | 100 | 0.42 |
| 3. Willoughby, "Family Similarities" | Palo Alto | Stanford Achievement and NIT | 141 | 0.40 [a] |
| 4. Outhit, "Resemblance of Parents" | U.S. and Canada | Army Alpha | 51 [b] | 0.74 |
| 5. Leahy, "Intelligence," Parents Raising Their Own Children | Minnesota | Binet Vocabulary | 164 | 0.43 |
| 6. Leahy, "Intelligence," Parents Raising Adopted Children | Minnesota | Binet Vocabulary | 174 | 0.61 |
| 7. Leahy, "Intelligence," Parents Raising Adopted Children | Minnesota | Otis Intelligence | 174 | 0.57 |
| 8. Conrad and Jones, "Second Study" | Rural New England | Army Alpha | 134 [c] | 0.52 |
| 9. Higgins, Reed, and Reed, "Intelligence and Family Size" | Minnesota | Diverse [d] | 1016 | 0.33 |
| Weighted Mean of Samples 1–3, 5, 6, and 8 | | Army Alpha and Binet | 887 | 0.50 |

[a] Reported value was 0.44, but this included a correction for attenuation.

[b] Basic sample $N = 51$, but couples were deliberately excluded where there was reason to expect a large discrepancy between spouses. Final $N$ not reported.

[c] Subsumes 105 pairs described by Jones, "First Study," where $r = 0.60$.

[d] Sample based on relatives of mental patients. IQ scores estimated by combining scores from diverse school records in many states.

tween fathers and mothers in a single study, $V_{BFM}$ is the variance between father-mother pairs in a single study, and $V_{WFM}$ is the variance within father-mother pairs in a single study. But, when we pool studies, $R_{FM} = (\overline{V}_{BFM} - \overline{V}_{WFM} + V_{BS})/(\overline{V}_{WFM} + \overline{V}_{BFM} + V_{BS})$, where $R_{FM}$ is the correlation for the pooled sample, $\overline{V}_{BFM}$ is the weighted mean of the between-pair variances for all studies, $\overline{V}_{WFM}$ is the weighted mean of the within-pair variances for all studies, and $V_{BS}$ is the variance between studies. Except in the unlikely event that all studies have the same mean and $\overline{V}_{BS} = 0$, $R_{FM}$ will exceed $\overline{r}_{FM}$ (where $\overline{r}_{FM}$ is the weighted mean of the $r$'s in different studies).[4]

For the six "acceptable" studies in Table A–1, $\overline{r}_{FM}$ is 0.50. The original studies summarized in Table A–1 do not, however, provide enough information to estimate $V_{BS}$. Thus, we cannot estimate $R_{FM}$ with certainty. Applying a rule of thumb that will be used again for other similar data, we will simply assume $V_{BS} = 0.05$. (This implies that if we take all studies, the standard deviation of the means will be $(15)(\sqrt{0.05}) = 3.4$ points.) If $V_{BS} = 0.05$, $R_{FM} = 0.524$. If we assume that the test reliability is about 0.92 for tests of the kind used in Table A–1, we have an implied true correlation of 0.57 between spouses.[5]

If the correlation between spouses' test scores were solely due to selection of mates on the basis of cognitive skill, the correlation between spouses' genotypes ($p$) would be:

$$p = r_{GF,IQF}\, r_{IQF,IQM}\, r_{IQM,GM} \tag{2}$$

Using Figure A–1, we can derive $r_{GF,IQF} = r_{GM,IQM} = h + se$, so we have

$$p = 0.57\ (h + se)^2 \tag{2a}$$

In practice, matters may not be so simple. Spouses select one another partly on the basis of cognitive skill but also partly on the basis of other factors that influence test scores. The selection may be more influenced by the environmental determinants of test scores than by the genetic determinants.

After a good deal of experimentation with rather complicated path diagrams, however, we have concluded that the effect of these "disturbances" is probably quite small.[6] Given the problematic and minor nature of this correction, we will simply assume $p = 0.57(h + se)^2$, i.e. that assortative mating is based entirely on IQ itself, not on the genetic or environmental determinants of IQ. This assumption allows us to calculate values for $q$, the correlation between father's and mother's environment, and for $t$, the correlation of one parent's genotype with the other's environment, in terms of $h$, $e$, and $s$. If all assortative mating is on IQ,

$$q = r_{EF,IQF}\, r_{IQF,IQM}\, r_{IQM,EM} = 0.57\ (e + hs)^2 \tag{3}$$

and,

$$t = r_{EF,IQF}\, r_{IQF,IQM}\, r_{IQM,GM} = r_{GF,IQF}\, r_{IQF,IQM}\, r_{IQM,EM} =$$
$$0.57\ (e + hs)\ (h + es) \tag{4}$$

We now have three of our unknown paths, $p$, $q$, and $t$, expressed in terms of the three variables we are trying to estimate, namely $h$, $e$, and $s$.

PARENT-CHILD CORRELATIONS

In order to estimate $w$ (the effect of parental cognitive skills on a child's environment) we need to disentangle the effects of $G$ and $E$. The most promising way to do this is to compare the relationship between parental IQ scores and children's IQ scores in situations where the degree of genetic connection between the parents and the children varies. This means comparing natural and adopted children.

We will look first at data on observed IQ correlations between natural parents ($NP$) and natural children ($NC$), and between adoptive parents ($AP$) and their adopted children ($AC$). We will then go through a series of calculations to determine the degree of genetic resemblance between adopting parents and their adopted children. These calculations will be based on data comparing the characteristics of natural and adopting parents. Finally, we will use this data to solve a series of equations generated by the path model. This gives us estimates of $h$, $e$, and $s$ in terms of $g$. We will check these estimates against data on natural parents and their children who have been placed for adoption.

Table A–2 shows the results of the six best studies reporting correlations between parents and natural children in somewhat representative American populations. We have ignored the results of the largest of these studies (Higgins, Reed, and Reed) because we suspect that the use of diverse school tests yielded less reliable estimates of IQ than the uniform testing procedures

### TABLE A–2
*Observed Correlations between Parents' IQ Scores*
*and Children's Stanford-Binet Scores*
*when Children Are Raised by Natural Parents[a]*

| Source | Parental Test | Number of Parents | Correlation |
|---|---|---|---|
| 1. Burks, "Nature and Nurture" | Stanford-Binet | 200 | .46 |
| 2. Leahy, "Intelligence" | Otis IQ | 366 | .51 |
| 3. Conrad and Jones, "Second Study" | Army Alpha | 441 | .49 |
| 4. Outhit, "Resemblance of Parents" | Army Alpha | 102 | .58 |
| 5. Willoughby, "Family Similarities" | Stanford Achievement and Army Alpha and NIT | 141 | .35 |
| 6. Higgins, Reed, and Reed, "Intelligence and Family Size" | Group Tests in School [b] | 2,032 | .44 |
| Weighted Mean of Samples 1–5 | | 1,250 | .48 |

[a] Correlations computed separately in original studies for fathers and mothers. Correlations shown here are means of virtually identical values. $N$ is total for both fathers and mothers.

[b] Results of diverse tests were transformed to a uniform scale, presumably lowering reliability and, hence, the observed correlation.

in the other studies. The weighted mean of the other five studies is 0.48. The average correlation is the same for mothers and fathers. Erlenmeyer-Kimling and Jarvik, in "Genetics and Intelligence," report an international median of 0.50 for twelve studies.

Just as with husbands and wives, we must inflate the mean observed correlation to take account of the fact that all the studies cover geographically restricted populations. Taking 0.48 as the correlation in local studies and again assuming that 5 percent of the total variance in American test scores is between the populations covered by local studies, we anticipate that a national study would yield a correlation of 0.505 between a parent and a natural child. Correcting for unreliability on the assumption that the tests have a reliability of 0.92, we estimate $R_{IQP,IQC} = 0.55$.

The reader should note that these two correction procedures will have contradictory effects on our eventual estimates of the heritability of IQ scores. Inflating correlations to take account of the restricted range of test score variation in local studies will lower our eventual estimates of heritability. This reflects the fact that the range of environments in the average community is narrower than in the nation as a whole. The studies summarized in Table A–2, like those used throughout this appendix, rarely deal with the South, especially the rural South. Most deal exclusively with either urban or rural subjects. The observed differences in test scores between regions and between types of communities (see, e.g. McNemar, *Revision,* and Coleman et al, *Equality of Educational Opportunity*) may, of course, be partly genetic. However, nobody has ever provided any evidence for this theory, whereas there is ample evidence that region and community influence a child's environment. Our correction procedures will therefore assume that the difference is environmental. This, in turn, means that the heritability of IQ scores is greater in any specific community, where environments are more equal, than they are in the nation as a whole. The reader who rejects this view can easily derive alternative estimates of heritability by reducing our final estimate of both the total variance and the environmental variance by 5 percent. The effect is trivial.

Correcting correlations for measurement error has precisely the opposite effect from correcting them for restriction of range. Instead of reducing the estimated heritability of test scores, this correction increases estimated heritability. This reflects the fact that measurement error is an environmental effect, and any reasonable analytic procedure treats it as such. Eliminating measurement error therefore increases the relative importance of genes.

The fact that the two corrections have opposite effects on heritability estimates may seem puzzling at first glance, since both corrections involve inflating observed correlations. The correction for restriction of environmental range only inflates the correlation for children raised by their own parents, however. It deflates the correlation among genetically related children raised by different parents. Furthermore, the correction for restriction of range has its largest effect when the observed correlation is low (e.g. between unrelated children reared together), whereas the correction for attenuation has its largest effect when the observed correlation is high (e.g. between identical twins reared together).

TABLE A–3

*Correlations between Characteristics of Adopting Parents*
*and Adopted Children's Stanford-Binet IQ Scores*

| Trait and Sources | Correlation | Number of Cases |
|---|---|---|
| **Father's IQ Score** | | |
| Burks, "Nature and Nurture" [a] | .07 | 178 |
| Freeman et al., "Influence" [b] | .37 | 180 |
| Leahy, "Intelligence" [c] | .19 | 178 |
| Weighted Mean | .21 | 536 |
| **Mother's IQ Score** | | |
| Burks, "Nature and Nurture" | .19 | 204 |
| Freeman et al., "Influence" | .28 | 255 |
| Leahy, "Intelligence" | .24 | 186 |
| Weighted Mean | .24 | 645 |
| **Father's Education** | | |
| Burks, "Nature and Nurture" | .01 | 173 |
| Leahy, "Intelligence" | .19 | 193 |
| Skodak and Skeels, "Final Follow-Up" [d] | .03 | 100 |
| Weighted Mean | .09 | 466 |
| **Mother's Education** | | |
| Burks, "Nature and Nurture" | .17 | 194 |
| Leahy, "Intelligence" | .25 | 192 |
| Skodak and Skeels, "Final Follow-Up" | .05 | 100 |
| Weighted Mean | .18 | 486 |
| **Father's Occupation** | | |
| Freeman et al., "Influence" | .34 | 394 |
| Leahy, "Intelligence" | .14 | 194 |
| Weighted Mean | .28 | 588 |
| **Family Income** | | |
| Burks, "Nature and Nurture" | .23 | 181 |

[a] All children placed before 12 months. Mean age at placement was 3 months.

[b] Study includes many late adoptions, some of whose IQ scores were known or could be guessed at the time of placement. Selective placement based on test scores was substantial (see Table A–4), but correlations between adopting parents' IQ scores and children's eventual scores were the same for children placed before 9 months, on whom IQ data was not available at the time of placement.

[c] All children placed before 6 months.

[d] All children placed before 6 months.

Table A–3 summarizes American research involving correlations between adopted children's Stanford-Binet scores and several characteristics of their adoptive parents. The mean correlation of an adopted child's IQ with that of its adoptive father is 0.21. The mean for adoptive mothers is 0.24. We will assume in subsequent analyses that the true correlations for fathers and mothers are equal ($r = 0.225$), since this view is consistent with the data on children reared by their natural parents and greatly simplifies the analysis. Correcting for unreliability yields a value of 0.244. Correcting for 5 percent variance between samples, this becomes $r_{IQAP,IQC} = 0.28$.

GENETIC RESEMBLANCE BETWEEN ADOPTIVE PARENTS AND CHILDREN

The correlation between a child's genotype and its natural parent's genotype can be deduced from Figure A–1 as $g + gp$ or $g(1 + p)$. The correlation between a child's genotype and its adoptive parents' genotype depends on the extent to which children are adopted by parents who resemble their natural parents genetically.

Table A–4 summarizes the results of American studies of selective placement. Where placement is delayed until the child is old enough to be given some kind of IQ test, the results are often used to place precocious children in what social workers view as good homes. Such test results are, however, a very poor indicator of later test scores or of genotype (see Chapter 3). Furthermore, such scores were not available for most of the children covered by the studies summarized in Table A–3, since almost all were adopted very early. We will therefore ignore selective placement based on children's test scores and concentrate on selective matching of natural and adoptive parents.

Table A–4 shows virtually no selective placement with regard to the occupations of natural and adoptive fathers, even when the former are known. There is, however, consistent evidence of selective placement with regard to the educational attainment of natural and adopting parents, especially mothers. The correlation between natural and adopting parents' educational attainments averages 0.29. Assuming the correlation between educational attainment and parental IQ is 0.68 (see Appendix B), and assuming no direct selectivity on the basis of IQ or its other correlates, the expected correlation between the IQ scores of natural and adopting parents would be about $(0.68)(0.29)(0.68) = 0.13$. To see if IQ does have an independent influence, we can look at the correlations between the natural mother's IQ score and the educational attainment of the adopting mother, as well as between the adopting mother's IQ score and the educational attainment of the natural mother. On the assumption that IQ has no influence independent of education, these correlations would be about $(0.29)(0.68) = 0.20$. Leahy, in "Intelligence," obtained a correlation of 0.20 between IQ scores of adoptive parents and the natural mother's education, suggesting that adoptive parents' IQ scores had no independent effect on placement. However, Skodak and Skeels, in "Final Follow-Up," obtained a correlation of 0.24 between the natural mother's test scores and the adoptive parents' average education, suggesting that the natural mother's scores, where available, might have had a small direct effect on placement. Still, matching of parents with respect to IQ is largely a matter of matching with respect to educational attainment. Assuming only slight matching with respect to factors other than education, we infer that the correlation between one natural and one adopting parents' IQ scores is about 0.15, instead of the 0.13 estimated on the basis of educational matching alone. This becomes 0.16 after correcting for attenuation. If we assume assortative mating among

TABLE A–4

*Correlations between Characteristics of Natural and Adopting Parents*

| Trait and Sources | Correlation | Number of Cases |
|---|---|---|
| Occupation of Natural and Adopting Fathers | | |
| Leahy, "Intelligence"—Minnesota | .09 | 89 |
| Leahy, "Selective Factors"—Minnesota | .08 | 1,046 |
| Burks, "Nature and Nurture"—California | –.02 | 86 |
| Education of Natural and Adopting Fathers | | |
| Leahy, "Selective Factors"—Minnesota | .31 | 124 |
| Education of Natural and Adopting Mothers | | |
| Leahy, "Intelligence"—Minnesota | .25 | 94 |
| Leahy, "Selective Factors"—Minnesota | .29 | 836 |
| Skodak and Skeels, "Final Follow-Up"—Iowa (Based on Midparent Education for Adopting Families) | .27 | 100 |
| Education of Natural Mother and Mean IQ of Adopting Parents | | |
| Leahy, "Intelligence"—Minnesota | .20 | 89 |
| IQ of Natural Mother and Mean Education of Adopting Parents | | |
| Skodak and Skeels, "Final Follow-Up"—Iowa | .24 | 100 |
| IQ of Child at Placement (Test Unknown) and Overall Rating of Adopting Parents | | |
| Freeman et al., "Influence"—Chicago | .34 | 74 |
| IQ of Child at Placement (Kuhlman-Binet) and Education of Adopting Mother | | |
| Leahy, "Intelligence"—Minnesota | .34 | 93 |

both natural and adopting parents at the 0.57 level, the correlation between the mean IQ scores of natural parents and the mean of adopting parents ($r_{\overline{IQNP},\overline{IQAP}}$) will be about 0.20.[7]

To estimate the likely correlation between the genotypes of adoptive parents and their adopted children ($r_{GAC,\overline{GAP}}$), we will assume that:

$$r_{GAC,\overline{GAP}} = r_{GAC,\overline{GNP}} \; r_{\overline{GNP},\overline{IQNP}} \; r_{\overline{IQNP},\overline{IQAP}} \; r_{\overline{IQAP},\overline{GAP}} \tag{5}$$

where:

$r_{GAC,\overline{GAP}} =$ the correlation between the genotype of an adopted child and the mean genotype of the adoptive parents.

$r_{GAC,\overline{GNP}} =$ the correlation between the genotype of the child and the mean genotype of its natural parents. This is equal to the multiple correlation of the child's genotype with the genotypes of its natural parents taken separately. This can be derived from Figure A–1 as $R^2_{GC.GF,GM} = g(g + gp) + g(g + gp)$. Simplifying and taking the square root yields $r_{GAC,\overline{GNP}} = \sqrt{2g^2_N (1 + p)}$, where $g_N$ is the regression of a child's genotype on one natural parent's genotype, holding the other parent's genotype constant.

$r_{\overline{GNP},\overline{IQNP}}$ = the correlation between the mean genotype of the natural parents and their mean IQ score. We will assume from Figure A–1 that this is equal to $h + se$.

$r_{\overline{IQNP},\overline{IQAP}}$ = the correlation between the mean IQ scores of natural and adopting parents, i.e. 0.20.

$r_{\overline{IQAP},\overline{GAP}}$ = the correlation between the mean IQ scores of the adopting parents and their mean genotype. This is again $h + se$.

Substituting, we obtain:

$$r_{\overline{GAC},\overline{GAP}} = 0.20 \sqrt{2g^2_N (1 + p)} (h + se)^2 \tag{5a}$$

But, in addition, the model in Figure A–1 assumes that:

$$r_{\overline{GAC},\overline{GAP}} = \sqrt{2g^2_A (1 + p)} \tag{6}$$

where $g_A$ is the regression of a child's genotype on one adoptive parent's genotype, holding the other parent's genotype constant. Setting equations (5a) and (6) equal to one another and simplifying, we get:

$$g_A = .20g_N (h + se)^2 \tag{7}$$

ESTIMATING HERITABILITY

From the data summarized in Tables A–3 and A–4, we now have estimates of the correlations between the IQs of natural parents and their children and between adopting parents and adoptive children. We also have in equation (7) a formula for the genetic resemblance between adopting parents and their adoptive children, expressed in terms of $g$. Using these estimates, we can calculate the value of $w$, which is the effect of parental test scores on a child's environment, in terms of $g$, $h$, $e$, and $s$. Knowing $w$, we can write three equations in these four unknowns. This will allow us to calculate $h$, $e$, and $s$ for alternative values of $g$.

Figure A–1 yields the general equation for the correlation between a parent's IQ score and a child's score, whether natural or adopted, namely:

$$r_{IQP,IQC} = ew(1 + r_{IQF,IQM}) + gh(h + se)(1 + r_{IQF,IQM}) \tag{8}$$

Since we assume $r_{IQF,IQM} = 0.57$, this reduces to:

$$r_{IQP,IQC} = 1.57\ ew + 1.57\ gh(h + se) \tag{8a}$$

In order to estimate $w$, we assume equilibrium, i.e. that the relationship between $G$ and $E$ is the same for parents as for children.

Thus:

$$r_{GC,EC} = r_{GF,EF} = r_{GM,EM} = s. \tag{8b}$$

From Figure A–1, we can derive:

$$r_{GC,EC} = 2wg (h + se) (1 + r_{IQF,IQM}) \tag{9}$$

Since $r_{GC,EC} = s$, and $r_{IQF,IQM} = .57$, we have:

$$s = 3.14\ wg\ (h + se) \tag{9a}$$

or

$$s = \frac{3.14\ wgh}{1 - 3.14\ wge} \tag{9b}$$

and

$$w = \frac{s}{3.14\ g\ (h + se)} \tag{10}$$

In order to use this formula with correlations and values of $g$ for both adoptive and natural relationships, we have to be able to assume that the value of $w$ is the same in natural and adoptive relationships. The actual value of $w$ for adoptive children ($w_A$) is probably a little less than for natural children ($w_N$), since parental IQ probably has some effect on prenatal environment. For reasons given in the section on "Children Reared Together," however, we doubt if the effect of parental IQ on prenatal environment is large. We will therefore assume that $w_A \cong w_N \cong w$.

We can now use the data in Tables A–2 and A–3 to write equations in $h$, $s$, $e$, and $g$ for natural and adoptive relationships. For natural parents and children, $r_{IQP,IQC} = 0.55$. Using this value in equation (8a), we have:

$$0.55 = 1.57\ ew_N + 1.57\ g_N h\ (h + se) \tag{11}$$

For adopted children, $r_{IQP,IQC} = 0.28$, and equation (8a) becomes:

$$0.28 = 1.57\ ew_A + 1.57\ g_A h\ (h + se) \tag{12}$$

In order to make equations (11) and (12) comparable we must express $w_A$, $w_N$, $g_A$, and $g_N$ in terms of $g$, $h$, $e$, and $s$. From equation (10), we have $w = s/3.14g\ (h + se)$. By assumption, $w_A \cong w_N$. From equation (7), we have $g_A = .20g_N\ (h + se)^2$. Using $g$ to denote $g_N$, we therefore have:

$$0.55 = \frac{se}{2g\ (h + se)} + 1.57\ gh\ (h + se) \tag{11a}$$

and

$$0.28 = \frac{se}{2g\ (h + se)} + 0.314\ gh\ (h + se)^3 \tag{12a}$$

In addition, we know from equation (1) that $h^2 + 2hes + e^2 = 1$. We therefore have three equations (11a, 12a, and 1) in four unknowns ($g$, $h$, $e$, and $s$). By assuming a series of alternative values for $g$, we can solve for $h$, $e$, and $s$.

Table A–5 estimates the values of $h$, $e$, and $s$ for values of $g$ ranging from 0.50 (the theoretical maximum for parent-child relationships) down to 0.25. It also shows the percentage of variance explained by heredity ($h^2$) and environment ($e^2$).[8]

TABLE A–5

Values of $h$, $e$, $s$, $h^2$, $e^2$, and $2hes$ for Alternative Values of $g$

| $g$ | $h$ | $e$ | $s$ | $h^2$ | $e^2$ | $2hes$ | $h^2 + 2hes + e^2$ |
|------|------|------|------|------|------|------|------|
| .50 | .54 | .72 | .25 | .29 | .52 | .19 | 1.00 |
| .45 | .58 | .69 | .24 | .34 | .47 | .19 | 1.00 |
| .40 | .63 | .64 | .25 | .40 | .41 | .19 | 1.00 |
| .35 | .69 | .58 | .24 | .47 | .34 | .19 | 1.00 |
| .30 | .77 | .48 | .26 | .59 | .23 | .19 | 1.00 |
| .25 | .87 | .24 | .28 | .76 | .06 | .18 | 1.00 |

Table A–5 shows that no matter what the assumed values of $g$, $h$, and $e$, the covariance term ($2hes$) is not only positive but substantial. In fact, it consistently accounts for 19 percent of the total variance.[9] This suggests that ignoring covariance (which many writers have done) when estimating the heritability of IQ will lead to substantial overestimates of both the genetic and the environmental components of variance. It also suggests when the correlation between $G$ and $E$ is reduced (as happens with adopted children) the variance in test scores should be reduced. Empirical studies sometimes confirm this expectation, but sometimes they do not. When Burks, in "Nature and Nurture," compared adopted children to a control sample, she found no difference in the IQ variance for two groups. Her control sample showed less variance on several background measures, however. Leahy, in "Intelligence," conducted a very similar study and found 34 percent less IQ variance in her sample of adopted children than in her control sample. The two samples were remarkably comparable in other respects. Newman, Freeman and Holzinger, in *Twins*, found 25 percent less variance among adopted identical twins than among identical twins reared by their natural parents. Burt, in "Genetic Determination," found no difference between the variance for 53 identical twins who had been adopted and the variance for 53 twins reared by their natural parents.[10] Skodak and Skeels, in "Final Follow-Up," found 7 percent less variance in the IQ scores of adopted children than in the IQ scores of their natural mothers, but this comparison is of limited value since the variance of the 1916 Binet changes with age. Thus, these data support the notion that the covariance is substantial in two out of four samples. The other two samples do not support this notion. Taking a mean of the four samples, we find an average reduction in variance of 14 percent. This is very close to what we expect from Table A–5, since we expect some covariance even among adopted children due to selective placement.

We can check the validity of our estimates of $h$, $e$, and $s$ by using them to estimate the likely correlation between a natural mother's IQ score and the IQ scores of her children when the children are adopted by another family at any early age.

Unfortunately, the only study providing data on this relationship is Skodak and Skeels, "Final Follow-Up." This study covered only 63 mothers. Most were tested after having decided to give up their baby for adoption.

The mothers' Stanford-Binet scores averaged 86. If assortative mating was the same for this sample as for the general population, the natural fathers of these children should have had mean IQ scores of $100 - (0.57)(100 - 86) = 92$. If there were no differences between the parents' average environment and the children's average environment, and if dominant genes did not affect IQ, the children would have ended up with mean IQ scores of $(86 + 92)/2 = 89$. Their actual IQ scores averaged 106.

The obvious inference from the very rough estimate of what the children's IQs should have been is that the children's environments were superior to their parents' environments and that this boosted the children's scores 17 points above the parents' scores. The children's environmental advantage could have taken several forms. The mothers could have had superior genotypes but could have had uniformly depressed scores. Alternatively, the children could have had inferior genotypes but could have had above-average scores because they had been placed in superior environments. A third explanation may also play some part, however. If IQ were influenced by dominant and recessive genes, the anticipated genotype of the children would be higher than 89. In this sample, for instance, the predicted mean for the children might be in the low 90s instead of 89. Still, environment must be the main factor in the children's doing better than their mothers.

Note, too, that if there were a strong relationship between mothers' IQ scores and their children's prenatal environments, these children should have been disadvantaged. There is no sign of this.

The correlations between children's test scores and their natural mothers' test scores in this study was zero on the infant tests. It rose to around 0.41 when the children were between 11 and 17.[11] Correcting for attenuation, $r_{IQNP,IQAC}$ (as estimated from this one study) becomes 0.446. Our formula for this relationship, derived from the general formula in equation (8), is:

$$r_{IQNP,IQAC} = 1.57 \, ew_{NA} + 1.57 \, gh \, (h + se) \tag{13}$$

where $w_{NA}$ is the effect of the natural mother's IQ score on the child's environment. We assume that $w_{NA} \cong 0.12$ Since $r_{IQNP,IQAC} = 0.446$, we have:

$$0.446 = 1.57 \, gh \, (h + se) \tag{13a}$$

None of the values of $g$, $h$, $e$, and $s$ in Table A–5 satisfy equation (13a). The value of $1.57 \, gh \, (h + se)$ in Table A–5 ranges from a low of 0.30 (for $g = 0.50$) to a high of 0.32 (for $g = 0.30$). The discrepancy between the observed and the predicted correlations is, thus, 0.13 to 0.15. How are we to explain this?

Although selective placement within the sample has no appreciable effect on the observed correlation, the fact that all mothers came from Iowa and all children were placed in Iowa may have had some effect. Had Skodak and Skeels found a national sample of mothers whose children were randomly distributed to homes all over the country, the observed correlation would almost certainly have been less than it was. Applying our rule of thumb, the within-pair variance might have been inflated 5 percent, making the correlation only 0.42, but this still implies a discrepancy of 0.10 to 0.12.

A second possibility is that we were wrong in assuming that the natural mother's IQ score had no effect on the child's prenatal environment. In order for this to make an appreciable difference, however, we have to assume that the overall effect of parental IQ on prenatal environment is quite large. This seems unlikely, given the pattern of correlations between children reared together. This will be discussed in the section on "Children Reared Together" in this appendix.

We therefore fall back on sampling error as an explanation. There is about one chance in three that if the true correlation is 0.32 for the overall population, the observed correlation in a sample of 63 will deviate from the true correlation by as much as it does in this case. Since our other correlations are based on much larger numbers of cases ($N = 887$ for natural children and $N = 1,181$ for adopted children), we will not attempt to adjust the estimates in Table A–5 to incorporate the 63 cases in this "deviant" study. Doing so would slightly inflate the estimated value of $h$ for any given value of $g$, but the change would be small, simply because of the small number of cases involved in the deviant study.

In summary, our analysis of parent-child correlations establishes two points. First, there is substantial correlation between the effects of heredity and the effects of environment. Second, the heritability of IQ scores can only be high if we assume that the genes influencing IQ scores are usually dominant or recessive (or that epistasis is important).

## Studies of Children Reared Together

Our analysis of the data on parents and children led us to estimates of $h^2$ which range from 0.29 to 0.76, depending on the value of $g$, i.e. the extent to which $G$ is affected by dominance and epistasis. In this section, we estimate heritability in a different way, using data on children reared together. Our aim is to narrow the range of estimates of $h^2$ more than we could using only parent-child data. Unfortunately, the estimates which we derive in this section are not internally consistent. As we shall see, the data on unrelated children leads to estimates of $h^2$ that are quite different from those calculated from other types of data. The findings of this section are, therefore, not conclusive.

Our procedure in this section is to compare different types of children reared together: $MZ$ twins, $DZ$ twins, siblings, and unrelated children. The procedure is somewhat different from the one we used with the parent-child data. We first describe the data on correlations between children reared together. We then use the path diagram in Figure A–2 to estimate the total variance in IQ scores for different types of children. We do this because we have reason to believe that the variance should differ for different types of children, and we do not have good empirical estimates. We then estimate the percentage of common variance for different types of children. To do this, we use the values for covariance ($2hes$), assortative mating ($r_{GF,GM} = p$), and the relationship of parents' genes to children's environment, which we derived in the first section of this appendix. This allows us to equate the observed correlation coefficients from studies of children reared together with the ratios of within-pair variance to total variance derived from Figure A–2. The resulting equations can then be solved for *h, s,* and *e.*

Estimates of the correlations between children are commonly derived from one of two sources. Erlenmeyer-Kimling and Jarvik, in "Genetics and Intelligence," conducted a quite comprehensive review of the literature published prior to 1963. They reported both the median value and the range of the correlations that had been reported for different kinds of relatives and nonrelatives on "intelligence" tests. Burt, in "Genetic Determination," published estimates based on his (nonrandom) sampling of English children and adults over 50 years. Burt's correlations closely approximate Erlenmeyer-Kimling and Jarvik's medians. Nonetheless, both series have three crucial defects for our purposes.

First, there are substantial discrepancies between the results of English and American studies. English studies generally imply that IQ scores are more influenced by heredity than American studies. This implies that (a) Burt's results are not applicable to America, and (b) that Erlenmeyer-Kimling and Jarvik's medians, which combine correlations from England, America and several other countries, are also inapplicable to America.

Second, even if the true correlations were the same for all the populations involved in the studies reviewed by Erlenmeyer-Kimling and Jarvik, the use of unweighted medians to estimate the true underlying correlations could have led to substantial error. Weighting by the size of the study somewhat reduces the likelihood of error. In addition, except where the extreme cases are completely spurious, a weighted mean estimates the underlying population value better than a weighted median.

Third, Erlenmeyer-Kimling and Jarvik's survey includes studies using many different tests, the heritabilities of which are likely to vary. If we want consistent results, we need correlations for a single test and for a consistently defined population.

In order to deal with these problems, we again reviewed the literature on correlations between relatives.[13] The results of the relevant studies of children reared together are shown in Tables A–6 to A–8.

Table A–9 summarizes the results of Tables A–6 to A–8. It also provides estimates of the true correlations for a national sample. These estimates make two assumptions:

1. We assume that the test-retest reliability of the 1916 Stanford-Binet is 0.92 (see Thorndike, "Effect of Interval," and Brown, "Time Interval") and that the reliability of the London Binet is 0.95 (see Burt and Howard, "Multifactorial Theory").

2. We assume that the variance between American studies is about 5 percent of the total variance.

The data on which these tables are based require some comment.

CORRELATIONS BETWEEN TWINS REARED TOGETHER

Considering the alleged importance of twin studies in estimating heritability, we were surprised to discover only 1 study of American twins which had adequate zygosity tests, reported correlations for both *MZ* and *DZ* twins, and used the Stanford-Binet. This study (Newman, Freeman, and

Holzinger, *Twins*) covers 50 pairs of *MZ* twins and 50 pairs of *DZ* twins.[14] Using a reliability of 0.92, we get $r_{IQMZT} = 0.97$ and $r_{IQDZT} = 0.68$. Correcting for regional restriction in the range of environments in this sample yields $r_{IQMZT} = 0.97$, and $r_{IQDZT} = .70$.

One simple formula for estimating heritability from data on children reared together is that used by Jensen, in "Limits of Heritability." The general formula is:

$$h^2 = \frac{r_{IQ1,IQ2} - r_{IQ3,IQ4}}{b_{GC1,GC2} - b_{GC3,GC4}} \tag{14}$$

where $r_{IQ1,IQ2}$ is the correlation between children reared together who share a given proportion of genes, $r_{IQ3,IQ4}$ is the correlation between children reared together who share fewer genes, and $b_{GC1,GC2}$ and $b_{GC3,GC4}$ are the presumed correlations between the children's genotypes. Jensen suggests that $b_{MZ} = 1.00$ and $b_{DZ} \cong 0.55$. The formula for estimating $h^2$ from comparisons of monozygotic and dyzygotic twins is, thus,

$$h^2 = \frac{r_{IQMZT} - r_{IQDZT}}{1 - .55}$$

Using this formula, Newman, Freeman, and Holzinger's data yields $h^2 = .60$ for observed IQ scores and 0.64 for true IQ scores (i.e. the scores we would get if we gave infinitely long tests under uniform conditions).

Vandenberg, "Hereditary Factors," reports results for 166 pairs of American *MZ* twins and 126 pairs of American *DZ* twins, using Thurstone's Primary Mental Abilities (PMA) test. Unfortunately, Vandenberg does not report simple correlations, and his implicit definition of heritability is not the same as Jensen's or ours. In general, his data suggest lower heritabilities for the PMA than for the Binet. He reports that the within-pair variance for *DZ* twins is 1.4 to 3.5 times as large as the within-pair variance for *MZ* twins, depending on the specific subtest. The average ratio is about 2.5:1. (Newman, Freeman, and Holzinger found that the within-pair variance for *DZ* twins was 3 times as large as for *MZ* twins.) Vandenberg, in "Hereditary Abilities," reports results for WISC vocabulary similar to those for the PMA.

Table A–6 also lists two other large American twin studies, both of which used group tests. Schoenfeldt has estimated correlations for the Project Talent test battery. He published results for five factor scores derived from this battery in "Hereditary-Environmental Components." He found a very high heritability for what Talent calls "Verbal Knowledges." The other four factors that contributed to success on the Talent tests had much lower heritabilities. We are not, however, interested in the heritability of separate factor scores. We are interested in the heritability of an overall test score. Schoenfeldt calculated these heritabilities but did not publish them. Table A–6 presents his results for four tests that are similar to those used in the Talent analyses reported in this volume. These correlations are based only on same-sex pairs and are corrected for attenuation. They are very similar to one another and to the Stanford-Binet correlations reported above. Table A–6 also shows the correlations for five a priori composite

TABLE A–6
*Correlations between Test Scores of Identical
and Fraternal Twins Reared Together*

| U.S. Studies | Tests | Identical Twins | | Fraternal Twins | |
|---|---|---|---|---|---|
| | | Cases | Corre-lation | Cases | Corre-lation |
| Holzinger, "Nature and Nurture" | Otis IQ | 25 | 0.92 | 26 | 0.63 |
| Holzinger, "Nature and Nurture" | Binet 1Q | 25 | 0.88 | 26 | 0.62 |
| Holzinger, "Nature and Nurture" | Word Meaning+ Arithmetic+ Nature Study+ History+ Literature+Spelling | 25 | 0.89 | 26 | 0.70 |
| Newman, Freeman, and Holzinger, *Twins*, corrected by McNemar, "Special Review" | Stanford-Binet | 50 | 0.89 | 50 | 0.63 |
| Newman, Freeman, and Holzinger, *Twins*, corrected by McNemar, "Special Review" | Otis IQ | 50 | 0.92 | 50 | 0.62 |
| Newman, Freeman, and Holzinger, *Twins*, corrected by McNemar, "Special Review" | Stanford Achievement Composite | 50 | 0.96 | 50 | 0.88 |
| Nichols, "National Merit" | NMSC Composite Achievement | 687 | 0.87 | 482 | 0.63 |
| Nichols, "National Merit" | Vocabulary | 687 | 0.86 | 482 | 0.64 |
| Schoenfeldt, unpublished tables | Project Talent "Vocabulary" (R-102) | 335 | 0.88 * | 156 | 0.70 * |
| Schoenfeldt, unpublished tables | Project Talent "Social Studies" (R-105) | 335 | 0.89 * | 156 | 0.56 * |
| Schoenfeldt, unpublished tables | Project Talent "Mathematics" (R-106) | 335 | 0.86 * | 156 | 0.58 * |
| Schoenfeldt, unpublished tables | Project Talent "Information" (R-190) | 335 | 0.87 * | 156 | 0.65 * |
| Schoenfeldt, unpublished tables | Project Talent "IQ Composite" (C-001) | 335 | 0.85 | 156 | 0.54 |

TABLE A–6 (Continued)
*Correlations between Test Scores of Identical
and Fraternal Twins Reared Together*

| U.S. Studies | Tests | Identical Twins | | Fraternal Twins | |
| --- | --- | --- | --- | --- | --- |
| | | Cases | Corre-lation | Cases | Corre-lation |
| Schoenfeldt, unpublished tables | Project Talent "General Academic Aptitude Composite" (C-002) | 335 | 0.84 | 156 | 0.60 |
| Schoenfeldt, unpublished tables | Project Talent "Verbal" (C-003) | 335 | 0.87 | 156 | 0.57 |
| Schoenfeldt, unpublished tables | Project Talent "Quantitative" (C-004) | 335 | 0.84 | 156 | 0.57 |
| Schoenfeldt, unpublished tables | Project Talent "Mechanical-Technical" (C-005) | 335 | 0.82 | 156 | 0.69 |
| *English Studies* | | | | | |
| Blewett, "Experimental Study" | Thurstone PMA | 26 | 0.76 | 26 | 0.44 |
| Burt, "Genetic Determination" | Burt's Binet | 95 | 0.92 | 127 | 0.53 |
| Burt, "Genetic Determination" | Burt's Group Intelligence | 95 | 0.94 | 127 | 0.55 |
| Burt, "Genetic Determination" | Burt's Reading and Spelling | 95 | 0.95 | 127 | 0.92 |
| Burt, "Genetic Determination" | Burt's Arithmetic | 95 | 0.86 | 127 | 0.75 |
| Burt, "Genetic Determination" | Burt's General Attainments | 95 | 0.98 | 127 | 0.83 |
| Eysenck and Prell, "Neuroticism" | Wechsler-Bellevue (Similarities and Digit Symbol) | 25 | 0.89 | 25 | 0.66 |
| Herman and Hogben, "Resemblance of Twins" | Otis Advanced Group Test | 65 | 0.84 | 234 | 0.49 |
| Weighted Mean of Four English Studies Using IQ Scores | | 211 | 0.87 | 412 | 0.51 |

\* Correlations based on unweighted mean of separate correlations for males and females, corrected for attenuation. Data not available for opposite-sex twins. Research design described in Schoenfeldt, "Hereditary-Environmental Components."

scores (that is, sums of separate tests, not factor scores) which summarize the overall results of the Talent battery. The correlations for four of these five composites are very similar. The fifth composite, which covers mechanical-technical knowledge, shows lower heritability than the other four. Using Jensen's formula (see equation 14), $h^2$ averages 0.58 for the four separate Talent tests and 0.55 for the overall composite scores. This suggests that tests of the kind given by Project Talent have heritabilities quite similar to the Stanford-Binet. Environmental variation between families appears a little less important for the Talent tests, while environmental variation within families appears a little more important. This may simply mean that Schoenfeldt overestimated the reliability of the Talent tests, inflating the within-family variance. Or it may mean that random events in school play a larger role in determining scores on the Talent tests than in determining scores on tests like the Binet. The Talent twins were older than most of Newman, Freeman, and Holzinger's twins.

Table A–6 also shows results from another large national twin study (see Nichols, "National Merit"). The sample is based on students who took the National Merit Scholarship Qualifying Test. This test is very similar to the SAT. Unfortunately, the NMSC tests were given primarily to students of above-average ability. This has two contradictory effects. First, it means that when twins' scores differed drastically, only 1 twin was likely to be in the sample. The mean within-pair difference is thus underestimated. Second, the overall variance is restricted. The effect of these biases on the $MZ$ twin results appears to be small. Nichols reports that the reliability of the NMSC subtests is "around 0.90," which implies that $r_{IQMZT} = 0.956$. This is not appreciably different from the estimated true correlation for $MZ$ twins on the Stanford-Binet or the London Binet. The bias may, however, be larger for the $DZ$ twins. Substantially more $DZ$ than $MZ$ twins were lost as a result of the sampling procedure. The observed value ($r_{IQDZT} = 0.64$) implies a true value of $r_{IQDZT} = 0.71$. This is the highest value reported in the literature for fraternal twins. We therefore suspect that the sampling procedure overestimates $r_{IQDZT}$. As a result, $h^2$ would be underestimated. We will therefore ignore Nichols' results.

When we turn to England, we find that each study used a different test. We have not attempted to estimate the reliabilities of all these tests. Using an average reliability of 0.90 and Jensen's formula for $h^2$, the English studies yield heritabilities that average about 0.10 to 0.30 higher than the American studies. Jensen's formula can be written for uncorrected data as:

$$h^2 = \frac{(r_{IQMZT} - r_{IQDZT})}{(1 - .55)r_{tt}}$$

where $r_{tt}$ is the reliability of the test and $r_{IQMZT}$ and $r_{IQDZT}$ are observed correlations such as those in Table A–6. Thus, for Burt's Binet:

$$h^2 = (0.92 - 0.53)/(0.45)(0.95) = 0.91.$$

For Newman et al.'s Binet results:

$$h^2 = (0.89 - 0.63)/(0.45)(0.92) = 0.63.$$

The difference between the English and the American studies emerges quite consistently for any reasonable estimate of $r_{tt}$.[15]

CORRELATIONS BETWEEN SIBLINGS REARED TOGETHER

The studies reported in Table A–7 cover diverse samples. We have listed only studies using Binet IQ tests. We have also listed only studies that tried to cover representative samples. (Studies of university-run laboratory schools are omitted, for example.) Nonetheless, all but one study in Table A–7 is restricted to a specific part of the country. No sample includes any appreciable number of nonwhites. This probably means that the environmental variance is restricted and that genes explain a larger proportion of the total variance than they would in a national sample. In addition, the observed correlations may be deflated by several other factors.

TABLE A–7

*Correlations between Binet IQ Scores of Siblings Reared Together*

| U.S. Studies | Test | Pairs of Cases | Correlation |
|---|---|---|---|
| Conrad and Jones, "Second Study" | Stanford-Binet | 312 | 0.50 |
| Hart, "Correlations" | Stanford-Binet and others | 399 | 0.45 |
| Madsen, "Some Results" | Stanford-Binet | 63 | 0.63 |
| McNemar, *Revision* | Stanford-Binet | 384 | 0.53 |
| Outhit "Resemblance of Parents" | Stanford-Binet and Army Alpha | 63 | 0.67 |
| Hildreth, "Resemblance of Siblings" | Stanford-Binet | 450 | 0.63 |
| Weighted Mean of Seven U.S. Studies | Stanford-Binet | 1,951 | 0.52 |
| English Study: | | | |
| Burt, "Genetic Determination" | London Binet | 264 | 0.53 |

One problem is that some of the children officially classified as siblings are probably half-siblings. Some are probably completely unrelated. We know no data on the frequency with which extramarital sex produces half-siblings who are then passed off as full siblings. Nor would we be optimistic about obtaining accurate estimates on this point. Nonetheless, this could be a factor of some consequence. In addition, adopted children and children from prior marriages may have been erroneously classified as siblings in some studies. This would lower the observed correlation.

Another problem is that the 1916 Revision of the Stanford-Binet, which was used in most of the research on correlations between relatives, had different standard deviations at different age levels. This meant that a child whose test score was consistently 1 standard deviation above the mean might have a score of 113 in one year, 115 in another year, and 117 in still another year. It also meant that two brothers who were both exactly 1 standard deviation above the mean might end up with scores that differed by several points. While most researchers tried to correct for this source of error, the correction procedures were (and are) imperfect. As a result, the correlation between siblings is systematically underestimated.

In light of all these considerations, we conclude that the true correlation between siblings could easily be higher than the 0.59 estimated in Table A–9.

### CORRELATIONS BETWEEN UNRELATED CHILDREN REARED TOGETHER

Table A–8 is divided into four panels. Panel 1 deals with pairs of adopted children reared in the same home ($r_{IQAAT}$). Panel 2 deals with pairs in which one child is adopted and one is natural ($r_{IQANT}$). Panel 3 deals with unrelated pairs in which no distinction is made between natural and adopted children ($r_{IQUNT}$). The correlations for pairs in which both members are adopted consistently exceed the correlations for pairs in which one is adopted and one is natural. This is precisely the opposite of what we would expect if selective placement led to genetic resemblance between natural and adopted children in the same home.[16]

One explanation for this puzzle might be that the average adopted child is genetically inferior to the average natural child in the same family. Another possible explanation might be that adopted children have inferior environments prior to adoption. Either way, there would be a difference in the means for natural and adopted children. This would lower the intraclass correlation, though it would not lower the product-moment correlation. Freeman et al. found such a difference in means. Skodak and Leahy did not. Since Freeman et al. included a number of late adoptions, while Leahy and Skodak did not, we infer (a) that adopted and natural children do not differ much genetically, and (b) that the IQ scores of children adopted after infancy may be depressed. We also infer that the difference between adopted-adopted and adopted-natural pairs is not entirely due to differences in the mean IQs of adopted and natural children.

Having rejected the theory that the observed difference between adopted-adopted and adopted-natural pairs might be due to differences in the means for adopted and natural children, we need an alternative theory. One possibility is that adopted children are treated differently from natural children in the same home, whereas pairs of adopted children are treated more alike. However, since there is no difference in means for adopted and natural children in Skodak or Leahy's data, we cannot assume that natural children are systematically favored over adopted children. Instead, we have to assume random favoring of one child or the other. At the same time, we have to assume less such random variation when both children are adopted. Such a theory seems tendentious and unconvincing.

Unable to devise a plausible explanation for the observed data, we turn to the theory that the data is spurious. The difference between adopted-adopted pairs and adopted-natural pairs is not statistically significant at the 0.01 level in any of the three studies that cover both sorts of children. (The difference reported by Skodak is, however, significant at the 0.02 level, using a one-tailed test.) Since we have no alternative explanation for the observed data, we will assume that the true correlations conform to the theoretically expected pattern, i.e. that the correlations are really higher for

TABLE A–8

*Correlations between Unrelated Children Reared Together*

| Panel 1: U.S. Studies in Which Both Children Are Adopted | Test | Cases | Average Correlation |
|---|---|---|---|
| Burks, "Relative Influence" | Stanford-Binet | 21 | 0.23 |
| Freeman, Holzinger, and Mitchell, "Influence of Environment" with Terman Cases | Stanford-Binet | 93 | 0.40 |
| Freeman, Holzinger, and Mitchell, "Influence of Environment" with Terman Cases | School Achievement | 74 | 0.18 |
| Leahy, "Nature-Nurture" | Stanford-Binet | 10 | 0.12 |
| Skodak, "Mental Growth" | Stanford-Binet | 41 | 0.65 |

| Panel 2: U.S. Studies in Which One Child Is Adopted and One Natural | | | |
|---|---|---|---|
| Freeman, Holzinger, and Mitchell, "Influence of Environment" with Terman Cases | Stanford-Binet | 47 | 0.38 |
| Leahy, "Nature-Nurture" | Stanford-Binet | 25 | 0.06 |
| Skodak, "Mental Growth" | Stanford-Binet | 22 | 0.21 |

| Panel 3: U.S. Studies Pooling Adopted-Adopted and Adopted-Natural Pairs | | | |
|---|---|---|---|
| Freeman, Holzinger, and Mitchell, "Influence of Environment" with Terman Cases | Stanford-Binet | 140 | 0.34 |
| Leahy, "Nature-Nurture" (calculated by Jencks) | Stanford-Binet | 35 | 0.08 |
| Skodak, "Mental Growth" (calculated by Jencks) | Stanford-Binet | 63 | 0.50 |

| Panel 4: English Study Pooling Adopted-Adopted and Adopted-Natural Pairs | | | |
|---|---|---|---|
| Burt, "Genetic Determination" | London Binet | 136 | 0.25 |
| Burt, "Genetic Determination" | Burt's "Group Intelligence" | 136 | 0.28 |
| Burt, "Genetic Determination" | Reading and Spelling | 136 | 0.55 |
| Burt, "Genetic Determination" | Arithmetic | 136 | 0.48 |
| Burt, "Genetic Determination" | General Attainments | 136 | 0.54 |

| | | | |
|---|---|---|---|
| Weighted Mean of All U.S. Studies of Unrelated Children in the Same Home | Stanford-Binet | 259 | 0.32 |
| Weighted Mean of Four U.S. Studies of Adopted-Adopted Pairs | Stanford-Binet | 165 | 0.42 |
| Weighted Mean of Three U.S. Studies of Adopted-Natural Pairs | Stanford-Binet | 94 | 0.26 |

natural-adopted than for adopted-adopted pairs. We will then assume that the observed correlations deviate from the expected pattern solely because of sampling error. The reader who can devise a more plausible theory that is compatible with the data in the original studies is invited to do so.

Panel 3 of Table A–8 shows the estimated correlations for all pairs of unrelated children in the same home. The weighted mean of these correlations (0.32) differs from the weighted mean of the correlation for adopted-adopted pairs (0.42) and for adopted-natural pairs (0.26) because the pooled correlation in the largest single study (Freeman et al.) is lower than the correlation for either adopted-adopted or adopted-natural pairs. This reflects the difference between adopted and natural children's mean scores in Freeman et al.'s data.

Table A–8 also shows an appreciable difference between America and England (Panel 4). Environmental differences between families again seem to be more important in America than in England. This could reflect sampling differences between the two countries. We have no information on how Burt's unsystematic sampling procedures might have affected the range of environments in which adopted children were raised, nor do we know at what age his children were adopted.

Since the U.S. studies all deal with geographically and socially restricted samples of adopting homes, the correlations are less than they would be in a full national sample. The effect of a correction for restriction of a range is larger for unrelated children than for siblings or twins, as can be seen in Table A–9. Yet the correction here may still be too small, since families that adopt children are disproportionately middle class. A more representative sample of families might yield a higher correlation between unrelated children in the same home.

The discrepancy between our results and those published by Erlenmeyer-Kimling and Jarvik is particularly marked for unrelated children. Their median was 0.23, whereas ours was 0.25, a trivial difference. However, when we eliminate the English results, our median rises to halfway between 0.25 and 0.34, or 0.295. Taking a weighted mean instead of an unweighted median yields 0.32. Correcting for attenuation yields 0.35. Correcting for restriction of range yields 0.38.

SUMMARY OF OBSERVED CORRELATIONS

We can summarize the above observations by saying that the quality of the data on correlations between children reared together is poor and that the results are often inconsistent. We feel reasonably confident that the true correlation between identical twins reared together is in excess of 0.90. We also feel reasonably confident that the true correlation between siblings reared together is between 0.50 and 0.60 for local samples, and that it would be between 0.55 and 0.65 for a fully representative national sample. The other correlations are much less certain. The value for fraternal twins varies substantially from one study to another. The value for unrelated children reared in random homes is uncertain, since adopting families are not likely to be representative of all families. All in all, the data base is far

## TABLE A-9
### Correlations among Children Reared Together on Various IQ Tests

| Relationship | Erlenmeyer-Kimling and Jarvik | London Binet | London Binet Corrected for Unreliability | U.S. Binet | U.S. Binet Corrected for Unreliability | U.S. Binet Corrected for Unreliability and Restriction of Range |
|---|---|---|---|---|---|---|
| Adopted-Natural Pairs Reared Together | NA | NA | NA | 0.26 (94) | 0.28 | 0.31 |
| Adopted-Adopted Pairs Reared Together | NA | NA | NA | 0.42 (165) | 0.46 | 0.48 |
| All Unrelated Children Reared Together | 0.23 | 0.252 (136) | 0.265 | 0.32 (259) | 0.35 | 0.38 |
| Siblings Reared Together | 0.49 | 0.498 (264) | 0.524 | 0.52 (1951) | 0.57 | 0.59 |
| DZ Twins Reared Together | 0.53 | 0.527 (127) | 0.555 | 0.63 (50) | 0.68 | 0.70 |
| MZ Twins Reared Together | 0.87 | 0.918 (95) | 0.966 | 0.89 (50) | 0.97 | 0.97 |

(Numbers in parentheses are the total number of pairs in the relevant studies.)

Source: Column 1: Erlenmeyer-Kimling and Jarvik, "Genetics and Intelligence."
Column 2: Burt, "Genetic Determination." Results are for "individual test," not "final assessment."
Column 3: Column 2/0.95.
Column 4: Tables A–6 to A–8 of this Appendix.
Column 5: Column 4/0.92.
Column 6: (Column 5 + 0.05)/(1 + 0.05).

shakier than one might imagine from reading that the studies "cover 30,000 individuals" and have been "replicated many times over."

One way to illustrate the difficulties with this data is to apply Jensen's formula for heritability ($h^2$) to the data in Table A–9, i.e.:

$$h^2 = \frac{r_{IQ1,IQ2} - r_{IQ3,IQ4}}{b_{GC1,GC2} - b_{GC3,GC4}} \tag{14}$$

Jensen assumes that $b = 0.55$ for fraternal twins and siblings. This appears to be roughly correct if $g$ is between 0.40 and 0.30.

Jensen makes no estimate of $b$ for unrelated children. As we shall see, the value of $b$ for unrelated children is lower when both are adopted than when one is natural and one is adopted. To simplify the analysis, we will pool both sorts of children and use a weighted mean of the values of $b$ for the two sorts of pairs. We can do this by anticipating some of the findings we explain further on in this section. Equations (28) and (29) show that the genetic correlations between natural-adopted pairs ($b_{NAT}$) is $0.40g^2$ $(h + se)^2$ $(1 + p)$, while the genetic correlation for adopted-adopted pairs ($b_{AA}$) is $0.20b_{NA}$. The genetic correlation for all unrelated children in the same home ($b_{UNT}$) will fall between $b_{NA}$ and $b_{AA}$. If we take a weighted mean, using $N_{AA} = 165$ and $N_{NA} = 94$, we get $b_{UNT} = 0.54b_{NA} = 0.216g^2$ $(h + se)^2$ $(1 + p)$. From equation (2) $p = 0.57(h + se)^2$. Substituting the values of $h$, $s$, and $e$ derived in Table A–5, we get values of $b_{UNT}$ between 0.035 to 0.022. We will use $b_{UNT} = 0.03$.

Table A–10 gives a series of alternative estimates of $h^2$ from Jensen's formula, using $b_{SIB} = 0.55$, $b_{UNT} = 0.03$, and the three data sets in Table A–9. Erlenmeyer-Kimling and Jarvik's medians have all been corrected on the assumption that they are based on tests with reliabilities of 0.92. The

TABLE A–10

*Values of $h^2$ Using Jensen's General Formula with Three Different Data Sets*

| Type of Comparison | General Formula | Estimate Using Erlenmeyer-Kimling and Jarvik Medians | Estimate Using Burt's Correlations | Estimate Using Jencks-Moore Means |
|---|---|---|---|---|
| $h^2$ MZ,DZ | $\dfrac{r_{IQMZT} - r_{IQDZT}}{1 - .55}$ | 0.82 | 0.91 | 0.60 |
| $h^2$ MZ,SIB | $\dfrac{r_{IQMZT} - r_{IQSIBT}}{1 - .55}$ | 0.92 | 0.98 | 0.84 |
| $h^2$ MZ,UNT | $\dfrac{r_{IQMZT} - r_{IQUNT}}{1 - 0.03}$ | 0.72 | 0.72 | 0.63 |
| $h^2$ DZ,UNT | $\dfrac{r_{IQDZT} - r_{IQUNT}}{0.55 - 0.03}$ | 0.63 | 0.60 | 0.62 |
| $h^2$ SIB,UNT | $\dfrac{r_{IQSIBT} - r_{IQUNT}}{0.55 - 0.03}$ | 0.54 | 0.50 | 0.40 |

results again illustrate the point that heritability depends on the country you study and the test you use. Burt's English data yields higher values of $h^2$ than the American data in four cases out of five. More important, however, is the dramatic variation in $h^2$ from one kind of comparison to another, with values varying from 0.40 up to almost unity.

We do not want to make too much of Table A–10, since it employs an oversimplified formula for $h^2$. It is, however, important to note that the comparison between siblings and unrelated children yields lower estimates of heritability than the comparisons involving twins. This is a recurrent finding in research on IQ heritability.

PATH MODEL FOR CHILDREN REARED TOGETHER

It is easy to show that Jensen's formula for estimating heritability yields inconsistent results when applied to different kinds of data. It is not easy to develop a formula which yields appreciably better results. Nonetheless, it is important to try. Figure A–2 illustrates a possible causal model of the sources of resemblance between children reared together. The variables for the first child are designated by the subscript 1, those for the second by the subscript 2. Figure A–2 alters the model shown in Figure A–1 by decomposing environment ($E$) into three separate sets of factors: the "uterine" factors ($EU$) that are shared by twins before birth, the "family" factors ($EF$) shared by all children raised in the same family, and the "random" factors ($ER$) not shared by children even when they have the same prenatal experience and the same upbringing. $EU$, $EF$, and $ER$ completely determine $E$. Together with $G$, they also completely determine $IQ$.

It is important to emphasize that our environmental variables do not mean exactly what their labels may seem to imply. The "uterine" environment, for example, does not include everything that happens to a child prior to birth. It includes only those things that are the same for twins prior to birth. All differences in the prenatal experience of twins are assigned to the "random" category. Similarly, "family" environment does not include every aspect of the home environment. It includes only those aspects of the home environment that are the same for all children raised in it. Furthermore, it also includes everything outside the home (e.g. the neighborhood and usually the schools) that is the same for all children raised in the same home. By definition, then, the correlation between two children's family environments is 1.00, if they are raised in the same family. Likewise, the correlation between twins' uterine environments (shown as $c$ in Figure A–2) is 1.00.

Note that we have not assumed any greater resemblance between the prenatal environment of siblings than between the prenatal environments of children in general. If siblings had more in common before birth than unrelated children, we would expect the correlation between siblings to exceed the correlation between unrelated children reared together by more than the amount expected on other grounds. As we have seen, however, the disparity between these two correlations is less than the disparity anticipated on the basis of other data. This may be because our theoretical model is deficient or because the data is inadequate. Nonetheless, the data offer no support for the theory that siblings with the same mother turn out more

FIGURE A–2

*Sources of Resemblance between Children Reared Together*

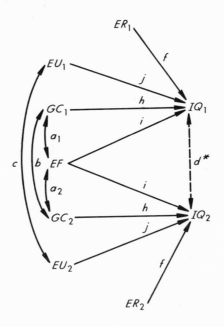

alike on that account. We therefore assume as much variation in prenatal conditions from one pregnancy to another as from one mother to another. This implies that for siblings, $c = 0$, and that variation in siblings' prenatal conditions simply inflates the "random" variance ($f^2$).[17]

Note, too, that we have assumed no correlation between *EU* and either *EF* or *GC*. This simplification derives from our notion that what twins have in common derives not from some fixed characteristic of the mother, like her genotype or her social status, but merely from the fact that twins both encounter the same random accidents. If a pregnant woman gets German measles, for example, both twins are likely to be affected. But the likelihood of her getting German measles in two successive pregnancies and thus creating a correlation between siblings is slight. If fixed characteristics of the mother *were* involved, $c$ would be greater than zero for siblings.

Another complication in Figure A–2 is that children raised together may have a direct effect on one another's test scores. Unlike the effects of parents on children, the reciprocal effects of children on one another cannot be easily incorporated into a path model. If reciprocal influences are incorporated into the model, the rules for estimating correlations and regression coefficients change. The reciprocal influence of children on one another is therefore shown with a dashed line, and the coefficient of this path is de-noted as $d^*$. (Such reciprocal influences provide the most parsimonious explanation for certain anomalies in the data, and we will assume their existence in certain contexts.)

Ignoring reciprocal effects for the time being, the correlation between the test scores of any two children reared together can be derived from Figure A–2 as:

$$r_{IQ1,IQ2} = i^2 + cj^2 + bh^2 + hia_1 + hia_2 \qquad (15)$$

In principle, if we know the values of $a$, $b$, $c$, $i$, and $j$, we can use the correlations between any two children, of whatever type, to estimate values of $h$. In order to make the standardized coefficients comparable from one analysis to another, however, we have to either assume that the variances are the same for different types of children or modify our calculations to take differences in variances explicity into account.

There are both theoretical and empirical reasons for supposing that the variance differs from one type of child to another. The discussion which follows will therefore deal first with estimating the total variance for different types of children and then with estimating the explained variance.

ESTIMATING THE TOTAL VARIANCE

Assuming that measurement error has been eliminated, Figure A–2 defines the total variance ($V_T$) in test scores for a population equally composed of children who have subscript 1 and children who have subscript 2 as:

$$V_T = h^2 + i^2 + j^2 + f^2 + hia_1 + hia_2 \qquad (16)$$

If the correlations between genotype and family environment for child 1 and child 2 are equal (i.e. $a_1 = a_2$) as they are for all but adopted-natural pairs, $hia_1 + hia_2 = 2hia$. The values of these components of variance are not constant for all sorts of children, however. We will take each up in turn:

1. The IQ variance due to genetic differences between children is defined as $h^2$. We will assume that the range of genetic variation is constant for twins, siblings, and adopted children. Some might argue that the range of genetic variation is restricted for adopted children, but the standard deviation of their mothers' IQ scores is the same as for the general population (see Skodak and Skeels, "Final Follow-Up").

2. The variance due to differences in the postnatal conditions provided by different families is defined as $i^2$. We will assume that the range of environmental variation between families is the same for twins, siblings, and adopted children. This last assumption might be questioned, since many adoption agencies refuse to place children with parents who seem likely to provide a very poor environment for the children. The variance in IQ scores among adopting parents appears fairly normal, however (see Burks, "Nature and Nurture," and Leahy "Intelligence").

3. The variance due to differences in the prenatal conditions encountered by different children is $j^2$. We will assume that $j^2$ is constant for all sorts of children.

4. The variance due to "random" environmental influences, i.e. to environmental characteristics that differ for children with the same mothers

and the same family environment, is $f^2$. Such variance is often referred to as "within-family" variance. We will assume that the within-family variance for adopted children ($f^2_A$) and siblings ($f^2_{SIB}$) is the same, but that the within-family variance for fraternal twins ($f^2_{DZ}$) and for identical twins ($f^2_{MZ}$) is less.

We might, of course, anticipate more environmental variance within pairs of unrelated children in the same family than within pairs of siblings, since genetic resemblance may lead parents and others to treat siblings more alike than unrelated children. As we indicated in Chapter 3, however, our estimates of the effects of genes on IQ scores necessarily include the effects of genes on the environments children encounter. If environmental differences between siblings and unrelated children are due to greater genetic resemblance between siblings than between unrelated children, we must attribute the resulting test score differences to genes rather than environment. Thus, we assume that $f^2$ includes only the effects of environmental characteristics that are unaffected by genotype, and that $f^2_A = f^2_{SIB}$.

We can think of several reasons for anticipating less environmental variation within families for twins than for siblings. Not all these reasons turn out to be empirically valid, however. It seems reasonable to suppose, for example, that parents change their approach to child-rearing as they grow older and wiser. In addition, a family's objective circumstances change over time. This should mean that twins, who are born at the same time, have environments that are more alike than siblings who are born at different points in time. If the theory were correct, however, siblings born close together would also resemble each other more closely than siblings born far apart. This is evidently not the case (see Finch, "Relation of Age Interval," and Outhit, "Resemblance of Parents"). Still, even if variation within sibling pairs is not reduced by their being born close together, it may be reduced by their being born simultaneously.

Another possible difference between twins and siblings is that twins may have more direct influence on one another than siblings. This could take one of two forms: differentiation or homogenization. While attempts at differentiation could have appreciable effects on personality traits and school grades, we doubt if they have much effect on performance on a test like the Stanford-Binet. On the contrary, we anticipate that interaction between both twins and siblings serves mainly to make their Binet scores more alike. When one twin or sibling acquires a bit of information or a simple skill of the kind measured on the Binet, he is likely to transmit it to the other. If this happens, the effects of random environmental differences between twins or siblings will be systematically reduced.

But if siblings had a systematic influence on one another, we would expect this to be greater when the siblings were born close together. This would produce higher correlations between siblings born close together than siblings born far apart. No such discrepancy is observed, so we will assume that siblings have little direct effect on one another. Whatever direct effect they do have reduces $f^2$ for all children, (except only children, on whom we have no data). It is therefore irrelevant when we compare different kinds of children.

Twins may, however, have more direct effect on one another than siblings. Thus we will entertain the possibility that $f^2_{DZ}$ and $f^2_{MZ}$ are less than $f^2_{SIB}$ and $f^2_A$. If this is so, the overall variance in twins' scores should also be somewhat less than the overall variance in siblings' scores.

Table A–9 shows that the correlation between fraternal twins exceeds the average correlation between siblings by 0.11 in American samples using the Stanford-Binet.

If the effects of differences between families were the same for twins and siblings, it would take a 16 percent reduction in the total variance to inflate the correlation from 0.59 to 0.70. The variance in Newman et al.'s twin sample appears fairly normal, but the sample was not drawn in such a way that we can compare the variance for the twins to the variance for non-twins in comparable families. Nor is Nichols' twin sample appropriate, since it excluded most low-ability students. This means that the variance was exogenously predetermined. If the variance for twins differed from the variance for other children, this would have affected the proportion of twins both of whom fell in the sample, but not the test score variance for such twins. In Schoenfeldt's Project Talent sample of 1,211 same-sex twins, the variable Talent labels "IQ" has 11.5 percent less variance than in the general population.[18] The same was true for other Talent tests. We will therefore assume that there is less effective within-pair environmental variance for twins than for siblings or unrelated children.

Finally, there is the question of whether environmental variation within pairs of fraternal twins exceeds environmental variation within pairs of identical twins. Using 832 identical twins from Project Talent, we found 5 percent more variance in what Talent labels IQ than for the 379 same-sex fraternal twins. For tests measuring high school achievement, we found 6 to 7 percent less variance for $MZ$ than $DZ$ twins, suggesting that $MZ$ twins influence one another's achievement scores slightly more than $DZ$ twins do. Overall, the data suggest little or no systematic difference in the within-family environmental variance of $MZ$ vs. $DZ$ twins. Nor have other studies reported appreciable differences in total variance for $MZ$ and $DZ$ twins.[19]

5. The last source of test score variance is the correlation between genotype and environment. This correlation $(a)$ inflates the total variance by $hia_1 + hia_2$. For natural children $a_1 = a_2 = a_N$, and the covariance is $2hia_N$. For reasons already discussed, we have assumed that the correlation between genotype and family environment is the only source of covariance. Thus, by definition, $2hia_N = 2hes$, the covariance term in Figure A–1. In Table A–5, $2hes \cong 0.19$ for all values of $g$, so $2hia_N \cong 0.19$.

For adopted children, the correlation between genotype and family environment $(a_A)$ is less than for natural children.

In general, comparing Figures A–1 and A–2:

$$ia = er_{GC,EC} = es \tag{17}$$

so:

$$2hia_A = 2her_{GCA,ECA} \tag{17a}$$

where $r_{GCA,ECA}$ is the correlation between an adopted child's genotype and its overall environment.

Assuming early adoption, such a correlation can arise only via a correlation between the natural parents' IQ scores and the environment created by the adoptive family. Using the notation of Figure A–1, we assume that:

$$r_{GCA,ECA} = r_{GCA,\overline{GPN}}\, r_{\overline{GPN},\overline{IQPN}}\, r_{\overline{IQPN},\overline{IQPA}}\, r_{\overline{IQPA},ECA} \tag{18}$$

Since $r_{IQPA,ECA}$ is equal to the multiple correlation of $ECA$ with the scores of the adoptive father and the adoptive mother, we can determine from Figure A–1 that:

$$r_{\overline{IQPA},ECA} = \sqrt{2w^2\,(1 + r_{IQF,IQM})} = w\sqrt{3.14} \tag{19}$$

Since equation (10) shows that $w = s/(3.14g)\,(h + se)$, we get:

$$r_{\overline{IQPA},ECA} = \frac{s\sqrt{3.14}}{3.14\,g\,(h + se)} \tag{19a}$$

In addition, equation (6) showed that:

$$r_{GCA,\overline{GPN}} = \sqrt{2g^2\,(1 + p)}$$

and Figure A–1 shows us that:

$$r_{\overline{GPN},\overline{IQPN}} = h + se$$

From the data in Table A–4, we concluded:

$$r_{\overline{IQPN},\overline{IQPA}} = 0.20.$$

Substituting into equation (18) we get:

$$r_{GCA,ECA} = (\sqrt{2g^2\,(1 + p)})\,(h + se)\,(.20)\left(\frac{s\sqrt{3.14}}{3.14\,g\,(h + se)}\right) \tag{18a}$$

or

$$r_{GCA,ECA} = .16\,s\sqrt{1 + p} \tag{18b}$$

Substituting (18b) into (17a) we get:

$$2hia_A = 0.32\,hes\sqrt{1 + p} \tag{17b}$$

Substituting $ia_N$ for $es$ and dividing by $2hi$, we have:

$$a_A = 0.16a_N\sqrt{1 + p} \tag{17c}$$

These manipulations allow us to express the total variance for different kinds of children in terms of the total variance for siblings.

Table A–11 summarizes the sources of variance for different kinds of children reared together. If we define the variance for siblings ($V_{SIB}$) as 1, we can say that:

$$V_{MZ} = V_{SIB} - f^2{}_{SIB} + f^2{}_{MZ} = 1 - (f^2{}_{SIB} - f^2{}_{MZ}) \tag{20}$$

$$V_{DZ} = V_{SIB} - f^2{}_{SIB} + f^2{}_{DZ} = 1 - (f^2{}_{SIB} - f^2{}_{DZ}) \qquad (21)$$

and

$$V_A = V_{SIB} - 2hes + 0.32 \sqrt{1+p}\; hes =$$
$$1 - 2hes\, (1 - 0.16 \sqrt{1+p}) \qquad (22)$$

where $V_{MZ}$ is the variance for $MZ$ twins, $V_{DZ}$ is the variance for $DZ$ twins, and $V_A$ is the variance for adopted children.

TABLE A–11

*Total Variance of Test Scores*
*For Different Kinds of Children Reared Together*

| | |
|---|---|
| *MZ* Twins Reared Together | $h^2 + i^2 + j^2 + f^2{}_{MZ} + 2\,hes$ |
| *DZ* Twins Reared Together | $h^2 + i^2 + j^2 + f^2{}_{DZ} + 2\,hes$ |
| Siblings Reared Together | $h^2 + i^2 + j^2 + f^2{}_{SIB} + 2\,hes$ |
| Adopted Children | $h^2 + i^2 + j^2 + f^2{}_{SIB} + 0.32\,hes\,\sqrt{1+p}$ |
| Samples in Which Half Are Adopted and Half Are Natural | $h^2 + i^2 + j^2 + f^2{}_{SIB} + (1 + 0.16\,\sqrt{1+p})\,hes$ |

CORRELATIONS BETWEEN GENOTYPES OF CHILDREN REARED TOGETHER

In order to use the observed correlations between children reared together to estimate $h$ in Figure A–2, we must know not only the total amount of variance in test scores for various types of children, but also the extent to which the variables that cause the variance are correlated. We must estimate the values of $a$, $b$, and $c$ (in Figure A–2) for identical twins, fraternal twins, siblings, adopted-natural pairs, and adopted-adopted pairs.

Equations (17) and (17c) provide values of $a$ for adopted and for natural children in terms of $e$, $s$, and $i$ (and $p$, which is a known function of $h$, $e$, and $s$). We have given our reasons for assuming that $c = 0$ for siblings and unrelated children. We have defined $c$ as 1 for both identical and fraternal twins. (Differences in twins' prenatal conditions merely inflate $f^2$.) This leaves the problem of estimating $b$, the correlation between genotypes.

For identical twins, $b_{MZ} = 1.00$.

For fraternal twins and siblings, the value of $b$ depends on two factors: the extent to which IQ scores are determined by dominant or recessive genes and epistasis (the value of $g$ in Figure A–1 or Table A–5), and the extent of assortative mating by genotype (the value of $p$ in Figure A–1).

If there were no dominance or epistasis, the correlation between siblings' genotypes could be derived by logical extension from Figure A–1. The correlation between a single child's genotype and a parent's genotype in Figure A–1 is:

$$r_{GC,GP} = g + gp \qquad (23)$$

The multiple correlation between a child and both parents is then:

$$R^2{}_{GC,GF,GM} = (g)\,(g + gp) + (g)\,(g + gp) = 2g^2\,(1 + p) \qquad (24)$$

However, the correlation between siblings' genotypes is equal to the percentage of variance in each sibling's genotype explained by whatever the two have in common, i.e. their parents' genotypes. Thus, in a model which assumes no dominance or epistasis:

$$r_{GSIB1,GSIB2} = R^2_{GC.GF,GM} = 2g^2 (1 + p) \tag{25}$$

In this model, $g = 0.50$, so we get:

$$r_{GC,GP} = 0.5 (1 + p) \tag{23a}$$

and

$$r_{GSIB1,GSIB2} = 0.5 (1 + p) \tag{25a}$$

If there were random mating and $p$ were 0, these expressions would reduce to the conventional value of 0.50. But since $p \cong 0.57 (h + se)^2$, the model implies:

$$r_{GC,GP} = 0.5 + 0.285 (h + se)^2 \tag{23b}$$

and

$$r_{GSIB1,GSIB2} = 0.5 + 0.285 (h + se)^2 \tag{25b}$$

When we assume that some genes are dominant or that there is epistasis, this line of reasoning ceases to be applicable. If the effects of genes are not strictly additive, $g$ will be less than 0.50, as we explained in the first section of this appendix. Siblings will, however, also have more in common than the strictly additive effects of genes lead us to expect. As a result, $r_{GSIB1,GSIB2}$ will exceed $2g^2 (1 + p)$. Under such circumstances, the simplest way to estimate the value of $r_{GSIB1,GSIB2}$ (which we will hereafter designate as $b_{SIB}$) is to abandon path models and to use a traditional analysis of variance. Let us call the proportion of the variance in genotypic values accounted for by an additive model $V_A$, and the proportion accounted for by dominance $V_D$. Ignoring epistasis, then, $V_A + V_D = 1$. The classic formulae of population genetics, which we will not derive here, show that the anticipated correlation between a parent's genotype and a child's genotype is then:

$$r_{GP,GC} = 0.5 (1 + p) V_A \tag{26}$$

These formulae also show that the anticipated correlation between siblings' genotypes is somewhat larger, namely:

$$b_{SIB} = 0.5 (1 + p) V_A + 0.25 V_D \tag{27}$$

Thus, if there is dominance, the genetic correlation between a parent and a child is invariably lower than the genetic correlation between siblings. The difference is $0.25 V_D$.[20] However, since $V_D = 1 - V_A$, it also follows that:

$$b_{SIB} = 0.5 (1 + p) V_A + 0.25 (1 - V_A) \tag{27a}$$

or

$$b_{SIB} = 0.25 + 0.25 V_A + 0.50pV_A \tag{27b}$$

Comparing equations (23) and (26), we can see that $g$ (in the path model) is equal to $0.5 V_A$ (in the analysis of variance model). Substituting $2g$ for $V_A$ in equation (27b) we get:

$$b_{SIB} = 0.25 + 0.5\,g + pg \tag{27c}$$

Substituting $0.57\ (h + se)^2$ for $p$ this becomes:

$$b_{SIB} = 0.25 + 0.5g + 0.57g(h + se)^2 \tag{27d}$$

The genetic correlation between unrelated children in the same home is more problematic. If children are placed young and cannot be tested, the correlation between the genotypes of children in the same home will derive entirely from the correlation between their parents' genotypes. This depends on the correlation between the natural and the adopting parents' mean IQ scores.

First, let us consider the case where one child is natural and one is adopted. We will designate the natural child as $C1$ and its parents as $P1$. We will designate the adopted child as $C2$ and its parents as $P2$. We will then assume that the correlation between the genotypes of the natural and the adopted child $(b_{NA})$ is given by:

$$b_{NA} = r_{GC1,\overline{GP1}}\ r_{\overline{GP1},\overline{IQP1}}\ r_{\overline{IQP1},\overline{IQP2}}\ r_{\overline{IQP2},\overline{GP2}}\ r_{\overline{GP2},GC2} \tag{28}$$

From equation (6) we have:

$$r_{GC1,\overline{GP1}} = r_{\overline{GP2},GC2} = \sqrt{2g^2\,(1 + p)}$$

From Figure A–1, we know:

$$r_{\overline{GP1},\overline{IQP1}} = r_{\overline{IQP2},\overline{GP2}} = h + se$$

From Table A–4, we have already derived:

$$r_{\overline{IQP},\overline{IQP2}} = 0.20$$

By substitution we therefore have:

$$b_{NA} = 0.40g^2\ (h + se)^2\ (1 + p) \tag{28a}$$

The correlation between genotypes for pairs of children in which both are adopted $(b_{AA})$ is lower than the correlation for pairs in which one is adopted and one is natural $(b_{NA})$. If the correlation between the mean IQ scores of natural and adopting parents is 0.20, the correlation between the mean scores of 2 sets of natural parents whose children are adopted into the same home will only be $(0.20)(0.20) = 0.04$. In general, then:

$$b_{AA} = r_{\overline{IQPN},\overline{IQPA}}\ b_{NA} \tag{29}$$

or

$$b_{AA} = 0.20\ b_{NA} \tag{29a}$$

or

$$b_{AA} = 0.08\ g^2\ (h + se)^2\ (1 + p) \tag{29b}$$

We now have the genetic resemblance between different kinds of children expressed in terms of the unknowns $h$, $e$, and $s$.

CORRELATIONS BETWEEN TEST SCORES OF CHILDREN REARED TOGETHER

Equation (15) gave the general formula for the correlation between two children, derived from Figure A–2. The correlation depends on eight parameters: $a_1$, $a_2$, $b$, $c$, $f$, $h$, $i$, and $j$. The absolute values of three of these parameters ($h$, $i$, and $j$) are presumed to be constant for all sorts of children. The values of $a$, $b$, $c$, and $f$ change from one kind of child to another. In two cases ($f$ and $a$), changes in the basic parameters affect not only the correlation between different kinds of children but also the total variance. If the absolute values of $h$, $i$, and $j$ are constant, and if the variance changes from one kind of child to another, the standardized values of $h$, $i$, and $j$ will change. In order to keep the standardized values of $h$, $i$, and $j$ constant, we will need to adjust the variance for adopted children and twins to make it comparable to the variance for siblings, parents, and children.

Equations (30) to (34) show the predicted correlation between various kinds of children reared together. The numerators represent the "explained" variance and are derived from equation (15) by substituting the values of $b$ which we have just derived and the values of $j$ and $c$ which we assume apply to different types of children. We also assume from equation (17) that $hia = hes$. The denominators are derived from the total variance estimates in Table A–11.

$$r_{IQMZT} = \frac{h^2 + i^2 + j^2 + 2\,hes}{h^2 + i^2 + j^2 + 2\,hes + f^2{}_{MZ}} \tag{30}$$

$$r_{IQDZT} = \frac{(0.25 + 0.5g + 0.57g\,(h + se)^2)h^2 + i^2 + j^2 + 2\,hes}{h^2 + i^2 + j^2 + 2\,hes + f^2{}_{DZ}} \tag{31}$$

$$r_{IQSIBT} = \frac{(0.25 + 0.5g + 0.57g\,(h + se)^2)h^2 + i^2 + 2\,hes}{h^2 + i^2 + j^2 + 2\,hes + f^2{}_{SIB}} \tag{32}$$

$$r_{IQANT} = \frac{(0.40g^2\,(h + se)^2\,(1 + p))h^2 + i^2 + (1 + 0.16\sqrt{1 + p})\,hes}{h^2 + i^2 + j^2 + (1 + 0.156\sqrt{1 + p})\,hes + f^2{}_{SIB}} \tag{33}$$

$$r_{IQAAT} = \frac{(0.08g^2\,(h + se)^2\,(1 + p))h^2 + i^2 + (0.32\sqrt{1 + p})\,hes}{h^2 + i^2 + j^2 + (0.312\sqrt{1 + p})\,hes + f^2{}_{SIB}} \tag{34}$$

These equations are more complicated and more ambiguous than Jensen's formula for $h^2$ in equation (14). Jensen's formula can, however, be derived from them, if we make three simplifying assumptions. First, assume that common prenatal factors have no effect on the degree of resemblance between twins. This makes $j^2 = 0$. Second, assume that twins have no direct effect on one another and that genetic resemblance between identical twins has the same effect, in additive terms, when the twins are reared together as it would if they were reared apart. This makes $f^2{}_{MZ} = f^2{}_{DZ} = f^2{}_{SIB}$. Third, assume that there is no correlation between genotype and environment. This makes $s = a = 0$. These three assumptions imply that the variance for all sorts of children, i.e. the denominators of equations (30) to (34), is the same.

Setting the variances equal to 1, the numerators of equations (30) to (34) all take the form

$$r_{IQ1,IQ2} = bh^2 + i^2 \tag{35}$$

where $b$ is the correlation between children's genotypes. Now, if we take two equations in which the value of $b$ differs, we can subtract one from the other and the $i^2$ term will drop out. Solving for $h^2$, we get equation (14), as follows:

$$r_{IQ1,IQ2} = b_{GC1,GC2} \, h^2 + i^2$$

$$r_{IQ3,IQ4} = b_{GC3,GC4} \, h^2 + i^2$$

so

$$r_{IQ1,IQ2} - r_{IQ3,IQ4} = b_{GC1,GC2} \, h^2 - b_{GC3,GC4} \, h^2$$

and

$$h^2 = \frac{r_{IQ1,IQ2} - _{IQ3,IQ4}}{b_{GC1,GC2} - b_{GC3,GC4}}$$

The only difficulty, as we saw in Table A–10, is that this simplified formula for $h^2$ yields different results when we compare different kinds of children. Considering $j^2$, $s$, and differences in $f^2$ allows us to eliminate some of these internal inconsistencies. However, even with the added parameters, the equations cannot be made completely compatible with the parent-child data in the first section of this appendix.

In order to see how values of $h$ can be derived from equations (30) to (34), we will first rewrite them in a somewhat different notation.

Defining the total variance as 1, we can rewrite equation (16) as:

$$h^2 + i^2 + j^2 + f^2 + hia_1 + hia_2 = 1 \tag{36}$$

Defining the total variance as 1 also allows us to rewrite the denominators of equations (30) to (34) using the estimates of the total variance in equations (20) to (22). In addition, $e^2$ (the environmental variance term in our parent-child calculation) can be divided into three components:

$$e^2 = i^2 + j^2 + f^2 \tag{37}$$

and, hence:

$$i^2 = e^2 - j^2 - f^2 \tag{38}$$

For clarity, we will also temporarily substitute $b_{SIB}$, $b_{NA}$ and $b_{AA}$ for the more complicated coefficients of $h^2$ shown in equations (30) to (34). Finally, we take values of $r_{IQMZT}$, $r_{IQDZT}$, $r_{IQSIBT}$, $r_{IQANT}$, and $r_{IQAAT}$ from Table A–9. Substituting all of this in equations (30) to (34), we get:

$$r_{IQMZT} = 0.97 = \frac{1 - f^2}{1 - f^2 + f^2_{MZ}} \tag{30a}$$

$$r_{IQDZT} = 0.70 = \frac{b_{SIB}h^2 + e^2 - f^2 + 2hes}{1 - f^2 + f^2_{DZ}} \tag{31a}$$

$$r_{IQSIBT} = 0.59 = \frac{b_{SIB}h^2 + e^2 - f^2 - j^2 + 2 \, hes}{1} \tag{32a}$$

$$r_{IQANT} = 0.31 = \frac{b_{NA}h^2 + e^2 - f^2 - j^2 + (1 + 0.16\sqrt{1 + p}) \, hes}{1 - (1 - 0.16\sqrt{1 + p}) \, hes} \tag{33a}$$

$$r_{IQAAT} = 0.48 = \frac{b_{AA}h^2 + e^2 - f^2 - j^2 + 0.32\sqrt{1 + p} \, hes}{1 - (2 - 0.32\sqrt{1 + p}) \, hes} \tag{34a}$$

Table A–5 shows that $2hes$ is equal to 0.19 for all plausible values of $g$. In addition, it implies that $\sqrt{1 + p}$ has values between 1.1 and 1.2 for plausible values of $g$. If we use $p = 1.15$, we get $0.16\sqrt{1 + p} \, hes = 0.035$.

Substituting and simplifying, we get:

$$0.97 = \frac{1 - f^2}{1 - f^2 + f^2_{MZ}} \tag{30b}$$

$$0.70 = \frac{b_{SIB}h^2 + e^2 - f^2 + 0.19}{1 - f^2 + f^2_{DZ}} \tag{31b}$$

$$0.40 = b_{SIB}h^2 + e^2 - f^2 - j^2 \tag{32b}$$

$$0.21 = b_{AN}h^2 + e^2 - f^2 - j^2 \tag{33b}$$

$$0.37 = b_{AA}h^2 + e^2 - f^2 - j^2 \tag{34b}$$

However, $b_{AA} = 0.20 \, b_{AN}$ (from equation (29a), so equations (33b) and (34b) are irreconcilable. We will therefore assume that the observed difference between adopted-adopted and adopted-natural pairs is spurious. (The statistical probability of this was discussed above.) Using the pooled data in Table A–9, $r_{IQUNT} = 0.38$ ($N_{AA} = 165$; $N_{AN} = 94$).

Taking the weighted mean of $b_{AN}$ and $b_{AA}$, we get $b_{UNT} = .49b_{AN}$. Taking the weighted mean of the covariance terms, which are $(1 + 0.16\sqrt{1 + p})hes$ and $(0.32\sqrt{1 + p})hes$, we get $(0.36 + 0.26\sqrt{1 + p})hes$. Combining equations (33a) and (34a) we, therefore, write:

$$r_{IQUNT} \cong \frac{0.49b_{AN}h^2 + e^2 - f^2 - j^2 + (0.36 + 0.26\sqrt{1 + p})hes}{1 - 2hes + (0.36 + 0.26\sqrt{1 + p})hes} \tag{39}$$

Substituting $hes = 0.095$, $\sqrt{1 + p} = 1.15$, $r_{IQUNT} = 0.38$, we get:

$$0.38 = \frac{0.49b_{AN}h^2 + e^2 - f^2 - j^2 + 0.062}{0.873} \tag{39a}$$

or

$$0.27 = 0.49b_{AN}h^2 + e^2 - f^2 - j^2 \tag{39b}$$

Subtracting (39b) from (32b) we get:

$$0.13 = (b_{SIB} - 0.49b_{AN})h^2 \tag{40}$$

Substituting the values of $b_{SIB}$ and $b_{AN}$ derived in equations (27c) and

(28a), and the value of $p$ derived in equation (2), we get a combined equation for unrelated children reared together:

$$0.13 = 0.25h^2 + 0.5gh^2 + 0.57gh^2 (h + se)^2 +$$
$$0.196g^2h^2 (h + se)^2 + 0.112g^2h^2 (h + se)^4 \qquad (40a)$$

There is no set of values for $g$, $h$, $s$, and $e$ in Table A–5 that satisfies equation (40a). If $g = 0.50$, the right side of equation (40a) is 0.18 and the discrepancy is 0.05. If $g = 0.30$, the right side of equation (40a) is 0.30 and the discrepancy is 0.17. Equation (40a) is only satisfied by values of $h^2$ below 0.25. Such values are too low to satisfy the equations relating parents' scores to their children's scores, unless we assume $g > 0.50$, which is impossible.

How can we explain this? The basic data on parents and on children and siblings is probably fairly accurate. This means that either the correlation between unrelated children in the same home is overestimated, or the analytic model is wrong. The reader will recall that the data on unrelated children also raised problems when we used Jensen's simpler analytic model (see Table A–10). A large, careful study of unrelated children in the same home is badly needed. If the data in Tables A–8 and A–9 proves correct, the analytic model used in this appendix will have to be revised, and our estimates of heritability will probably have to be lowered. Given the small number of cases, however, the most reasonable conclusion, at present, is that the true value of $r_{UNT}$ is considerably less than 0.38. We would guess that it is around 0.20.

The main reason we think $r_{UNT}$ is less than 0.38 is that the correlations between siblings and twins imply values of $h^2$ that seem quite consistent with the values implied by parent-child comparisons. In order to show that this is true, however, we must make some further manipulations in equations (30) to (32).

Multiplying both sides of (31b) by $1 - f^2 + f^2_{DZ}$, subtracting the resulting equation from (32b), and simplifying, we get:

$$0.11 = 0.70(f^2 - f^2_{DZ}) + j^2 \qquad (41)$$

This equation "explains" the difference between siblings and fraternal twins. As it stands, it is indeterminate. The actual values of $f^2 - f_{DZ}$ and $j^2$ have some effect on our estimates of $h^2$ and $e^2$. If fraternal twins have no more direct influence on one another than siblings, $f^2 = f^2_{DZ}$ and $j^2 = 0.11$. We will call this the "prenatal hypothesis." If prenatal resemblance is no greater for twins than for siblings, $j^2 = 0$ and $f^2 - f^2_{DZ} = 0.157$. We will call this the "reciprocal influence" hypothesis.

Let us first consider the prenatal hypothesis. Substituting $f^2 - f^2_{DZ} = 0$ and $j^2 = 0.11$ into (32b) we have

$$0.51 = b_{SIB}h^2 + e^2 - f^2 \qquad (32c)$$

If, in addition, the restriction in the range of environments encountered by identical twins in the same home is an additive function of (a), the restriction for any two children in the same home, and (b), the restriction for any two children with the same genes, we can say $f^2_{MZ} = f^2_{DZ}$. Still assuming $f^2_{DZ} = f^2$, we can write the equation for $MZ$ twins as:

$$0.97 = 1 - f^2 \tag{30c}$$

and $f^2 = 0.03$. Substituting $f^2 = 0.03$ and $j^2 = 0.11$ into equation (32c) we get:

$$0.54 = b_{SIB}h^2 + e^2 \tag{32d}$$

Now, let us consider the reciprocal influence hypothesis, i.e. $f^2 - f^2_{DZ} = 0.157$ and $j^2 = 0$. Again assuming $f^2_{MZ} = f^2_{DZ}$, we get:

$$0.97 = \frac{1 - f^2}{1 - 0.157} \tag{30d}$$

This yields $f^2 = 0.182$, which, in turn, implies $f^2_{MZ} = f^2_{DZ} = 0.025$. Substituting $f^2 = 0.18$ and $j^2 = 0$ into equation (32b), we get:

$$0.58 = b_{SIB}h^2 + e^2 \tag{32e}$$

Using equation (27d) to express $b_{SIB}$ in terms of $h$, $e$, and $s$, and using Table A–5 to derive values of $h$, $e$, and $s$ for values of $g$, we can now solve equations (32d) and (32e). Equation (32d) implies $g = 0.30$ and $h^2 = 0.59$. Equation (32e) implies $g = 0.33$ and $h^2 = 0.52$.

The most reasonable assumption is probably that the difference between fraternal twins and siblings is due partly to resemblance in twins' prenatal conditions and partly to twins' reciprocal influence on one another. (As noted earlier, part of the difference may also be due to measurement error in siblings' scores.) If we arbitrarily assume that $j^2 = 0.06$, for example, equation (41) implies $f^2 - f^2_{DZ} = 0.07$. If we still assume $f^2_{MZ} = f^2_{DZ}$, substitution in equation (30) yields $f^2 = 0.10$, which implies:

$$0.56 = b_{SIB}h^2 + e^2 \tag{31e}$$

This, in turn, implies $g = 0.315$ and $h^2 = 0.55$.

Up to this point, we have been assuming that $f^2_{MZ} = f^2_{DZ}$, i.e. that genetic resemblance reduces the environmental variance about twice as much for identical twins as for fraternal twins. (We have made no assumptions about the absolute effect of genotype on environment. We have only assumed that the effect was consistent in all situations and, hence, that doubling the degree of genetic resemblance doubled whatever effect genetic resemblance had on environmental resemblance.) If this assumption is wrong, $f^2_{MZ}$ will be less than $f^2_{DZ}$. Unless we can estimate the magnitude of the difference from external evidence, equations (30) to (32) become indeterminate. The only evidence that seems relevant is the total variance for identical as against fraternal twins. As noted above, these variances are almost always quite similar. At most, we might argue that $f^2_{MZ} - f^2_{DZ} = 0.05$ or so. If we assume $f^2_{DZ} - f^2_{MZ} = 0.05$, and if we follow our earlier compromise and assume $j^2 = 0.06$ and $f^2_{SIB} - f^2_{DZ} = 0.07$, we get $f^2 - f^2_{MZ} = 0.12$. Substituting in (30b), we get $f^2 = 0.144$. If $f^2 = 0.144$ and $j^2 = 0.06$, equation (32b) becomes:

$$0.60 = b_{SIB}h^2 + e^2 \tag{32f}$$

Solving this as before, with the aid of Table A–5, $g = 0.35$ and $h^2 = 0.47$.

In the absence of precise estimates of the variances for identical twins, fraternal twins, siblings, and adopted children, we can see no way to carry this particular line of inquiry any further. Assessing the evidence on children reared together, we can say that comparisons of identical and fraternal twins point to heritabilities in the 0.45 to 0.60 range, with a value of about 0.55 seeming most likely. Comparisons of siblings and unrelated children point to heritabilities of less than 0.25. We have more faith in the twin data than in the data on unrelated children, but both comparisons involve several uncertainties. The most reasonable compromise value for $h^2$ is probably around 0.45.

## Studies of Related Children Reared Apart

The data we have examined so far has yielded the following estimates:

$0.29 < h^2 < 0.76$ from the parent-child data
$0.45 < h^2 < 0.60$ from comparisons of identical and fraternal twins
$h^2 < 0.25$ from comparisons of siblings and unrelated children.

There is one additional body of data to be examined: that on related children reared apart. In this section, we look at the data on identical twins reared apart and on siblings reared apart. Unfortunately, such data is extremely hard to find. There has been only one American study of identical twins reared apart, only two American studies of siblings reared apart, and no studies of half-siblings reared apart. The dearth of twin studies is easy to explain, since such twins are hard to locate. The dearth of sibling studies is more puzzling, since they yield almost equally valuable data and are much easier to locate.

Such data as we have can be analyzed using the same procedures as with children reared together. A path model is shown in Figure A–3. This data yields estimates of $h^2$ consistent with estimates based on twins reared together and with data on parents and children. The results are not consistent with data on unrelated children reared together.

### IDENTICAL TWINS REARED APART

Internationally, there have been four studies of identical twins reared apart. One covers an American sample; two cover English samples; one covers a Danish sample. The results are summarized in Table A–12. Jensen, in "Identical Twins," argues that the results of these four studies are sufficiently similar to justify pooling the results. He bases this conclusion on the fact that the interpair (i.e. genetic) variances in the four studies do not differ enough to be significant at the 0.05 level. This is a rather weak test, since the U.S. study involved only 19 pairs of twins. Yet even with 19 pairs, unpublished calculations by Richard Light and Paul Smith show that the intrapair (i.e. environmental) variance is significantly larger in the U.S. sample than in the English samples. Once again, then, we have evidence that variation in environmental conditions is greater in the U.S than in England.

**TABLE A-12**

*Correlations between Identical Twins Reared Apart*

| Source | Country | Test | Pairs | Correlation |
|--------|---------|------|-------|-------------|
| Burt, "Genetic Determination" | England | Burt's Binet | 53 | 0.86 |
| Burt, "Genetic Determination" | England | Burt's Group Intelligence | 53 | 0.77 |
| Burt, "Genetic Determination" | England | Burt's Reading and Spelling | 53 | 0.60 |
| Burt, "Genetic Determination" | England | Burt's Arithmetic | 53 | 0.71 |
| Burt, "Genetic Determination" | England | Burt's General Attainments | 53 | 0.62 |
| Juel-Nielsen, "Individual and Environment" | Denmark | Raven's Progressive Matrices | 12 | 0.73 |
| Juel-Nielsen, "Individual and Environment" | Denmark | Wechsler Bellevue Verbal | 12 | 0.78 |
| Juel-Nielsen, "Individual and Environment" | Denmark | Wechsler Bellevue Performance | 12 | 0.49 |
| Newman, Freeman, and Holzinger, *Twins* | U.S. | Stanford-Binet IQ | 19 | 0.69 |
| Newman, Freeman, and Holzinger, *Twins* | U.S. | Otis IQ | 19 | 0.73 |
| Newman, Freeman, and Holzinger, *Twins* | U.S. | Stanford Achievement | 19 | 0.51 |
| Shields, *Monozygotic Twins* | England | Nonverbal Intelligence ("Dominoes") | 38 | 0.77 |
| Shields, *Monozygotic Twins* | England | Mill-Hill Vocabulary | 38 | 0.74 |
| Weighted Mean of Four Sources Above | Denmark, U.S., England | First "Intelligence" Test Listed in Each Study Above | 122 | 0.81 |

The American study also poses another problem. The authors originally reported a correlation of 0.670 between the Binet IQ scores of their 19 pairs. McNemar's "Special Review" noted that this estimate would have been higher if (a) the authors had taken account of the fact that the mean and variance of the Binet changed with age, and (b) if they had corrected for the fact that the standard deviation for separated twins was only 13 points (compared to 15 points for twins reared together). The first correction is appropriate and raises the correlation to 0.69. The second correction is harder to justify, and we have not made it.

The proper correction for restriction in range depends on what caused the restriction. Three possibilities come to mind:

1. All the "missing" sources of variance might be ones that would, if present, increase the amount of variation *between* separated pairs but not the variation *within* separated pairs. This could happen if parents who gave up children for adoption were more alike genetically than the norm for the society. If this were the case, the estimated correlation between separated twins in a more representative population would be 0.767. This was the estimate presented by McNemar and used by many hereditarians since then. We know no theoretical reason to suppose that parents who give up identical twins are more genetically homogeneous than the general population, but this could have been the case with this particular sample of 19 pairs.

2. All the missing sources of variance might be ones that would, if present, increase the amount of variance within pairs. This could happen if the range of environmental differences between families that adopted these twins were less than the range in the general population. This seems quite possible, not only because of sampling error, but because adoption may have been restricted to certain kinds of families. If all the missing variance were environmental, a representative group of twins assigned to random families would have test scores that correlated only 0.48.

3. The missing source of variance could be the absence of a correlation between genotype and family background. As we saw in previous sections, such covariance accounts for about 19 percent of the total variance. There is not much selective placement, so we expect about 15 percent less variance in a population of adopted children than in the general population. If this accounts for the reduced variance among these twins, the observed correlation should not be corrected. Estimates of $h^2$ and $e^2$ based on the observed correlation should, however, be corrected by the methods used in the section on "Children Reared Together."

All in all, we can see at least as much reason for revising the observed correlation downward as for revising it upward. The correlations in Table A–12 were therefore calculated from Newman et al.'s Table 87, by comparing mean differences within pairs to the mean difference in the sample (taken as 1.13 times the reported standard deviation). This corrects for age but not for restriction in range. If we correct the resulting correlation of 0.69 for unreliability, we get an estimated true correlation of 0.75.

The general analytic model for predicting correlations among identical twins reared apart is shown in Figure A–3. (Figure A–3 differs from Figure A–2 in that $GC_1$ is assumed to equal $GC_2$, $EU_1 = EU_2$, and $EF_1 \neq EF_2$.)

### FIGURE A-3
*Sources of Resemblance between Identical Twins Reared Apart*

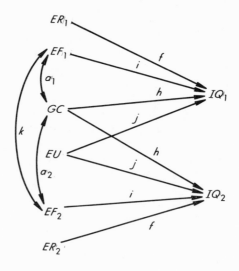

The correlation can be derived as:

$$r_{IQMZS} = h^2 + j^2 + hia_1 + hia_2 + ki^2 \tag{42}$$

From our calculations in the previous section, we have values of $a$ in terms of $h$, $e$, and $s$. We also have some estimates of $j^2$. To solve the equations we need a value for $k$.

First, let us consider cases in which both twins are placed for adoption in different homes. Let us make the assumption that placement of identical twins follows the same pattern as placement of other adopted children. In such a situation, the correlations between each twin's genotype and its family environment ($a_1$ and $a_2$) should be the same as for other adopted children, i.e. $a_A$. From equation (17c), $a_A = 0.16\ a_N\sqrt{1+p}$. In addition, from (17b), $hia_A = 0.16\sqrt{1+p}\ hes$.

The correlation between the two twins' family environments will depend on the pattern of selective placement. Let us assume that the only source of resemblance between the adoptive homes of the twins is the resemblance between each adoptive home and the home that would have been provided by the natural parents. Finally, assume that the resemblance between the overall environment provided by natural and adoptive homes is equal to the correlation between the mean IQ scores of natural and adoptive parents, i.e. about 0.20. It follows that $k = (0.20)(0.20) = 0.04$.

This value may be low, but there is no good empirical basis for assuming a higher value. In the one study which provides a correlation between the homes of identical twins reared apart (Burt, "Genetic Determination"), the correlation between the occupational statuses of the natural and the adoptive fathers was −0.06.[21] Only one of the two twins in each of Burt's 53 pairs was adopted. The other was raised by the natural parents. Many of the adopted twins were raised by relatives of the natural parents. It would therefore be rash to assume that the correlation between Burt's twins' overall environments was as low as the correlation between their fathers' occupational statuses. Still, there is no evidence for a higher correlation. In the absence of evidence, we will accept 0.04 as an estimate of $k$ when both twins are adopted. Thus we have:

$$r_{IQMZAA} = h^2 + j^2 + 0.32 \ hes\sqrt{1 + p} + 0.04i^2 \tag{43}$$

where $r_{IQMZAA}$ is the correlation between identical twins both of whom are adopted.

Next, let us consider situations in which one twin is placed for adoption and one is raised by its natural parents. This pattern accounts for the majority of twins covered by studies of separated twins. The correlation between such twins' scores will be higher than when both are adopted. More specifically, if $r_{IQMZAN}$ is the correlation between identical twins where one is adopted and one is raised by its natural parents, and if $hia_N = hes$, from equation (17), $hia_A = 0.16hes\sqrt{1 + p}$ from equation (17b), and $k = 0.20$ from Table A–4, then we can rewrite equation (42) as:

$$r_{IQMZAN} = h^2 + j^2 + hes + 0.16hes\sqrt{1 + p} + 0.20i^2 \tag{44}$$

In order to derive these correlations using values of $h$, $e$, and $s$ from the general population, we must adjust the predicted correlation upward to take account of the expected reduction in total variance among adopted children. Using the variances in Table A–11, we get:

$$r_{IQMZAA} = \frac{h^2 + j^2 + 0.32 \ hes\sqrt{1 + p} + 0.04i^2}{1 - 2 \ hes \ (1 - .16\sqrt{1 + p})} \tag{43a}$$

and

$$r_{IQMZAN} = \frac{h^2 + j^2 + (1 + 0.16\sqrt{1 + p}) \ hes + 0.20i^2}{1 - hes \ (1 - .16\sqrt{1 + p})} \tag{44a}$$

As a check on the validity of these adjustments, we inspected the variances for Burt's twins, half of whom were adopted and half of whom were reared by their natural parents. We expected a reduction in variance for the adopted twins of about 15 percent. The actual reduction was nil. For samples of this size (53 pairs), a population difference of 15 percent will result in samples with no observed difference, or with differences in the opposite direction from the one anticipated on theoretical grounds, in more than one sample out of four. Thus, while the data does not provide any support for our expectations, neither does it completely discredit them.

If we persist in assuming that our equations are correct, and if we substitute the values of $h$, $e$, and $s$ derived from Table A–5 in equations (43a) and (44a), we can predict the values of $r_{IQMZAA}$ and $r_{IQMZAN}$ for various values of $g$. If we assume that $f^2 = 0.10$ and $j^2 = 0.06$, as we did in the previous section, we get the predicted values of $r_{IQMZAA}$ and $r_{IQMZAN}$ shown in Table A–13. Our best estimate of the true correlation from the data we

TABLE A–13

*Predicted Correlations between Identical Twins Reared Apart, Using Alternative Values of g, Population Values of h, e, and s from Table A-5, and $f^2 = .10$ and $j^2 = 0.06$*

| g | $h^2$ | $r_{IQMZAA}$ | $r_{IQMZAN}$ |
|---|---|---|---|
| .50 | .29 | .47 | .60 |
| .45 | .34 | .53 | .64 |
| .40 | .40 | .59 | .69 |
| .375 | .43 | .64 | .72 |
| .35 | .48 | .68 | .76 |
| .325 | .53 | .74 | .80 |
| .30 | .59 | .81 | .85 |

have is 0.75. This value implies a value of $h^2$ between 0.47 and 0.55, depending on the proportion of cases in which one twin is raised by its natural parents. If we have underestimated the environmental similarity between twins, it implies an even lower value of $h^2$.

This conclusion differs from the conclusions drawn by hereditarians from the same data. Most hereditarians argue that the correlation between identical twins reared apart is itself an estimate of $h^2$. Our estimates suggest that a correlation of 0.75 implies $h^2 \cong 0.50$. The reason for this difference is not that we have assumed a great deal of selective placement. We have assumed a correlation of only 0.04 between the family environments of twins where both were adopted. Neither have we assumed that shared prenatal conditions had a substantial effect ($j^2 = 0.06$). The main difference between our estimates and others is that we have assumed a significant degree of covariance between genotype and environment in the normal population, while assuming a much lower correlation among adopted children. This means that the expected variance among adopted children is lower. It follows that the proportion of this variance explained by genotype will be quite high for adopted twins, even though the value of $h^2$ in the general population is more modest.

Our assumptions about the effects of covariance have, it is true, received only sporadic support from the data on adopted children, which sometimes shows restricted variance and sometimes does not. Nonetheless, the indirect evidence for covariance presented in the first section of this appendix seems quite convincing. Only the precise amount is uncertain. Those who reject our assumptions about covariance must, moreover, devise some alternative explanation for the restricted variance among Newman et al.'s separated twins. If they discount covariance, they must assume either a restricted range of environments or a restricted range of genotypes. On its face, the idea that these twins had relatively similar environments seems considerably more plausible than the idea that they had a restricted range of genotypes. If the missing variance were mostly environmental, the observed data would again be consistent with heritability estimates of around 0.50.

SIBLINGS REARED APART

In light of the fact that siblings reared apart are far more common than identical twins, and the fact that the correlations among siblings reared apart tell us nearly as much as the correlations among twins reared apart, it is both surprising and unfortunate that we do not have better data on such siblings.[22] The two American studies are almost useless for our purposes. Freeman et al., in "Influence of Environment," worked with a sample which included some children who were not separated until the age of 6. Hildreth's sample, described in "The Resemblance of Siblings," shows a very restricted range of test scores. Burt gives no details on his English sample, but many of the separations may well have been quite late. In light of these difficulties, we have not tried to analyze this data.

## Conclusions

Our analyses of heritability suggest that the data base for making generalizations about the heritability of IQ scores is still too weak to justify a precise estimate. Our best guess is that genotype explains about 45 percent of the variance in IQ scores, that environment explains about 35 percent, and that the correlation between genotype and environment explains the remaining 20 percent. For adopted children, both genotype and environment probably play a larger role, since the correlation between the two is smaller. As a guess, we would say that this estimate of heritability had a standard error of about 0.10. In gambler's terms, this means we think the chances are about two out of three that the heritability of IQ scores, as we have defined the term, is between 0.35 and 0.55, and that we think the chances are about 19 out of 20 that heritability is between 0.25 and 0.65.[23]

A brief review of the empirical basis for our overall estimate may help the reader decide whether or not to accept it. First, we examined data on correlations between parents and children. The number of cases involved in these studies is large, which makes the estimates more precise than many others used in this appendix. These parent-child studies strongly support the notion that there is substantial covariance between genotype and environment. The studies do not, however, yield a definitive estimate of $h^2$. They yield a series of alternative estimates, the magnitudes of which depend on the extent to which we assume IQ scores are influenced by dominant genes or epistasis.

Next, we examined correlations among children reared together. Comparisons of identical and fraternal twins in America yield estimates of $h^2$ between 0.45 and 0.60. Comparisons of siblings and unrelated children reared in the same home yield estimates of $h^2$ below 0.25. The data on unrelated children reared together is, however, full of internal contradictions, and cannot be weighed too heavily.

Finally, we looked at genetically related children who had been separated early in life. Almost all the separated identical twins studied by psychologists have been reared in England, where environmental differences appear to be less marked than in the United States. The data on American twins is subject to a wide range of interpretations, depending on how we explain the restricted range of these twins' scores. It is, however, relatively easy to reconcile the data with a heritability estimate of 0.50 or 0.45.

All in all, an estimate of $h^2 = 0.45 \pm 0.10$ seems to come closer to explaining the overall pattern of correlations between relatives and nonrelatives than does either a higher or a lower estimate. Nonetheless, the margin of uncertainty remains considerable.

Two other points also require emphasis. First, our estimates of heritability deal with true IQ scores, adjusted to exclude the effects of measurement error. As a practical matter, measurement error can only be eliminated by repeated testing of the same individual. If we are interested in the heritability of scores on a single test, we have to lower our estimate by 5 to 10 percent.

Second, our estimates of heritability are based on Stanford-Binet scores in the United States. The heritability of some other aptitude and ability tests appears to be rather similar to the Binet, but others appear to be lower. Furthermore, heritability will be higher in local samples, where the environmental variance is restricted. We will return to this issue in Appendix B.

# NOTES

1. This definition is not precisely comparable to others in common use. For discussions of several alternative definitions, see Jensen, "Limits of Heritability" and Jinks and Fulker, "Comparison."

2. For more details, see, for example, Li, *Population Genetics,* or Falconer, *Quantitative Genetics.*

3. The high value reported by Outhit, in "Resemblance of Parents," comes from a very heterogeneous sample in which the author deliberately excluded cases in which one or both spouse's scores was thought to be deviant. The low value (see Higgins et al., "Intelligence and Family Size") comes from a sample of relatives of mental patients and is based on test scores gathered from school records. We do not know whether the relatives of mental patients can be viewed as representative of the general population. In any event, the use of school records means that scores on diverse tests must have been transformed to a single uniform scale. Such transformations substantially reduce the reliability of individual scores. This reduces the observed correlations between individuals. Higgins et al. do not report the reliability of their IQ estimates. The correlation between a parent and a child was, however, also appreciably lower than that reported elsewhere (see Table A-2). The correlation between siblings was about equal to that reported elsewhere, but in most cases both siblings probably took the same test. Transformation errors would then inflate rather than deflate the sibling correlation. For these reasons, we decided to eliminate both Outhit's data and Higgins et al.'s data from further consideration.

4. Throughout this appendix, we have calculated the weighted mean of

correlations without using the $z$ transformation. The $z$ transformation affects the results only when the correlations are very large, or very different from one another. This is almost never the case with our data.

5. The rationale and procedure for correcting for unreliability are described at some length in Appendix B.

6. The correlation between the occupational statuses of spouses' fathers is about 0.30. The correlation between spouses' educational attainments is about 0.60. See Blau and Duncan, *The American Occupational Structure*. James Crow (in correspondence) has pointed out that the assumptions made here also ignore the effects of dominance. If $g < 0.50$, $p < 0.57$ $(h + se)^2$. We have not worked out all the implications of this.

7. This correlation is most easily derived by calculating the multiple correlations, which equal the correlations between means when the coefficients of the independent variables are equal.

8. It should be noted that if we had used data derived from local studies and made no correction for variance between studies, the value of $h^2$ would be higher for any given value of $g$. Thus, for $g = .50$, $h^2$ would rise from 0.29 to 0.32. For $g = 0.30$, $h^2$ would rise from 0.59 to 0.64.

9. In the absence of a correction for variance between studies, the covariance term explains from 16 to 17 percent of the total variance.

10. The original study is reported by Burt, in "Genetic Determination." The variances were not reported, but the original data was made available to CEPR and was analyzed by Randall Weiss and Jencks.

11. The child's score on the 1916 revision of the Binet correlated 0.38 with the mother's score on the 1916 revision. The child's score on the 1937 revision correlated 0.44 with the mother's score on the 1916 revision. The discrepancy between the two results is statistically insignificant and is in the opposite direction from what we would theoretically expect. We will therefore assume that the discrepancy was due to chance and that the correlation is 0.41.

12. Skodak and Skeels found a correlation of 0.24 between the natural mother's Binet score and the educational attainment of the adopting mother. This suggests some selective placement. But they also found correlations of 0.02 to 0.10 between the education of the adopting mother and the child's scores. This means that if selective placement had been based only on educational matching, the correlation between the natural mother's IQ and the child's environment would have been on the order of $(0.24)(0.10) =$ 0.024. The same pattern held when Skodak and Skeels looked at the effects of the adoptive parents' occupational status on the child's scores. This implies that the natural mother's IQ scores had no appreciable effect on any relevant aspect of the child's postnatal environment in this study.

13. We are indebted to Carol Ann Moore for reviewing most of the studies on twins and siblings.

14. The 51 pairs reported by Holzinger, in "Nature and Nurture," were apparently incorporated into Newman et al.'s results, in *Twins*.

15. We have not attempted to correct any of the foregoing correlations for errors in diagnosis of zygosity. In general, eliminating such errors will increase $r_{IQMZT}$, reduce $r_{IQDZT}$ and increase the estimated heritability of test scores.

16. Compare equations (34) and (35).

17. As Jensen has noted, the role of prenatal environments could be greatly clarified by obtaining correlations between half-siblings. Fifty percent of such children share the same prenatal environment, while fifty percent share only their father's genes. Given the frequency of broken families, such data would not be difficult to obtain.

18. We compared the means and variances for Project Talent's twins to the means and variances for the general population from which the twins were drawn, i.e. all students in ninth to twelfth grades in 1960. We examined the distribution of five a priori composite scores, which Talent labels C-001, C-002, C-003, C-004, and R-100. C-001 is what Talent somewhat misleadingly calls "IQ," and includes Reading Comprehension, Abstract Reasoning, and Basic Arithmetic. C-002 is what Talent calls "Academic Aptitude," and includes English, Math, Vocabulary, Reading Comprehension, Abstract Reasoning, and a short test labeled "Creativity." C-003 is what Talent labels "Verbal" and includes Literature Information, English, and Vocabulary. C-004 is what Talent labels "Quantitative," and includes a series of mathematical tests. R-100 is a General Information test, covering everything from vocabulary to knowledge about the Bible. Table 3–1 of Flanagan et al.'s *The American High School Student* gives means and standard deviations for these composites by grade level and sex for all high school students, along with more information about the characteristics of the composites. Talent's original file on same-sex twins was made available to us by Lyle Schoenfeldt and was analyzed by Marsha Brown.

The means for the Talent twins exceed the means for others of their grade and sex by an average of 0.1 standard deviations. (Most twins average 0.2 or 0.3 standard deviations below the population mean.) Of the same-sex pairs with "IQ" data, 69 percent were diagnosed as monozygotic. This is much higher than in most other twin samples. The twins are also female in 59 percent of all cases. All this suggests that the results should be treated with caution. Nonetheless, the variances for twins are all restricted to roughly the extent we would expect on theoretical grounds. If we define the population variances as 100, the twin variances are as follows: C-001 = 88.5, C-002 = 86.4, C-003 = 83.6, C-004 = 98.2, and R-100 = 86.1.

The only other comparable source of data is Husen's study of 2,935 male twins examined for military service in Sweden between 1948 and 1952 (see *Psychological Twin Research*). The variance for all these twins on the Swedish military's "intelligence" test was 4 percent larger than the population variance.

19. Using the same Talent twins as in note 18, the variances for *MZ* vs. *DZ* twins are as follows: 90.2 vs. 85.9 for C-001; 85.4 vs. 91.0 for C-002; 78.2 vs. 96.3 for C-003; 93.8 vs. 109.6 for C-004; and 85.0 vs. 91.0 for R-100. The variance for *MZ* twins is thus 5 percent larger than that for *DZ* twins on what Talent labels "IQ," but smaller on all the other composites. For the two composites covering broad ranges of subjects (C-002 and R-100), the difference is 6 percent. Such differences are not statistically significant at the 0.05 level.

Husen's twin sample included an appreciable fraction of males whose zygosity could not be diagnosed, and they had an unusually high variance. Among those who were diagnosed, the *MZ* twins had a variance 8 percent smaller than the same-sex *DZ* twins, and 2 percent larger than the male *DZ* twins with female partners.

Overall, the evidence does not suggest much difference in the environmental variance within families for *MZ* as against *DZ* twins. There could, however, easily be a difference of 5 percent.

20. The reader who finds this discrepancy puzzling should consult a genetics text in which derivations are shown. Li, in *Population Genetics*, has a good presentation. The formulae for situations with assortative mating are derived in Crow and Felsenstein, "Assortative Mating."

21. Calculated by Randall Weiss from data supplied to CEPR by the late Sir Cyril Burt.

22. One of the tables in Burt, "Genetic Determination," which has been widely reproduced, reports the existence of forty-two studies of siblings reared apart. This is a typographical error. So far as we can discover, there are only two studies other than Burt's.

23. This conclusion does not contradict Jensen's heritability estimate of 0.80 as sharply as it seems to do. Jensen's formula for $h^2$ arbitrarily partitions the covariance between heredity and environment. This means that both $h^2$ and $e^2$ are higher than when a covariance term enters. This strikes us as an undesirable simplification, but it precludes direct comparisons between his estimates of $h^2$ and ours.

# APPENDIX B

## Path Models of Intergenerational Mobility

This appendix analyzes the determinants of educational attainment, occupational status, and income. The analytic method and much of the data derive directly from the work of Otis Dudley Duncan, to whom we owe an enormous debt. We have, however, made a number of extensions and alterations of his models, for which he is obviously not responsible.

The basic analytic method is path analysis. The presentation assumes familiarity with this approach. Readers who want an introduction should consult Duncan, "Path Analysis," and the sources cited there.

### Variables

The analyses presented here are concerned with the variables which are defined below:

1. *Father's Occupational Status (POPOC)*. This background variable is a rating of the father's occupation, measured on the Duncan scale when data is available in that form, and adjusted to approximate the Duncan scale when data is not available in that form.

2. *Father's Educational Attainment (POPED)*. This is the highest grade of school or college completed by the respondent's father.

3. *Father's IQ (POPIQ)*. This is the father's score on either the Binet Vocabulary, the Otis IQ test, or a military aptitude test.

4. *Educational Attainment (ED)*. This is the highest grade of school or college completed by the respondent. No correction is made for the quality of schooling or for how much the respondent learned in school. These differences are either captured by test scores or lost.

5. *Early Test Scores (IQ-11)*. Although we have used the label "IQ" for the sake of easy recognition, the test scores in these analyses are almost all group tests, and they often purport to measure aptitude rather than intelligence. The correlations between scores on group aptitude tests and individual IQ tests tend to be very high, however, especially after correction for measurement error. Wherever possible, we have based our estimates on tests administered in the sixth grade.

6. *Adult Test Scores (AFQT)*. These are scores on one of the military classification tests, such as the *AFQT, AGCT,* or Army Alpha. These tests are similar but not identical in content to the group tests used for assessing scholastic aptitude. The results correlate very highly with scholastic aptitude test scores and also with scores on individually administered IQ tests. Data are only available for males. Data are from tests given at the time men were examined for military service, usually between 18 and 26.

**320**

7. *Occupational Status (OC)*. Occupational status is measured using the Duncan scale, which is described in Chapter 6 and in Duncan, "Properties and Characteristics," and "Socioeconomic Index."

8. *Income (INC)*. The definition of income is that used by respondents in the Current Population Survey. Only money income is covered, and only the income of the respondent, not the income of his entire family.

9. *Family Background (EF-IQ and EF-ED)*. This is a hypothetical variable which cannot be measured directly. The quality of an individual's family background must be inferred by looking at the average effect of growing up in his family on all the children who did so. Family background is, thus, a weighted combination of all the nongenetic characteristics that make siblings alike. These characteristics include economic status, parental education, family size, parental interest in education, attitudes toward achievement, neighborhood characteristics, schools, region, and so forth.

If we had exact measures of all the factors making siblings alike, and if we understood all the interactions between these factors, we could write an equation which would predict the average result for all siblings in a family with complete accuracy. The coefficients of the variables would, however, vary according to the outcome we were predicting. The family background characteristics that influenced educational attainment, for example, might be somewhat different from those that influenced test scores. As a result, the hypothetical index of family background that predicts test scores (which we will label *EF-IQ*) is not perfectly correlated with the hypothetical index that predicts educational attainment (which we will label *EF-ED*). These 2 indices are, therefore, treated as separate variables, even though they embody many of the same underlying family attributes. Their correlation is unknown. *EF-IQ* is synonymous with *EF* in Appendix A.

10. *Parental Genotype (GP)*. Genotype here refers only to those aspects of an individual's genotype that influence test scores. We will use *GP* to denote parental genotype, *GF* to denote father's genotype, and *GM* to denote mother's genotype.

11. *Respondent's Genotype (GC)*. This is the IQ genotype of the individual respondent.

## Data Sources

Wherever possible, we will use a single data set, namely white nonfarm males covered by the March 1962 Current Population Survey on "Occupational Change in a Generation." The results of this survey have been reported extensively in Blau and Duncan, *The American Occupational Structure,* Duncan, Featherman, and Duncan, *Socioeconomic Background,* and elsewhere. This survey does not, however, provide test score data, so the results reported there will be supplemented by the results of other surveys.

The careful reader will note numerous discrepancies between the correlations reported in the text and notes of this book and the correlations reported in this appendix. These discrepancies derive (we hope) from differences in the samples under discussion. The text often tries to describe gross relationships for the entire American population. Data on the entire population is not available for all the relevant relationships, however, and we have therefore concentrated our detailed analyses on a more limited population for which relatively consistent data is available, i.e. nonfarm whites born between 1897 and 1936. The exclusion of farm-born whites and of all blacks restricts the range of variation in most variables and lowers the correlations somewhat. A comparison between correlations reported in Duncan, Featherman, and Duncan, *Socioeconomic Background,* for white males, white nonfarm males, and black males and correlations reported in Blau and Duncan, *The American Occupational Structure,* for all nonfarm males suggests that the differences between nonfarm whites and the total population are quite small. The results for blacks are, however, quite different from those for whites.

In order to conduct an analysis of the type attempted in this appendix, we need a matrix of true correlations. We begin by presenting a matrix of observed correlations, i.e. correlations that are not adjusted to take account of measurement error. We will then discuss the process by which we adjusted the observed correlation to estimate the true correlations.

Our "observed" matrix is shown in Table B–1. The key to the source of each correlation is given beside the correlation:

a. $r_{POPED,POPOC}$; $r_{POPED,ED}$; $r_{POPED,OC}$; $r_{POPED,INC}$; $r_{POPOC,ED}$; $r_{POPOC,OC}$; $r_{POPOC,INC}$. These correlations were estimated by averaging the correlations for men aged 25–34, 35–44, 45–54, and 55–64 reported on p. 57 of Duncan, Featherman, and Duncan, *Socioeconomic Background,* for non-Negro, nonfarm males in the civilian labor force in March 1962. For most pairs of variables, the correlations averaged across age groups are very similar to those derived from pooling all men aged 25–64. The main exception is education, which is correlated with age.

TABLE B–1
*Observed Correlations between Characteristics
of Native White Nonfarm Males*

|  | 1 | 2 | 3 | 4 | 5 | 6 | 7 | 8 |
|---|---|---|---|---|---|---|---|---|
| 1. *POPED* | 1.00 | | | | | | | |
| 2. *POPOC* | .509a | 1.00 | | | | | | |
| 3. *POPIQ* | .630b | .450b | 1.00 | | | | | |
| 4. *IQ–11* | .300c | .300c | .480e | 1.00 | | | | |
| 5. *ED* | .382a | .420a | – | .550f | 1.00 | | | |
| 6. *AFQT* | .305d | .314d | – | .830g | .630i | 1.00 | | |
| 7. *OC* | .303a | .369a | – | .460h | .612j | .450l | 1.00 | |
| 8. *INC* | .184a | .238a | – | – | .330k | .310m | .399n | 1.00 |

*Additional Correlations*

$r_{IQ8IBT} = 0.520$ o

$r_{EDSIBT} = 0.541$ p

$r_{OCSIBT} = 0.292$ q

$r_{GC,EF-IQ} = 0.334$ (corrected for attenuation) r

$r_{GC,IQ-11} = 0.823$ (corrected for attenuation) r

$r_{EF-IQ,IQ-11} = 0.584$ (corrected for attenuation) r

For the source of each correlation, see textual note indicated by corresponding letter. For key to abbreviations, see text.

b. $r_{POPED,POPIQ}$; $r_{POPOC,POPIQ}$. These correlations were set equal to the observed correlations for sons (see below). No correction was made for possible reductions in the correlations for fathers because of restriction in the range of variation for fathers. This may lead to a slight overestimate of the correlations. On the other hand, the available data suggest that $r_{ED,AFQT}$ may actually have declined over time. For education, then, the bias introduced by restriction of range is in the opposite direction from the bias introduced by assuming stability over time. For occupation, we have no trend data. The amount of error introduced by ignoring changes over time is unlikely to exceed ± 0.05.

c. $r_{POPED,IQ-11}$; $r_{POPOC,IQ-11}$. The literature is replete with studies reporting correlations between test scores and measures of socio-economic background. Values for large samples range between around 0.20 (see e.g. Duncan, "Ability and Achievement") to around 0.40 (see e.g. Shaycoft, *Cognitive Growth*). Differences between samples, tests, and background measures account for the diverse results. Our estimates are based primarily on data reported by Coleman et al., *Equality of Educational Opportunity, Supplemental Appendix,* for white sixth graders. Coleman et al. report a correlation of 0.312 between parental education and verbal scores for a national sample of whites. Eliminating farm children would slightly reduce the estimate. Eliminating girls does not affect the estimate. We, therefore, take 0.30 as a reasonable estimate of the correlation between father's education and the scores of white nonfarm sixth graders on a verbal test of the EEOS type. For northern urban whites, Smith obtained correlations of 0.300 between verbal scores and mother's education, 0.275 between verbal scores and father's education, and 0.278 between verbal scores and a dichotomous measure of occupational status (white collar vs. blue collar). We estimate that a more precise occupational classification would inflate the correlation between father's status and a child's test scores to roughly 0.30. These correlations are within ± 0.02 of the observed correlations in our sample of ninth graders in Project Talent.

d. $r_{POPED,AFQT}$; $r_{POPOC,AFQT}$. The correlations between $AFQT$ scores of veterans aged 25–34 in 1964 and their reports of their father's education and occupation were taken from the 1964 NORC veterans survey. We are grateful to William Mason for supplying us with this data. We have used Duncan's correction for restriction in the range of variation for veterans' $AFQT$ scores. (Our results for nonfarm whites agree closely with Duncan's for all whites.) We have also checked these correlations to see whether they vary according to the type of military test used, since some veterans had taken a test other than the $AFQT$. No systematic differences appear.

e. $r_{POPIQ,IQ-11}$. This correlation is taken from Table A–2 in Appendix A of this volume.

f. $r_{IQ-11,ED}$. There has never been a national study of the association between test scores in elementary or junior high school and subsequent years of schooling. We do, however, have four local studies. Benson, in "Scholastic Success," followed up 1,680 out of 1,989 students who had taken the Haggerty Intelligence Test as sixth graders in Minneapolis in 1923. She reported a correlation of 0.57 between test scores and attainment. Duncan, in "Ability and Achievement," reestimated this value at 0.54.

Benson's initial sample does not adequately represent the bottom end of the nation's ability distribution. This is even more true of her final sample. Median IQ was 105 for the initial sample and 108 for those who were successfully followed up. On this basis we expect the Minneapolis follow-up sample to be about $(0.54 \times 8/15) = 0.29$ standard deviations above the national mean on educational attainment. It is. The mean attainment of the Minneapolis sample was 11.2 years, with a standard deviation of 2.3 years. The national mean for the same group was 10.1 years with a standard deviation of 3.6 years. (See Chapter 2, Table 2–1.) The national mean for those with 5 or more years of schooling (i.e. those eligible for Benson's sample) was 10.3 years, and the standard deviation was 3.0 years.

The restriction of range in the Minneapolis test scores is about what we would expect if the mean were inflated 0.29 standard deviations by dropping cases in the bottom portion of the distribution. The restriction of range in educational attainment is, however, much greater than we would expect on the basis of either the fact that the initial sample had all reached sixth grade or the restriction of range in test scores. This suggests that some of the noncognitive factors that produced diversity in attainment around the country (e.g. differential access to higher education) were absent in Minneapolis (which had a large, cheap, public university). Had these factors been operational, test scores might have been relatively less important in determining attainment.

Bajema, in "A Note," and in "Relation of Fertility" followed up 989 out of 1,144 students who had taken the Terman Group Intelligence Test as sixth graders in Kalamazoo in 1928. He reported a correlation of 0.58 for males, 0.61 for females, and 0.58 overall. Mean attainment was 11.76 years for males and 12.22 years for females. The grand mean was 11.99 vs. about 11.4 for the nation as a whole at the time. The standard deviation of attainment was not published, but the breakdown that was published is quite similar to that for the entire nation. No data on the test score distribution was published. There was a public college in Kalamazoo, so money was presumably less of a barrier to entering college for these students than for many others. This would increase the correlation between test scores and attainment.

Thorndike, in *Vocational Success,* gave 2,225 eighth grade boys and girls in New York City the Thorndike-McCall Reading Scale and the I.E.R. Arithmetic Tests in 1922. He followed up 80 percent of them. A composite of the 2 test scores correlated 0.42 with boys' educational attainment and 0.50 with girls' attainment. A clerical test showed similar correlations. The multiple correlation of the 3 tests with attainment was in excess of 0.5. These students' mean attainment was almost 2 years above national norms, but the standard deviation was only about 10 percent less than for the nation as a whole. We have no norms for judging the representativeness of the test score distributions. Given the large fraction of immigrants in New York at this time, eighth grade testing may have missed many low-scoring dropouts. Ethnic differences may also have influenced attainment more in New York than in the nation as a whole, reducing the relative importance of test scores.

Finally, Conlisk, in "A Bit of Evidence," reported a correlation of 0.45 between early IQ scores and later attainment for 79 males in the Berkeley Guidance Study. The means and standard deviations of the relevant variables are not reported.

Taking the 3 large samples together, we infer that the observed correlation between tests of academic aptitude in grades 6–8 and educational attainment for local samples was about 0.55 before World War II. If we had data for a full national sample, the correlation might have been higher, but this is far from certain. We will take 0.55 as the national value, but this estimate should be treated as having a standard error of perhaps ±0.05.

Results from Project Talent's ninth graders, who were tested in 1960 and followed up in 1968, 5 years after they would normally have finished high school, provide a useful check on the above estimates. Using a weighted sample, the correlation between projected educational attainment (based on actual attainment, plus an increment for those still in school or college) and a composite aptitude score (based on vocabularly, social studies information, reading comprehension, and arithmetic) was 0.567.

g. $r_{IQ-11,AFQT}$. We know of no data on the stability of group test scores between the ages of 11 and, say, 21 when the $AFQT$ is typically administered. (We have shorter term stability estimates for students who remain in school, but these are not pertinent.) Bradway and Thompson, in "Intelligence at Adulthood," report that for 111 reasonably representative individuals, scores on the Stanford-Binet administered in early adolescence correlated 0.85 with Stanford-Binet scores 15 years later and 0.81 with Wechsler Adult Intelligence Scale scores 15 years later. Using a sample of 40 high-ability Berkeley children, Bayley, in "Learning in Adulthood," found an average correlation of 0.83 (0.69 for females and 0.97 for males) between IQ at 16 and 36. Jones, in "Problem Solving," reports an average correlation of 0.87 (0.84 for males and 0.90 for females) for 83 individuals in Oakland. A reasonable estimate for individual IQ tests might, thus, be 0.85. The correlation between group tests like the EEOS verbal test and the $AFQT$ might be a little lower than 0.85, since the tests are less reliable. (To the extent that tests at 11 and 21 measure different skills, the correlations would be lower than between tests that measure the same skills. We have assumed tests that try to measure the same skills.) We have used 0.83 because, given our assumptions about the reliability of $IQ-11$ and $AFQT$, it yields a true correlation of 0.92. This is equal to the true correlation implied by the Binet results.

h. $r_{IQ-11,OC}$. This estimate is from the Kalamazoo sample described by Bajema in "A Note." We have not attempted to determine the representativeness of this figure, since it is not used in our calculations. If the figure in Table B–1 is correct, some of the other correlations in the table are wrong, or some important variables are omitted from the model, for the use of this correlation yields a positive direct path from $IQ-11$ to $OC$. We know no data on the correlation between early IQ scores and later income, although it can be inferred from the models presented hereafter.

i. $r_{ED,AFQT}$. Yerkes, in *Psychological Examining*, reports a correlation of 0.68 between years of schooling and Army Alpha scores for literate whites inducted during World War I. He estimates that if a truly representative sample of American adults had been tested, their Army Alpha scores would have correlated 0.75 with the number of years of schooling they had completed. The correlation would have been lower for native-born, nonfarm whites.

The Adjutant General's Office, in "The Army General Classification Test," reported a correlation of 0.73 between *AGCT* scores and years of schooling for World War II draftees. Tuddenham, in "Soldier Intelligence," reported that years of schooling correlated 0.74 with the *AGCT* and 0.75 with Army Alpha, when the same sample took both tests. (For details on the sample, see Chapter 3, note 23. There was some restriction in the range of schooling.) Fulk and Harrell, in "Army Test Scores," reported data implying a correlation of 0.66 between years of schooling and *AGCT* scores for white Air Force recruits. For recruits who did not finish elementary school, however, the relationship was nil. This suggests that military selectivity at the bottom of the scale was a problem. If we look only at whites with more than 7 years of schooling, the correlation was 0.75. The relationships for blacks were a little weaker.

Cutright, in "Military Service," studied a representative group of draftees registered with Selective Service in 1953. He found a correlation of 0.68 between *AFQT* and years of schooling for whites. His sample excluded volunteers and men who avoided the draft by staying in school. The mean education for his white sample was only 10.7 years, compared to 12 years for all white males of the same age. The standard deviation in Cutright's white sample is 2.68 years, compared to 3.1 for all white males of the same age. This implies that his correlations underestimate the population value, but no more than earlier military studies. Cutright found weaker correlations for blacks than for whites.

Karpinos, in "Mental Qualification," also provides *AFQT* scores for whites by years of schooling prior to induction. Duncan, in "Ability and Achievement," calculated a correlation of 0.63 from this data and inferred that the correlation with eventual years of schooling was close to 0.66.

The correlation between *AFQT* and years of schooling for white males covered by the 1964 NORC veterans survey is 0.49. Correcting for restriction of range yields 0.57. We have no good explanation for the discrepancy between these results and those reported by Cutright and Karpinos.

The trend of the correlations over time is clearly downward. We attribute this to two factors. First, the range of cultural differences among military recruits has probably declined since 1917, both because of urbanization and because of reduced immigration. This helps explain the reduced variance in educational attainment (see Chapter 2, Table 2–1.) (The regression of test scores on years of schooling has, if anything, risen, as shown in Chapter 3, note 85.) Second, automatic promotion has become more and more widespread in schools. This reduces the correlation between test scores and highest grade completed. (For correlations between test scores and years enrolled, see the Adjutant General's Office, "The Army General Classification Test.") In addition, the *AFQT* may include more items that are unrelated to schooling than the *AGCT* or the Army Alpha.

The mean correlation between test scores and education for white males aged 25–34, 35–44, 45–54, and 55–64 in 1962 was presumably somewhere between the value for white men in 1917 (around 0.70), and the value estimated by Duncan from Karpinos 50 years later (0.66). We will use 0.67 as a reasonable compromise. The value for nonfarm white veterans in the NORC survey was 0.03 lower than for all white veterans (0.46 vs. 0.49). Applying a proportional correction to 0.67, we estimate the correlation for all nonfarm whites at 0.63. This estimate should probably be viewed as having a standard error of ±0.05.

For correlations between educational attainment and adult scores on intelligence tests see, e.g. Weisenburg, Roe, and McBride, *Adult Intelligence;* Shakow and Goldman, "Effect of Age"; Lorge, "Last School Grade"; Lewinski, "Vocabulary"; and Wechsler, *Adult Intelligence.* The mean correlation in these studies is $0.63 \pm .03$. The variance in all these samples appears to be restricted. Yerkes, in "Psychological Examining," reports a correlation of 0.65 between Stanford-Binet scores and educational attainment for native white males, which is comparable to the correlations between years of schooling and Army Alpha for the same group. These estimates support our choice of 0.63 as a reasonable value for white non-farm males.

Miner, in *Intelligence,* however, found a correlation of only about 0.55 between education and vocabulary for a representative national sample. Similarly, Duncan and Featherman, in "Psychological and Cultural Factors," report a correlation of only 0.57 between educational attainment and adult scores on the similarities subtest of the WAIS, using data from the Detroit Area survey. These tests probably have much lower reliabilities than the military tests, especially since they were not given under uniform conditions.

j. $r_{ED,OC}$. Estimate derived as in (a). The correlations are slightly higher for the younger men. One possible interpretation of this is that educational attainment plays a larger role in determining status today than in the past. If that were the case, averaging across age groups would be a mistake. Comparisons between Censuses do not, however, support this interpretation (see Folger and Nam, "Trends in Education"). Neither is any such trend visible in the correlations between occupation and education when sons of varying ages report their father's education and his occupation when the son was 16. These correlations pertain to the father's occupation when the average age was 44. We therefore infer that there has been no increase in $r_{ED,OC}$ since 1900, but that educational attainment has more influence on the occupational status of workers when they are young than when they get older. This makes sense, since we expect later status to be somewhat influenced by performance on the job. Blau and Duncan, in *The American Occupational Structure,* offer a formal interpretation along these lines. If this interpretation is correct, averaging correlations across age cohorts gives us an estimate of the average occupational advantage conferred by a given level of educational attainment. (It does not, however, give us an estimate of the correlation between educational attainment and mean status averaged over a lifetime. The correlation between educational attainment and mean status must be appreciably higher than 0.61.)

k. $r_{ED,INC}$. Estimate derived as in (a). The correlation is lower for the group aged 25–34, higher for those aged 35–44 and 45–54, and lower for those aged 55–64. As with occupation, the use of an average coefficient gives the average relationship between education and annual income over a lifetime, not the relationship of educational attainment to lifetime income.

l. $r_{AFQT,OC}$. This correlation is taken from Duncan's reworking of the 1964 NORC veterans survey in "Ability and Achievement." Duncan, Featherman, and Duncan, in *Socioeconomic Background,* report r = 0.424 using *AGCT* scores and preinduction occupations of World War II men studied by Harrell and Harrell, in "Army General Classification," and r = 0.446 using similar data reported by Stewart in *"AGCT* Scores." Thorndike and Hagen, in *10,000 Careers,* followed up 10,000 Air Force veterans who had been given a variety of tests during World War II and reported that 23 percent of the variance on their academic test scores fell between occupational categories. This is almost identical to Harrell and Harrell's results and to Stewart's results. For nonacademic tests (e.g. those measuring manual skills) Thorndike and Hagen reported lower percentages of variance between occupational categories. There is some restriction of range in all the military samples, but the *AFQT* estimate is corrected for this.

It can be argued that the *AFQT,* which has "vocational knowledge" subtests, might predict success better than a purer measure of IQ genotype would. However, Duncan and Featherman reported r = 0.43 between the similarities subtest and occupational status in the 1966 Detroit Area Survey. These values are all remarkably consistent. Only the GATB results reported in Duncan, Featherman, and Duncan, in *Socioeconomic Background,* seem inconsistent, and the inconsistencies in that data set seem likely to be due to sampling.

m. $r_{AFQT,INC}$. This is taken from Duncan's reworking of the NORC veterans survey data on *AFQT* scores and earnings. We have reanalyzed the data to see whether alternative measures, such as family income or expected income for the current year, correlate better with *AFQT.* They do not. Neither does a composite income index based on all available information. Because the intercorrelations among these income measures were distressingly low, we have also examined data on draftees collected by Cutright. He estimated annual earnings from the total earnings reported in Social Security Administration records, using the month in which the individual reached the taxable limit to estimate total earnings for those who exceeded the taxable limit. Cutright found correlations averaging 0.34 for men in their late twenties and early thirties.

Since the correlation between education and income rises in middle age, the correlation between *AFQT* scores and income may do the same. We have no direct evidence that this happens, however, and we do have direct evidence from both Cutright and from the NORC veterans survey that the correlation between income and *AFQT* is almost identical to the correlation between income and education. Thus, if we assume that the correlation between income and *AFQT* is more than 0.31 for nonfarm whites aged 25–64, we must also assume that the correlation between income and education is more than 0.33 for these men. The reader who reestimates the models in this appendix using correlations of, say, 0.36 for $r_{INC,AFQT}$ and 0.38 for $r_{INC,ED}$ will not find that this alters the conclusions very much.

n. $r_{OC,INC}$. Estimate derived as in (a). Like others involving income, it is higher for the middle-aged and lower for the young and old.

The correlations in Table B–1 allow us to estimate the relationship between the measurable characteristics of respondents. We are also interested in the effects of several unmeasured variables, namely genotype and family background. To estimate these effects with confidence, we need correlations between relatives who share different proportions of genes and who have been raised either together or apart. We have several such correlations for test scores but not for other variables.

We can extend our analysis much further with the aid of a simplifying assumption. We will assume that genes have no effect on educational attainment except via their effect on IQ scores. This allows us to attribute all educational resemblance between brothers to 1 of 3 factors: (1) similar IQ scores, (2) family background (*EF-ED*), or (3) brothers' effects on one another. This assumption allows us to estimate the effects of family background from correlations between brothers.

o. $r_{IQSIBT}$. Appendix A, Table A–7, gives the correlation between siblings' IQ scores in local samples as 0.520. The correlation for brothers is the same. For reasons discussed below, we assume the correlation between white nonfarm males is about equal to the average for local samples.

p. $r_{EDSIBT}$. Tables B5–B8 in Duncan, Featherman, and Duncan, *Socioeconomic Background,* report correlations averaging 0.541 between respondents' educational attainment and their older brother's attainment for non-Negro nonfarm men aged 25–34, 35–44, 45–54, and 55–64 in the civilian labor force in 1962. Since many men in small families did not have older brothers, this correlation is based on a disproportionately lower-class sample. The average level of education for those families is less than for the overall white nonfarm sample, but the variance is not appreciably reduced. The expected reduction in the correlation due to restriction in range is trivial.

q. $r_{OCSIBT}$. We know no published national data on the correlation between the occupational statuses of brothers. Hodge (in correspondence) reports 0.292 from an unpublished survey. Excluding blacks and farm-born whites might lower the value slightly. Hermalin, in "Homogeneity," collected data on the siblings of 312 older male employees of an eastern utility company. Despite the restriction of range potentially implicit in such a sample, he found correlations between brother's educational attainments that closely resembled those reported by Duncan, Featherman, and Duncan, in *Socioeconomic Background,* for a national sample. This suggests that his findings about brothers' occupational statuses may also be similar to the national pattern. He reports correlations that average around 0.30 between brothers' occupational statuses.

r. $r_{GC,EF-IQ}$, $r_{GC,IQ}$, $r_{EF-IQ,IQ-11}$. Our estimates of the correlations between family environment, genotype, and test scores are derived by the same method as in Appendix A. Our estimates differ from those in Appendix A, however, because we are now dealing with nonfarm whites rather than a full national sample. Appendix A assumed that the test score variance due to environment would be 5 percent greater for a full national sample than for the local samples covered by most studies. We based this judgment on the fact that most local samples excluded southerners, ethnic minorities, and either big cities or rural areas. In estimating the effects of environment on native white nonfarm males, we will assume that the range of environments is 5 percent less than for the nation as a whole, i.e. the same as the range in the average local sample cited in Appendix A, Tables A–1, A–2, A–3, A–6, A–7, and A–8. Using the notation of Appendix A, we, thus, have:

$$r_{IQF,IQM} = 0.54$$
$$r_{IQNP,IQC} = 0.52$$
$$r_{IQAP,IQC} = 0.24$$
$$r_{IQSIBT} = 0.57$$

(All these are true correlations, corrected for attenuation. The uncorrected correlations are given in Appendix A, Tables A–1, A–2, A–3, and A–7.)

We have used these values of $r_{IQF,IQM}$, $r_{IQNP,IQC}$, and $r_{IQAP,IQC}$ to reestimate Table A–5 (Appendix A). In general, we get values of $h$ slightly lower than those in Table A–5 and values of $e$ slightly higher than those in Table A–5. The covariance term ($2hes$) hovers around 0.165 instead of 0.19 for all values of $g$.

In Appendix A our efforts to balance data on parents, unrelated children in the same home, siblings, and twins led us to an estimate of $h^2 = 0.45 \pm 0.10$ for a national sample. For a local sample, this same balancing act yields $h^2 = 0.50 \pm 0.10$, if $2hes = 0.165$, $e^2 = 0.335$, and $s = 0.20$. Using an ersatz version of Table A–5, this implies $g = 0.36$.

Since we plan to work with brothers, we need a set of values for $h$, $i$, and $a$ which will yield $r_{IQSIBT} = 0.566$. However, from Appendix A we know that $r_{IQSIBT} = b_{SIB}h^2 + i^2 + 2hia$, that $b_{SIB} = 0.25 + 0.5g + r_{IQF,IQM}g$ $(h + se)^2$ and that $2hia = 2hes$. For local samples he have $h^2 = 0.50$, $h = 0.707$, $2hes = 0.165$, $s = 0.200$, $e^2 = 0.336$, $e = .580$, $g = 0.36$, and $r_{IQF,IQM} = 0.543$. It follows that $b_{SIB} = .562$, and that $r_{IQSIBT} = (0.562)(0.50) + i^2 + 0.164$. Since $r_{IQSIBT} = 0.566$, $i^2$ must be 0.121, and $i$ must be 0.348. Since $ia = es$, $a$ must be 0.334. Note that this makes $e^2 - i^2 = 0.204$. Thus, 20.4 percent of the total variance is imputed to environmental differences within families. This seems high, but lower values are hard to reconcile with the sibling data used here. We suspect that the explanation is that $r_{IQSIBT} > 0.566$ in a sample of this kind, but we have not doctored the data in this way. The true correlations are thus taken as:

$$r_{GC,EF-IQ} = a = 0.334$$
$$r_{GC,IQ-11} = h + ia = 0.823$$
$$r_{EF-IQ,IQ-11} = i + ha = 0.584$$

## Measurement Error

The most frequent approach to measurement error is indifference. Errors are presumed to exist and to inflate the standard error of regression equations, but not to bias the estimated path coefficients. Or, if they do bias the path coefficients, the bias is expected to be small and uniform. This expectation seems unwarranted for data of the kind discussed here.

A second common approach is to make corrections for measurement error on the assumption that all errors are random. This has two effects. First, it makes all relationships look stronger. Second, it inflates the estimated effects of poorly measured variables relative to well-measured variables. Thus, there is good reason to believe that when respondents provide information about events or situations that existed many years ago, their recollections will be less accurate than their recollection about more recent events. If these errors are random, the apparent association between distant events and current events will be reduced more than the apparent association between recent events and current events. More specifically, a man's retrospective reports about his father's occupation and education are likely to be less accurate than his reports about his own occupation and education. If his errors are random, parental status will look less important than it is in determining a son's life chances. If the errors are nonrandom, however, their effects may be the opposite.

Since the treatment of measurement errors seems to influence the conclusions that can be drawn about the rate of social mobility in America, disagreement about technical problems often follows political lines. Conservatives have generally followed Otis Dudley Duncan's lead in assuming that the effects of measurement error are problematic and probably minor. Radicals (e.g. Bowles, "Schooling and Inequality") have assumed that the effects of measurement error were large and that they resulted in serious underestimates of the effects of background on life chances.

Measurement errors can have any of the following characteristics:

1. Errors can be correlated with some other measured characteristic of the respondent. Highly educated respondents may, for example, exaggerate the status of the job they hold. This will inflate the correlation between educational attainment and occupational status. Alternatively, highly educated respondents may understate the status of their job, lowering the correlation between educational attainment and occupational status. In general, we expect errors of this type to inflate observed correlations above the true level, because we expect people to make their responses to a survey more consistent than they really are.

2. Errors can be correlated with the characteristic actually being measured. Individuals with high incomes may underreport them, for example, while individuals with low incomes overreport them. This may either increase or reduce the variance of the characteristic in question, depending on the sign of the correlation and the size of the errors. In most cases, errors of this type will also reduce a variable's correlation with other variables, but this is not always the case. Sometimes such errors actually inflate the observed correlation.

Consider sons' reports of their fathers' occupational status. Men usually hold a variety of different jobs during their lifetimes. The status of these jobs varies considerably. Some of the jobs—and statuses—are temporary. This is particularly likely to be true of certain low-status "interim" jobs, which are held while looking for something better. When a son is asked to report his father's occupation when the son was 16, he may well be confronted with a choice between reporting the low-status job that his father held at the time the son was actually 16, or the higher-status job that the father held during most of the son's childhood. Confronted with such a choice, many sons undoubtedly decide that the survey is not really interested in a job their father held for only a few weeks or months but in the father's usual occupation during that period of their lives. A father who usually worked as a bricklayer but was temporarily employed as a delivery truck driver is thus reported as a bricklayer, and so forth. Technically speaking, this is "measurement error." However, if the father in question acted like a bricklayer when his son was growing up, even when he worked as a truck driver, his son's "error" will give us a better picture of the father's real status than would an accurate report.

3. Errors can be uncorrelated with the respondent's true characteristics, but can be correlated with errors in the measurement of other variables. Individuals who overreport their incomes, for example, may also overreport their educational attainment and their occupational status. Errors of this type will inflate the variance of the variable under study. In general, if the correlations between errors are larger than the correlations between the true values of the same variables, the errors will also inflate the observed correlations between the two variables. If the correlations between errors are smaller than the correlations between true values, or if they have opposite signs, the errors will deflate the observed correlations. The magnitude of the effect depends on the relative size of the error variance and the true variance.

4. Errors can be uncorrelated with either the true values of other variables or with errors in other variables but can still be correlated with themselves over time. An individual who overreports his 1949 income in the 1950 Census may also overreport it in the Post-Enumeration Survey. The effect of such errors will generally be to increase the observed variance in the variable under study and to deflate its correlation with other variables.

5. Errors can be uncorrelated with anything. This is particularly likely to happen if the errors are not made by the respondent himself but by keypunch operators, coders, and others involved in turning questionnaire data into cards or tape. Errors made by respondents can also have a substantial component that is uncorrelated with anything else.

In practice, most errors are a mixture of all the above species. The relative magnitude of the various correlations has not been investigated in a systematic way for survey data of the kind discussed here, and inferences about the relationship between observed correlations and true correlations are therefore highly conjectural. Nonetheless, the problem is sufficiently important so that we have tried to determine the sensitivity of our calculations to what we regarded as plausible degrees of measurement error.

One common strategy for dealing with measurement error is to look at the correlation between information obtained at one point in time and information about the same characteristic obtained at an immediately subsequent point in time. Testers, for example, often administer two forms of a test to the same individual on two successive days. They assume that the student has the same underlying true score on both days and that this is the sole source of resemblance between his two scores. They then infer the correlation between his observed scores and his true score from the correlation between the two observed scores. The correlation between the observed scores is known as the "reliability coefficient." It is the square of the correlation between the observed score and the true score. The reliability coefficient is therefore equal to the percentage of variance in the observed scores explained by the true score. The rest of the variance is imputed to measurement error and is presumed to be random. If this assumption is correct, i.e. if the errors are all Type 5, an observed correlation between two variables must be divided by the geometric mean of the two reliabilities to get a true correlation.

This approach to correcting measurement errors in questionnaire data has two pitfalls. First, differences in response to one question can easily be correlated with differences in response to another question, i.e. the errors can be Type 3 rather than Type 5. Type 3 errors can, at times, inflate observed correlations rather than deflate them. Yet the standard correction procedure assumes that errors are all of Type 5. Applying a correction appropriate for a Type 5 error to a Type 3 error may make the final true correlation less accurate than the observed correlation. The likelihood of such mishaps is unknown.

The second problem is that the correlation between sequential measures of the same variable tells us very little about the extent of Type 1, Type 2, and Type 4 errors. Response biases that are a function of a respondent's true characteristics will be repeated from one survey to the next. When this happens, the correlation between successive responses will approach unity, and we will not detect any error at all.

In the absence of good data on the actual character and frequency of measurement errors in this type of research, further speculation is not likely to take us very far. Indeed, the reader who has gotten this far may well feel that we have already taxed his patience. Instead of trying to resolve the problem, we must try to sidestep it. We will first analyze our data on the assumption that there are no measurement errors. We will then correct our correlation matrices on the assumption that all discrepancies between successive reports and scores are due to Type 5 (i.e. random errors), and that other types of error are either absent or cancel one another out. Having corrected our correlation matrices in this way, we will compare the results with those derived from uncorrected matrices. The differences do not seem large enough to warrant serious concern.

The best study of error in demographic data of the type analyzed in this appendix is Siegel and Hodge, "A Causal Approach." They report the following correlations between the Census and the Post-Enumeration Survey: 0.933 for educational attainment, 0.873 for occupational status, and 0.847 for income. They conclude, however, that the Current Population Survey is more reliable than the full Census, presumably because the interviewers are better trained. Siegel and Hodge estimate the reliability of the CPS at 0.977 for educational attainment and 0.896 for income. The comparable Census reliabilities are 0.892 for education and 0.809 for income. Since the data discussed in this appendix comes mostly from the Current Population Survey, we will use the estimated CPS reliabilities. We will assume that the reliability of CPS reports of occupational status has the same relationship to the CPS reliabilities for education and income as in comparisons between the Census and the PES. Thus, the Census-PES correlation for occupational status exceeds that for income by 0.0258 and falls short of the Census-PES for education by 0.0606. If the ratio for the CPS is the same, CPS occupational measures have a reliability of 0.913.

The foregoing results should be compared with those of Bowles, in "Schooling and Inequality," who reports 1950 Census-PES correlations of 0.83 for occupational status, 0.86 for educational attainment, and 0.80 for income. We have preferred Siegel and Hodge's results because they appear to be based on fuller and more recent information. (Bowles also assumes some correlated errors and assumes that these imply a uniform downward bias to observed correlations. This creates a further disparity between his results and ours.)

We also need an estimate of the reliability of respondents' reports of parental status. We have proceeded as follows. Using Siegel and Hodge's reliabilities for respondents' reports of their own education and occupation, we estimated the true correlation between these variables at $0.612/\sqrt{(0.913)(0.977)} = 0.646$. Using Duncan, Featherman, and Duncan's data from the 1962 CPS, we get a mean correlation of 0.509 between respondents' reports on their fathers' education and occupation. The variance of fathers' education is restricted by the fact that poorly educated fathers tend to have more sons than well-educated fathers. The restriction is small, however, and the presumed true correlation between father's occupation and education is still 0.64. Thus, the reliabilities of reports about fathers must have a geometric mean of $0.509/0.64 = 0.795$. If we assume that the ratio of the reliability of retrospective reports on father's education and father's occupation is the same as the ratio of the reliability of current reports on these variables (i.e. 0.977/0.913), the reliability of father's occupation must be 0.769 and the reliability of father's education must be 0.823. We will use these reliabilities, despite the evidence cited by Bowles that sons' reports on their fathers correlate considerably less than $\sqrt{0.769}$ with the fathers' actual statuses. Bowles' data may well be correct. However, if it is, some of the errors must be Type 2, i.e. they must be correlated with one another. Otherwise, sons' reports of their fathers' education and occupation would correlate less than 0.509. Using a reliability less than $\sqrt{0.769}$ for retrospective data would imply a true correlation between education and occupation in excess of 0.64. This seems unwarranted in light of Siegel and Hodge's evidence on the reliability of current reports.

The accuracy of sixth graders' reports about their parents is even more problematic than the accuracy of adults' reports about their parents. Having estimated the reliability of adult reports on parental education at 0.824, we first assumed that sixth graders' reports had even lower reliabilities. In EEOS, for example, the value could be 0.60 or less (see Jencks, "Quality of the Data"). Such figures must, however, be applied with some caution. The correlation between white northern urban sixth graders' reports on their mother's educational attainment and their father's educational attainment, for example, is 0.632 in EEOS. If we assume that sixth graders' reports have the same reliability as adults' retrospective reports (i.e. 0.796), an observed correlation of 0.632 implies a true correlation of 0.794. If we assume that sixth graders' reports have a reliability of 0.60, the implied true correlation between mother's and father's education is in excess of 1.00. The correlations between spouses' reports of their own educational attainments range from 0.55 to 0.62 for those in the right age bracket to have had sixth grade children in EEOS (see Blau and Duncan, *The American Occupational Structure*). Unless we are prepared to believe that children's reports are more accurate than their parents', we have to conclude that the errors in children's reports are more highly correlated than the true values. This is a Type 3 error. Applying a standard correction for unreliability would make our estimate of the correlation less accurate, not more so.

The reader should not conclude that all errors are correlated or that correction for attenuation is always unwarranted. He should simply recognize the importance of exercising judgment in deciding when and how to adjust correlations. Thus, EEOS sixth graders' reports on their father's education and their reports on whether he had a white-collar job correlated 0.278. The true correlation between these two variables is in excess of 0.4. The low observed correlation suggests a great deal of random error. We infer that when sixth graders are given nonanalogous questions (education vs. occupation) to deal with, their errors are less likely to be correlated than when they are given analogous questions (mother's education and father's education). The same is very likely true of adults.

We are left with the problem of how large a correction we should apply to children's reports about parents. Our solution was to assume that twelfth graders' reports about their parents were as accurate as young adults' retrospective reports. Next, we assumed that the true correlation between background measures and test scores in the sixth grade was equal to that in the ninth and twelfth grades. In EEOS, the average correlation between parental education and the four tests given in sixth, ninth, and twelfth grades is 0.267 for sixth grade whites, 0.292 for ninth grade whites, and 0.249 for twelfth grade whites (see Coleman et. al., *Equality of Educational Opportunity, Supplemental Appendix*). The same pattern holds when we restrict ourselves to whites in the North. The average reliability of the tests is 0.855 in sixth grade, 0.830 in ninth grade, and 0.845 in twelfth grade (see Jencks, "Quality of the Data Collected"). Lacking a good explanation for the decline in the correlations between ninth and twelfth grade (the variance in parental education declines only 4 percent), we conclude that the average correlation in ninth and twelfth grades exceeds the sixth grade correlation by only 0.004. This hardly suggests that errors in the measurement of parental education are depressing the observed correlation in sixth grade more than they do later. If sixth graders make more errors than ninth and twelfth graders, which seems likely, these errors must be related to their test scores in a way that maintains an observed correlation at almost 0.3. We will therefore use the same correction for random errors in children's reports on their parents as for random errors in adults' reports on their parents. This means we will assume that 20.5 percent (1–0.795) of the response variance is random error.

We also need reliabilities for the test scores used in our analyses. Many reported reliabilities are "internal," i.e. based on correlations between the separate items in a test. Reliabilities of this type allow us to estimate correlations for tests that are infinitely long. They do not tell us about error due to variations in testing conditions and the condition of the test taker. For this we need test-retest correlations. The internal reliabilities of individually administered intelligence tests are often as high as 0.95. The test-retest reliabilities of the Stanford-Binet run closer to 0.92 (see e.g. Thorndike, "The Effect of the Interval," and Brown, "Time Interval"). The internal reliability of the EEOS group tests for sixth graders ranges from a high of 0.94 for the verbal test to a low of 0.78 for the nonverbal test (estimated by the Educational Testing Service; reported in more detail in Jencks, "The Quality of the Data"). We will assume, on the basis of admittedly inadequate evidence, that the test-retest reliability of the EEOS verbal test is about 0.90.

When we turn to the *AFQT* and similar tests, we again find a very high internal reliability. The Adjutant General's Office, in "The Army General Classification Test," reports internal reliabilities of 0.94–0.97 and alternate form reliabilities of 0.89–0.92 for the *AGCT*. It also reported a test-retest reliability for the *AGCT* in the low 80s, but when this is corrected for restriction of range in the sample it becomes 0.95. Given the amount of variation in military testing conditions, the reliability of test results for random veterans is likely to be less than the reliability reported in the literature. In the absence of evidence on this, we will assume a test-retest reliability of 0.88. This is just below the *AGCT* alternate-form reliability, and allows for some clerical error in military record keeping.

Using the foregoing reliabilities, we have transformed the observed correlations in Table B–1 into the true correlations in Table B–2. Scanning the two tables shows few important differences. As we shall see, the results of regression analyses are also quite similar for both matrices. We conclude that random measurement error is of relatively little importance in research of the kind described here. Nonrandom error and failure to measure the right variables may, of course, be far more important.

## Analytic Models

The use of correlations from disparate sources limits the kinds of models we can use to describe the determinants of economic status. We cannot, for example, investigate nonlinear relationships. Blau and Duncan have, however, explored nonlinear relationships among measures of occupational status and educational attainment of fathers and sons, using multiple-classification analysis, in *The American Occupational Structure*. In general, multiple classification does not provide appreciably more accurate predictions than linear regression. Neither does multiple classification alter our picture of the relative importance of different variables. Jencks investigated nonlinear relationships between cognitive skills, status, and education, using

TABLE B–2

*Estimated True Correlations between Characteristics of Native White Nonfarm Males*

|        | 1      | 2      | 3      | 4      | 5      | 6      | 7      | 8      |
|--------|--------|--------|--------|--------|--------|--------|--------|--------|
| 1. POPED | (.823) |        |        |        |        |        |        |        |
| 2. POPOC | .640   | (.769) |        |        |        |        |        |        |
| 3. POPIQ | .680   | .502   | (.920) |        |        |        |        |        |
| 4. IQ–11 | .345   | .357   | .522   | (.920) |        |        |        |        |
| 5. ED    | .426   | .485   | –      | .580   | (.977) |        |        |        |
| 6. AFQT  | .358   | .382   | –      | .924   | .680   | (.880) |        |        |
| 7. OC    | .350   | .440   | –      | –      | .648   | .502   | (.913) |        |
| 8. INC   | .214   | .287   | –      | –      | .353   | .349   | .441   | (.896) |

*Additional Correlations*

$r_{IQSIBT} = 0.566$ (see Appendix A, Table A–9, no correction for restriction in range)
$r_{EDSIBT} = 0.553$ $(0.541/0.977)$
$r_{OCSIBT} = 0.320$ $(0.292/0.913)$
$r_{GC,EF-IQ} = 0.334$
$r_{GC,IQ-11} = 0.823$
$r_{EFIQ,IQ-11} = 0.584$

Source: Correlations in Table B–1, divided by geometric mean of reliabilities in the diagonal. (Except that $r_{POPOC,POPED} = r_{OC,ED}$ adjusted for restriction of range; $r_{POPIQ,POPED} = r_{AFQT,ED}$; $r_{POPIQ,POPOC} = r_{AFQT,OC}$; and $r_{AFQT,IQ-11} = 0.85/0.92$, since the 0.85 estimate in Table B–1 involves Binet scores with presumed reliabilities of 0.92, not *AFQT* scores.)

EEOS data on early test scores and the NORC veterans data on *AFQT* scores. Again, nonlinear relationships were of modest importance.

A more serious limitation derives from our inability to explore non-additive relationships between the various determinants of adult economic success. Nonadditive relationships have not been explored in detail elsewhere, either. Jencks examined the NORC veterans survey for evidence of nonadditive relationships between education, *AFQT* scores, and later economic success. Such relationships have been found in other data sets (see e.g. Taubman and Wales, "Effects of Education"). Jencks found interactions only for the relationship of education to income for men from different class backgrounds (see Chapter 7). We doubt if nonadditive interactions will prove important so long as the analyses involve clear hierarchical scales, like IQ, status, and income. Nonadditive interactions may be quite important when qualitative measures of family environment are used.

A third limitation is our inability to deal with heteroscedasticity. Thus, when we predict occupational status from *AFQT* scores, the errors in prediction are larger for men with high scores than for men with low scores. This suggests that cognitive skills may be a necessary but not sufficient condition for advancement. To the extent that this is so, an additive regression equation will be somewhat misleading.

Recognizing these limitations, we nonetheless think that simple path models summarize the relationships between men's characteristics as accurately as any alternative model now available and that they do so in a way which makes the overall character of these relationships much clearer than more complicated models. Furthermore, additive models are the only ones that allow us to combine data from diverse sources, since researchers rarely publish enough of their data to allow more sophisticated extrapolations.

Figures B–1 and B–2 present a simple path model of the causal connections between different characteristics. Figure B–1 uses the observed correlations in Table B–1, while Figure B–2 uses the true correlations in Table B–2.

The model is taken directly from Duncan's "Ability and Achievement" and is more or less self-explanatory. It assumes that father's education (*POPED*) and father's occupation (*POPOC*) influence a child's early cognitive skills (*IQ-11*). Father's education, father's occupation, and the child's cognitive skills all influence the child's educational attainment (*ED*). Educational attainment and early cognitive skills then determine later cognitive skills (*AFQT*). We also investigated the possibility that parental status (*POPOC* and *POPED*) had a direct effect on *AFQT* scores. In the model based on observed correlations, these paths are negative. In the model based on true correlations, they are zero.

The model assumes that education, cognitive skills, and father's occupation all influence occupational status (*OC*). We also investigated the effect of father's education on a son's status, but it was virtually nil. Finally, cognitive skills, occupational status, and father's occupational status all influence the respondent's income (*INC*).

We originally expected that education would also have a direct influence on income, over and above its influence on occupational status and cognitive skills. Duncan, in "Ability and Income," found that after controlling occupational status and *AFQT* the direct path from education to earnings was 0.09. Since his estimates were not adjusted to correct for measurement error, they presumably overstate the effect of education (which has a high reliability) relative to other variables (which have lower reliabilities). In our analysis, the path from education to income is only 0.03 before correcting for measurement error. This reflects small differences between our unadjusted correlations (based on income and averaged for men aged 25–64) and Duncan's (based on earnings and covering men aged 25–34). We suspect that Duncan's estimate is more realistic than ours, since it involves a single data set. However, when we correct our estimate for measurement error, it falls from 0.03 to –0.01, and the same thing happens when we correct Duncan's matrix. We infer, then, that the direct path from education to income is trivial (i.e. around 0.05), and we will omit it from our model.

Figures B–1 and B–2 include measures of parental status (*POPED* and *POPOC*) but no other measures of family environment. This is a serious limitation. In Figure B–3, we use the same two status measures to predict a son's IQ, but supplement them with a measure of father's cognitive skill (*POPIQ*). Unfortunately, the results are not at all plausible. One of the two status measures (father's education) takes on an appreciable negative coefficient. This suggests that we have underestimated the correlation between father's education and son's IQ, overestimated the correlation between

FIGURE B–1

*Relationships between Characteristics of Native White Nonfarm Males
Aged 25–64 in 1962, Based on Observed Correlations*

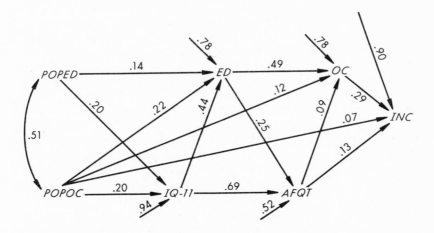

FIGURE B–2

*Relationships between Characteristics of Native White Nonfarm Males
Aged 25–64 in 1962, Based on "True" Correlations*

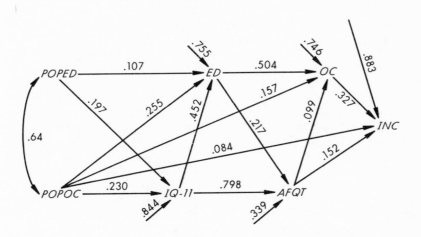

father's education and father's IQ, or both. It also underlines the hazards of synthesizing data from disparate studies. We conclude that synthetic data cannot be used to disentangle the effects of specific background characteristics.

An alternative strategy is to estimate the overall effect of all aspects of family background, without making any specific assumptions about the relative importance of different family characteristics or about how they interact. We can do this to some extent by using data on the resemblance

FIGURE B-3

*Path Coefficients for Determinants of Son's IQ Scores*

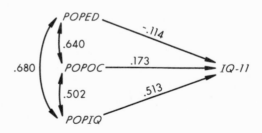

between brothers. Figure B-4 presents a model of the sources of resemblance between brothers' test scores and educational attainments. As in Appendix A, we denote unknown paths with lower case letters. We use the values of $h$, $i$, and $a$ derived in the first section of this appendix. This leaves $m$, $n$, $p$, and $q$ unknown.

Note that we assume no direct relationship between genotype and educational attainment. This reflects our definition of *GC*, which is IQ genotype, not a general measure of genetic advantage. The effects of athletic ability, sex, appearance, and so forth are thus excluded.

Note, too, that *EF-IQ* cannot affect educational attainment and *EF-ED* cannot affect IQ. This is again a matter of definition. If the factors that influence IQ also influence attainment, as they obviously do, this simply inflates $m$, the correlation between the two sets of factors. In the extreme case, if the two sets of factors are the same, $m = 1$.

Finally, note that we have not entertained the possibility that an older brother's educational attainment has a direct effect on his younger brother's educational attainment. If brothers do affect each other, we cannot estimate any of the parameters in Figure B-4 with much confidence. We will return to this problem later.

In general, Figure B-4 implies that:

$$r_{ED1,IQ1} = r_{ED2,IQ2} = p + q(mi + nh) \tag{1}$$

$$r_{ED1,ED2} = p^2 r_{IQ1,IQ2} + q^2 + 2pq(hn + im) \tag{2}$$

Substituting $r_{IQ1,IQ2} = 0.566$, $r_{ED1,ED2} = 0.553$, and $ha + i = 0.584$, and assuming $n = am$, we get:

$$0.580 = p + 0.584qm \tag{1a}$$

and

$$0.553 = 0.566p^2 + q^2 + 1.168mpq \tag{2a}$$

We now have two equations in three unknowns. In order to estimate the two path coefficients ($p$ and $q$), we need a value for $m$, the correlation between the family background characteristics influencing a son's test scores, and the family background characteristics influencing his educational attainment. The only way to obtain such data empirically would be to correlate the differences in brothers' IQ scores with differences in their educational attainment. We know no data set which allows us to do this. In the absence of evidence, we will consider three possible values for $m$: 1.00, 0.75, and 0.50. (Lower values seem quite improbable.) Solving equations (1a) and (2a) simultaneously, we find that:

If  $m = 1.00$,  $q = 0.604$  and  $p = 0.227$
If  $m = 0.75$,  $q = 0.573$  and  $p = 0.329$
If  $m = 0.50$,  $q = 0.566$  and  $p = 0.415$

The value of $q$ is thus quite insensitive to the presumed correlation between family background characteristics influencing educational attainment and those influencing cognitive skills. The value of $p$, in contrast, is quite sensitive to this correlation. This reflects the fact that $r_{EF\text{-}IQ,IQ\text{-}11}$ is exogenously determined. It implies that as much as half the correlation between cognitive skill and educational attainment may be explained by the fact that both are determined by unmeasured features of the home environment.

Using these estimates of $p$ and $q$, we can now extend the causal model in Figure B–4 to include adult test scores ($AFQT$). This model is shown in Figure B–5. The paths from IQ and education to $AFQT$ scores are calculated directly from the correlations in Table B–2 and are the same as those shown in Figure B–2. In addition, we have entertained the possibility

FIGURE B–4

*Model of Sources of Resemblance between Brothers' IQ Scores and Educational Attainments, Assuming Brothers Do Not Influence One Another*

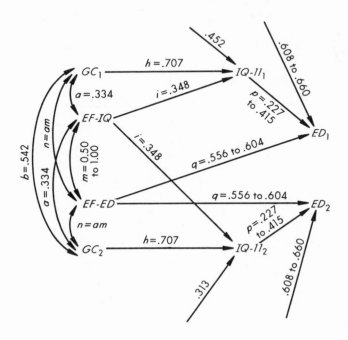

that genetically determined characteristics exert some direct influence on adult cognitive skill, over and above their influence on test scores at age 11. We have no empirical basis for determining whether or not this hypothesis is correct. The implications of accepting it do, however, deserve brief comment.

If we reject the idea that genes exert a continuing influence on cognitive growth, the correlation between genotype and adult test scores will inevitable be lower than the correlation between genotype and scores at 11. The heritability will also be lower. If there is no direct path from genotype to *AFQT* (i.e. $v = 0$ in Figure B–5), the heritability of *AFQT* scores in this model will range from $0.72h^2$ to $0.79h^2$. Since we assume that $h^2 = 0.50$ for white nonfarm men, the implied heritability of *AFQT* scores will be 0.36 to 0.395. This estimate is consistent with our argument that the amount of schooling people get influences their test scores more than does the quality of their schooling. If that is true, the range of environmental variation among 11 year olds is effectively less than among older men, since 11 year olds have all had about the same amount of schooling.

The analytic model used in the first section of Appendix A assumed that $h$, $e$, and $s$ were the same for adults and children, i.e. that $v > 0$. If we assume that $v = 0$ and that the heritability of adult scores is lower than the heritability of children's scores, the estimates in Appendix A would have to be slightly modified by not assuming that all values of $h$ are equal. We

FIGURE B–5

*Determinants of Early IQ Scores, Educational Attainment, and Adult Test Scores*

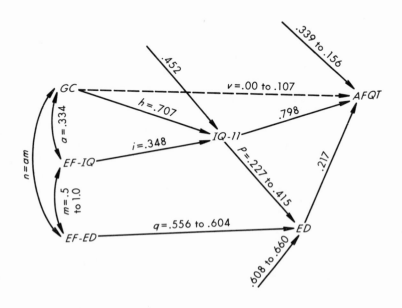

have not done this. If $p = 0.227$ (our "low" estimate), we need $v = 0.107$ to make the heritability of *AFQT* scores as high as the heritability of 11 year old IQ scores. If $p = 0.414$ (our "high" value), we need $v = 0.077$ to make the heritabilities equal. Note that if we assume $v = 0.107$, genotype, early scores, and educational attainment explain 97 percent of the variance in *AFQT* scores. This seems unlikely. We will, however, estimate the relationship between IQ, genotype, and other variables both on the assumption that the heritability of adult scores is 0.50 (i.e. that $v \cong 0.107$) and on the assumption that it is 0.36 to 0.39 (i.e. that $v = 0$).

FIGURE B–6

*Sources of Resemblance between Brothers' Occupational Statuses*

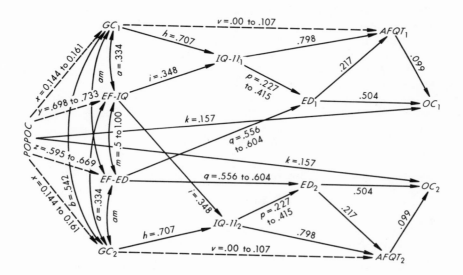

Figure B–6 extends our analysis to include occupational status. Note that we have not created a new hypothetical variable, *EF-OC,* to describe the combination of family background characteristics that make brothers' occupational statuses alike. The correlation between brothers' occupational statuses can be almost completely explained on the basis of similarities in their educational attainment, cognitive skill, and father's occupation, without resorting to hypothetical variables. The implied correlation between brothers' occupational statuses in Figure B–6 ranges from 0.304 to 0.315, depending on our estimates of $m$ and $v$. The true correlation is estimated as 0.320 or less (see Table B–2 and note $r$ to Table B–1). Inventing variables to explain this discrepancy seems superfluous.

A second feature of Figure B–6 also requires comment. We have introduced father's occupation into this model to explain part of the resemblance between brothers' statuses. We have also estimated the effect of father's occupation on each of our three hypothetical variables: genotype (*GC*), family environment as it affects IQ scores ($EF\text{-}IQ$), and family environment as it affects educational attainment ($EF\text{-}ED$). Father's occupation accounts for only part of the correlation between these hypothetical variables. The actual correlations are shown with double-headed arrows. The effects of father's occupation are shown with dashed lines. (This model is presented in a way that differs from the usual conventions of path analysis and should be used with caution.)

In order to estimate the path from father's occupation to son's genotype ($x$ in Figure B–6), we assume:

$$x = r_{POPOC,GC} = r_{POPOC,GF}\, r_{GF,GC} \tag{3}$$

where $r_{POPOC,GF}$ is the correlation between father's occupation and father's genotype, and $r_{GF,GC}$ is the correlation between father's genotype and son's genotype. From Figure A–1 in Appendix A we know that $r_{GF,GC} = g + gp = g(1 + r_{IQF,IQM}\, r^2_{IQ,GC})$, where $r_{IQF,IQM}$ is the correlation between spouses' scores, and $r_{IQ,GC}$ is the correlation between an individual's test scores and his genotype. From Table B–2 of this appendix, $r_{IQ,GC} = 0.823$, and we have estimated $r_{IQF,IQM}$ at 0.543. We have estimated $g$ at 0.36, so $r_{GF,GC} = 0.493$. We also assume $r_{POPOC,GF} = r_{OC,GC}$. Thus, we have:

$$x = 0.493 r_{OC,GC} \tag{3a}$$

From Figure B–6, we also have:

$$r_{OC,GC} = .504 r_{ED,GC} + .099 r_{AFQT,GC} + .157x \tag{4}$$

Substituting $0.493 r_{OC,GC}$ for $x$, we get:

$$r_{OC,GC} = .504 r_{ED,GC} + .099 r_{AFQT,GC} + .077 r_{OC,GC} \tag{4a}$$

or

$$r_{OC,GC} = .546 r_{ED,GC} + .107 r_{AFQT,GC} \tag{4b}$$

We can derive $r_{ED,GC}$ and $r_{AFQT,GC}$ from Figure B–6. The implied values are shown in Table B–3. Using these values we can derive $r_{OC,GC}$, the implied values of which are also shown in Table B–3. Substituting these values into equation (3a), we obtain values of $x$ between 0.144 (if $m = 1$ and $v = 0$) and 0.161 (if $m = 0.50$ and $v = 0.107$).

TABLE B–3

*Estimated Correlations between IQ Genotype and Other Traits*

| | Correlation of Genotype with | | | | |
| --- | --- | --- | --- | --- | --- |
| | IQ–11 | Education | AFQT | Occupation | Income |
| If $m=1$ and $v=0$ | .823 | .389 | .741 | .292 | .220 |
| $m=.75$ and $v=0$ | .823 | .414 | .747 | .306 | .226 |
| $m=.50$ and $v=0$ | .823 | .435 | .751 | .319 | .232 |
| $m=1$ and $v=.107$ | .823 | .389 | .848 | .304 | .240 |
| $m=.75$ and $v=.092$ | .823 | .414 | .838 | .316 | .244 |
| $m=.50$ and $v=.079$ | .823 | .435 | .830 | .326 | .246 |

We also need to estimate $y$ and $z$, the paths from father's occupation to *EF-IQ* and *EF-ED*. To do this we write two additional equations:

$$r_{POPOC,IQ-11} = yi + xh \tag{5}$$

and

$$r_{POPOC,ED} = zq + pr_{POPOC,IQ-11} \tag{6}$$

Using $x = 0.144$ to .161, $h = 0.707$, $i = 0.348$, $q = 0.566$ to 0.604, $p = 0.227$ to 0.415, $r_{POPOC,IQ} = 0.357$, and $r_{POPOC,ED} = 0.485$, equation (5) yields values of $y$ between 0.698 (if $m = 1$ and $v = 0$) and 0.733 (if $m = .50$ and $v = 0.107$). Equation (6) yields values of $z$ ranging from 0.669 (if $m = 1.00$) to 0.595 (if $m = 0.50$).

The estimated correlation between father's occupational status and the overall family environment, $y$, is surprisingly high (0.700 to 0.735). This is a by-product of the fact that the overall correlation between a father's status and a son's test scores is taken to be 0.357 and that only 30 percent of this ($xh = 0.102$ to 0.114) is accounted for by the genetic advantages of high-status children. This leaves 70 percent to be explained by family environment. Yet the total estimated effect of family environment, $i$, is only 0.348 in this model. Father's occupation must therefore be very highly correlated with the other family characteristics that influence IQ. The idea that father's occupation is the key determinant of a child's environment does not, however, receive much support from studies of adopted children (see sources in Appendix A, Table A–3). The reader should therefore treat our estimate of $y$ with some caution. Estimates of $r_{POPOC,IQ-11}$ vary substantially according to the type of test and the occupational classification system, and estimates of $i$ are subject to a multitude of vagaries described in Appendix A and earlier in this appendix. We may well have underestimated $i$ and overestimated $r_{POPOC,IQ-11}$. If we used a higher value for $i$, a lower value for the "within-family" variance in environment, and a higher value for $r_{IQSIBT}$, as we probably should, the correlation of father's occupation with the overall family environment would fall.

Figure B–7 extends our model to include income. It also eliminates the presumption of a causal connection between father's occupation and overall family environment and simply shows correlations between the two. This makes manipulations of the diagram more straightforward for those familiar with the conventions of path analysis, although it makes it less satisfactory as a causal model.

Since we have no data on the correlation between brothers' incomes, we cannot estimate the overall effect of family background on income. Given our findings about occupational status, however, we assume that the size of the estate left by parents is the only unmeasured family characteristic that has much direct effect on a son's income. Even inheritance is only important to 1 or 2 percent of the population (see Chapter 7). We therefore infer that the actual correlation between brothers would not be very different from the correlation implied by the path model in Figure B–7, which ranges from 0.119 (if $m = 0.50$ and $v = 0$) to 0.130 (if $m = 1$ and $v = 0.107$). For simplicity, we have presented Figure B–7 for a single individual rather

FIGURE B–7

*Relationships between Characteristics of White Nonfarm Men, Assuming Resemblance between Brothers Is Due Entirely to Family Environment*

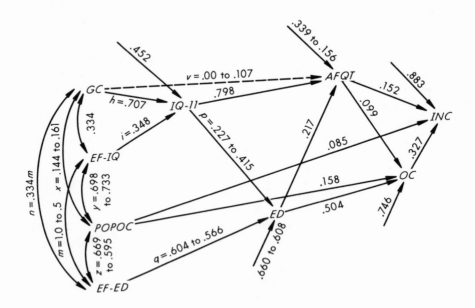

Note: Where two values are given on a path, the first value is derived by assuming $m = 1.0$ and $v = 0$, while the second is derived by assuming $m = 0.50$ and $v = 0.107$. Intermediate values of $m$ and $v$ produce intermediate values for all paths.

than for two brothers. Figure B–7 represents our best effort at describing the determinants of adult success in America, and it is used throughout the text as a basis for descriptive generalization.

There is, however, another alternative model that deserves brief discussion. Up to this point, we have been imputing all resemblance between brothers to common background factors. An alternative model assumes that resemblance between brothers is partly due to the direct effect of one brother on the other. Appendix A argued that if siblings had a direct effect on each other's test scores, siblings born close together should be more alike than siblings born further apart. Since this was not true, we inferred that siblings had relatively little influence on one another's test scores. This argument does not seem applicable to educational attainment, however. It is easy to imagine that older brothers serve as role models for younger brothers, and this could happen regardless of age disparities.

If brothers have a direct effect on one another, we must modify Figure B–4 by including a direct path, $t$, from one brother's education to the other's. Figure B–8 shows such a model. The subscript 1 is for older brothers while 2 is for younger brothers.

FIGURE B–8
*Model of Sources of Resemblance between Brothers'*
*Educational Attainments, Assuming Brothers Influence One Another*

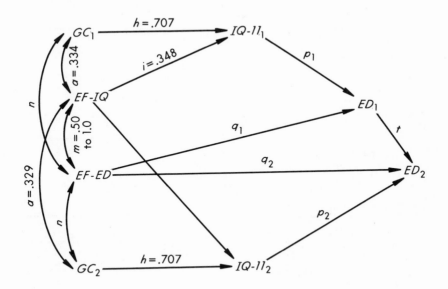

We can derive two relationships from Figure B–8:

$$r_{ED1,IQ1} = p_1 + q_1hn + q_1im \tag{7}$$

$$r_{ED2,IQ2} = p_2 + q_2hn + q_2im + tp_1r_{IQ1,IQ2} + tq_1hn + tq_1im \tag{8}$$

Setting $i + ha = 0.584$, $r_{IQ1,IQ2} = 0.566$, and assuming that $n = am$, we get:

$$r_{ED1,IQ1} = p_1 + 0.584q_1m \tag{7a}$$

$$r_{ED2,IQ2} = p_2 + 0.584q_2m + 0.566p_1t + 0.584q_1mt \tag{8a}$$

Thus, if $p_1 = p_2$, $q_1 = q_2$, and if $t$ is positive, $r_{ED2,IQ2}$ must be greater than $r_{ED1,IQ1}$. To obtain data on the actual correlation between early IQ scores and later educational attainment for older as against younger brothers, we compared the regression equations for older and younger brothers' educational attainments from Project Talent's follow-up on the high school class of 1961. These students were tested in the eleventh grade and followed up 6 years later—a year after they would normally have finished college if they had remained in school throughout the interval. The means, standard deviations, and correlations of the relevant variables are shown separately for older and younger brothers in Table B–4.

The correlations are lower than those in Tables B–1 and B–2 because the Project Talent data covers a restricted sample. The test scores are actually orthogonal factor scores, which accounts for the low correlation be-

TABLE B–4

*Means, Standard Deviations, and Correlations*
*for Older and Younger Brothers in Project Talent*

| Older Brothers (Unweighted *N*=3,675) | Mean | Standard Deviation | 1 | 2 | 3 | 4 | 5 |
|---|---|---|---|---|---|---|---|
| | | | | Correlations | | | |
| 1. Father's Education | 12.08 | 3.16 | 1.000 | | | | |
| 2. Father's Occupation | 36.71 | 18.96 | 0.493 | 1.000 | | | |
| 3. Verbal | 108.47 | 14.96 | 0.293 | 0.216 | 1.000 | | |
| 4. Math | 115.39 | 18.82 | 0.293 | 0.182 | 0.189 | 1.000 | |
| 5. Education at 22 | 14.15 | 1.89 | 0.317 | 0.283 | 0.371 | 0.500 | 1.000 |

| Younger Brothers (Unweighted *N*=2,704) | Mean | Standard Deviation | 1 | 2 | 3 | 4 | 5 |
|---|---|---|---|---|---|---|---|
| | | | | Correlations | | | |
| 1. Father's Education | 11.45 | 3.29 | 1.000 | | | | |
| 2. Father's Occupation | 33.73 | 19.06 | 0.459 | 1.000 | | | |
| 3. Verbal | 104.90 | 14.74 | 0.270 | 0.191 | 1.000 | | |
| 4. Math | 115.75 | 18.36 | 0.205 | 0.138 | 0.197 | 1.000 | |
| 5. Education at 22 | 14.13 | 1.90 | 0.342 | 0.311 | 0.384 | 0.445 | 1.000 |

Source: Project Talent eleventh grade sample, tested in 1960, followed up in 1966. Sample includes only first and second born males in families of two or more. Sample is *not* based on older and younger brothers in same family.

Variables: Father's occupation recoded using Duncan scores. Verbal is "Verbal Knowledges" factor score (see Lohnes, *Measuring Adolescent Personality*) from overall Project Talent battery. Math is a supposedly orthogonal factor score from same source. Education at 22 is the highest grade completed by respondents in 1966, or probable highest grade for those still in school, assuming those still in 4-year colleges will get an average of 15 years and those in graduate school will get 18 years.

tween them and other variables. The regression equations are:

$$ED_1 = 0.0378\ POPED_1 + 0.0123\ POPOC_1 + $$
$$0.0620\ MATH_1 + 0.0471\ VERBAL_1\ (R^2 = 0.353) \quad\quad (9)$$

$$ED_2 = 0.0765\ POPED_1 + 0.0154\ POPOC_1 + $$
$$0.0539\ MATH_1 + 0.0486\ VERBAL_1\ (R^2 = 0.344) \quad\quad (10)$$

The coefficients for *POPED*, *POPOC*, and *MATH* are significantly different at the 0.01 level. The coefficients for *VERBAL* are not significantly different.

The correlations between educational attainment and the two test scores in Table B–4 for younger brothers average 95 percent of those for older brothers. Let us, therefore, assume that $r_{ED2,IQ2} = 0.95\ r_{ED1,IQ1}$. The regression coefficients for the background measures in equation (10) average 164 percent of those in equation (9). Let us, therefore, assume that $q_2 = 1.64\ q_1$. The regression equations for the ability measures in equation (10) average 94.3 percent of those in equation (10). Let us, therefore, assume $p_2 = 0.943\ p_1$.

Substituting these values into equation (8a) we get:

$$0.95\, r_{ED1,IQ1} = 0.943p_1 + 0.928q_1m + 0.566p_1 + 0.584q_1mt \tag{8b}$$

Multiplying equation (7a) by 0.95 and subtracting (8b) from the result we get:

$$0 = 0.007p_1 - 0.373q_1m - 0.566p_1t - 0.584q_1mt \tag{11}$$

or

$$t = \frac{0.007p_1 - 0.373q_1m}{0.566p_1 + 0.584q_1m} \tag{11a}$$

Thus, $t$ must be negative for reasonable values of $p$ and $q$. This implies that brothers try to become unlike one another. We doubt if this inference is correct, but it is at least clear that the Project Talent data provides no support for the theory that older brothers have a strong positive influence on their younger brothers.

## Conclusions

The purpose of this appendix was to investigate the determinants of economic status for white nonfarm men. The precision of our estimates has been limited by the fact that we had to synthesize data from disparate sources and by the fact that we could not be sure whether unmeasured variables affected the observed relationships.

We began by examining the relationships among measurable variables. These relationships were summarized in Figure B–2. The most potentially misleading feature of Figure B–2 is probably the estimated effect of early IQ scores on later educational attainment. The path shown in Figure B–2 is 0.45. When we allow for the fact that educational attainment and IQ are both influenced by unmeasured variables that do not appear in Figure B–2, the estimated coefficient falls somewhat. The actual value of this path (shown as $p$ in Figures B–4 to B–7), may be as low as 0.225. Its value depends on the extent to which the factors causing resemblance between brothers' educational attainments are the same as the factors causing resemblance in brothers' test scores.

Having examined measurable variables, we tried to estimate the probable effect of several unmeasured variables, namely IQ genotype and family background. The magnitude of their effect depends on two factors: the effect of genotype on cognitive skills and the effect of cognitive skills on adult status. Both these estimates are subject to a considerable margin of error.

The effect of genotype on IQ scores is shown as $h$ in Figures B–4 to B–8. For white nonfarm males, our best estimate of $h^2$ was 0.50. This meant that our best estimate of $h$ was 0.71. We assumed, however, that our estimate of $h^2$ had a standard error of $\pm 0.10$, which means that our estimate of $h$ has a standard error of about $\pm 0.07$. This means we must entertain the possibility that $h$ is anywhere between 0.60 and 0.80. Our uncertainty is further increased by not having any information on the heritability of adult

TABLE B-5

*Compound Paths from IQ Genotype to Other Traits*
*Using Various Causal Models from Figure B-7*

|  | IQ-11 | Education | AFQT | Occupation | Income |
|---|---|---|---|---|---|
| If $m=1.00, v=0,$ | .707 | .161 | .600 | .140 | .137 |
| $m=.75, v=0,$ | .707 | .233 | .614 | .179 | .152 |
| $m=.50, v=0,$ | .707 | .293 | .628 | .210 | .164 |
| $m=1.00, v=0.107,$ | .707 | .161 | .707 | .151 | .157 |
| $m=.75, v=0.092,$ | .707 | .233 | .707 | .188 | .169 |
| $m=.50, v=0.079$ | .707 | .293 | .707 | .218 | .179 |

Source: Compound paths from $GC$ to relevant variable in Figure B-7.

test scores. If unequal exposure to schooling means that adults have been exposed to more variable environments than children, genotype will have relatively less effect on adult scores than on children's scores. The compound paths from genotype to $AFQT$ scores might therefore be as low as 0.51 (if the path from genotype to $IQ$-$11$ were 0.60 and if $m$ were 1.00, so that $p$ was 0.227). Alternatively, the paths from genotype to $AFQT$ scores might be as high as 0.80 (if we assume $h = 0.80$ and $v$ is greater than 0).

The effect of cognitive skill on adult status is also difficult to estimate. We do not know how much of the observed correlation between early test scores and educational attainment is due to the common influence of unmeasured family background characteristics on both educational attainment and IQ scores. This makes our estimates of the effect of cognitive skill on adult status problematic.

Nonetheless, we can at least set upper and lower limits on the probable effects of genotype on adult status. Table B-5 suggests such limits. Table B-5 is derived by calculating the compound paths from genotype to the relevant adult trait. The resulting coefficients indicate the effect of genotype holding family background constant. If our linear additive model is correct, this is equivalent to the effect of genotype on differences within families. Thus, the coefficients in Table B-5 estimate the average difference on various indices between two white nonfarm brothers whose genotypes differ by 1 standard deviation.

Table B-5 assumes that the heritability of test scores for native white nonfarm men is 0.50 and that $h = 0.707$. If $h \cong 0.60$, the estimated effects of genotype on other traits will be reduced about 15 percent. If $h \cong 0.80$, the estimated effects of genotype will be increased about 13 percent. (These estimates are not exact, since changing our estimate of $h^2$ from 0.50 to 0.36 or 0.64 would require a number of other changes in the model.) A 1 standard deviation difference between brothers' genotypes thus implies an average difference of 0.14 to 0.33 standard deviations in the brothers' educational attainments, a difference of 0.12 to 0.25 standard deviations in their occupational statuses, and a difference of 0.12 to 0.20 standard deviations in their incomes.

# APPENDIX C

## A Layman's Guide to Statistical Terms

This appendix tries to provide a layman's explanation of four statistical concepts used in the text: the standard deviation, the coefficient of variation, the correlation coefficient, and explained variance.

STANDARD DEVIATION

Imagine three different ways of dividing up $25,000 among five people.

|          | A     | B     | C     |
|----------|-------|-------|-------|
| person 1 | 5,000 | 4,000 | 1,000 |
| person 2 | 5,000 | 4,500 | 4,000 |
| person 3 | 5,000 | 5,000 | 5,000 |
| person 4 | 5,000 | 5,500 | 6,000 |
| person 5 | 5,000 | 6,000 | 9,000 |

The mean for each group is $5,000. Nonetheless, the distributions are clearly different. Distribution A is clearly more equal than Distribution C. The standard deviation (S.D.) provides a way of describing the degree of inequality.

The standard deviation is calculated by finding out how much each individual deviates from the mean of the distribution. We can calculate these deviations by subtracting the mean for the whole distribution from each individual's value. Thus, in our 3 income distributions the deviations are:

|          | A | B       | C       |
|----------|---|---------|---------|
| person 1 | 0 | −1,000  | −4,000  |
| person 2 | 0 | − 500   | −1,000  |
| person 3 | 0 | 0       | 0       |
| person 4 | 0 | 500     | 1,000   |
| person 5 | 0 | 1,000   | 4,000   |

For reasons too complicated to explain here, a standard deviation is calculated by squaring each deviation, taking the "sum of squares," dividing by the number of individuals, and taking the square root of the resulting "mean square."

$$\text{S.D. (Group A)} = \sqrt{\frac{(0)^2 + (0)^2 + (0)^2 + (0)^2 + (0)^2}{5}} = 0$$

$$\text{S.D. (Group B)} = \sqrt{\frac{(-1,000)^2 + (500)^2 + (0)^2 + (500)^2 + (1,000)^2}{5}} = 707$$

S.D. (Group C) =

$$\sqrt{\frac{(-4,000)^2 + (-1,000)^2 + (0)^2 + (100)^2 + (4,000)^2}{5}} = 2,608$$

Differences in the sizes of the standard deviation allow us to say that one distribution is more equal or unequal than another. They also give us a numerical measure of the degree of inequality.

### COEFFICIENT OF VARIATION

Sometimes we can compare distributions by looking only at standard deviations. We said, for example, that Distribution C was more unequal than Distribution B merely by looking at the 2 standard deviations. Sometimes, however, looking only at standard deviations is misleading. Knowing that the standard deviation of income was $4,000 in 1940 and $6,000 in 1970, for example, does not necessarily mean that inequality increased between 1940 and 1970. It may merely mean that there was a lot of inflation. In order to compare 1940 to 1970, we need to know the mean of the distribution. We can then calculate the "coefficient of variation"—the ratio of the standard deviation to the mean—in order to make our comparisons. Suppose, for example, that mean income was $6,000 in 1940 and $10,000 in 1970. Then the coefficient of variation for 1940 would be 4,000/6,000 = 0.667. The coefficient for 1960 would be 6,000/10,000 = 0.600. This would mean that, according to our definition, inequality had decreased by 10 percent, because (0.667 − 0.600)/0.667 = 10.0.

We can also compare the amount of inequality in distributions of different things, as long as both variables have real rather than arbitrary values. This book talks about 2 variables—educational attainment and income—which have real values, i.e., dollars of income and years of schooling. We talk about 2 other variables—test scores and occupational status—whose means and standard deviations are established by an arbitrary convention. The average IQ score, for example, is defined as 100. Occupational status is usually defined in such a way that the mean is just over 40. An IQ score of 120 is high relative to other people, but we cannot say that someone who scores 120 is "20 percent smarter" than a person with an average IQ score. Scores can be used to rank people, but they cannot be used to say whether people's cognitive skills are more unequal than their incomes. The same is true of status scores. It makes sense to compare coefficients of variation for real variables, and we do so in the chapters on years of schooling and income. It also makes some sense to compare the coefficient of variation for IQ scores in one group to the coefficient in another group, assuming the 2 groups have taken the same test and that the test was scored the same way for both. (Since the means are presumed to be the same, comparing coefficients of variation for IQ is like comparing standard deviations. If the means are not the same, the comparison becomes very dangerous.) However, it makes no sense to compare the coefficient of variation for IQ scores to the coefficient for anything else, including other tests of cognitive skills. For example, IQ tests have an arbitrary mean of 100 and a standard deviation of 15. SAT tests have an equally arbitrary mean of 500 and a standard deviation of 100. To say that because of this decision the distribution of SAT scores is less equal than the distribution of IQ scores is absurd.

USES OF THE STANDARD DEVIATION

We can use standard deviations to estimate the number of people who fall at certain places in a distribution, e.g. the number who have IQ scores above 120, the number who have incomes below $3,000, and so forth. To do this, however, we must usually assume that things are "normally distributed." This is a statistical term for a specific distribution in which most people fall in the middle and a few people fall at the extremes. Suppose, for example, that you stop 500 men on the street and measure their height. The shortest might be 5 feet tall, the tallest might be 7 feet tall. You would be very surprised, however, if more than 1 or 2 men were close to 7 feet, or if more than 1 or 2 were only 5 feet, even though you would not be at all surprised if there were many men around 6 feet tall. The distribution of heights would probably look something like what is shown in Figure C–1. Since many things are more or less normally distributed, and since normal distributions have convenient statistical properties, we often treat variables as if they were normally distributed, even when they really are not.

FIGURE C–1

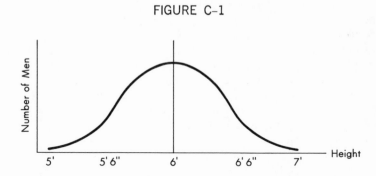

The distinctive feature of a normal distribution is that the percentage of people who fall in any given interval is always the same when the intervals are expressed in standard deviations. These percentages are shown in Figure C–2. If something is normally distributed, 68 percent of the population falls within 1 standard deviation of the mean. IQ scores, for example, have a mean of 100 and a standard deviation of 15. This means that 68 percent of the population has scores between 85 $(100-15)$ and 115 $(100+15)$. Moreover, we can convert any given score to a percentile equivalent:

An IQ score of 120 is 1.33 standard deviations above the mean, since

FIGURE C–2

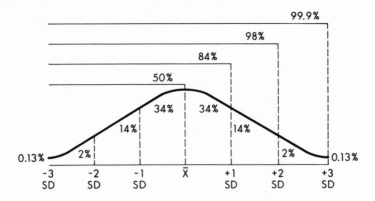

$(120 - 100)/15 = 1.33$. A score that is 1.33 standard deviations above the mean is in the ninety-first percentile (i.e. above 91 percent of the population). A score of 98 is in the forty-fifth percentile.

If something is normally distributed, the difference between the top and bottom fifth of the distribution or between random individuals can also be expressed in terms of the standard deviation. The top fifth of a normal distribution averages 1.4 standard deviations above the mean; the bottom fifth averages 1.4 standard deviations below the mean. Thus, the top fifth of the IQ distribution has an average score of $100 + (1.4)(15) = 121$ and the bottom fifth has an average score of $100 - (1.4)(15) = 79$. The difference is 42 IQ points, or 2.8 standard deviations $(42/15 = 2.8)$. The difference between random individuals is equal to $2/\sqrt{\pi} = 1.13$ standard deviations. Thus, random individuals differ by 17 IQ points.

We use all these methods—standard deviations, percentiles, differences between top and bottom fifths, differences between random individuals—to describe many different kinds of inequality. The validity of the *description* does not depend on the distributions being normal. The validity of some of our *estimates* does, however, depend on their being normal. Thus estimates that deal with educational attainment tend to be quite accurate, since the distribution is quite normal. Estimates that deal with income may be less accurate because the distribution is skewed and the degree of skewness varies.

CORRELATION COEFFICIENTS

Correlation coefficients range from −1.0 to +1.0. The closer the coefficient is to +1.0 or −1.0, the stronger is the relationship between variables. The closer it is to 0, the weaker the relationship. Positive correlations indicate that high values of one variable are associated with high values of the other. Negative correlations indicate that low values of one variable are associated with high values of the other. The size of the coefficient tells us how well we can predict one thing if we know another.

A correlation coefficient also allows us to estimate the average value of a variable if we know the value of another variable. In addition, it tells us how much inequality there is in one variable if the other is held constant. To understand how this works, let us consider some examples.

First, let us suppose we know people's shoe sizes and that we want to predict their IQ scores. If we had information on both IQ scores and shoe sizes for 50 individuals and plotted the information on a graph, it might look something like Figure C–3.

FIGURE C–3

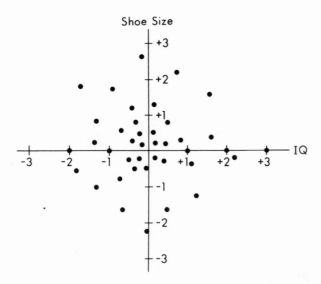

Figure C–3 indicates that IQ and shoe size are not related. People with size 9 shoes have about the same average IQ as people with size 12 shoes. Furthermore, the range of IQ scores for people with the same size shoe is about the same as the range for the population as a whole. (In this graph, as in others, we have used "standardized" scores, i.e. we have transformed all shoe sizes by subtracting the mean and dividing by the standard deviation. This creates a mean of 0 and a standard deviation of 1.)

If we calculated the correlation coefficient for the distribution, we would find that it was very close to 0. This would tell us several things:

1. There is no observable association between IQ and shoe size.

2. There is as much variation in IQ at each level of shoe size as there is in the whole sample. The standard deviation of IQ for size 7, 9, or 13 is equal to the standard deviation of the entire sample.

3. The best predictor of IQ for an individual is the mean IQ for the group. The best predictor of shoe size is mean shoe size. Knowing shoe size adds nothing to our ability to predict IQ, and vice versa.

Now let us consider a very different case. Suppose we looked at the relationship between adults' shoe sizes in one year and their shoe sizes the preceding year. In almost every case, these 2 measures would be the same. If we plotted standard scores on a graph similar to the one we used before, we would find that the graph would look like Figure C–4. If there were no cases in which shoe size changed from year *A* to year *B* (or if

FIGURE C–4

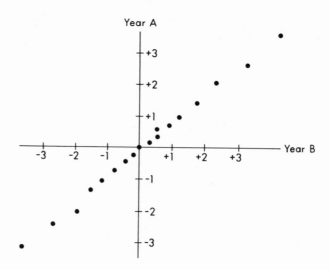

everyone's shoe size changed exactly the same amount), the correlation co-efficient would be 1.0. If there were a minute number of changes the correlation might be 0.98 or 0.99. A correlation of 1.00 tells us:

1. An individual's shoe size is perfectly predicted by his shoe size the previous year, and vice versa.
2. The standard deviation of present shoe size for those who had equal shoe sizes the previous year is 0.

There are, of course, almost no correlations in the social world that are equal to 1.0. There is almost always some variation in one variable among people who are the same with respect to another variable. Such associations, in which knowing one variable tells you something but not everything about the other variable, are represented by correlation coefficients that fall between 0 and ±1.0.

To illustrate, let us look at Figure C–5 which represents an imperfect association between, let us say, IQ and occupational status. Suppose we calculate the mean status of individuals who are 1 standard deviation above the mean on IQ and then for the group who are 2 standard deviations above the mean. The graph shows that an increase of 1 standard deviation in IQ is associated with an average increase of about 0.5 standard deviations in

FIGURE C–5

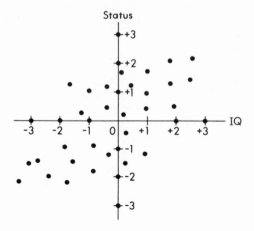

occupational status. If we looked at the graph from the opposite point of view, we would see that a 1 standard deviation increase in status was associated with an increase of 0.5 standard deviations in average IQ. More generally, a correlation coefficient of 0.XX means that people who differ by 1 standard deviation on one variable (e.g. by 15 IQ points) will differ by an average of 0.XX standard deviations on the other variable.

EXPLAINED VARIANCE

A second way of looking at the correlation coefficient is as a measure of the accuracy with which we can predict one variable if we know another. Our graph shows, for example, that there is less inequality in status at a given IQ level than there is in the population as a whole. The people who are 2 standard deviations above the mean on IQ are almost all concentrated above the mean on status. The people whose IQ's fall 2 standard deviations below the mean almost all have statuses below the mean. The correlation coefficient tells us how much restriction we can expect in the range of statuses among people with the same IQ score. Without trying to explain why it should be so, we can simply say that the square of the correlation coefficient (in this case $0.5^2 = 25$ percent) is the percentage of "variance" in one variable "explained" by the other. The rest of the variance (in this case $1 - 0.25 = 75$ percent) is "unexplained" by the other. The standard deviation of status scores for people with the same IQ will average out to be the square root of the unexplained variance (i.e., $\sqrt{.75} = 0.87$), multiplied by the standard deviation of the overall population (i.e. $0.87 \times 15 = 13$).

We can summarize the meaning of a correlation coefficient of, say, 0.5, by 3 propositions:

1. A correlation coefficient of 0.5 between 2 measures means that if individuals differ by 1 standard deviation on either of the 2 measures, they

will differ by an average of 0.5 standard deviations on the other measure. Some will differ by more, some by less.

2. A correlation coefficient of 0.5 means that if people are the same on 1 of 2 measures, their scores on the other measure will have a standard deviation that is $\sqrt{1 - 0.5^2} = 87$ percent of the overall standard deviation for the entire population.

3. A correlation coefficient of 0.5 means that if we compare random pairs of individuals and find that they differ by a specified amount on one measure, we can expect that, on the average, differences on the other measure will "explain" $0.5^2 = 25$ percent of this difference. This does not, of course, mean that differences in the second measure really cause 25 percent of the observed difference on the first. It merely tells us that if the relationship were causal, and if there were no other complicating factors, the second measure would cause 25 percent of the observed differences. Putting it the other way round, we can say that a correlation of 0.5 means that $1 - 0.5^2 = 75$ percent of the difference between random individuals on the first measure, caused by factors that are uncorrelated with the second measure.

CHOICE OF STATISTICS

How data is presented makes a big difference in how important a problem seems to be. As an example, consider the following statements about the relationship of parental status and years of schooling, all of which are more or less true:

1. Eighty-seven percent of those high school seniors whose parents make more than $15,000 a year enter college, while only 20 percent of those whose parents make under $3,000 per year do so.

2. Individuals whose parents are in the top fifth of the income distribution receive, on the average, 14 years of schooling, while those whose parents are in the bottom fifth receive an average of 10 years of schooling.

3. The correlation of years of schooling with parental income is probably about 0.43.

4. If an individual is 1 standard deviation above the mean in terms of parental income and at the mean in terms of IQ, he will be 0.30 standard deviations above the mean in terms of schooling.

5. Parental income explains 9 percent of the variance in years of schooling, independent of IQ.

The first statement might give a reader the impression that the problem was very large. The last statement might give a quite different impression. Since all 5 statements are correct, it is hard to say whether the "big problem" response is more appropriate than the "trivial problem" response. We have presented our data in a number of different ways, but it should be clear that the problem of interpretation remains a large one.

# REFERENCES

Acland, Henry. "The Effects of Schooling in the Elementary Grades." Harvard Center for Educational Policy Research, 1972.

———. "Social Determinants of Educational Achievement: An Evaluation and Criticism of Research." Ph.D. thesis in progress, Oxford University.

———. "Streaming in British Junior Schools." Harvard Center for Educational Policy Research, 1972.

Adjutant General's Office, Classification and Replacement Branch, Personnel Research Section. "The Army General Classification Test." *Psychological Bulletin* 42 (1945): 760–768.

Alexander, C. Norman, Jr., and Campbell, Ernest Q. "Peer Influences on Adolescent Educational Aspirations and Attainments." *American Sociological Review* 29 (August 1964): 568–575.

Alker, Hayward, and Russet, Bruce. "On Measuring Inequality." *Behavioral Science* 9 (July 1964): 207–218.

Alkin, Marvin C., and Benson, Charles S. "Economy of Scale in the Production of Selected Educational Outcomes." *Administrator's Notebook* 16 (May 1968).

Anderson, John E. "The Limitations of Infant and Preschool Tests in the Measurement of Intelligence." *Journal of Psychology* 8 (Oct. 1939): 351–379.

Armor, David. "The Racial Composition of Schools and College Aspirations of Negro Students." In U.S. Commission on Civil Rights, *Racial Isolation in the Public Schools*. Vol. 2. Washington, D.C.: U.S. Government Printing Office, 1967.

———. "School and Family Effects on Black and White Achievement: A Reexamination of the USOE Data." In *On Equality of Educational Opportunity*, edited by Frederick Mosteller and Daniel P. Moynihan. New York: Random House, 1972.

———. "The Evidence on Busing." *The Public Interest*, Summer 1972, pp. 90–126.

Ashenfelter, Orley. "Changes in Labor Market Discrimination Over Time." *Journal of Human Resources* 5 (Fall 1970): 403–430.

Astin, Alexander W. "College Dropouts: A National Profile." *American Council on Education Research Reports*, vol. 7, no. 1, 1972.

———. " 'Productivity' of Undergraduate Institutions." *Science* 136 (April 13, 1962): 129–135.

———. "Undergraduate Achievement and Institutional 'Excellence.' " *Science* 161 (August 16, 1968): 661–668.

**359**

Averch, Harvey; Carroll, Stephen; Donaldson, Theodore; Kiesling, Herbert; and Pincus, John. "How Effective is Schooling? A Critical Review and Synthesis of Research Findings." Santa Monica: The Rand Corporation, 1972.

Bajema, Carl Jay. "Estimation of the Direction and Intensity of Natural Selection in Relation to Human Intelligence By Means of the Intrinsic Rate of Natural Increase." *Eugenics Quarterly* 10 (December 1963): 175–187.

———. "Relation of Fertility to Educational Attainment in a Kalamazoo Public School Population: A Follow-up Study." *Eugenics Quarterly* 13 (1966): 306–315.

———. "A Note on the Interrelations Among Intellectual Ability, Educational Attainment, and Occupational Achievement: A Follow-up Study of a Male Kalamazoo Public School Population." *Sociology of Education* 41 (Summer 1968): 317–319.

Barkai, Haim. "The Kibbutz As Social Institution." *Dissent,* Spring 1972, pp. 354–370.

Baron, Harold M. "Race and Status in School Spending: Chicago, 1961–1966." *Journal of Human Resources* 6 (Winter 1970):1–24.

Bayley, Nancy. "Consistency and Variability in the Growth of Intelligence from Birth to 18 Years." *The Pedagogical Seminary and Journal of Genetic Psychology* 75 (December 1949): 165–196.

———. "Learning in Adulthood: The Role of Intelligence." In *Analyses of Concept Learning,* edited by Herbert J. Klausmeier and Chester W. Harris. New York: Academic Press, 1966.

———. "Research in Child Development: A Longitudinal Perspective." *Merrill-Palmer Quarterly of Behavioral Development* 11 (July 1965): 183–208.

Becker, Gary S. *Human Capital.* New York: National Bureau of Economic Research, Columbia University Press, 1964.

Benson, Charles S. et al. "State and Local Fiscal Relationships in Public Education in California." Report of the Senate Fact-Finding Committee on Revenue and Taxation. Sacramento: Senate of the State of California, 1965.

Benson, Viola E. "The Intelligence and Later Scholastic Success of Sixth Grade Pupils." *School and Society* 55 (February 1942): 163–167.

Bereiter, Carl. "An Academic Preschool for Disadvantaged Children: Conclusions from Evaluation Studies." Paper presented at Hyman Blumberg Memorial Symposium on Research in Early Childhood Education, Johns Hopkins University, 1971.

Berg, Ivar E. *Education and Jobs: The Great Training Robbery.* New York: Praeger, 1970.

Bergmann, Barbara R., and Lyle, Jerolyn R. "The Occupational Standing of Negroes by Areas and Industries." *Journal of Human Resources* 5 (Fall 1971): 411–433.

Bissell, Joan S. "The Cognitive Effects of Pre-School Programs for Disadvantaged Children." Unpublished Ed.D. thesis, Harvard Graduate School of Education, 1970.

Blau, Peter, and Duncan, Otis Dudley. *The American Occupational Structure.* New York: John Wiley, 1967.

Blauner, Robert. "Work Satisfaction and Industrial Trends in Modern Society." In *Labor and Trade Unionism,* edited by Walter Galenson and Seymour Martin Lipset, pp. 339–360. New York: John Wiley, 1960.

Blewett, D. B. "An Experimental Study of the Inheritance of Intelligence." *Journal of Mental Science* 100 (October 1954): 922–933.

Bloom, Benjamin Samuel. *Stability and Change in Human Characteristics.* New York: John Wiley, 1964.

————. "The 1955 Normative Study of the Test of General Educational Development." *School Review* 64 (March 1956): 110–124.

Blum, Zahava, and Coleman, James S. "Longitudinal Effects of Education on the Incomes and Occupational Prestige of Blacks and Whites." Baltimore: Johns Hopkins University Center for the Study of Social Organization of Schools, June 1970.

Bowles, Samuel. "Schooling and Inequality from Generation to Generation." *Journal of Political Economy* 80 (May/June 1972): S219–S251.

Bowles, Samuel, and Levin, Henry M. "The Determinants of Scholastic Achievement—An Appraisal of Some Recent Evidence." *Journal of Human Resources* 3 (Winter 1968): 3–24.

————. "More on Multicollinearity and the Effectiveness of Schools." *Journal of Human Resources* 3 (Summer 1968): 393–400.

Boyd, J. "Project Head Start—Summer 1966, Section 2: Facilities and Resources of Head Start Centers." Princeton: Educational Testing Service, 1966.

Boyle, Richard P. "On Neighborhood Context and College Plans, 3." *American Sociological Review* 31 (October 1966): 706–707.

————. "The Effect of the High School on Students' Aspirations." *American Journal of Sociology* 71 (May 1966): 628–639.

Bradway, Katherine, P., and Thompson, Clare W. "Intelligence at Adulthood: A Twenty-five Year Follow-Up." *Journal of Educational Psychology* 53 (February 1962): 1–14.

Bradway, Katherine P.; Thompson, Clare W.; and Cravens, Richard B. "Preschool IQ's After 25 Years." *Journal of Educational Psychology* 49 (October 1958): 278–281.

Break, George F. "Income Taxes and Incentives to Work." *American Economic Review* 47 (September 1957): 529–549.

Brown, Ralph R. "The Time Interval Between Test and Re-Test in its Relation to the Constancy of the Intelligence Quotient." *Journal of Educational Psychology* 24 (February 1933): 81–96.

Bruck, H. W. "Results of a Study of Patterns of Discrimination in Budget Allocations to Elementary Schools in the Chicago School District." Cambridge: Massachusetts Institute of Technology, Urban Systems Laboratory, 1971.

Budd, Edward C., and Radner, Daniel B. "The OBE Size Distribution Series: Methods and Tentative Results for 1964." *American Economic Review* 59 (May 1969): 435–449.

Burkhead, Jesse; Fox, Thomas G.; and Holland, John W. *Input and Output in Large City High Schools.* Syracuse: Syracuse University Press, 1967.

Burks, Barbara S. "The Relative Influence of Nature and Nurture Upon Mental Development: A Comparative Study of Foster Parent–Foster Child Resemblance and True Parent–True Child Resemblance." *27th Yearbook of the National Society for the Study of Education,* pt. 1, pp. 219–316. Bloomington: Public School Publishing Co., 1928.

Burrows, James C. "Some Determinants of High School Educational Achievement." Mimeographed. Washington, D.C.: Bureau of the Budget, October 1966.

Burt, Sir Cyril. "Ability and Income." *British Journal of Educational Psychology* 13 (June 1943): 83–98.

———. "The Genetic Determination of Differences in Intelligence: A Study of Monozygotic Twins Reared Together and Apart." *British Journal of Psychology* 57 (May 1966): 137–153.

———. "Inheritance of General Intelligence." *American Psychologist* 27 (March 1972): 175–190.

———. "Quantitative Genetics in Psychology." *The British Journal of Mathematical and Statistical Psychology* 24 (May 1971): 1–21.

Burt, Sir Cyril, and Howard, Margaret. "The Multifactorial Theory of Inheritance and Its Application to Intelligence." *British Journal of Statistical Psychology* 9 (November 1956): 95–131.

Cain, Glen G., and Watts, Harold W. "Problems in Making Policy Inferences from the Coleman Report." *American Sociological Review,* 35 (April 1970): 228–242.

Campbell, Ernest Q., and Alexander, Norman C. "Structural Effects and Interpersonal Relationships." *American Journal of Sociology* 71 (November 1965): 284–289.

Centers, Richard. *The Psychology of Social Classes.* Princeton: Princeton University Press, 1949.

Chamberlin, Dean; Chamberlin, Enid; Drought, Neal E.; and Scott, William E. *Did They Succeed in College? The Follow-up Study of the Graduates of the Thirty Schools. Adventures in American Education,* vol. 4, New York: Harper, 1942.

Chase, Clinton, and Pugh, Richard C. "Social Class and Performance on an Intelligence Test." *Journal of Educational Measurement* 8 (Fall 1971): 197–202.

Chomsky, Noam. "The Fallacy of Richard Herrnstein's I. Q." *Social Policy,* May 1972.

Claudy, John G. "Educational Outcomes." In Flanagan, John C. et al., *Five Years After High School,* Palo Alto: Project Talent, American Institutes for Research and University of Pittsburgh, 1971.

Clem, O. M., and Dodge, S. B. "The Relationship of High School Leadership and Scholarship to Post-school Success." *Peabody Journal of Education* 10 (1933): 321–329.

Cohen, David K. "Children and Their Primary Schools: Vol. 2." *Harvard Educational Review* 38 (Spring 1968): 329–340.

Cohen, David K.; Pettigrew, Thomas F.; and Riley, Robert. "Race and the Outcomes of Schooling." In *On Equality of Educational Opportunity,* edited by Frederick Mosteller and Daniel P. Moynihan. New York: Random House, 1972.

Cohn, Elchanan. "Economies of Scale in Iowa High School Operations." *Journal of Human Resources* 3 (Fall 1968): 422–434.

Coleman, James S. *The Adolescent Society: The Social Life of the Teenager and its Impact on Education.* New York: The Free Press of Glencoe, 1961.

———. "Equality of Educational Opportunity: Reply to Bowles and Levin." *Journal of Human Resources* 3 (Spring 1968): 237–246.

———. "The Evaluation of Equality of Educational Opportunity." In *On Equality of Educational Opportunity,* edited by Frederick Mosteller and Daniel P. Moynihan. New York: Random House, 1972.

———. "Reply to Cain and Watts." *American Sociological Review* 35 (April 1970): 242–249.

Coleman, James S. et al. *Equality of Educational Opportunity.* Washington, D.C.: U.S. Government Printing Office, 1966.

Conlisk, John. "A Bit of Evidence on the Income–Education–Ability Interaction." *Journal of Human Resources* 6 (Summer 1971): 358–362.

Connecticut Citizens for the Public Schools. "A Study of Factors Related to Academic Achievement in Public Schools." Hartford, 1957.

Conrad, Herbert S., and Jones, Harold E. "A Second Study of Familial Resemblance in Intelligence: Environmental and Genetic Implications of Parent–Child and Sibling Correlations in the Total Sample." *39th Yearbook of the National Society for the Study of Education,* pt. 2, pp. 97–141. Bloomington: Public School Publishing Co., 1940.

Coons, John E. "Chicago." In U.S. Commission on Civil Rights, *Civil Rights USA: Public Schools North and West.* Washington, D.C.: U.S. Government Printing Office, 1962.

Coons, John E.; Clune, William H.; and Sugarman, Stephen D. *Private Wealth and Public Education.* Cambridge: Harvard University Press, 1970.

Corrazzini, Arthur J. et al. "Study of Higher Education, Metro 2." Mimeographed. Boston: Tufts University, 1969.

Crain, Robert L. *The Politics of School Desegregation.* Chicago: Aldine Publishing Co., 1968.

———. "School Integration and the Academic Achievement of Negroes." *Sociology of Education* 44 (Winter 1971): 1–26.

———. "School Integration and Occupational Achievement of Negroes." *American Journal of Sociology,* 75 (January 1970): 593–606.

Crandall, James Henry. "A Study of Academic Achievement and Expenditures on Instruction." Ed.D. Dissertation, University of California, Berkeley, 1961.

Crow, J. F., and Felsenstein, J. "The Effect of Assortative Mating on the Genetic Composition of a Population." *Eugenics Quarterly* 15 (June 1968): 85–97.

Crowley, John J. "High School Backgrounds of Successful Men and Women Graduates." *School Review* 48 (March 1940): 205–209.

Cutright, Phillips. "Achievement, Military Service and Earnings." Mimeographed. Bloomington: University of Indiana, 1972.

———. "Occupational Inheritance: A Cross-National Analysis." *American Journal of Sociology* 73 (January 1968): 400–416.

Daniere, Andre. "Social Class Competition in American Higher Education." Boston: Boston College Institute of Human Sciences, Xerox, 1971.

Davenport, K. S., and Remmers, H. H. "Factors in State Characteristics Related to Average A-12 V-12 Test Scores." *Journal of Educational Psychology* 41 (February 1950): 110–115.

Davis, James A. "The Campus as A Frog Pond: An Application of the Theory of Relative Deprivation to Career Decisions of College Men." *American Journal of Sociology* 72 (July 1966): 17–31.

DeCecco, John P. "Class Size and Co-ordinated Instruction." *British Journal of Educational Psychology* 34 (February 1964): 65–74.

Deck, Leland P. "Buying Brains by the Inch." *Journal of the College and University Personnel Association* 19 (May 1968): 33–37.

DeGroot, A. D. "War and the Intelligence of Youth." *Journal of Abnormal and Social Psychology* 46 (October 1951): 596–597.

Denison, Edward F. *Why Growth Rates Differ.* Washington, D.C.: Brookings Institution, 1967.

Domas, Simeon J., and Tiedeman, David V. "Teacher Competence: An Annotated Bibliography." *Journal of Experimental Education* 19 (December 1950): 101–218.

Douglas, James W. B.; Ross, J. M.; and Simpson, H. R. *All Our Future.* London: Peter Davies, 1968. Mimeographed appendices available from author, London School of Economics.

Dreeben, Robert. *On What Is Learned in Schools.* Reading, Mass.: Addison-Wesley, 1968.

Dugan, Willes E. "Follow-up Study of Gifted High School Graduates." In *Talent and Education,* edited by Ellis P. Torrance. Minneapolis: University of Minnesota Press, 1960.

Duncan, Beverly. "Trends in Output and Distribution of Schooling." In *Indicators of Social Change,* edited by E. B. Sheldon and Wilbert E. Moore. New York: Russell Sage Foundation, 1968.

Duncan, Otis Dudley. "Ability and Achievement." *Eugenics Quarterly* 15 (March 1968): 1–11.

———. "Discrimination Against Negroes." *Annals of the American Academy of Political and Social Science* 371 (May 1967): 85–103.

———. "Inheritance of Poverty or Inheritance of Race?" In *On Understanding Poverty: Perspectives from the Social Sciences,* edited by Daniel P. Moynihan. New York: Basic Books, 1968.

———. "Path Analysis: Sociological Examples." *American Journal of Sociology* 72 (July 1966): 1–16.

———. "Properties and Characteristics of the Socioeconomic Index." In Albert J. Reiss, *Occupations and Social Status.* New York: Free Press, 1961.

————. "A Socioeconomic Index for All Occupations." In Albert J. Reiss, *Occupations and Social Status*. New York: Free Press, 1961.

Duncan, Otis Dudley, and Featherman, David L. "Psychological and Cultural Factors in the Process of Occupational Achievement." Ann Arbor: Population Studies Center, University of Michigan, 1971.

Duncan, Otis Dudley; Featherman, David L; and Duncan, Beverly. *Socioeconomic Background and Occupational Achievement: Extensions of a Basic Model*. Washington, D.C.: U.S. Office of Education, Bureau of Research, Final Report, Project No. 5–0074 (EO–191), Contract No. OE–5–85–072, 1968.

Duncan, Otis Dudley; Haller, Archibald O.; and Portes, Alejandro. "Peer Influences on Aspirations: A Reinterpretation." *American Journal of Sociology* 74 (September 1968): 119–137.

Duncan, Otis Dudley, and Hodge, Robert W. "Education and Occupational Mobility: A Regression Analysis." *American Journal of Sociology* 68 (May 1963): 629–644.

Eckland, Bruce K. "Genetics and Sociology: A Reconsideration." *American Sociological Review* 32 (April 1967): 173–194.

Ekstrom, Ruth B. *Experimental Studies of Homogeneous Grouping*. Princeton: Educational Testing Service, 1959.

Erickson, E. "A Study of the Normative Influence of Parents and Friends." In Wilbur Brookover et al., *Self-Concept of Ability and School Achievement*, vol. 3, Cooperative Research Project 2831. East Lansing: Human Learning Research Institute, Michigan State University, 1967.

Erlenmeyer-Kimling, L., and Jarvik, Lissy F. "Genetics and Intelligence: A Review." *Science* 142 (December 13, 1963): 1477–1479.

Eysenck, H. J., and Prell, D. B. "The Inheritance of Neuroticism: An Experimental Study." *Journal of Mental Science* 97 (July 1951): 441–465.

Falconer, Douglas S. "Genetic Consequences of Selection Pressure." In *Genetic and Environmental Factors in Human Ability*, edited by James E. Meade and A. S. Parkes. Edinburgh, London: Oliver & Boyd, 1966.

————. *Introduction to Quantitative Genetics*. New York: Ronald Press, 1960.

Finch, F. H. "A Study of the Relation of Age Interval to Degree of Resemblance of Siblings in Intelligence." *Pedagogical Seminary and Journal of Genetic Psychology* 43 (December 1933): 389–403.

First National City Bank of New York. "Public Education in New York City." New York: November 1969.

Flanagan, John C., and Cooley, William W. *Project Talent: One Year Follow-up Studies*. Pittsburgh: University of Pittsburgh, Project Talent, 1966.

Flanagan, John C., and Jung, Steven M. "Progess in Education: A Sample Survey, 1960–1970." Palo Alto, Project Talent, American Institutes for Research, 1971.

Flanagan, John C. et al. *The American High School Student*. Pittsburgh: University of Pittsburgh, Project Talent, 1964.

Fleming, Charlotte M. "Class Size as a Variable in the Teaching Situation." *Educational Research* 1 (February 1959): 35–48.

Floud, Jean, and Halsey A. H. "Intelligence Tests, and Selection for Secondary Schools." *British Journal of Sociology* 8 (March 1957): 33.

Fogel, Walter. "The Effect of Low Educational Attainment on Incomes: A Comparative Study of Selected Ethnic Groups." *Journal of Human Resources* 1 (Fall 1966): 22–40.

Folger, John K., and Nam, Charles B. *Education of the American Population* (A 1960 Census Monograph). Washington, D.C.: U.S. Government Printing Office, 1967.

———. "Trends in Education in Relation to the Occupational Structure." *Sociology of Education* 38 (Fall 1964): 19–33.

Fox, Thomas G., and Miller, S. M. "Economic, Political and Social Determinants of Mobility: An International Cross-Sectional Analysis." *Acta Sociologica,* 9 (1966): 76–93.

Freeman, Frank N.; Holzinger, Karl J.; and Mitchell, Blythe C. "The Influence of Environment on the Intelligence, School Achievement, and Conduct of Foster Children." *27th Yearbook of the National Society for the Study of Education,* pt. 1, pp. 103–217. Bloomington: Public School Publishing Co., 1928.

Freeman, Roger A. *Financing the Public Schools.* Washington, D.C.: Institute for Social Science Research, 1960.

Friedman, Milton. *A Theory of the Consumption Function,* Princeton: Princeton University Press, 1957.

Fulk, Bryon E., and Harrell, Thomas W. "Negro-White Army Test Scores and Last School Grade." *Journal of Applied Psychology* 36 (February 1952): 34–35.

Gage, Nathaniel L., ed. *Handbook of Research on Teaching.* Chicago: Rand McNally, 1963.

Garms, Walter. "A Benefit-Cost Analysis of the Upward Bound Program." *Journal of Human Resources* 6 (Spring 1971): 206–220.

Garvey, George. "Inequality of Income: Causes and Measurement," *Studies in Income and Wealth* 15 (1952): 27–47.

Gawkoski, R. S. "The Use of Community Characteristics for Obtaining Local Norms on Standardized Achievement Tests." Ph.D. dissertation, Columbia University, 1955.

Gerard, Harold, and Miller, Norman. "Factors Contributing to Adjustment and Achievement in Racially Desegregated Schools." Los Angeles: Department of Psychology, University of California at Los Angeles, 1971.

Ghiselli, Edwin E. "The Validity of Commonly Employed Occupational Tests." *University of California Publications in Psychology* 5 (May 1949): 253–288.

Gintis, Herbert. "Education and the Characteristics of Worker Productivity." *American Economic Review* 61 (May 1971): 266–279.

———. "Towards a Political Economy of Education:A Radical Critique of Ivan Illich's *De-Schooling Society.*" *Harvard Educational Review* 42 (February 1972): 70–97.

Gittell, Marilyn. *New York City School Fact Book*. Flushing, N.Y.: Institute for Community Studies, Queens College, 1971.

Goldberg, Miriam L.; Justman, Joseph; and Passow, A. Harry. *The Effects of Ability Grouping*. New York: Horace Mann–Lincoln Institute of School Experimentation, Teachers College, Columbia University, 1966.

Goldsmith, Selma P. "Changes in the Size Distribution of Income." *American Economic Review* 47 (May 1957): 504–518.

Goldsmith, Selma P.; Jaszi, George; Kaitz, Hyman; and Liebenberg, Maurice. "Size Distribution of Income since the Mid-Thirties." *Review of Economics and Statistics* 36 (1954): 1–32.

Goodman, Paul. *Compulsory Mis-education*. New York: Horizon Press, 1964.

Goodman, Samuel M. "The Assessment of School Quality." Albany: New York State Education Department, 1959.

Gorseline, Donald E. *The Effect of Schooling upon Income*. Bloomington: 1932.

Gray, Susan W., and Klaus, Rupert A. "An Experimental Preschool Program for Culturally Deprived Children." *Child Development* 36 (1965): 887–898.

Greeley, Andrew, and Rossi, Peter. *The Education of Catholic Americans*. Chicago: Aldine, 1966.

Green, Robert L. et al. "The Educational Status of Children in a District without Public Schools." Cooperative Research Project 2321. Washington, D.C.: U.S. Office of Education, 1964.

Grubb, W. Norton, and Michelson, Stephan. "States and Schools: The Political Economy of School Resource Inequities." Harvard Center for Educational Policy Research, work in progress, 1972.

Guilford, J. P. "The Structure of Intelligence." In Dean K. Whitla, *Handbook of Measurement and Assessment in Behavioral Sciences*. Boston: Addison–Wesley, 1968.

Gurin, Gerald; Veroff, J.; and Feld, Sheila. *Americans View Their Mental Health*. New York: Basic Books, 1960.

Guthrie, James W. "A Survey of School Effectiveness Studies." In *Do Teachers Make a Difference?*, edited by Alexander Mood. Washington, D.C.: U.S. Office of Education, 1970.

Guthrie, James W. et al. *Schools and Inequality*. Cambridge: Massachusetts Institute of Technology Press, 1971.

Haller, A., and Butterworth, C. "Peer Influences on Levels of Occupational and Educational Aspirations." *Social Forces* 38 (May 1960): 289–295.

Hanna, F. A. "The Accounting Period and the Distribution of Income." *Studies in Income and Wealth* 9 (1948): 155–256.

Hanoch, Gioria. "An Economic Analysis of Earnings and Schooling." *Journal of Human Resources* 2 (Summer 1967): 310–329.

Hansen, W. Lee. "Total and Private Rates of Return to Investment in Schooling." *Journal of Political Economy* 71 (April 1963): 128–140.

Hansen, W. Lee, and Weisbrod, Burton A. *Benefits, Costs, and Finance of Public Higher Education*. Chicago: Markham, 1969.

Hanushek, Eric. "The Education of Blacks and Whites." Ph.D. dissertation, Department of Economics, Massachusetts Institute of Technology, 1968.

———. "Teacher Characteristics and Gains in Student Achievement: Estimation Using Micro-Data." *American Economic Review* 61 (May 1971): 280–288.

Hanushek, Eric, and Kain, John F. "On the Value of *Equality of Educational Opportunity* as a Guide to Public Policy." In *On Equality of Educational Opportunity,* edited by Frederick Mosteller and Daniel P. Moynihan. New York: Random House, 1972.

Harnqvist, K. "Relative Changes in Intelligence from 13 to 18." *Scandinavian Journal of Psychology* 9 (1968): 50–82.

Harrell, Thomas W., and Harrell, Margaret S. "Army General Classification Test Scores for Civilian Occupations." *Educational and Psychological Measurement* 5 (Autumn 1945): 229–239.

Hart, Hornell. "Correlations Between Intelligence Quotients of Siblings." *School and Society* 20 (September 1924): 382.

Hause, John C. "Ability and Schooling as Determinants of Lifetime Earnings, or If You're So Smart Why Aren't You Rich?" *American Economic Review* 61 (May 1971): 289–304.

Hauser, Robert M. "Schools and the Stratification Process." *American Journal of Sociology* 74 (May 1969): 587–611.

Havemann, Ernest, and West, Patricia Salter. *They Went to College: The College Graduate in America Today.* New York: Harcourt Brace, 1952.

Hayes, Donald P., and Grether, Judith. "The School Year and Vacations: When Do Students Learn?" Washington, D.C.: The Urban Institute, 1969.

Henson, Mary F. "Trends in the Income of Families and Persons in the United States: 1947–1964." Washington, D.C.: U.S. Bureau of the Census, Technical Paper 17, 1967.

Hermalin, Albert Isaac. "The Homogeneity of Siblings on Education and Occupation." Ph.D. thesis, Princeton University, 1969.

Heron, Alexander R. *Why Men Work.* Stanford: Stanford University Press, 1948.

Herriot, Robert. "Some Social Determinants of Educational Aspiration." *Harvard Educational Review* 33 (Spring 1963): 157–177.

Herriot, Roger A., and Miller, Herman P. "Who Paid Taxes in 1968?" Paper prepared for the National Industrial Conference Board, New York Meeting, March 18, 1971.

Herrman, Louis, and Hogben, Lancelot. "The Intellectual Resemblance of Twins." *Proceedings of the Royal Society of Edinburgh* 53 (1932–1933): 105–129.

Herrnstein, Richard. "IQ." *The Atlantic Monthly,* September 1971, pp. 43–64.

Heyns, Barbara. "Curriculum Assignment and Tracking Policies in Forty-Eight Urban Public High Schools." Ph.D. dissertation, University of Chicago, 1971.

Hieronymus, A. N. "Achievement in the Basic Skills as Related to Size of School and Type of Organization." School of Education, State University of Iowa, Iowa City, 1960.

Higgins, J. V.; Reed, E. W.; and Reed, S. C. "Intelligence and Family Size: A Paradox Resolved." *Eugenics Quarterly* 9 (June 1962): 84–90.

Hildreth, Gertrude. "The Resemblance of Siblings in Intelligence and Achievement." *Contributions to Education,* no. 186. New York: Teacher's College, 1925.

Hochbaum, Godfrey; Darley, John G.; Monachesi, E.D.; and Bird, Charles. "Socioeconomic Variables in a Large City." *American Journal of Sociology* 61 (July 1955): 31–38.

Hodge, Robert W. "The Status Consistency of Occupational Groups." *American Sociological Review* 27 (June 1962): 336–343.

Hodge, Robert W.; Siegel, Paul M. "The Classification of Occupations: Some Problems of Sociological Interpretation." *American Statistical Association, Proceedings of the Social Statistics Section,* 1966, pp. 176–192.

————. *Occupational Prestige in the United States,* forthcoming.

Hodge, Robert W.; Siegel, Paul M.; and Rossi, Peter H. "Occupational Prestige in the United States, 1925–63." *American Journal of Sociology* 70 (November 1964): 286–302.

Hodge, Robert W.; Treiman, Donald; and Rossi, Peter H. "A Comparative Study of Occupational Prestige." In *Class, Status and Power,* edited by Reinhard Bendix and Seymour Martin Lipset. New York: Free Press, 1966.

Holland, John L., and Lutz, Sandra W. "Predicting a Student's Vocational Choice." *American College Testing Program, Research Report,* no. 18, Iowa City, March 1967.

Holzinger, Karl J. "The Relative Effect of Nature and Nurture Influences on Twin Differences." *Journal of Educational Psychology* 20 (April 1929): 241–248.

Honzik, Marjorie P. "Developmental Studies of Parent-Child Resemblance in Intelligence." *Child Development* 28 (June 1957): 215–228.

Honzik, Marjorie P.; Macfarland, J. W.; and Allen, L. "The Stability of Mental Test Performance between Two and Eighteen Years." *Journal of Experimental Education* 17 (December 1948): 309–324.

Hoyt, Donald. "The Relationship between College Grades and Adult Achievement: A Review of the Literature." *American College Testing Program, Research Report,* no. 7. Iowa City, September 1965.

Hsia, Jayjia. "Integration in Evanston, 1967–1971: A Longitudinal Evaluation." Evanston, Illinois: Educational Testing Service, August 1971.

Hu, Teh-Wei; Lee, Maw Lin; and Stromsdorfer, Ernst W. "Economic Returns to Vocational and Comprehensive High School Graduates." *Journal of Human Resources* 6 (Winter 1971): 25–50.

Hunt, Shane. "Income Determinants for College Graduates and the Return to Educational Investment." *Yale Economic Essays* 3 (Fall 1963): 305–357.

Husén, Torsten. "The Influence of Schooling upon IQ." *Theoria* 17 (1951): 61–88.

—————. *International Study of Achievement in Mathematics.* New York: John Wiley, 1967.

—————. *Psychological Twin Research, 1, A Methodological Study.* Stockholm: Almqvist and Wiksell, 1959.

—————. "Talent, Opportunity, and Career: A Twenty-Six-Year Follow Up." *School Review* 76 (June 1968): 190–209.

Illich, Ivan. *De-Schooling Society.* New York: Harper and Row, 1971.

Jencks, Christopher S. "The Coleman Report and the Conventional Wisdom." In *On Equality of Educational Opportunity,* edited by Frederick Mosteller and Daniel P. Moynihan. New York: Random House, 1972.

—————. "Student Achievement in Desegregated Elementary Schools: A Further Analysis of the Equality of Educational Opportunity Survey." Harvard Center for Educational Policy Research, 1972.

—————. "The Effects of High Schools on Their Students." Harvard Center for Educational Policy Research, 1972.

—————. "The Quality of the Data Collected by the Equality of Educational Opportunity Survey." In *On Equality of Educational Opportunity,* edited by Frederick Mosteller and Daniel P. Moynihan. New York: Random House, 1972.

Jencks, Christopher, S., and Riesman, David. *The Academic Revolution.* New York: Doubleday, 1968.

Jensen, Arthur R. "Estimation of the Limits of Heritability of Traits by Comparison of Monozygotic and Dizygotic Twins." *Proceedings of the National Academy of Science* 58 (1967): 149–156.

—————. "How Much Can We Boost IQ and Scholastic Achievement?" *Harvard Educational Review* 39 (1969): 1–123.

—————. "IQ's of Identical Twins Reared Apart. *Behavior Genetics* 1 (1970): 133–146.

Jinks, J. L., and Fulker, D. W. "Comparison of the Biometrical Genetical, MAVA, and Classical Approaches to the Analysis of Human Behavior." *Psychological Bulletin* 73 (May 1970): 311–349.

Johnston, John. *Econometric Methods.* New York: McGraw-Hill, 1963.

Jones, F. Lancaster. "Occupational Achievement in Australia and the United States: A Comparative Path Analysis." *American Journal of Sociology* 77 (November 1971): 527–539.

Jones, Harold Ellis. "A First Study of Parent-Child Resemblance in Intelligence." *27th Yearbook of the National Society for the Study of Education,* pt. 1, pp. 61–72. Bloomington: Public School Publishing Co., 1928.

—————. "Intelligence and Problem Solving." In *Handbook of Aging and the Individual,* edited by James E. Birren. Chicago: University of Chicago Press, 1959.

Juel-Nielson, N. "Individual and Environment: A Psychiatric-Psychological Investigation of Monozygous Twins Reared Apart." *Acta Psychiatrica et Neurologica Scandinavica,* Monograph Supplement 183, Copenhagen, Munksgaard, 1965.

Karpinos, Bernard D. "The Mental Qualification of American Youths for Military Service and its Relationship to Educational Attainment." *Proceedings of the American Statistical Association, Social Statistics Section*, 1966.

Katz, Irwin, and Greenbaum, Charles. "Effects of Anxiety, Threat and Racial Environment on Task Performance of Negro College Students." *Journal of Abnormal and Social Psychology* 66 (June 1963): 562–567.

Katzman, Martin T. "Distribution and Production in a Big City Elementary School System." Ph.D. dissertation, Economics Department, Yale University, 1967.

———. *The Political Economy of Urban Schools*. Cambridge: Harvard University Press, 1971.

Kemp, Leslie C. D. "Environmental and Other Characteristics Determining Attainments in Primary Schools." *British Journal of Educational Psychology* 25 (June 1965): 67–77.

Kiesling, Herbert J. "High School Size and Cost Factors." Washington, D.C.: U.S. Office of Education, Bureau of Research, Project 6–1590, March 1968.

———. "Measuring a Local Government Service: A Study of School Districts in New York State." *Review of Economics and Statistics* 49 (August 1967): 356–367.

Klatzky, Sheila R., and Hodge, Robert W. "A Canonical Correlation Analysis of Occupational Mobility." *Journal of the American Statistical Association* 66 (March 1971): 16–22.

Klineberg, Otto. *Negro Intelligence and Selective Migration*. New York: Columbia University Press, 1935.

Kolko, Gabriel. *Wealth and Power in America*. New York: Praeger, 1962.

Kornhauser, Arthur. *Detroit as the People See It*. Detroit: Wayne University Press, 1952.

Krauss, Irving. "Sources of Educational Aspirations Among Working Class Youth." *American Sociological Review* 19 (December 1964): 867–879.

Kravis, Irving B. *The Structure of Income*. Philadelphia: University of Pennsylvania Press, 1962.

Kreitlow, Burton W. "Long Term Study of Educational Effectiveness of Newly Formed Centralized School Districts in Rural Areas." Washington, D.C.: Educational Resources Information Center, USOE Cooperative Research Project, no. 375.

———. "Long Term Study of Educational Effectiveness of Newly Formed Centralized School District in Rural Areas, pt. 2." Washington, D.C.: Educational Resources Information Center, USOE Cooperative Research Project, no. 1318.

Kuznets, Simon. *Shares of Upper Income Groups in Income and Savings*. New York: National Bureau of Economic Research, 1953.

Lamson, Edna E. "To What Extent Are Intelligence Quotients Increased by Children Who Participate in a Rich, Vital School Curriculum?" *Journal of Educational Psychology* 29 (January 1938): 67–70.

Lansing, John B.; Lorimer, Thomas; and Moriguchi, Chikashi. *How Peo-*

*ple Pay for College.* Ann Arbor: University of Michigan, Survey Research Center, 1960.

Lazerson, Marvin. *Origins of the Urban School: Public Education in Massachusetts, 1870–1915.* Cambridge: Harvard University Press, 1971.

———. "Social Reform and Early Childhood Education: Some Historical Perspectives." *Urban Education* 2 (April 1970): 84–102.

Leahy, Alice M. "Nature-Nurture and Intelligence." *Genetic Psychology Monographs* 17 (August 1935): 236–308.

———. "A Study of Certain Selective Factors Influencing Prediction of the Mental Status of Adopted Children." *The Pedagogical Seminary and Journal of Genetic Psychology* 41 (December 1932): 294–329.

Leech, Don R. "Scholarship and Success in Later Life." *School Review* 38 (March 1930): 222–226.

Lennon, R. T. "Prediction of Academic Achievement and Intelligence from Community and School-System Characteristics." Ph.D. thesis, Columbia University, 1952.

Lesser, Gerald S.; Fifer, Gordon; and Clark, Donald H. "Mental Abilities of Children from Different Social Class and Cultural Groups." *Monographs of the Society for Research in Child Development,* vol. 30, no. 4, 1965.

Levin, Henry. "A Cost-Effectiveness Analysis of Teacher Selection." *Journal of Human Resources* 5 (Winter 1970): 24–33.

———. "A New Model of School Effectiveness," In *Do Teachers Make a Difference?,* edited by Alexander Mood, USOE, 1970.

Lewinski, Robert J. "Vocabulary and Mental Measurement: A Quantitative Investigation and Review of Research." *The Pedagogical Seminary and Journal of Genetic Psychology* 72 (June 1948): 247–281.

Li, C. C. *Population Genetics.* Chicago: University of Chicago Press, 1955.

Light, Richard J., and Smith, Paul V. "Social Allocation Models of Intelligence: A Methodological Inquiry." *Harvard Educational Review* 39 (August 1969): 484–510.

Lindsay, Carl A., and Gottleib, David. "High School Racial Composition and Educational Aspirations." Mimeographed. Pennsylvania State University, 1969.

Lipset, Seymour Martin, and Bendix, Reinhard. *Social Mobility in Industrial Society.* Berkeley: University of California Press, 1959.

Lohnes, Paul R. *Measuring Adolescent Personality.* Pittsburgh: Project Talent, University of Pittsburgh, 1966.

Lorge, Irving. "The 'Last School Grade Completed' as an Index of Intellectual Level." *School and Society* 56 (November 1942): 529–531.

———. "The Prediction of Vocational Success." *Personnel Journal* 12 (1933): 189–197.

———. "Schooling Makes a Difference." *Teachers College Record* 46 (May 1945): 483–492.

McDavid, John W. "Innovations in Education of the Disadvantaged Child: What Have We Learned." Mimeographed. University of Miami, 1969.

McDill, Edward L., and Coleman, James. "High School Social Status, College Plans and Interest in Academic Achievement: A Panel Analysis." *American Sociological Review* 28 (December 1963): 905–918.

McDill, Edward L.; Rigsby, Leo C.; and Meyers, Edmund D. "Institutional Effects on the Academic Behavior of High School Students." *Sociology of Education* 40 (Summer 1967): 181–199.

McNemar, Quinn. *The Revision of the Stanford-Binet Scale: An Analysis of the Standardization Data.* Boston: Houghton-Mifflin, 1942.

———. "Special Review, Newman, Freeman, and Holzinger's Twins: A Study of Heredity and Environment." *Psychological Bulletin* 35 (1938): 237–249.

McPartland, James. "The Segregated Student in Desegregated Schools." Baltimore: Johns Hopkins University, Center for the Study of Social Organization of Schools, Report no. 21, June 1968.

Madsen, I. N. "Some Results with the Stanford Revision of the Binet-Simon Tests." *School and Society* 19 (1924): 559–562.

Mahan, Thomas W. "Project Concern—1966 to 1968." Hartford: Board of Education, 1968.

Marklund, Sixten. "Scholastic Attainments As Related to Size and Homogeneity of Classes." *Educational Research* 6 (November 1963): 63–67.

Martin, David, and Morgan, James. "Education and Income." *Quarterly Journal of Economics* 77 (August 1963): 423–437.

Mayeske, George W.; Tabler, Kenneth A.; Weinfeld, Frederic D.; and Proshek, John M. "Correctional and Regression Analyses of Differences between the Achievement Levels of Ninth Grade Schools from the Educational Opportunities Survey." Technical Note 61. Washington, D.C.: U.S. Office of Education, National Center for Educational Statistics, 1968.

Mayeske, George W.; Weinfeld, Frederic D.; and Beaton, Albert E. "Correlational and Factorial Analyses of Items from the Educational Opportunities Survey Teacher Questionnaire." USOE National Center for Educational Statistics. Technical Note 49. Washington, D.C.: U.S. Office of Education, National Center for Educational Statistics, 1968.

Mayeske, George W.; Weinfeld, Frederic D.; Beaton, Albert E.; David, Walter; Fetters, William B.; and Hixson, Eugene. "Item Response Analyses of the Educational Opportunities Survey Student Questionnaire." Technical Note 64. Washington, D.C.: U.S. Office of Education, National Center for Educational Statistics, 1968.

Mayeske, George W. et al. *A Study of Our Nation's Schools.* Washington, D.C.: U.S. Office of Education, 1969.

Mercer, Jane, and Brown, Wayne Curtis. "Racial Differences in IQ: Fact or Artifact." Xerox. Riverside: University of California, 1972.

Meyer, John W. "High School Effects on College Intentions." *American Journal of Sociology* 76 (July 1970): 59–70.

Michael, John A. "High School Climates and Plans for Entering College." *Public Opinion Quarterly* 25 (Winter 1961): 585–595.

Michelson, Stephan. "The Association of Teacher Resourceness with Children's Characteristics." In *Do Teachers Make a Difference?*, edited by Alexander Mood. Washington, D.C.: U.S. Office of Education, 1970.

————. "Equal Protection and School Resources." *Inequality in Education,* December 5, 1969, pp. 9–16.

————. "Principal Power." *Inequality in Education,* June 30, 1970, pp. 7–10.

Miller, Herman P. *Income Distribution in the United States* (A 1960 Census Monograph). Washington, D.C.: U.S. Government Printing Office, 1966.

————. "New Evidence Regarding the Understatement of Income in the Current Population Survey." *American Statistical Association, Proceedings of the Business and Economic Statistics Section,* 1962, pp. 25–28.

Miner, Jerry. *Social and Economic Factors in Spending for Public Education.* Syracuse: Syracuse University Press, 1963.

Miner, John B. *Intelligence in the United States.* New York: Springer, 1957.

Mollenkopf, William G., and Melville, Donald S. "A Study of Secondary School Characteristics As Related to Test Scores." Research Bulletin, 56-6. Princeton: Educational Testing Services, 1956.

Morgan, James N., and Smith, James D. "Measures of Economic Well-Offness and Their Correlates." *American Economic Review* 59 (May 1969): 450–462.

Morgan, James N.; David, Martin H.; Cohen, Wilbur J.; and Brazer, Harvey E. *Income and Welfare in the United States.* New York: McGraw-Hill, 1962.

Morris, Joyce. *Standards and Progress in Reading,* Slough, England: National Foundation for Educational Research in England and Wales, 1966.

Morse, Nancy, C. and Weiss, Robert. S. "The Function and Meaning of Work and The Job." *American Sociological Review* 20 (April 1955): 191–198.

Mosteller, Frederick, and Moynihan, Daniel P. eds. *On Equality of Educational Opportunity.* New York: Random House, 1972.

Moynihan, Daniel P. "The Schism in Black America." *The Public Interest,* Spring 1972, pp. 3–24.

Nachman, Marvin, and Opochinsky, Seymour. "The Effects of Different Teaching Methods: A Methodological Study." *Journal of Educational Psychology* 49 (October 1958): 245–249.

Nam, Charles B.; Rhodes, Lewis A.; and Herriot, Robert E. "School Retention by Race, Religion, and Socio-Economic Status." *Journal of Human Resources* 3 (Spring 1968): 171–190.

National Center for Educational Statistics. "Correlation and Regression Analyses of School Achievement for Schools of Varying Racial Composition." Xerox. Washington, D.C.: U.S. Office of Education, 1967.

National Education Association, Research Division. *Ability Grouping.* Research Summary 1968–S3. Washington, D.C.: 1968.

————. "Teacher Opinion Poll: Ability Grouping." *NEA Journal,* February 1968, p. 53.

————. "The Three R's Hold Their Own at the Mid Century." Washington, D.C.: National Education Association 1951.

National Society for the Study of Education. *39th Yearbook*. Bloomington: Public School Publishing Co., 1940.

Newman, H. H.; Freeman, F. N.; and Holzinger, K. J. *Twins: A Study of Heredity and Environment*. Chicago: Chicago University Press, 1937.

Nichols, Robert C. "The National Merit Twin Study." In *Methods and Goals in Human Behavior Genetics,* edited by Steven G. Vandenberg. New York: Academic Press, 1965.

Orshansky, Mollie. "Counting the Poor." *Social Security Bulletin* 28 (January 1965): 3–29.

Outhit, Marion Currie. "A Study of the Resemblance of Parents & Children in General Intelligence." *Archives of Psychology,* April 1933, no. 149, pp. 1–60.

Owen, John D. "The Distribution of Educational Resources in Large American Cities." *Journal of Human Resources* 7 (Winter, 1972): 171–190.

Owens, William A. "Age and Mental Abilities: A Longitudinal Study." *Genetic Psychology Monographs* 48 (1953): 3–54.

Panos, Robert J., and Astin, Alexander. "Attrition Among College Students." *American Council on Education Research Reports,* vol. 2, no. 4, 1967.

Payne, Arlene. "The Selection and Treatment of Data for Certain Curriculum Decision Problems: A Methodological Study." Ph.D. dissertation, University of Chicago, 1963.

Peaker, Gilbert F. *The Plowden Children Four Years Later*. Slough, England: National Foundation for Educational Research, 1971.

———. "The Regression Analysis of the National Survey." In Central Advisory Council for Education, *Children and Their Primary Schools,* vol. 2, appendix 4, London: Her Majesty's Stationery Office, 1967.

———. "Standards of Reading of 11-Year Olds." In Central Advisory Council for Education, *Children and Their Primary Schools,* vol. 2, appendix 7, London: Her Majesty's Stationery Office, 1967.

Pechman, Joseph. A. "The Rich, the Poor, and the Taxes They Pay." *The Public Interest,* Fall 1969, pp. 21–43.

Peterson, O. L.; Andrews, L. P.; Spain, R. S.; and Greenberg, B. G. "An Analytical Study of North Carolina General Practice." *Journal of Medical Education* 31 (1956): 1–165.

Piccariello, Harry. "Evaluation of Title I." Xerox. U.S. Office of Education, 1969.

Pritchard, Miriam C.; Horan, Kathryn M.; and Hollingworth, Leta S. "The Course of Mental Development in Slow Learners Under an 'Experience Curriculum.'" National Society for the Study of Education, *39th Yearbook,* pt. 2, pp. 245–254. Bloomington: Public School Publishing Co., 1940.

Public Education Association. "The Status of the Public School Education of Negro and Puerto Rican Children in New York." Mimeographed. New York, 1955.

Purl, Mabel, and Dawson, Judith. "The Achievement of Pupils in Desegregated Schools." Xerox. California: Riverside Unified School District, 1971.

Quinn, Robert P. "Survey of Working Conditions, 1969, Final Report on Univariate and Bivariate Tables." Ann Arbor: Survey Research Center, University of Michigan, 1970.

Rainwater, Lee. *It's a Living: Explorations in the Social Meaning of Low Incomes,* forthcoming.

Raymond, Richard. "Determinants of the Quality of Primary and Secondary Public Education in West Virginia." *Journal of Human Resources* 3 (Fall 1968): 450–470.

Reed, Ritchie, and Miller, Herman. "Some Determinants of the Variation in Earnings for College Men." *Journal of Human Resources* 5 (Spring 1970): 177–190.

Reiss, Albert J. *Occupations and Social Status.* New York: Free Press, 1961.

Reymert, Martin L., and Hinton, Ralph T. "The Effect of a Change to a Relatively Superior Environment upon the IQ's of One Hundred Children." In National Society for the Study of Education, *39th Yearbook,* pt. 2, pp. 255–268. Bloomington: Public School Publishing Company, 1940.

Rhodes, Lewis. "Dropouts and the Socio-Economic Composition of Schools in a Metropolitan System." *Social Science Quarterly* 49 (September 1968): 237–252.

Rice, J. M. "The Futility of the Spelling Grind." *The Forum* 23 (1897): 163–172.

Richards, James M., Jr.; Taylor, Calvin W.; and Price, Philip B. "The Prediction of Medical Intern Performance." *Journal of Applied Psychology* 46 (April 1962): 141–146.

Riew, John. "Economies of Scale in High School Operation." *Review of Economics & Statistics* 48 (August 1966): 280–287.

Riley, Robert T., and Cohen, David K. "Comparison or Conformity: The Effect of School Environments on Educational Aspirations." Harvard Center for Educational Policy Research, 1969.

Rist, Ray C. "Student Social Class and Teacher Expectations: The Self-Fulfilling Prophecy in Ghetto Education." *Harvard Educational Review* 40 (August 1970): 411–451.

Rogers, Daniel C. "Private Rates of Return of the United States." *Yale Economic Essays* 9 (Spring, 1969): 89–136.

Rogoff, Natalie. "Local Social Structure and Educational Selection." In A. H. Halsey, Jean Floud, and C. Arnold Anderson, *Education, Economy and Society.* New York: Free Press, 1961.

Rolfe, J. F. "The Measurement of Teaching Ability, Study Number Two." *Journal of Experimental Education* 14 (1945): 52–74.

Rosenshine, Barak. "The Stability of Teacher Effects Upon Student Achievement." *Review of Educational Research* 40 (December 1970): 647–662.

Rosteker, L. E. "The Measurement of Teaching Ability, Study Number One." *Journal of Experimental Education* 14 (1945): 6–51.

St. John, Nancy. "Desegregation and Minority Group Performance." *Review of Educational Research* 40 (February 1970):111–133.
―――. "Thirty-six Teachers: Their Characteristics, and Outcomes for Black and White Pupils." Xerox. Harvard Graduate School of Education, November 1970.
―――. "The Effects of School Desegregation on Children." Xerox. Harvard Graduate School of Education, 1972.
St. John, Nancy, and Lewis, Ralph. "The Influence of School Racial Context on Academic Achievement." Harvard Graduate School of Education. Xerox. 1970.
St. John, Nancy, and Smith, Marshall, "School Racial Composition, Achievement, and Aspiration." Harvard Center for Educational Policy Research, mimeo, 1969.
Scarr-Salapatek, Sandra. "Race, Social Class, and IQ." *Science* 174 (December 24, 1971): 1285–1295.
Schoenfeldt, Lyle. "Hereditary-Environmental Components of the Project Talent Two-Day Test Battery." *Measurement and Evaluation in Guidance* 1 (Summer 1968): 130–140.
Schrader, William B. "Test Data as Social Indicators." Princeton: Educational Testing Service, September 1968.
Schultz, Theodore W. "Capital Formation by Education," *Journal of Political Economy* 68 (December 1960): 571–583.
―――. "Education and Economic Growth." In *Social Forces Influencing American Education,* edited by N. B. Henry. Chicago: University of Chicago Press, 1961.
Schutz, Richard E. "A Factor Analysis of Educational Development in the United States." *Educational and Psychological Measurement* 16 (1956): 324–332.
Sewell, William H.; Haller, Archibald O.; and Ohlendorf, George W. "The Educational and Early Occupational Status Attainment Process: Replication and Revision." *American Sociological Review* 35 (December 1970): 1014–1027.
Sewell, William H., and Shah, Vimal P. "Socioeconomic Status, Intelligence, and the Attainment of Higher Education." *Sociology of Education* 40 (Winter 1967): 1–23.
Sewell, William, and Armer, Michael. "Neighborhood Context and College Plans." *American Sociological Review* 31 (April 1966): 159–168.
Sexton, Patricia. *Education and Income.* New York: Viking, 1961.
Shakow, David, and Goldman, Rosaline. "The Effect of Age on the Stanford-Binet Vocabulary Score of Adults." *Journal of Educational Psychology* 29 (April 1938): 241–256.
Shane, Harold G. "We Can Be Proud of the Facts." *The Nation's Schools* 60 (September 1957): 44–47.
Shannon, J. R. "The Post-School Careers of High-School Leaders and High-School Scholars." *School Review* 37 (November 1929): 656–665.
Shannon, J. R., and Farmer, James C. "The Correlation of High School

Scholastic Success with Later Financial Success." *School Review* 39 (February 1931): 130–133.

Shapiro, Sherman. "Some Socio-Economic Determinants of Expenditures for Education: Southern and Other States Compared." *Comparative Education Review* 6 (October 1962): 160–166.

Shaycoft, Marion F. *The High School Years: Growth in Cognitive Skills.* Pittsburgh: American Institutes for Research and University of Pittsburgh, Project Talent, 1967.

Shields, J. *Monozygotic Twins Brought Up Apart and Brought Up Together.* London: Oxford University Press, 1962.

Shuey, Audrey Mary. *The Testing of Negro Intelligence.* New York: Social Science Press, 1966.

Shutz, Robert R. "On the Measurement of Income Inequality." *American Economic Review* 41 (March 1951): 107–122.

Siegel, Paul. "Prestige in the American Occupational Structure." Ph.D. dissertation, University of Chicago, 1971.

Siegel, Paul M., and Hodge, Robert W. "A Causal Approach to the Study of Measurement Error." In Hubert M. Blalock and Ann B. Blalock, *Methodology in Social Research.* New York: McGraw-Hill, 1968.

Skodak, Marie. "Mental Growth of Adopted Children in the Same Family." *The Pedagogical Seminary and Journal of Genetic Psychology* 77 (1950): 3–9.

Skodak, Marie, and Skeels, Harold M. "A Final Follow-up Study of 100 Adopted Children." *The Pedagogical Seminary and Journal of Genetic Psychology* 75 (September 1949): 85–125.

Smith, Marshall S. "The Brookline Study." Harvard Center for Educational Policy Research, 1971.

———. "Equality of Educational Opportunity: The Basic Findings Reconsidered." In *On Equality of Educational Opportunity,* edited by Frederick Mosteller and Daniel P. Moynihan. New York: Random House, 1972.

———. "Equality of Educational Opportunity: Comments on Bowles and Levin." *Journal of Human Resources* 3 (Summer 1968): 384–389.

Smith, Marshall S., and Bissell, Joan. "Report Analysis: The Impact of Head Start." *Harvard Educational Review* 40 (February 1970): 51–104.

Smith, Paul V. "Models of the Determination of Intelligence." Ed.D. qualifying paper, Harvard Graduate School of Education, May 1970.

Sontag, Lester; Baker, Charles; and Nelson, Virginia. "Mental Growth and Personality: A Longitudinal Study." *Monographs of the Society for Research in Child Development* 32, no. 2 (1958): 1–143.

Stanley, Julian. "Predicting College Success of the Educationally Disadvantaged." *Science* 171 (February 19, 1971): 640–647.

Start, K. B., and Wells, B. K. "The Trend in Reading Standards." Slough, England: National Foundation for Educational Research, 1972.

Stearns, Marian Sherman. "The Effects of Preschool Programs on Children and Their Families." Xerox. Santa Monica: The Rand Corporation, 1971.

Stewart, Naomi. "AGCT Scores of Army Personnel Grouped by Occupation." *Occupations* 26 (1947): 5–41.

Stodolsky, Susan S., and Lesser, Gerald. "Learning Patterns in the Disadvantaged." *Harvard Educational Review* 37 (1967): 546–593.

Summers, Robert. "An Econometric Investigation of the Lifetime Size Distribution of Lifetime Average Annual Income." Cowles Foundation Discussion Paper 9. Summary in *Econometrica* 24 (July 1956): 346–347.

Super, Donald E., and Crites, John O. *Appraising Vocational Fitness by Means of Psychological Tests.* New York: Harper, 1962.

Taubman, P., and Wales, T. "Effects of Education and Mental Ability on Income: The Evidence from the Wolfe-Smith Data." National Bureau of Economic Research, November 1969.

Terman, Lewis Madison, and Oden, Meltita H. *The Gifted Group at Mid-Life.* Palo Alto: Stanford University Press, 1959.

Thomas, J. A. "Efficiency in Education: A Study of the Relationship Between Selected Inputs and Test Scores in a Sample of Senior High Schools." Ph.D. dissertation, School of Education, Stanford University, 1962.

Thompson, Claude E. "Selecting Executives by Psychological Tests." *Educational and Psychological Measurement* 7 (Winter 1947): 773–778.

Thorndike, Edward L. *Prediction of Vocational Success.* New York: The Commonwealth Fund, 1934.

Thorndike, Robert L. "Community Variables as Predictors of Intelligence and Academic Achievement." *Journal of Educational Psychology* 42 (October 1951): 321–338.

————. "Retest Changes in the IQ in Certain Superior Schools." In National Society for the Study of Education, *39th Yearbook,* pt. 2, pp. 351–362. Bloomington: Public School Publishing Co., 1940.

————. "The Effect of the Interval between Test and Retest on the Constancy of the I.Q." *Journal of Educational Psychology* 24 (October 1933): 543–549.

Thorndike, Robert L., and Hagen, Elizabeth. *10,000 Careers.* New York: John Wiley, 1959.

Thornhill, R. W., and Landis, Carney. "Extra-Curricular Activity and Success." *School & Society* 28 (July 1928): 117–120.

Thurow, Lester C., and Lucas, Robert E. B. "The American Distribution of Income: A Structural Problem." A study prepared for the use of the Joint Economic Committee, U.S. Congress. Washington, D.C.: U.S. Government Printing Office, March 17, 1972.

Traxler, Arthur E. "Reading Growth of Secondary School Pupils During a Five Year Period." *Educational Records Bulletin* 54 (July 1950): 96–107.

Trent, James W., and Medsker, Leland L. *Beyond High School.* Berkeley: Center for Research and Development in Higher Education, University of California, 1967.

Tuckman, Howard P. "High School Inputs and Their Contribution to School Performance." *Journal of Human Resources* 6 (Fall 1971): 490–509.

Tuddenham, Read D. "Soldier Intelligence in World Wars I and II." *American Psychologist* 3 (February 1948): 54–56.

Turner, Ralph H. *The Social Context of Ambition.* San Francisco: Chandler, 1964.

U.S. Bureau of the Census. *Current Population Reports.* Series P–20, no. 110. "School Enrollment, and Education of Young Adults and their Fathers: October, 1960," Washington, D.C.: U.S. Government Printing Office, 1961.

————. *Series Census-ERS* (P–27), no. 32. "Factors Related to College Attendance of Farm and Non-Farm High School Graduates: 1960," Washington, D.C.: U.S. Government Printing Office, 1962.

————. *U.S. Census of Population: 1960.* "Subject Reports, Occupational Characteristics." Final Report PC (2)–7A, Washington, D.C.: U.S. Government Printing Office, 1963.

————. *U.S. Census of Population: 1960.* Vol. 1. "Characteristics of the Population, Part 1, United States Summary," Washington, D.C.: U.S. Government Printing Office, 1964.

————. *Current Population Reports.* Series P–20, no. 132. "Educational Change in a Generation," Washington, D.C.: U.S. Government Printing Office, 1964.

————. *Historical Statstics of the United States: Colonial Times to 1957,* Washington, D.C.: U.S. Government Printing Office, 1965.

————. *Current Population Reports.* Series P–20, no. 185. "Factors Related to High School Graduation and College Attendance: 1967." Washington, D.C.: U.S. Government Printing Office, 1969.

————. *Current Population Reports.* Series P–60, no. 66. "Income in 1968 of Families and Persons in the United States." Washington, D.C.: U.S. Government Printing Office, 1969.

————. *Statistical Abstract of the United States.* Washington, D.C.: U.S. Government Printing Office, 1970.

————. *Current Population Reports.* Series P–20, no. 194. "Educational Attainment: March 1969." Washington, D.C.: U.S. Government Printing Office, 1970.

————. *Current Population Reports.* Series P–60, no. 75. "Income in 1969 of Families and Persons in the United States." Washington, D.C.: U.S. Government Printing Office, 1970.

————. *Current Population Reports.* Series P–23, no. 39. "Differences between Incomes of White and Negro Families by Work Experience of Wife and Region: 1970, 1969, and 1959." Washington, D.C.: U.S. Government Printing Office, 1971.

————. *Current Population Reports.* Series P–20, no. 229. "Educational Attainment: March 1971." Washington, D.C.: U.S. Government Printing Office, 1971.

————. *Current Population Reports.* Series P–60, no. 80. "Income in 1970 of Families and Persons in the United States." Washington, D.C.: U.S. Government Printing Office, 1971.

————. *Current Population Reports.* Series P–20, no. 222. "School Enrollment: October 1970." Washington, D.C.: U.S. Government Printing Office, 1971.

————. *Current Population Reports.* Series P–23, no. 38. "The Social and

Economic Status of Negroes in the United States, 1970." Washington, D.C.: U.S. Government Printing Office, 1971.

————. *Statistical Abstract of the United States.* Washington, D.C.: U.S. Government Printing Office, 1972.

U.S. Commission on Civil Rights. *Racial Isolation in the Public Schools.* Washington, D.C., 1967.

U.S. Department of Commerce. *Survey of Current Business,* Washington, D.C.: U.S. Government Printing Office, April 1964.

U.S. Department of Health, Education and Welfare. *Digest of Educational Statistics,* 1970.

————. *Digest of Educational Statistics,* Washington, D.C.: U.S. Government Printing Office, 1965.

————. News Release, June 18, 1971.

Vandenberg, Steven G. "Hereditary Factors in Psychological Variables in Man, with a Special Emphasis on Cognition." In *Genetic Diversity and Human Behavior,* edited by J. N. Spuhler. New York: Viking Fund Publications in Anthropology no. 45, 1967.

————. "The Hereditary Abilities Study: Hereditary Components in a Psychological Test Battery." *American Journal of Human Genetics* 14 (1962): 220–237.

Walster, Elaine; Cleary, T. Anne; and Clifford, Margaret. "Research Note: The Effect of Race and Sex on College Admission." *Sociology of Education* 44 (Spring 1971): 237–244.

Warburton, F. W. "Attainment and the School Environment." In Stephen Wiseman, *Education and Environment.* Manchester, England: Manchester University Press, 1964.

Wechsler, David. *The Measurement and Appraisal of Adult Intelligence.* Baltimore: Wilkins & Wilkins, 1958.

Weikart, David P. et al. "Longitudinal Results of the Ypsilanti-Perry Preschool Project." Ypsilanti (Michigan): High/Scope Educational Research Foundation, 1970.

Weinberg, Meyer. *Desegregation Research: An Appraisal.* 2d ed. Bloomington: Phi Delta Kappa, 1970.

Weisbrod, Burton, and Karpoff, Peter. "Monetary Returns to College Education, Student Ability, and College Quality." *Review of Economics and Statistics* 50 (November 1968): 491–497.

Weisenberg, Theodore; Roe, Anne; and McBride, Katherine E. *Adult Intelligence: A Psychological Study of Test Performances.* New York: The Commonwealth Fund, 1936.

Weiss, Leonard, and Williamson, Jeffrey. "Black Education, Earnings, and Interregional Migration: Some New Evidence." Madison: University of Wisconsin, Institute for Research on Poverty, Discussion Paper, 1971.

Westinghouse Learning Corporation/Ohio University. *The Impact of Head Start.* Springfield, Virginia: Clearinghouse for Federal Scientific and Technical Information, U.S. Department of Commerce, June 12, 1969.

Wheeler, Lester R. "A Comparative Study of the Intelligence of East Tennessee Mountain Children." *Journal of Educational Psychology* 33 (May 1942): 321–334.

Wilensky, Harold L. "Varieties of Work Experience." In *Man in a World at Work,* edited by Henry Borow. Boston: Houghton Mifflin, 1964.

Willoughby, Raymond R. "Family Similarities in Mental Test Abilities." *27th Yearbook of the National Society for the Study of Education,* pt. 1, pp. 55–59. Bloomington: Public School Publishing Co., 1928.

Wilson, Alan B. "Residential Segregation of Social Classes and Aspirations of High School Boys." *American Sociological Review* 24 (December 1959): 836–845.

———. "Educational Consequences of Segregation in a California Community." In U.S. Commission on Civil Rights, *Racial Isolation in the Public Schools,* vol. 2. Washington, D.C.: U.S. Government Printing Office, 1967.

Wiseman, Stephen. "The Manchester Survey." In Central Advisory Council for Education, *Children and Their Primary Schools,* vol. 2, Appendix 9. London: Her Majesty's Stationery Office, 1967.

Wolfle, Dale, and Smith, V. G. "The Occupational Value of Education for Superior High School Graduates." *Journal of Higher Education* 27 (April 1956): 201–214.

Worbois, G. M. "Changes in Stanford-Binet IQ for Rural Consolidated and Rural One-Room School Children." *Journal of Experimental Education* 2 (December 1942): 210–214.

Wright, Sewell. "Path Coefficients and Path Regressions." *Biometrics* 16 (1960): 189–202.

Yerkes, Robert M. "Psychological Examining in the U.S. Army." *Memoirs of the National Academy of Science,* vol. 15. Washington, D.C.: U.S. Government Printing Office, 1921.

Young, Michael, and Gibson, John. "In Search of an Explanation of Social Mobility." *British Journal of Statistical Psychology* 16 (May 1963): 27–36.

# INDEX

ability grouping, 33, 34, 36, 96, 106–109
ability, nonverbal, 54
access, to schooling, 17–23, 31, 40, 67, 143–144, 255, 257, 258
achievement tests, 55–56, 57, 63, 81, 95, 104
adopted children: and adoptive parents, 300; genetic factors and, 278, 297; IQ, 276, 281, 290–292; and natural children, 274, 293, 299, 303; reared together, 301; test scores, 79–80
adults' reports, on parents, 334–336
adult status, and cognitive skills, 349, 350
adult test scores, 60, 320; and genetic factors, 342
Alabama, school expenditures, 24
alternative services, for schools, 17, 23, 137
Appalachia, 82
aptitude, academic, 145–146
aptitude tests, 55–56, 57, 63, 144, 258
Armed Forces Qualification Test (*AFQT*) scores, 63; and educational attainment, 142, 146, 343; heritability of, 342, 343; and income, 220, 328; internal reliability of, 336; and IQ genotype, 344, 349–350; and occupational status, 337; parental status and, 338; and schooling, 326
Army Alpha, 63, 82, 186, 325–326
Army General Classification Test (*AGCT*) scores, 63; and occupational status, 328; and schooling, 326; test-retest reliability and, 336
aspirations, educational, 35; occupational, 140, 176, 183–185, 194, 195
assortative mating, 74, 271–273, 277–278

Bentham, Jeremy, 9, 11
biological development, and genes, 270

**383**

blacks, 4, 81, 82; *AFQT* scores, 326; *AGCT* scores, 326; cognitive skills, 52; curriculum assignment, 35–37; desegregation, 8, 16, 32, 35, 97–103, 104, 105, 106, 189, 253; educational attainment, 141–143, 153–156, 159; incomes, 216–219, 223, 224, 229; middle class, 190–191; occupational status, 190–191, 193, 194, 195; school expenditures for, 27–28; schooling, 18, 19, 22, 27–28, 30, 31, 35–36, 40–41, 86–87, 88, 141–143, 153–156, 257, 258–259; test scores, 53, 64, 81–84, 87–88, 106, 142–143, 159

"blending," 271

Boston, 155; school expenditures, 28

Brookline, Massachusetts, 103, 105

brothers, economic status of, 7–8; and family background, 143, 346; genetic factors and, 350; influenced by brothers, 347–349; IQ scores and educational attainment, 340–341; occupational status of, 179, 181, 198, 219–220, 329; *see also* siblings

busing, 28, 30, 40, 99, 102, 105, 155, 257, 259, 260

central financing, of schools, 258

Chicago, school expenditures, 28

children, IQ and parental IQ, 268, 279; reared together, 283–309; related, reared apart, 271, 274, 309–315; unrelated, 290–292, 293, 294, 307; working, 211; *see also* adopted children, natural children

children's reports, on mother's and father's educational attainment, 335

Chomsky, Noam, 83

church attendance, and parochial schooling, 133

Civil Rights Act, 1964, 193

civil rights movement, 141, 190, 217

civil service, wages in, 230–231

coefficient of variation, 352–353

cognitive skills, 6, 7, 104, 253, 337, 338; and adult status, 349, 350; of blacks, 52; educational attainment, 144–145, 146, 159, 160, 254, 341; environment, 64, 72–76; equalization of, 11, 109–110, 263–265; family background, 254; genetic fac-

tors, 61, 64, 72–76, 342; heredity vs. environment, 66–72; and income, 63, 209, 214, 219, 220–221, 223, 226, 227, 254, 262, 263; and IQ, 52–53; occupational status, 176, 180, 181, 182, 185–186, 191, 195, 254; parental, 269–270; rich vs. poor children, 52; schooling, 88, 89; tracking and curriculum assignment, 34; variations over time, 63; verbal ability, 52, 84, 85; *see also* test scores
Coleman, James, 100, 103
college, *see* higher education
community, and IQ scores, 275; and schools, 7, 258
compensatory opportunity, 75, 255
compensatory schooling, 7, 94
competence, on the job, 8, 9, 11, 143–144, 227, 228, 254, 263
Contra Costa County, California, 101, 103, 105, 106
correlation coefficients, 354–358
cost-benefit analysis, of schooling, 223–224
covariance, 314; and heritability of IQ, 281
cultural differences, range of, 326
culture-free tests, 79
Current Population Survey (CPS), 333–334
curriculum assignment, 16, 33–37, 41, 107, 108–109, 145, 156–158, 159, 253

Department of Health, Education and Welfare, 32
desegregation: blacks, 8, 16, 32, 35, 97–103, 104, 105, 106, 189, 253; busing, 28, 30, 40, 99, 102, 105, 155, 257, 259, 260; economic, 105, 106; vs. integration, 98–99; internal, 106–109; middle-class whites, 103–106; poor whites, 103, 104; working class, 105–106
Detroit, school expenditures, 28
differentiation, 298
diligence, and schooling, 139
dominance, 271, 301–302; and epistasis, 266, 271; and recessiveness, 270
dropouts, 149, 150, 156–157, 181, 184, 221, 222, 224, 259, 324
Duncan, Otis Dudley, 331
Duncan scale, 178

economic inequality, 13, 110; brothers, 7–8; equal opportunity, 9; need, 10; schooling, 29

economic status, and IQ, 77–81

education, *see* schooling, schools

educational aspirations, 140–141, 145, 147, 148, 151–153, 153–155, 160, 194

educational attainment, 320, 354; academic aptitude, 145–146; adult test scores, 185; and *AFQT* scores, 343; amount of schooling, 136–137, 141, 156–157; blacks, 141–143, 153–156, 159; and brothers, 340–341, 348–350; cognitive skills, 144–145, 146, 159, 160, 254, 341; college entrance rates, 148, 149, 150, 151–153, 153–155, 156–158; credentials, 136, 156, 160; curriculum assignment, 145, 150, 156–158, 159; diligence, 139; dropouts, 149, 150, 156–157, 181, 184; economic background, 138–141, 146; educational aspirations, 140–141, 145, 147, 148, 151–153, 153–155; 160, 194; elementary school quality, 147–148; elementary school test scores, 144; equalization of, 11; family background, 143, 159, 176, 254, 262, 344; of father, 320; genetic factors, 329, 340; guidance counselors, 149–150; high school quality, 146–147, 148, 152, 159; high school resources, 149–151; income, 214, 216, 218–219, 222, 223, 225, 226, 227, 255; IQ, 145, 325, 342; intervention programs, 150–151; job satisfaction, 247, 248, 249, 255; and mean status, 327; middle vs. working classes, 139, 140, 141, 151–153, 159–160; natural and adopting parents, 277; occupational status, 138, 176, 180–185, 185–188, 191, 192, 193, 198, 254, 327, 331; school day length, 149; school resources, 158, 159, 255; siblings, 151, 155; test scores, 145, 146; tracking, 157; and unmeasured variables, 349; Upward Bound, 150–151

educational credentials, 12, 135–137, 159; competence vs. effort, 143–144; distribution of, 261; educational attainment, 136, 156, 160; income, 209, 221–225, 254; occupational status, 192, 193, 195; as privilege rationing, 184–185; quality of, 136–137

Educational Testing Service, 55, 153

egalitarianism, 10, 11, 16, 23, 27, 38, 41, 72, 73, 197, 230, 261, 262, 263–265

Elementary and Secondary Education Act, 94

elementary schools, 18, 22, 85, 87–88, 89, 90–91, 93, 94, 100, 101, 103, 104, 105, 144, 147–148, 255

England, 70–72; and America (studies), 284, 292; school tracking, 35, 193

environment: and cognitive skills, 64, 72–76; families and, 292; and genetic factors, 266–269, 304–308, 315; IQ, 65, 66–73, 82; range of, 330; variables in, 295, 297–299, 320–330; *see also* family background

environmental variation, between and within families, 288; and selective placement of identical twins, 312–314

epistasis, 283, 301–302; and dominance, 266, 271

Equality of Educational Opportunity Survey (EEOS), 32, 34, 35, 54, 55, 56, 81, 82, 86, 90–91, 92, 94, 96, 100, 101, 103, 105, 106, 146, 147, 149, 150, 152, 154, 184, 334–335; test-retest reliability of, 336

equalization: of cognitive skills, 11, 109–110, 263–265; of educational attainment, 11; of income, 11–12, 230–232, 260–261, 262, 263; of occupational status, 262; of opportunity, 195–199; of school expenditures, 29; of test scores, 261

equal opportunity, 3, 4, 7, 9, 52, 72–73, 109–110, 192, 220, 227, 263; access to schooling, 30–31; blacks, 4; vs. compensatory, 75, 255; curriculum assignment, 34, 37; for higher education, 19–20

error variance, 332

ethnic differences, 324

Evanston, Illinois, busing, 102

executives, job satisfaction, 249

factory, vs. family model for schools, 256

families, adopting, 292

family background, 295, 321, 339; brothers, 346; cognitive skills, 254; educational attainment, 138–141, 143, 146, 159, 176, 254, 262, 340–341, 344, 350; father, 345; genetic factors and, 297–298, 311, 314; income, 209, 215, 219–220, 222, 223, 226, 227, 229, 254, 262, 263, 345; IQ, 64, 76–78, 344, 350; occupational status, 176, 179, 191, 192, 198, 199, 254, 262; siblings, 346; test scores, 53, 61; *see also* environment

family income, 209, 211, 212, 217, 219, 328; and adopted children's IQ, 276

father, educational attainment of, 320; and family background, 345; IQ of, 276, 320; schooling of, 276, 334, 348

father's status, and income, 213, 214, 215, 217, 219; and occupational status, 131, 194, 195, 278, 320, 334, 338, 343–345, 348

federal government, and control of economy, 264

federal support, of schools, 24–25, 38, 257–258

fraternal twins, 292; and identical twins, 286–287, 299, 308–309, 315; IQ of, 293, 301; and siblings, 307, 308

freedom of choice, educational, 40, 41

general information, tests of, 54, 84–85, 90, 108

genetic engineering, 64, 73

genetic factors: and adopted children, 278, 297; and adult cognitive skills, 342; and adult test scores, 342; and brothers, 350; and children reared together, 301–303; and educational attainment, 329, 340; and environment, 266–269, 304–308, 315; and family background, 297–298, 311, 314; and father's occupational status, 343–344; and identical twins, 304; and income, 209, 215, 254, 262; and IQ, 270, 304, 349, 350; and natural child, 278; and occupational status, 176, 179–180, 188; and siblings, 302; and test scores, 53, 61, 62, 63, 65–72, 80, 253

genetic resemblance, between adoptive parents and children, 277–279 genotype, *see* heritability, IQ

German measles, 296

*Griggs v. Duke Power Company,* 192–193

group tests, 57

group, vs. individual inequalities, 14

guidance counselors, 149–150

half-siblings, and prenatal environment, 318

Head Start program, 18, 22

heredity, vs. environment, 66–72, 283; *see also* cognitive skills, IQ, test scores

heritability, of *AFQT* scores, 342, 343; of IQ scores, 59, 64–69, 69–72, 76, 82–83, 266–269, 271, 275, 279–283, 316; *see also* IQ

heteroscedasticity, 337

higher education, access to, 19–20, 22, 31, 67, 143–144, 255, 258; entrance rates, 148, 149, 150, 151–153, 153–155, 156–158; financing of, 39, 259–260

Higher Education Act, 1972, 258

high school equivalency examination, 135–136

Holland, 87

homogenization, 298

identical twins, 292; and adoption, 281; and fraternal twins, 286–287, 299, 308–309, 315; genetic factors and, 304; IQ of, 293, 301; reared apart, 309–314

Illich, Ivan, 260

illiteracy, 6, 63

immigration, 326

income, 321, 328, 354; blacks, 216–219, 223, 224, 229; brothers, 219–220, 254, 350; civil service, 230–231; cognitive skills, 53, 209, 214, 219, 220–221, 223, 226, 227, 254, 262, 263; dropouts, 221, 222, 224; earners per family, 211; educational attainment, 214, 216, 218–219, 222, 223–225, 226, 227, 255; educational credentials, 209, 221–225, 254; equalization of, 9–10, 11–12, 230–232, 260–261, 262, 263; family, 209, 211, 212, 217, 219; family background, 209, 215, 219–220, 222, 223, 226, 227, 229, 254, 262, 263, 345; father's education, 213, 214, 215, 217, 219; father's occupational

income (*cont'd*)
status, 212, 214, 215, 217; genetic factors, 209, 215, 254, 262; high school grades, 186; income insurance, 228–230; individual, 211, 212, 217, 218; inheritances, 214; IQ, 131, 220, 229, 350; job competence, 8, 9, 11, 227, 228, 254, 263; job satisfaction, 247, 248, 255; luck, 8, 9, 131, 227, 228; middle vs. lower class, 213–214, 215–216, 223, 224; occupation, 184, 225–226, 227, 254; parental income, 214, 219; parental status, 131, 216; property, 212; racial discrimination, 218, 219, 229; rich vs. poor, 210–211, 215, 216; schooling, 14, 131–132, 136, 182, 216, 223, 227, 263, 328–329, 338, 358; school quality, 216; social security, 211–212; test scores, 52, 77–81, 156, 216, 218, 219, 221, 222, 223, 227, 254, 255–256, 261, 328; top vs. bottom fifth, 27, 209, 210–211, 212, 213, 214, 216, 220, 262; transfer payments, 212; unearned, 212, 217; wage control, 230–231, 263; welfare, 211–212; women, 211, 213, 216, 217, 219, 221, 224, 226, 262; working children, 211; *see also* family income

income insurance, 228–229; compulsory, 230

individual incomes, 211, 212, 217, 218

individual, vs. group inequalities, 14

infant tests, 59

inheritance: of occupational status, 179–180, 185; of capital assets, 214, 345

integration, vs. desegregation, 98–99

intelligence quotient (IQ), 56–57, 63; of adopted children, 276–281; vs. aptitude scores, 59–60; and assortative mating, 271, 273; blacks, 81, 82; of brothers, 340–341, 349; cognitive skills, 52–53; computation of, 58–59; coefficient of variation for, 352–353; and community, 275; and covariance, 281; early and adult test scores, 342; early and educational attainment, 325, 342; economic status, 77–81; educational attainment, 145; environment, 65, 66–73, 82; family background, 64, 76–78, 344; of father, 276, 320; of fraternal twins, 293, 301; genetic

factors and, 270, 304, 349, 350; heritability, 64–69, 69–72, 76, 82–83, 266–269, 271, 275, 279–283, 316; heritability, England vs. America, 70–72; husbands and wives, 74, 272, 273; identical vs. fraternal twins, 70, 76, 293, 301; identical twins reared apart, 70–71, 76, 82, 293, 301; income, 131, 220, 229; mean IQ, 355; of natural and adopted children, 290–292; of natural and adopting parents, 277; occupational status, 83–84, 131, 186, 188, 191, 356–357; parents and children, 69, 268, 271, 274–276, 279, 281; parents and infants, 59; and region, 275; schooling, 88; and schooling of parents, 278; school resources, 96; siblings, 70, 76, 77, 289–290, 292, 293, 301; of sons, 340; and standard deviation, 353, 354; and status, 357; test scores, 56–57, 63, 254; top vs. bottom fifth, 77, 81; unmeasured variables, 349; unrelated children reared together, 70, 76; *see also* test scores
intervention programs, in schools, 150, 151
Israel, kibbutz, 228, 231, 263

Japan, wage distribution, 231
Jensen, Arthur, 65
Jensen's formula, 285, 288, 294, 295, 304, 319
job competence, 8, 9, 11, 143–144, 227, 228, 254, 263
job relevance, and test scores, 186, 193
job satisfaction: challenge of job, 248–249; educational attainment, 247, 248, 249, 255; executives, 249; income, 247, 248, 255; occupational status, 247, 248, 249, 255; professionals and managers, 247–248
Johnson, Lyndon B., 5, 263

Kennedy, John F., 263
kibbutz, 228, 231, 263

labor unions, 183, 197, 230
logical inference, tests of, 84–85, 90
long- vs. short-term effects, of schooling, 16–17, 23–24, 29, 30, 31, 255–257

lower classes, and schooling, 22, 35, 36, 78, 79, 80, 81, 89, 248, 258
luck, 131, 227, 228; and economic success, 8, 9

malnutrition, in childhood, 62
managers, job satisfaction, 247–248
matching, selective, 277–279
mathematical skills, tests of, 52, 54, 83–84, 90, 101, 110, 147, 257
measurement error, 275, 316, 330–336
meritocratic vs. non-meritocratic discriminations, 67, 68
middle class, 103–106, 139, 140, 141, 151–153, 159–160, 213–214, 215–216, 223, 224; schools, 26–27, 32, 78, 79, 80, 81, 86–87, 89, 100, 101, 253, 257, 258
mother, education of, 276; IQ of, 276
mother, natural (IQ), and adopted children's IQ, 281; and adopting mother's educational attainment, 315; and children's prenatal environment, 282; and child's postnatal environment, 317
motivation, for test passing, 55

National Education Association, 33, 35, 107
National Foundation for Educational Research, England, 108
National Opinion Research Corporation, 132, 176
National Welfare Rights Organization, 5
natural children: and adopted children, 274, 290–293, 299, 303; genetic factors and, 278
New York City, 87, 88, 91; school expenditures, 28
New York State, school expenditures, 24
Nixon, Richard M., 263
noncognitive traits, 131, 159, 198; effects of schooling, 12, 13, 132; public vs. parochial schools alumni, 132–133, 189–190
nonlinear relationships, 336–337
nonverbal ability, 54
NORC veterans survey, 326, 327

occupation, and income, 225–226, 227, 254
occupational aspirations, 140, 176, 183–185, 194, 195

occupational status, 10–11, 12, 321, 332,
352; and *AFQT* scores, 337; and *AGCT*
scores, 328; black middle class, 190–191;
brothers, 179, 181, 198, 329, 343, 350;
cognitive skills, 180, 181, 182, 185–188,
191, 195, 254; desegregation, 189; Duncan scale, 178, educational attainment,
138, 176, 180–185, 185–188, 191, 192,
193, 198, 254, 327, 331; educational
credentials, 180–185, 192, 193, 195;
equalization of, 262; equalization of opportunity, 195–199; family background,
176, 179, 191, 192, 198, 199, 254, 262;
of father, 320, 338, 343–345, 348; father's cognitive skills, 176; father's genes,
176; father's schooling, 176, 334; father's
status, 131, 194, 195; genetic factors,
176, 179–180, 188; income, 186; inheritance of, 179–180, 185; IQ, 83–84, 131,
186, 187, 188, 191, 350; job satisfaction,
247, 248, 249, 255; labor unions, 183,
197; luck, 131; occupational aspiration,
140, 176, 183–185, 194, 195; parochial
schooling, 189–190; prediction of, 192;
vs. prestige, 177–178; race, 190–191, 193,
194, 195; schooling, 23, 131–132, 133–
134, 136, 176, 180–185, 191, 198, 199,
254; school quality, 176, 180, 188–190,
198; social mobility, 176, 180, 194, 195,
196, 199; stability of, 192; and status
rankings, 177–178; and test scores, 52;
176, 180, 185–188, 191, 192, 193, 194,
195, 197–198; top and bottom fifths,
179–180
open enrollment, 30, 40, 194

parental income, 214, 219
parental IQ, and children's IQ, 279, 268
parental status, 80, 131, 216; and *AFQT*
scores, 338; and schooling, 358
parents: and adopted children, 276, 300;
and adopted children's IQ, 276; cognitive
skills, 269–270; natural and adopting, IQ,
277; natural, and children's IQ, 274–275;
schooling, and children's IQ, 278
parochial schooling, 132–133, 189–190; and
church attendance, 133
path analysis, 14
performance contracts, 231

Plowden survey, England, 96, 105
poverty, definitions of, 4–6; schooling, 7–8; war on, 3, 4, 7, 8, 150
poverty line, 4, 5
prenatal environment, 297; of siblings, 295–296
prenatal factors, and twins, 304
prenatal hypothesis, 307–308
preschool, 18, 22, 59, 60–61, 85–87, 89
prestige, vs. status, 177–178
Prince Edward County, 87
professional competence, and college grades, 187
professionals, and job satisfaction, 247–248
Project Concern, Hartford, 102, 259
Project Talent, 89–90, 92, 94, 96, 103, 105, 108, 141, 142, 146, 147, 149, 150, 152, 153, 154, 157, 285, 288, 318, 325, 347–349
promotion, automatic (schools), 326
property, income from, 212

racial discrimination, 72, 218, 219, 229
Rainwater, Lee, 232
"random" factors, in environment, 295–296, 297–298
reading, tests of, 29, 31, 52, 54, 55, 74, 84, 85, 87, 90, 101, 109, 110, 147, 257
recessiveness, and dominance, 270
reciprocal influence hypothesis, 307, 308
region, and IQ, 275
regression, toward mean, 59, 61
related children, reared apart, 309–315
relatives, and nonrelatives, 316
reliability coefficient, 333–336
rich, vs. poor, 26–27, 52, 86–87, 88, 100, 101, 210–211, 215, 216
rising expectations, 5
Riverside, California, busing, 102
Roosevelt, Franklin D., 5

St. John, Nancy, 101
SAT tests, 353
Scholastic Aptitude Test, 56
school day length, 149
schooling: adult income, 14; and *AFQT* scores, 326; and *AGCT* scores, 326; amount of, 8, 23, 131–132, 133–134,

136–137, 141, 156–157, 180–185, 191, 198, 199, 254, 342; blacks, 18, 19, 22, 27–28, 30, 31, 35–36, 40–41, 86–87, 88, 141–143, 153–156, 257, 258–259; cognitive skills, 88, 89, 338; compensatory, 7, 94; cost-benefit analysis, 223–224; educational aspiration, 35; of father, 276, 334, 348; income, 131–132, 136, 182, 216, 223, 227, 263, 328–329, 338, 358; and IQ genotype, 344, 350; lifetime inequalities in, 26–27; long- vs. short-term effects, 16–17, 23–24, 29, 30, 31, 255–257; lower classes, 22, 35, 36, 78, 79, 80, 81, 89, 258; money from home, 139, 259; noncognitive outcomes, 12, 13, 131, 132–133, 159, 189–190, 198; occupational status, 23, 131–132, 133–134, 136, 176, 180–185, 191, 198, 199, 254, 338; and parental status, 358; of parents and children's IQ, 278; rich vs. poor children, 7–8, 26–27, 86–87, 88, 100, 101; test scores, 85–89, 91–92, 326; top vs. bottom fifths, 137; women, 22; years completed, by different groups, 20–22

school policies, 95–97, 255

school quality, 29–30, 89–93, 136–137, 146–147, 148, 152, 159, 216, 254; occupational status, 176, 180, 188–190, 198

schools: ability grouping, 33, 34, 36, 96, 106–109; academic segregation, 32–33; access to, 17–23, 30–31, 40, 67, 257, 258; alternative services, 17, 23, 137; as certification agencies, 135–137, 159; community control, 7, 258; curriculum assignment, 16, 33–37, 41, 107, 108–109, 253; dropouts, 149, 150, 156–157, 181, 184, 221, 222, 224, 259; economic segregation, 32; factory vs. family models, 256; elementary, 18, 22, 85, 87–88, 89, 90–91, 93, 94, 100, 101, 103, 104, 105, 144, 255; higher education, 19–20, 22, 32, 39, 67, 143–144, 148, 149, 150, 151–153, 153–155, 156–158, 187, 255, 258, 259–260; internal desegregation, 106–109; internal inequality, 250; leaving age, 63; middle class, 26–27, 32, 78, 79, 80, 81, 86–87, 89, 100, 101, 253, 257, 258; per-

schools (*cont'd*)

   formance contracts, 231; preschools, 18, 22, 59, 60–61, 85–87, 89; quality of, 29–30, 89–93, 136–137, 146–147, 148, 152, 159, 176, 180, 188–190, 198, 254; racial segregation, 8, 16, 32, 35; resources, 96, 149–151, 158, 159, 253, 255; vs. public services, 38–39; reform of, 255; secondary, 19, 22, 85, 88–89, 89–90, 93, 94, 100–101, 132, 143–144, 159, 186, 253; tracking, 16, 33–37, 41, 106–109, 157, 193

schools, expenditures for, 8, 30, 37–38, 149; blacks, 27–28; central financing, 258; by districts, 25, 38; equalization of, 29; federal support, 24–25, 38, 257–258; state aid, 24, 28, 38, 40; and test scores, 93–95, 255; within districts, 26, 38

secondary schools, 19, 22, 85, 88–89, 89–90, 93, 94, 100–101, 132, 143–144, 159, 186, 253

segregation, academic, 32–33; economic, 32, 105, 106; pupil preferences, 31; racial, 8, 16, 32, 35; and test scores, 97–104; *see also* blacks, desegregation

selective placement, 277, 278, 282, 312–314, 317

siblings, 151, 155, 316; classification of, 289; and family background, 346; and fraternal twins, 307, 308; genetic factors and, 302; IQ of, 70, 76, 77, 289–290, 292, 293, 301; prenatal conditions of, 295–296; reared apart, 315; reared together, 300; and twins, 298–299; and unrelated children, 295, 298, 309, 315; *see also* brothers

skills, measurement of, 325

socialism, 265

social mobility, 176, 180, 194, 195, 196, 199

social security, 211–212

sons, income, and father's occupational status, 338; IQ scores, 340; test scores, and father's occupational status, 345

son's reports, on fathers' occupational status, 331–332

spouses, IQ of, 273

standard deviation, 59, 351–352; uses of, 353–354

Stanford-Binet test, 88, 289, 316; test-retest reliability of, 336
state aid, for schools, 24, 28, 38, 40
success, adult, 346
success, economic, 337
Survey Research Center (SRC), University of Michigan, 247, 248, 249
Sweden, 88

taxation, 3, 9, 10, 38, 39, 229, 230, 259, 260, 263; of capital assets, 232
test-retest reliability, and *AGCT* scores, 336
test scores, 6, 8, 12, 52, 64; adopted vs. natural children, 79–80; achievement, 55–56, 57, 63, 81, 95, 104; adult, 60, 185; aptitude, 55–56, 57, 63, 144, 258; aptitude vs. IQ, 59–60; blacks, 53, 64, 81–84, 87–88, 106, 142–143, 159; class status, 81; culture-free tests, 79; curriculum assignment, 34–37; early, 320; economic status, 77–81, 156; educational attainment, 145, 146, 324; effects of segregation, 97–104; elementary school, 85, 87–88, 89, 90–91, 93, 94, 100, 101, 103, 104, 105, 255; equalization of, 261; family background, 53, 61; father's occupation, 80; general information, 54, 84–85, 90, 108; genetic factors, 53, 61, 62, 63, 64, 65, 72, 79, 80, 253; group tests, 57; heritability, 59, 64–69, 69–72, 76, 82–83; income, 52, 216, 218, 219, 221, 222, 223, 227, 254, 255–256, 261; infant, 59; IQ, 56–57, 63, 254; job relevance, 186, 193; logical inference, 84–85, 90; mathematical, 52, 54, 83–84, 90, 101, 110, 147, 257; motivation, 55; nonverbal ability, 54; occupational status, 52, 176, 180, 185–188, 191, 192, 193, 194, 195, 197–198; parents' education, 80; preschool, 59, 60–61, 85–87, 89; reading, 52, 54, 55, 74, 84, 85, 87, 90, 101, 109, 110, 147, 257; regression toward mean, 59, 61; rich vs. poor, 138–139; schooling, 85–89, 91–92; school expenditures, 93–95, 255; school policies, 95–97, 255; school quality, 254; secondary school, 85, 88–89, 89–90, 93, 94, 100–101, 253; sex differences, 67; social class, 64; socio-

test scores (*cont'd*)
economic background, 323; stability of, 53, 58–62; tracking, 106–109; U. S. military, 63, 82, 142, 146, 186, 220; verbal ability, 54, 56, 67, 82, 106–107, 147; vocabulary, 60, 80, 90, 108; *see also* cognitive skills, IQ

Title I programs, 94

tracking, educational, 16, 33–37, 41, 106–109, 157, 193

transfer payments, 212

twins, adopted, 312–314; IQ scores, 70–71, 76, 82; and population mean, 318; prenatal factors and, 304; reared together, 284–288; and siblings, 298–299; *see also* fraternal twins, identical twins

unearned income, 212, 217

university, *see* higher education

Upward Bound, 150–151

urbanization, 326

U.S. Army, tests, 63, 82, 186

U.S. Supreme Court, 22, 26, 32, 192–193, 257, 264–265

"uterine" environment, 295

variables, measurable, 349; unmeasured, 349

variance, explained, 357–358; true, 332; within-family, 298, 299; within-pair, 285, 288

verbal ability, 52, 54, 56, 67, 82, 84, 85, 106–107, 147

vocabulary tests, 60, 80, 90, 108

wage control, 230, 231, 263

WAIS similarities subtest, 327

Washington, D. C., school expenditures, 28

wealth, as relative, 6

welfare, 211–212

Westinghouse-Ohio Survey of Head Start graduates, 86

white nonfarm males, native, 322, 337, 339, 346; economic status for, 349–350

whites, *AFQT* scores for, 326; *AGCT* scores for, 326

whites, poor, 103, 104, 105–106

white supremacy, 83–84

Wilson, Alan, 101, 103, 105, 106
women, 22, 67, 211, 213, 216, 217, 219, 221, 224, 226, 262
Wood, Evelyn, 261
working class, 139, 140, 141, 151–153, 159–160